CRIMINOLOGICAL AND FORENSIC PSYCHOLOGY

HELEN GAVIN

Los Angeles | London | New Delhi
Singapore | Washington DC

Los Angeles | London | New Delhi
Singapore | Washington DC

SAGE Publications Ltd
1 Oliver's Yard
55 City Road
London EC1Y 1SP

SAGE Publications Inc.
2455 Teller Road
Thousand Oaks, California 91320

SAGE Publications India Pvt Ltd
B 1/I 1 Mohan Cooperative Industrial Area
Mathura Road
New Delhi 110 044

SAGE Publications Asia-Pacific Pte Ltd
3 Church Street
#10-04 Samsung Hub
Singapore 049483

Editor: Michael Carmichael
Editorial assistant: Keri Dickens
Production editor: Imogen Roome
Proofreader: Elaine Leek
Indexer: W.D. Farrington
Marketing manager: Alison Borg
Cover design: Wendy Scott
Typeset by: C&M Digitals (P) Ltd, Chennai, India
Printed and bound in Great Britain by Ashford
Colour Press Ltd

First published 2014

Library of Congress Control Number: 2013938304

British Library Cataloguing in Publication data

A catalogue record for this book is available from
the British Library

ISBN 978-1-84860-700-2
ISBN 978-1-84860-701-9 (pbk)

CRIMINOLOGICAL AND FORENSIC PSYCHOLOGY

This book is dedicated to the memory of the man who told me I could be anything I wanted to be, no matter what anyone else said. Thanks Dad.

Contents

Introduction

This book is designed to support final-year students in Psychology who are taking modules in criminal psychology. It also would be appropriate for postgraduate students in forensic psychology or similar courses. Having taught these topics for some years, and being an active researcher and consultant in criminal psychology for more, the author has written this book with the express intention of it being another form of support to those embarking on research or practice careers, or those who are simply interested in the psychology of crime and want something a bit more technical than the true crime section of the library. Its scope is broader than simply forensic psychology and will support courses in other aspects of criminal psychology or criminology.

Most of the chapters, where appropriate, examine a case study in each of the crime areas under examination. For example, the chapter on juvenile offenders considers the sad case of Jamie Bulger, killed by two 10-year-old boys, and what happened to them in the criminal justice system as they were tried, convicted and imprisoned. The chapter on psychology in investigation examines some rather gruesome murders that took place in the East End of London in the nineteenth century, and how modern psychology might have helped the police in their then unsuccessful investigation. Serial murderer Stephen Griffiths is the case study in the chapter on homicide, perhaps an atypical case due to the fact he was reading for a PhD in Criminology. However, serial murder is not a typical activity and is not carried out by typical people. The Central Park Jogger case was a brutal attack on a young woman in New York, and termed by the governor, Mario Cuorno, as 'the ultimate shriek of alarm' (Pitt, 1989). What happened next as a result of that alarm is of interest to psychology, however, and Chapter 14 examines how and why people confess to a crime they did not commit. In this way, each topic hopefully comes more alive and real for the reader, and shows how all the techniques and theories of psychology can be used to examine and attempt to explain real life crimes.

At the beginning of each chapter there is a list of terms or concepts that cover the key themes discussed within it. These terms are also listed in the glossary at the end of the book. Highlighted boxes within the text explain further terms that are important but are not included in the main text to avoid confusion. Section 1 takes the reader through the process of becoming a forensic psychologist, but also sets out how to be a researcher in the wide areas of criminal psychology. Chapter 1 defines forensic psychology and briefly looks at where the psychologist works, and then considers the training which needs to be completed before anyone can call themselves a forensic psychologist. Chapter 2 looks at the broader issues of researching in the psychology of crime and the difficulty of accessing and working with forensic samples.

Section 2 examines the psychological explanations of crime and criminals. It takes a broad look at the theories available to explain crime in Chapter 3, and then considers, in more depth, questions of the criminal mind in Chapter 4 and the juvenile offender in Chapter 5.

Section 3 looks at specific crimes in more detail and provides the psychological explanations for homicide, sexual crimes, terrorism, arson, theft and fraud. Defining each topic, these chapters look at the legal aspects of these crimes in brief and then provide a more in-depth examination of the psychological explanations for them. The chapter on homicide covers the act of killing people, from genocide to manslaughter, with a look at single, multiple and serial homicide in between. Serial murder is then examined in more detail, evaluating the ways in which several psychological theories can or cannot explain why people kill over and over again. Chapter 7 considers why people kill for a cause, sometimes including themselves, and what theoretical perspectives in psychology can tell us about political or social violence, as distinct from person-to-person killing.

Carrying on with the theme of crimes against the person, Chapter 8 examines rape, sexual assault and child molestation, looking at some of the crimes that are deemed so heinous that those convicted of them are often kept in isolation from other prison inmates. Sexual crimes cause a great deal of anger and revulsion, but the social scientist will always question their own feelings and those of others to try to understand why this is the case and why some people still carry them out. This chapter does not set out the answer, but looks at the ways in which psychology is attempting to find it.

Crimes against property are those that do not have a personal victim, except as the result of the loss of property or money. Arson, while dangerous and potentially lethal, is not directed at a person as such, but against houses, cars and other building or structures. In Chapter 9, the definition of arson, and the distinction from pyromania, is discussed, along with psychological theories that may explain why people set fires. Chapter 10 examines another property crime, theft, and the range of activities that come under that heading. While kleptomania is an explanation for some stealing, it is not the whole story. Stealing on a large scale, however, comes under the heading of fraud or white-collar crime. This includes fraudulent money-making schemes, embezzlement, and generally conning people out of their hard-earned cash. The psychology of the fraudster is examined in Chapter 11.

Section 4 moves on to the more forensic element of criminal psychology and follows the route of the psychology of crime from investigation to imprisonment. It is concerned with the psychology of the investigation process and covers profiling and crime scene analysis (Chapter 12) interviewing witnesses and victims (Chapter 13), and identification and interrogation of suspects, and what can go wrong at this stage (Chapter 14).

Section 5 puts psychology in the court room. Chapter 15 outlines what happens in court, how evidence is handled and how testimony from both eyewitnesses and expert witnesses is managed. Chapter 16 looks at the mind of the defendant, paying particular attention to the insanity plea and the application of the M'Naghten rules in the case of a man who thought he had got away with his murders as there were no bodies to examine. Chapter 17 looks at how the jury sees the court and what happens in both the court room and the jury room, and how to research this aspect of the criminal justice system.

Section 6 is concerned with what many see at the endpoint of criminal justice – prison and what happens there. Chapter 18 is concerned with questions about imprisonment: why do we imprison our criminals? What is prison for? And what happens in there? The role of the prison psychologist is briefly examined here. Chapter 19 looks at the major issue of mental disorder within prison. There is a high proportion of people within both the prison system and secure hospitals who have commited a crime but who are mentally ill. How we treat them is a controversial and costly issue. Chapter 20 looks at the case of the long-term prisoner, the life prisoner and the capital prisoner, and the psychology of each of the categories of incarceration.

In addition to the main textbook, there is also a companion website, access to which is granted on adoption or purchase. The website contains lecturer resources, consisting of PowerPoint slides for each chapter, a test bank of multiple-choice and short-answer questions for each chapter, and student resources, with multiple-choice questions for a self-assessment test bank and a glossary of key terms. In this way, users of the textbook are supported with resources to aid learning via both the textbook's structures and the linkages to areas for self-assessment and tutor assessment. The website can be found at www.sagepub.co.uk/gavinCFP

Section 1

Defining Criminological and Forensic Psychology

This section introduces the concepts fundamental to the psychological study of crime. In terms of defining what forensic psychology is, and its relationship with other psychological approaches to crime, Chapter 1 defines the topics to be examined and outlines what forensic psychologists do, and how that is different from the wider psychological perspectives. Chapter 2 examines how research in psychology and the methods of psychological research can be applied to the study of crime. This chapter relates to the research dimension and core role 2 (research), but also core role 1 (applications) because it introduces the elements of research and research practice that are important to forensic psychologists. The need to remain informed about developments in the discipline is a fundamental component of professional practice, as well as contributing to research where possible.

1

Defining Forensic Psychology

What is forensic psychology?

History of forensic psychology

What do forensic psychologists do and how do I become one?

Becoming a forensic psychologist in the UK, the USA and in other countries

Definitions and terminology

The relationship between psychology and the law

Knowledge and skills required
Dimensions
Knowledge, research and practice
Core roles
Applications, research, communications and training

The pathways to qualifications, and the acquisition of knowledge and skills

Psychology in investigation – an example of forensic psychology in action

Imagine a granite-faced Scotsman, moodily smoking a cigarette and staring at a murder suspect with ill-disguised distaste. Or a group of impossibly attractive people flying across country in a jet to solve crimes for other police officers. Or a beautiful young woman who can 'see' crime scenes through the eyes of others, usually the perpetrator.

Familiar images? Yes, probably, if you have ever watched any TV programme about a forensic psychologist. Truthful images? Well, no, they are made for dramatic effect and contain only a germ of the truth. So, what does it mean to be a forensic psychologist, and what is the truth behind the drama and mayhem portrayed on the TV screen?

WHAT IS FORENSIC PSYCHOLOGY?

The term 'psychology' was probably first used by Goclenius, a German philosopher, who wrote about various philosophical positions in 1590 in a book called *Problematum Logicorum* (Dyck, 2009). The word itself comes from the Greek for 'soul' or 'spirit' (*psyche*), so 'psychology' was originally termed to describe the study of the soul. However, in modern use, 'psychology' is, for many people, a science, albeit a special kind of science.

There are various specialisms within the broad field of psychology, and forensic psychology is one of them. The word 'forensic' is from the Latin term *forensis* meaning 'of the forum'. Ancient Rome's forum was where the law courts were held. We now refer to forensic sciences as the application of scientific principles to the adversarial law process.

Forensic psychology is the application of psychology to the legal process

Where does such terminology leave forensic psychology? Forensic psychology is strictly the term describing the application of psychology to the legal process, and it has a long, long history.

HISTORY OF FORENSIC PSYCHOLOGY

The relationship between psychology and the law is an ancient one. The Greek philosopher Aristotle stated, in his books *Nicomachean Ethics*, that a person should only be considered morally responsible for a criminal act if he has knowledge of the circumstances and acted without external compulsion (Pakaluk, 2005). Such philosophical positions took centuries to be incorporated into any form of legal system, and the history is littered with what to twenty-first-century eyes appears to be injustice. The concept of insanity as mitigation in English law was not considered until the fourteenth century, and then only in cases of 'absolute madness' (Allnutt et al., 2007). This is the point at which common law courts were directed that defendants must be capable of assisting in their own defence. If they were deemed incompetent due to insanity or mental defect, then the court would not proceed with the prosecution (Otto, 2006). There is little record of what happened to the defendant after that decision was made though.

According to Spielvogel (2007), it is during the Age of Enlightenment that we find the first acceptance of the status of expert witness testimony in court. In 1723, 'The Wild Beast Test' became the standard exemption from punishment, meaning that a man 'that is totally deprived of his understanding and memory, and doth not know what he is doing, no more than an infant, than a brute, or a wild beast, such a one is never the object of punishment' (Taylor, 1997: 103). This was followed by the development of systematic criminal investigation in the eighteenth and nineteenth centuries. This is also the time, perhaps coincidently, when experimental psychology was beginning to emerge as a scientific discipline and clinical psychology became established as a profession in its own right.

Forensic psychology, as a specialism within clinical psychology, or as a distinct discipline, grew out of the need for psychological evidence to be used in law and the legal process. Forensic psychology is strictly seen to be concerned with psychological aspects of legal processes, but the term can also be applied to investigative and criminological psychology, in which theory is applied to criminal investigation, psychological explanations of crime, and the treatment of criminals.

The first recorded event of expert psychological testimony being used in court is not until 1896, when Albert von Schrenk-Notzing argued against the conviction of a man accused of murder. He testified that, due to the huge pre-trial publicity the case had attracted, the witnesses would be unable to distinguish between what they actually witnessed and what was reported in the newspapers. It is also in the nineteenth century that psychology and the study of the mental state was first examined rigorously, and Hugo Munsterberg published the first essays in forensic psychology in 1908. In the USA, perhaps the first systematic study of legal testimony was carried out by Cattell in 1895, starting a process that leads us to today's knowledge about witnesses and their memory (Brown & Campbell, 2010). Therefore, although forensic psychology can claim to be a discipline with hundreds of years of history, in reality, as a recognised professional practice, it is little over 100 years old. This means it is a mere child in comparison to the use of medicine in law; the first forensic medicine textbook was written in China in 1247 by a man regarded as the father of forensic science, Song Ci (Peng & Pounder, 1998). Even this is predated by fifth-century European laws specifying the employment of physicians to determine cause of death (Wecht, 2005).

However well-established forensic psychology might be, it is a misunderstood practice, mainly due to the romanticising of the discipline in the media, and the somewhat prurient interest of the public in anything to do with crime, criminals and detection.

WHAT DO FORENSIC PSYCHOLOGISTS DO AND HOW DO I BECOME ONE?

A forensic psychologist can be involved in a variety of activities. Both the British Psychological Society (BPS, www.BPS.org.uk) and the American Psychological Association (APA, www.APA.org) describe these tasks as being central to legal processes, and covering aspects from crime scenes to testimony in court. As forensic psychology is the interface between matters legal and matters psychological, it follows that forensic psychologists are both subject to the law and have influence on it. In fact, forensic psychology is now a term used to represent any application of psychology to any aspect of the legal and criminal process, although when psychology is used in the detection and investigation of crime, it is now quite often referred to as investigative psychology (see Canter & Youngs, 2003). If an academic researcher is investigating causes of crime in order to understand criminality or how to prevent crime, rather than the detection and prosecution of criminals, this is more likely to be referred to as criminological psychology.

Activities in forensic psychology

- Statistical analysis of crime trends
- Statistical analysis for offender profiling
- Crime scene analysis
- Providing expert testimony in court
- Assessing suspects for fitness to be charged, questioned or tried
- Hostage negotiation
- Offender treatment programmes
- Academic/practice research programmes

Psychology in investigation

Once a crime has been committed, psychology can play some interesting roles in the investigation process, including crime scene analysis and profiling. These roles are perhaps the areas that have been depicted most in fiction, but despite this, or maybe because of it, are particularly misunderstood functions of forensic psychology (Aamodt, 2008). Profiling involves the understanding of human behaviour and psychopathology, and requires study of aspects of a crime scene in order to build a picture of an offender. Such profiles can be very accurate, and hence can be used to guide investigatory processes. The problem is that they can also be viewed as over-accurate; investigators sometimes use the profile as if it were physical evidence, rather than a means to narrow searches and eliminate suspects.

In 1992, Rachel Nickell was sexually assaulted and stabbed to death on Wimbledon Common, the only witness being her 2-year-old son. As Leppard (2007) reports, this was a high-profile case, possibly due to the victim's youth and attractiveness, or the horror attached to the idea of a young child witnessing such a terrible attack. There were few suspects, but the investigation alighted on Colin Stagg, a loner who appeared to have violent sexual fantasies and who frequented the Common. At the same time, the police had asked a well-known psychologist to compile a profile, based on sexually deviant aspects of the crime. The profile was accepted as an accurate assessment not of the *type* of person who would have committed the crime, but of *Stagg's* personality and behaviour (Herndon, 2007). The police set up what became known as a 'honey trap' – an undercover female police officer attempted to trap Stagg into revealing he had killed Rachel Nickell. He did reveal some sexual fantasies, but nothing in his conversations with the police officer ever suggested he killed the woman. Nevertheless, the police were convinced that they had their man and proceeded to charge and prosecute Stagg for the murder. Their major evidence comprised the profile and communications with the policewoman. As the trial approached, in 1994, the presiding judge, Mr Justice Ognall, decided that the material demonstrated manipulation of the accused in a reprehensible manner, an attempt to incriminate by police deception (Gregory, 2007). In other words, the police set out to find evidence to cause Stagg to look guilty based on the profile, and the manner in which they did this constituted entrapment. The judge ruled that the evidence was inadmissible under section 78 of the Police and Criminal Evidence Act 1984. The prosecution case collapsed and Stagg was formally acquitted. Robert Napper, a serial rapist who had attacked and killed another woman and her daughter since Rachel's death, was charged in 2007 with the murder of Rachel (Leppard, 2007), and on 18 December 2008, he pleaded guilty to Rachel's manslaughter on the grounds of diminished responsibility.

Profiling took a severe blow, its theoretical and empirical foundations shaken. The unwise way in which the profile was used, the advice of the profiler being followed slavishly, was subjected to harsh scrutiny and criticism by the media. The hitherto magical darling of fiction was shown for what it was – an instrument that needed skilful hands or it would damage what it was supposed to build. However, when used properly, crime scene analysis and resulting profiles are an effective aid to police and security agency investigations. For example, Dean (2007) suggests that profiling can be used to outline the process by which terrorists are formed, rather than trying to build a profile of individual extremists. This may be a more fruitful way of applying profiling, as a prevention rather than detection process, and remove the temptation of law enforcement officers and psychologists to use it as a piece of hard evidence.

Psychology can also be helpful once the investigation identifies witnesses or a suspect. The psychological research around eyewitness memory and the fallibility of testimony has helped, as police officers now know that they need to corroborate such evidence independently and with different forms of evidence seeking. Psychology has also revealed the problems of mental incapacity to be interviewed or charged, false confession and suspect/ witness suggestibility, and police officers are trained in interview techniques designed to minimise these effects.

Once a suspect has been identified and charged, psychologists may enter the realm of the courts. Defendants may need to be assessed for competency to stand trial for example, and a clinical psychologist with forensic training may provide the assessment rather than a psychiatrist. Psychologists tend to have more training in the use of psychometric tests and their application in legal settings, and be able to determine whether someone is mentally incapacitated or legally insane, in which case the prosecution and trial become very different matters. The psychological expert may be called on to give this opinion in court and hence become an expert witness. There are various other types of expert testimony a forensic psychologist might give. For example, the research on problems with eyewitness memory or the possibility of false confessions has not only aided the process of evidence gathering, but can be presented in court to support issues around the presentation of evidence.

After the trial, psychologists may be involved with those convicted of a crime. According to Durcan (2008), a large proportion of those in prison have mental health problems 'together with a complex mix of other issues, including substance misuse, poverty and a history of abuse' (p. 7). In this case, the care of prisoners does need input from psychological services, and forensic psychologists are best placed to provide these – understanding crime, what crime does to those involved in it, and the psychological outcomes of incarceration.

Forensic psychologists may also be asked to bring their expertise to bear in civil cases, such as proceedings involving child custody or compensation. This role is not covered in any detail in this book as it concentrates on criminological applications of psychology; however, it bears mention here, as it could be something you encounter in your professional life. While crime is a controversial and difficult area, when family or civil matters reach court it can be even more problematic, due to the emotional turmoil represented. This is the legal aspect of divorce and child custody, compensation and workers' rights, and impinges on abuse, trauma and blame, and all their attendant difficulties. The very nature of this turmoil often leads psychologists away from this area of practice and back to the criminal courts, as experts of course.

Typical cases where a psychologist may be consulted are those involving employment discrimination, sexual harassment, personal injury, workplace stress, in which they need to carry out evaluation of individuals alleging psychological damage, or in divorce proceedings, where assessment of the parties involved is required after allegations of abuse or disputes over child custody.

BECOMING A FORENSIC PSYCHOLOGIST IN THE UK, THE USA AND IN OTHER COUNTRIES

Becoming a forensic psychologist in the UK

A great many of the forensic psychologists working in the UK are employed by the Prison Service, the Home Office research units, and the health service, but they can also be found in many other settings, including universities, the social services, the Probation Service and private consultancy.

In order to become a forensic psychologist, you will need to undertake the training identified by the country/state in which you want to work. The following summarises the information found in the British Psychological Society (BPS) publications on recognised qualifications (e.g. BPS, 2013). In the UK, this means having a degree recognised by the British Psychological Society, which is the professional body that also accredits undergraduate programmes, providing the Graduate Basis for Registration (GBR) or, more recently, Graduate Basis for Chartership (GBC). This should be followed by either:

a. an accredited Masters qualification in Forensic Psychology, followed by two years' supervised practice

or

b. a professional Doctorate in Forensic Psychology, incorporating supervised practice.

A graduate will normally need to have attained at least an upper second classification in their first degree to gain a place on a postgraduate programme of this nature.

The courses qualify a graduate in the academic component of the required competences to be a Chartered Forensic Psychologist, but the whole programme should have the academic training followed by practical experience under the supervision of a Chartered Forensic Psychologist. An alternative academic route is to undertake a Doctoral programme in Forensic Psychology, which combines the taught and research-based elements with the required practice-based elements of training.

The training in forensic psychology is complex because, in addition to acquiring advanced knowledge of psychology and criminology, it also involves acquiring an awareness of the legal system. For example, when specialising in forensic issues, a practitioner in forensic psychology might be called on by a court to assess a defendant's competency to stand trial. There is also the possibility of being called on to assess the state of mind of the defendant at the time of the offence. Such an assessment is a legal one and not simply a psychological one, so it requires someone with the ability to transpose their psychological expertise into legal framework and language and then explain this to a jury of lay people. In the UK, the training is regulated by the BPS, which outlines the training for forensic psychology in terms of competences to be acquired in order to qualify for the Diploma in Forensic Psychology. Completion of an accredited course and the required supervised practice qualifies a candidate to apply for the Society's Diploma.

In order to satisfy the Society that you have met these requirements, you need to demonstrate that you have achieved a satisfactory standard in three dimensions:

- Knowledge Dimension – the underpinning knowledge base (Stage 1)
- Research Dimension – the research element of training (Stages 1 & 2)
- Practice Dimension – a period of supervised practice (Stage 2)

These standards are assessed by the production of portfolios that demonstrate competence in:

- Core Role 1 Conducting Applications and Interventions
- Core Role 2 Research
- Core Role 3 Communicating with Other Professionals
- Core Role 4 Training Other Professionals

Trainee forensic psychologists must show understanding of the conceptual basis within which psychological knowledge is applied in forensic contexts, i.e. understanding of the link between psychology and criminal behaviour, appreciation of the legal framework of the law and the civil and criminal justice systems, methodological issues and appreciation of the ethical and professional considerations of forensic practice. They must also show understanding of applications of psychology to processes within the criminal and civil justice systems in the UK, i.e. how psychology is applied to the process of investigation, the legal process, the custodial process and through care.

There are often specific client groups encountered in forensic psychology, and applicants for registration as forensic psychologists need to show that they appreciate that interventions with specific client groups are appropriate, such as the assessment and intervention with victims of offences, offenders, litigants, appellants and individuals seeking arbitration and mediation, etc.

The use and communication of information in psychological practice is a key element of practice and a forensic psychologist must understand the nature and style of the information required within forensic settings, such as approaches to assessment, criteria for professional report production, giving expert testimony, consultancy, project management and organisational interventions.

In order to demonstrate the knowledge, skills and experience necessary for registration with the professional body, a trainee must undertake the academic training together with supervised practice. For details, you are referred to the registration body's literature, but this book is concerned with the academic component of the training.

Becoming a forensic psychologist in the USA

The major professional body that certifies forensic psychologists in the USA is the American Board of Forensic Psychology (ABFP). Although other organisations offer Board Certification, the ABFP advises on the integrity and credibility of programmes offered by other organisations and is the only nationally recognised body. The following information is a summary of the ABFP guidance on obtaining the board certification (ABFP, 2010). In order to apply for registration/certification, an applicant needs to demonstrate that s/he has undertaken 1,000 hours of qualifying experience in forensic psychology over a minimum of a four-year period, although the substitution of a specified degree can be claimed as long as 1,000 hours have been undertaken in the remaining time. In addition, 100 hours of specialised training in forensic psychology are required, either under direct supervision by a qualified forensic professional, or in continuing education activities, and/or relevant classroom activities at a graduate or postgraduate level. Workshops presented by the American Academy of Forensic Psychology count on a

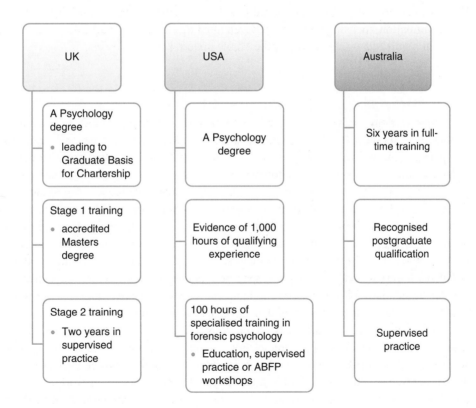

Figure 1.1   Becoming a forensic psychologist

two-for-one basis towards the required 100 hours. After meeting all those criteria, an applicant is eligible to apply for the Diploma and to undertake a written examination. The exam shows whether a candidate possesses a sufficient depth and breadth of core knowledge in forensic psychology, and demonstrates a psycho-legal knowledge at a sufficient level of competence, proficiency and professionalism. The examination currently consists of 200 multiple-choice questions focusing on:

- Ethics, Guidelines and Professional Issues
- Law, Precedents, Court Rules, and Civil and Criminal Procedure
- Testing and Assessment, Judgment and Bias, and Examination Issues
- Individual Rights and Liberties, Civil Competence
- Juvenile, Parenting and Family/Matrimonial Matters
- Personal Injury, Civil Damages, Disability and Workers' Compensation
- Criminal Competence
- Criminal Responsibility

If applicants pass this, they are required to submit Practice Samples, and then submit to an oral examination, focusing on the practice element of the work. Finally, they need to submit a written report of a research project they have undertaken.

Forensic psychology across the world

The above sections give an overview of the training in forensic psychology in two nations, but a quick analysis shows that the programmes are remarkably similar – several years studying and practising under supervision, leading to a scrutiny by a designated professional body in order to acquire recognition. Where forensic psychology is recognised as a discipline in its own right, the training and recognition of practitioners is similar in nature to those found in the UK and the USA. For example, in Australia, forensic psychologists need to complete at least six years of full-time university training, including a recognised postgraduate forensic psychology qualification together with supervised practice. They then are required to be registered with the Psychologist Registration Board in their State or Territory and with a national registration board. As in the UK and USA, there are specified standards of competence and ethical practice and strict guidelines for professional conduct, and practitioners are required to undertake continuing professional development, with a particular focus on forensic psychology.

Some countries call the practice of psychology within the legal or criminal justice system something other than forensic psychology. For example, in Canada, the Canadian Psychological Association (Société Canadienne de Psychologie) has a Criminal Justice Psychology section, which represents members of the Canadian Psychological Association working in a variety of criminal justice and forensic settings, including correction, law enforcement, the courts, hospitals, community mental health, and academic settings. It also has a section geared towards the study and prevention of extremism and terrorism. However, it is not the body that certifies psychologists in practice, as there are provincial regulatory bodies that do this.

If a psychologist were wishing to practise in a particular country, it would be wise to consult the professional psychological body in that country to determine what training would be required and acceptable, and under what title a practitioner would work. At the end of this chapter is a list of bodies that provide some form of network for psychologists in a specific country. Some countries do not officially recognise forensic psychology as a separate area of study or practice. As a general rule of thumb, if a country does not have a psychological association of some sort, then it is unlikely to recognise forensic psychologists. However, having an association does not necessarily mean that there is such a designation in that country.

There are moves to build internationally recognised bodies that can draw these together and ensure that a suitably qualified person can practise in other parts of the world. See the International Academy of Investigative Psychology, for example.

THIS BOOK

As our brief history of forensic psychology shows, the concept of psychological elements of crime and legal processes has had an impact for centuries, even though its recognition as an identifiable discipline is somewhat more recent. Crime has always been with us, although understanding how the criminal mind works, and how the legal process influences and affects the criminal, victim, witness and professional legal person is a relatively recent development. The place of the forensic psychologist in this world is central, and therefore the training of forensic psychologists must be rigorous and evident. This book is intended to introduce and develop knowledge in the areas of criminological and forensic psychology, and support students wishing to attain these on the way to acquiring qualifications in forensic or criminal psychology. The chapters reflect knowledge and understanding of the academic components that underpin the competences required by the British Psychological Society in order to register as a Chartered Forensic Psychologist and which reflect those elsewhere in the world. They will therefore cover elements that aid the attainment of an understanding of psychology and criminal behaviour, and how that knowledge is applied in forensic contexts. Hence the book will cover all of the areas that would be addressed in an academic training in forensic psychology, but will not directly support the practice element of the postgraduate training, i.e. the supervision of work in a forensic setting.

The academic training includes elements of the four key roles:

- Conducting psychological applications and interventions
- Research (the design, conduct, analysis and evaluation of applied psychological research in forensic settings)
- Communicating psychological knowledge and advice to other professionals
- Training other professionals in psychological skills and knowledge

These are addressed in relevant sections of the book, not simply as a description of the various topics needed to be understood in order to demonstrate the core competences of

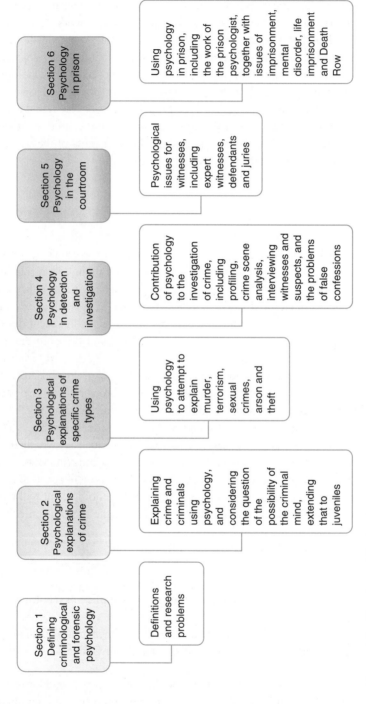

Figure 1.2　Structure of the book

a Chartered Forensic Psychologist. Instead, it will embed this knowledge by examining famous cases in terms of the relevant topic being explored. In addition to these cases, as each chapter makes explicit the link between the material under discussion and the competency to be addressed by learning and applying that material.

SUMMARY

This chapter has discussed the definitions of forensic psychology and outlined the educative process of entering this area of practice. The next chapter introduces the component of research inherent in each of the academic and applied areas. An understanding of research and the ability to undertake it are vital, as forensic psychology is a growing discipline, moving forward by research, and the best people to undertake that research are those who understand the way in which forensic psychology impinges on the world and everyone in it.

List of psychological bodies

Afghan Psychological Association

American Psychological Association, Association for Psychological Science, US National Committee for Psychology

Argentinian Association of Behavioral Therapy

Association of Albanian Psychologists

Association of German Professional Psychologists

Association of Greek Psychologists

Association of Liechtenstein Psychologists

Australian Psychological Society

Azerbaijan Psychological Association

Bahamas Psychological Association

Bangladesh Psychological Association

Belgian Association for Psychological Science

Belgian Federation of Psychologists

Brazilian Psychological Society

British Psychological Society

Bulgarian Psychological Society

Cambodian Psychology Society

Cambodian Transcultural Psycho Social Organization

Canadian Psychological Association

Chinese Psychological Society

Collegium of Chilean Psychologists

Colombian Psychological Society

Croatian Psychological Association

Cyprus Psychologists Association, Pancyprian Society of Psychologists

Czech-Moravian Psychological Society

Danish Psychological Association

Dominican Psychologists' Society

Egyptian Association for Psychological Studies

Emirates Psychological Association

Ethiopian Psychologists' Association

(Continued)

(Continued)

Federation of Austrian Associations of
    Psychologists
Federation of Swiss Psychologists
Finnish Psychological Society
French Psychological Society, Federation
    of French Psychologists
Georgian Psychological Association
German Psychological Association
Guam Psychological Association
Guatemalan Psychological Association
Hellenic Psychological Society (Greece)
Hong Kong Psychological Society
Hungarian Psychological Association
Icelandic Psychological Society
Indian Psychological Association
Indonesian Psychology Association
Iranian Association of Psychology
Iraqi Educational and Psychological
    Association
Israel Psychological Association
Italian Network of Professional
    Psychologists Associations, Italian
    Psychological Society
Jamaica Psychological Society
Japanese Psychological Association
Jordanian Psychological Association
Kenya Psychological Association
Korean Psychological Association
Latvian Professional Psychologists
    Association
Lebanese Psychological Association
Lithuanian Psychological Association
Malaysian Psychological Association
Mexican Psychological Association
Mongolian Psychologists Association
Moroccan Psychological Association
National Syndicate of Psychologists (Portugal)
Nepalese Psychological Association
Netherlands Institute of Psychologists
New Zealand Psychological Society

Nicaraguan Psychological Association
Nigerian Psychological Association
Norwegian Psychological Association
Organization of Psychologists of San Marino
Pakistan Psychological Association
Panamanian Association of Psychologists
Peru Psychological Association
Polish Psychological Association
Portuguese Psychological Society
Psychological Association of Barbados
Psychological Association of Namibia
Psychological Association of the Philippines
Psychological Society of Ireland
Psychological Society of South Africa
Psychologists Union of Cuba
Psycho-Pedagogical Association of Vietnam
Puerto Rico Psychological Association
Romanian Psychologists Association
Russian Psychological Society
Saudi Educational and Psychological
    Association
Serbian Psychological Society
Singapore Psychological Society
Slovenian Psychological Association
Spanish Federation of Psychological
    Associations, Spanish Psychological
    Association
Sudanese Psychological Society
Swedish Psychological Association
Swiss Psychological Society
Thai Psychological Association
Turkish Psychological Association
Uganda National Psychological
    Association
Ukranian Psychological Society
Union of Estonian Psychologists
Union of Psychologists of Armenia
Uruguay Psychological Society
Yemen Psychological Association
Zimbabwe Psychological Association

Research Methods in Forensic Psychology

Identifying research questions	Designing the study	Ethical considerations	Dissemination

Literature reviewing
Literature databases

Quantitative designs
Experimental and correlational designs

Qualitative designs
Ethnography
Phenomenology
Grounded Theory

Sampling

Analysis

Psychology is an evidence-based discipline. This means that knowledge about psychology is derived from clearly articulated and empirically supported theories. That empirical support is a result of rigorous, openly discussed and reviewed research that adds to theory or moves it on. To be any type of psychologist, a person must be able to interpret and use the results of research in his or her own work, and for some, that means carrying out that research, interpretation and dissemination. This chapter examines the forms of research design and methodology that are supportive of the practice of forensic psychology

KEY THEMES

- Identifying research questions
- Reviewing the literature
- Designing research
- Quantitative designs
- Qualitative designs
- Ethical considerations in research
- Data collection
- Experimental designs
- Correlation designs surveys
- Psychometrics
- Sampling
- Analysis

  - Qualitative analysis
  - Quantitative analysis

- Dissemination

One of the major skills needed as a forensic psychologist is carrying out and understanding research and the way it can be applied in forensic settings. The core role associated with these skills is the ability to design and conduct applied psychological research, analyse the data derived from the research, and evaluate such research. A competent forensic psychologist needs to be able to generate ideas for research and formulate the research questions that derive from those ideas, define parameters and identify resources for research, plan, design and prepare research investigations and the tools needed to carry them out, negotiate for access and resources to conduct research, collaborate with other professionals and collect and analyse data, and provide appropriate interpretation and evaluation of results. Having done all that, there is the need to formulate recommendations based on the outcomes of research. These skills are an integral part of the qualification in forensic psychology in many jurisdictions.

The types of research question that might face a forensic or criminological psychologist include: those examining the nature of crime; criminal types or personalities; social, biological or psychological causes of crime; reliability of witness testimony; fear of crimes and the consequence of that fear, etc. Specific to a forensic psychologist are questions such as the reliability of psychological profiles of criminals, or the effectiveness of punishment, treatment or rehabilitation.

Throughout an undergraduate course in psychology, a student is told that the use of research methods is an underpinning skill and competency that needs to be acquired before psychology can be truly understood. It also seems to be the most difficult part of the discipline that students encounter. This chapter will summarise the use of research methods and refresh knowledge of the area.

In order to carry out psychological research, a researcher must identify the phenomenon under examination, determine the question to be investigated and the theoretical framework in which the question is to be set, and the appropriate design to investigate the question.

IDENTIFYING FORENSIC PSYCHOLOGICAL RESEARCH QUESTIONS

The first step in research is to decide what is to be researched. Once a piece of research is decided upon, the researcher must search out relevant material about the topic in a structured and focused manner.

The literature search and review

A literature search is an essential start to a project and is a planned search for relevant publications on a topic. This means that researchers look for the evidence on the subject and can see what has been done to investigate it and how, and avoid repeating work that has already been carried out. Finding literature allied to your research question means that you can identify what still needs to be investigated (and previous research may include suggestions for this) and how new research will advance understanding within the specified area. However, a literature search should be selective, and identify the most relevant resources to support the work. The judgement on relevancy does mean that new researchers must familiarise themselves with the general area of research and methods used, and a good place to start, beyond textbooks, are review articles that summarise research and argument in a given area. For example, Grubb and Harrower (2008) reviewed several studies that addressed factors affecting judgements of rape victims. Their conclusions contributed an overview of some of the ways in which people attribute blame to victims of serious sexual assault and identified methodological limitations across the field of rape study. Such articles are invaluable in terms of identifying the theoretical and methodological framework of your chosen area of study. From there, the search can move into more specific pieces of work that are relevant to the research question.

Searching the literature

In order to identify the literature to be used, a familiarity with the search resources is essential, as there are several sources of information about the topic. Journals are the best source for recent information that has been peer-reviewed and accepted by the research community. Some of the most relevant journals in the forensic psychology literature are included in a list at the end of this chapter. The review process means that journal editors only accept the most relevant research for publication. However, due to the review and editing process that journals undertake, it might be up to two years before a piece of research is published. So a more up-to-date source might be conference proceedings. Conferences are arenas in which the latest findings are presented to colleagues interested in a research area, in the form of papers or posters. The proceedings are the published papers or abstracts of the conference. They can be useful in providing information on the latest research or research that has not been published. They are also helpful in providing information on which people are currently involved in which research areas, and can therefore be helpful in tracking down other work by the same researchers.

The fastest growing source of information is the Internet. While this is a valuable asset in any researcher's world, there are some very important difficulties to be aware of. First, anyone with access to a computer and the relevant authoring software can design a website, and just about anyone can post information on the Internet, so the quality of content may not be reliable. Secondly, the information posted may be intended for a general audience and so not be suitable for inclusion in your literature review. It is very easy to place information on the Internet and those who do so may have various motivations for doing so. Some people may have a political agenda to meet; some may simply be posting up their own opinions without any reference to other viewpoints. It is safest to view each website with more than a little scepticism until the information can be verified by another source. Sites such as Wikipedia have been shown to be unreliable. In 2005, the founder of Wikipedia admitted that the quality of the information placed on it was suspect at best and subject to serious errors. Wikipedia is based on open and collaborative insertion and editing of entries, and this very openness and accessibility can cause problems with reliability of topics. It should be noted than many universities do not allow the use of Wikipedia as a primary source, but this may extend to encyclopedias in general. However, many of the articles on such sites are invaluable to readers new to a topic. These can be viewed as useful introductions to the topics in easily readable and accessible forms before moving on to more reliable sources of data. Many refereed electronic journals (e-journals) are appearing on the Internet – if they are refereed it means that there is an editorial board that evaluates the work so the quality should be more reliable.

Carrying out a search of the literature in the area provides the context for the current research and will also provide clues about how to write up work. There are some conventions about writing up research papers and every researcher should be aware of them. The majority of research articles and other sources of research literature are now in electronic format, although hard copies of books and papers are still available through your academic library. The major repository for psychological and related literature is PsycINFO. This is a database containing all the information from *Psychological Abstracts*, the key secondary reference journal. It contains non-evaluative summaries (abstracts) of the literature in more than 1,300 periodicals. PsycINFO does not provide full-text access to sources, although the library to which you subscribe may have access to these, and can provide them for you through links in PsycINFO. However, reading abstracts is a very good place to start choosing articles to include in your review or deciding which sources to eliminate.

Another useful resource is the Social Sciences Citation Index (SSCI), which uses cited reference searching. If you start with a specific source, such as a key review article, the SSCI will identify all articles that have cited the original. The assumption is that if an article cited your original, it could be relevant. You also need to be clear about where you are searching as books and articles in peer-reviewed journals have undergone a rigorous process of review and amendment, whereas other publications might not have.

Most students will also be already familiar with online search engines such as Google. There is an extension of Google called Google Scholar, which, fairly obviously, searches only within scholarly literature, but across a range of disciplines. Using Google Scholar might give you a taste of articles and authors in order to limit your search in something like PsycINFO.

The problem with these search engines, as with all other search engines, academic or not, is that they only search for what you ask. This means you need to learn how to limit your search terms so that you do not end up with thousands of 'hits' in the database the engines search. Take, for example, a search using Google Scholar and the search term 'sex offenders'. This returned almost 30,000 hits. Even using PsycINFO, the same term brought up almost 5,500 publications, 3,700 of those in peer-reviewed journals. Clearly, no one wants to spend several hours (days?) sifting through these. A more refined and focused search strategy is needed.

One way of doing this is to use more search terms and combine them using 'Boolean operators'. This refers to the ways in which you combine your search terms and will determine how focused your results will be. Choosing to use the advanced search tool in PsycINFO allows you to combine search terms readily. Combining 'sex offenders' AND 'medical treatment' found 31 published works, of which ten were in peer-reviewed journals. So, what is the Boolean bit? Well, if we had used OR instead of AND, the search would have brought us over 76,000 hits in PsycINFO, almost 17,000 in Google Scholar and 13,900,000 in Google. This is because we are asking for all articles that include any of these phrases. Think about how you are combining your search terms, or you may end up even more confused and frustrated.

Once you have your refined search results, examine the article title. If it seems relevant, read the abstract. At this point you should be choosing to include or exclude articles from your search, and a highly relevant abstract should be followed up in terms of acquiring the full text of the article. This might be quite easy, as the library you are a member of may have online or paper subscriptions to the journals. A paper subscription means a trip to the library and its periodical section to copy the article, but an online subscription means you can download the article to your own computer. Not having a subscription means a bit of a wait, though, but you can request it through interlibrary loans. Your university might make a small charge for this, and even limit the number you can request as a student, so make sure you are requesting the most relevant for your research question and literature review.

Table 2.1 Choosing a research approach in forensic and criminological psychology

Consideration	Qualitative research	Quantitative research	Choices
Scientific method	Bottom-up New hypotheses, and possibly new theories, are generated from data Example: How the familial context of sex offenders affects their empathy	Top-down Testing hypotheses and theory with data. Example: Accuracy of fingerprint analysts and the effect of confidence in ability	Do you have specific hypotheses to test or more broad ideas to examine?
Viewpoint on human behaviour	Fluid, situational, social and personal The familial context is fluid and socially and personally constructed	Regular and predictable Fingerprint analysts work within certain limits, which can be measured and predicted	Do you view any behaviours as being subject to influences that are outside the person, or do you view it as being possible to predict in a given set of circumstances?
Research objectives	Description, exploration and discovery Describing how these offenders behave allows discovery of their personal viewpoints with respect to their victims and may lead to new theoretical positions	Description, explanation and prediction of human behaviour The ways in which this sample of analysts behave will predict how other similar people will behave	Do you want to discover aspects of behaviour as yet unknown, or wish to make predictions about how someone will behave in similar situations?
Research focus	Broad and deep with respect to people under observation The ways in which offenders view their victims and their offences	Narrow and specific Accuracy of fingerprint identification compared to level of confident in accuracy	Can you operationalise specific variables or not?
Context	Naturalistic	Controlled conditions	Can you control the environment sufficiently to say it can be relocated, or is it more open to other influences?
Nature of reality	Subjective	Objective	Do you view reality as something different people will agree on when it is observed in a given set of circumstances, or that each person has their own worldview?
Data collection	Unstructured Offenders' reports in answer to researcher's questions Written accounts of views – letters of apology to the victim	Precise measurements, calibrated outside the researcher's purview Accuracy levels and confidence levels	Are you making measurements or observations?
Data	Words, aims and categories	Measurements	What form is your data and how will you transform it into ways understood by others?
Analysis	Patterns, themes and holistic features Offenders' ways of expressing apology	Statistical relationships or differences between variables Correlation between accuracy and confidence	Can you make statistical analysis or will you look for recurring configurations of meaning?
Results	Present multiple perspectives Offenders' familial context led to the personal construction of their view of the offences and victims	Generalisation of findings Analysts' accuracy may be affected by confidence	

One thing that new researchers often fall foul of is keeping track of what has been read and where each piece of information has been was found. A 'running matrix' is often a good idea. This is a database in which the salient details of each article or other items found can be recorded, such as the list shown in Table 2.1. This way, all items can be kept together in some easily accessible way and the items can be ordered by date or by author – a really useful device when it comes to checking citations and references.

Having gathered all the previous work in the area that you need, the next thing to do is to examine the theoretical and methodological issues within those papers. You can then align yourself within that framework and even make decisions about your own research and what form it will take. Previous writers in the area will have made clear what their objectives were, but also what they think the limitations in the area are and what future research is necessary. From this, you can build the rationale for your own work and move on to design your own study or studies.

DESIGNING THE STUDY

Both quantitative and qualitative methods are used in forensic psychology; the choice depends on the question being investigated. Researchers do not always have the autonomy to choose the method as the research may be carried out as part of a commission. Sometimes, professional psychologists may be asked to carry out research on behalf of someone else, or a particular agency. For example, the UK Home Office might commission research on the usefulness of prison treatment programmes or the effective recruitment of police officers. Security agencies might ask for confidential psycholinguistic or discourse analysis of terrorist communications. All of these studies can be carried out using the research methodology of psychology.

Quantitative research design

Most empirical quantitative research belongs clearly to one of two general categories. In correlational research, we do not (or at least try not to) influence any variables, but only measure them and look for relations (correlations) between some set of variables, such IQ

Table 2.2   Example of a running matrix

Year	Authors	Method	Findings	Journal
2010	Gavin/Porter	Review	Stats & causes	TVA
2011	schlomer et al	Review & theory appn	Conflict theory/ evolution	Psy Rev

and amount of criminal behaviour. If we see a relationship (and it is established that IQ and crime are negatively correlated), we might conclude that low IQ increases criminal behaviour or criminal behaviour decreases IQ. So correlation research does not seek to establish causal relationships between variables, just the strength and direction of the relationship.

In experimental research, we manipulate some variables and then measure the effects of this manipulation on other variables. For example, to investigate the effect of weight gain on cholesterol levels, a researcher might have participants deliberately increase their weight and then record cholesterol level (not the most ethical of studies!). Only experimental data can conclusively demonstrate causal relations between variables. For example, if we found that whenever we change variable A, then variable B changes, then we could conclude that A influences B. Data from correlational research can only be interpreted in terms based on known theories; correlational data cannot conclusively prove causality.

In order to claim causality we need three elements:

- Temporal precedence
- Covariation of cause and effect
- No alternative explanation

Temporal precedence

In order to be able to say that one thing caused another, the first thing has to happen before the second. This might not be quite as easy as you think and it could be a classic case of chicken and egg. For example, our study of obesity factors must establish which state happened first, the weight gain or the high cholesterol.

Covariation

As well as establishing that our cause happens before the effect, we need to show that there is actually a relationship between them. In logic, we would express this as if A then B; if not A then not B. So if we can observe that whenever A is present, B is too, and whenever A is absent, B is too, then we have demonstrated that a relationship exists between them. However, this might not be reasonable. For example, in the days before family planning (and probably electric lighting and widely available heating), more babies were born in the months July to September (in the Northern Hemisphere). They are also the months when, in Europe, storks migrate. A plausible explanation might be that storks deliver babies... hmm. So, it can be dangerous to simply accept the causality of a relationship without examining the veracity of its nature. Simply because one thing happens before another, or seemingly at the same time, does not mean there is a relationship between them.

Alternative explanation

So, we have a relationship between two variables, we can show one happened before the other, but we still do not know that the relationship is a causal one. There is always the possibility that there is another variable/factor that is causing the outcome. This is the 'missing variable' problem, allied to the idea of extraneous or confounding variables, and is the core of internal validity.

Internal validity

For research that measures the effects of treatments or interventions (independent variables), internal validity is a primary consideration. It is the ability to be able to say that your manipulation of the variables has led to an observed difference, such as it changes memory performance (a mnemonic strategy) or lowers aggression (a new therapy), for example. But there may be many reasons, other than our intervention, that explain why memory scores improve or anger is more controlled. So we need to ask whether our observed changes can be attributed to our manipulations of differences in the levels of our independent variable and not to other possible causes.

Plausible alternative explanations or threats to internal validity can include flaws in design, such as only testing one group of people (there may be something special about this group that makes the results peculiar to them) or several groups of people who may not be comparable. There are also social threats, threats that arise because social research is conducted in real-world contexts where people will react not only to what affects them, but also to what is happening to others around them. This is termed 'demand characteristics'.

In order for us to argue that we have demonstrated internal validity, we have to eliminate the plausible alternative explanations. This can be done by making our research design as good as we can get it, by minimising flaws. It can be demonstrated by ensuring that it is possible to find the same results again when the study is replicated, thus ensuring that our findings are reliable.

Replicability and reliability

In order for quantitative research and its findings to be accepted, not only must there be no meaningful alternative explanation (or that must be taken into account), but it must also be possible to find the same effect if the research is repeated in the same circumstances. This repetition is called replication. A study is only replicable if the researcher clearly exposes his or her procedure to people reading about it. This means explaining how the design of the study was arrived at, how the sample was drawn, how the data was collected, etc. Everything pertinent to someone repeating the study must be explained. If this can be done, and the study can be repeated with (statistically) similar results, then the findings are said to be reliable. In order to make causal statements about the research findings any procedures and instruments must be reliable, i.e. stable and/or repeatable and unbiased.

We will encounter reliability and validity in more detail when we look at psychometric measurements.

The final point about the utility and application of causal relationships is that of external validity.

External validity

Researchers using quantitative methods, particularly experimentation, need to ensure that the setting for the experiment has ecological validity, i.e. the attempt to ensure that the experimental procedures resemble real-world conditions. This is linked to the concept of external validity but should not be confused with it. External validity means whether or not experimental results can be generalised to a real-world situation. A study may possess external validity but not ecological validity, and vice versa.

If we have drawn a representative sample from our population, we should be able to generalise any findings from the sample to the population. However, it is not always possible to ensure the sample is truly representative. One way of improving external validity is to improve the sampling procedure used. Demonstrating external validity can be done by carrying out the study in a variety of places, with different people and at different times. So, external validity will become more credible the more replications with variation of the study are performed, and the better the sampling procedure used.

Sampling

In psychology, quantitative research is almost exclusively carried out on samples drawn from populations. Here the term 'population' has a slightly different meaning from the one we use in everyday speech. It need not refer only to people or creatures – for example, the rural population of Poland, or the number of hedgehogs in Huddersfield. In research, we can also refer to a population of objects, events, procedures or observations. A population is thus an aggregate of things.

We must always clearly define the population we are interested in, but we may not be able to describe and enumerate it exactly. For example, we might want to know the average IQ of psychology students, but who are these people? At any one time, the population of psychology students may contain people of different sexes, ages, socio-economic and ethnic background, etc. Also, at one time, every psychology lecturer has been a psychology student. The researcher needs to provide a precise definition of a population and the constraints on that definition (such as time and location) in order to draw valid inferences from the sample that was studied to the population being considered. Statistics that we will consider when taken from populations are referred to as 'population parameters'. They are often denoted by Greek letters: the population mean is denoted by μ (mu) and the standard deviation denoted by σ (lower case sigma).

Even if a population can be defined, it will usually contain too many individuals to study, so research investigation is commonly confined to one or more samples drawn from it. A good sample will contain the information that the population does, so there must be an effective relation between the sample and the population. One way of providing this is to ensure that everyone in the population has a known chance of being included in the sample. It also seems reasonable to make these chances equal. We also want to be certain that the inclusion of one population member does not affect the chance of others being included. So the choice is made by some element of chance, such as spinning a coin or, in large populations and samples, by use of tables of random numbers. These are widely published alongside other tables used in statistical analysis.

Forensic samples

The most difficult point in using forensic samples is defining what they are. There are many definitions, such as people in prison, serial killers on Death Row, victims of crime. So, the sample will be drawn from a population that is defined by the research's objectives, questions, protocols and design.

In order to draw samples effectively there are a few things to bear in mind. Research can vary widely in sample size and sampling design; it can be large-scale, small-scale or cross-cultural, and the approach and design will also determine the constraints of a sample size. Large-scale probability samples are the ideal, and the target population would be a whole country, such as the United Kingdom. Typical large-scale surveys of a national population can use a sample size of 1,000 respondents, but can be much larger, as with the British Crime Survey. Small-scale surveys have a typical sample size of 200–300 respondents, although researchers on tight budgets often use smaller samples. Comparative or cross-cultural surveys usually involve 3–6 nations and sample sizes that typically involve 1,000 people per nation.

The sample size required for a study partly depends on the statistical quality needed for the findings. This then relates to how the results will be used. However, there is no simple rule for sample size that can be used for all research as much depends on the resources available. Researchers often find that a moderate sample size is sufficient statistically. For example, national polls in the UK typically use a properly selected sample of only 1,000 individuals. This is deemed to reflect various characteristics of the total population. Ideally, we would use the whole population, but it is not feasible to include all of its members, and we need to have a small but carefully chosen sample to represent the population from which it is drawn.

The first thing we need to determine is if we can construct a sampling frame. This is a procedure by which all the potential members of a population can be identified, and a sample then drawn. If our population is all the people in prison in a particular year, the sampling frame would be drawn from prison records across the country, and our sample would be taken from that.

Sampling methods can lead to probability or non-probability samples. When we select a probability sample each member of the population had has a known probability of being selected. Probability methods include random sampling, systematic sampling and strati-fied sampling. If we cannot employ such methods, then we have to use a non-probability sampling method in which members of the sample are selected on a non-random basis. Such methods include convenient opportunity sampling, judgement sampling, quota sam-pling and snowball sampling. Non-probability sampling means that we cannot calculate a sampling error, the degree to which a sample might differ from the population. When we make inferences about the population based on samples' behaviour, we would like to do it in terms of sampling error, but non-random non-probability sampling means that the sam-pling error remains unknown. Therefore, the sampling method of choice would always be random sampling if possible. Here we have each member of the population having an equal and known chance of being selected in the sample, thus reducing bias. As an alternative, systematic sampling might be used. This is also called the Nth name selection technique. If we have a list of population members, every Nth record is selected (for example after every 10 names the next name is selected). If the list does not contain any order, such as being in descending age, systematic sampling becomes as effective at representativeness as random sampling, but is so much simpler.

Qualitative research design

There are various reasons why we might choose to use qualitative methods. They allow us to approach research questions with flexibility and possibly allow access to participants who would not usually be comfortable taking part in more structured forms of research. They can also be carried out in a natural setting, placing participants and data in a natural context. Qualitative methods also allow access to more subjective perceptions, but this also means there is the danger that the researcher's own subjective perceptions will affect the process or outcomes of the research. To attempt to minimise this lack of neutrality there are theoreti-cal tools that allow researchers to address any methodological and philosophical issues that may arise.

Reflexivity

No data collection can be truly neutral or free from the subjective perceptions of the data collector. This is a major criticism that qualitative researchers level at the experimental paradigm – that objectivity is impossible, so why attempt to achieve it. Conversely, quali-tative research is criticised for the same thing, that it is too open to subjectivity and non-neutrality. The response is that qualitative research allows a researcher to be *reflexive*. This means that the researcher acknowledges that s/he will affect the behaviour and interpretation of the behaviour of any system being observed or theory being formulated. Any observations cannot, therefore, be independent of the participation of the observer. Popper (1959) said that reflexivity presents a problem for science because if a prediction can lead to changes in the observed behaviour, it becomes difficult to assess scientific hypotheses. In psychology, this causes us a dilemma as we are observing ourselves when we examine human behaviour. Qualitative researchers view this not as a threat to the validity of the data and analysis, but as an opportunity to explore and reflect on their own views. In other words, researchers can afford to make critical reflections on the research process and their own input to it. According to Willig (2001), personal reflexivity means that we have to reflect on how our personal values, experiences and beliefs shape the research and how the research has affected us. She then suggests there is an alternative, *epistemological reflexivity*, in which we should think about whether the research question we have generated has limited the design and outcome and whether it could have been conducted differently. Would this, then, have stimulated a different view of the phenomenon?

This all suggests that a qualitative researcher spends a lot of time on the reflection rather than the performance of research. This is not really the case, but each is given sufficient value in the process to ensure the research is of good quality. When, in quantitative research, value is given to the design, the representativeness of the sampling and the generalisability of the results, this is establishing, or attempting to establish, the reliability and validity of any subsequent interpretation. There is a similar set of processes in qualitative research that attempts to ensure its integrity.

Validity in qualitative research

Some qualitative researchers reject the concept of, and adherence to, validity that is fundamental to quantitative research. Qualitative research is unconcerned with the idea of an external unitary reality to which we can *extrapolate* our findings. If we are to reject the assumption that there is a reality external to our perception of it, then it does not make sense to be concerned with the falsehood of an observation with respect to an external reality. Therefore, we need different standards for judging the quality of research.

Guba and Lincoln (1981) proposed four criteria for judging the veracity of qualitative research and said that these reflected the underlying assumptions better than the concepts of reliability and validity that quantitative research applies:

- **Credibility** (analogous to internal validity). This involves establishing that the results of qualitative research are credible or believable from the perspective of the participant. The participant, then, is the only one who can judge this.
- **Transferability** (analogous to external validity). This is the degree to which the results of qualitative research can be transferred to other contexts or settings. In a quantitative research perspective, this would mean generalising to a population's parameters from a sample's statistics. The researcher may not be the person doing the transferring; therefore, it is the responsibility of whoever wishes to do this to ensure that it is done properly. The person who wishes to place the results in a different context to the original is responsible for making the judgement of how sensible the transfer is.

- **Dependability** (analogous to reliability). The quantitative view of reliability is based on replicability. To what extent are we sure we will find the same result on repetition of the research? This is based on a possibly erroneous assumption that we can create the same situation and control the environment to such an extent that the same conditions prevail. In order to estimate reliability, quantitative researchers construct various hypothetical concepts (such as measurement error) to try to get around this fact. Dependability, though, emphasises that the researcher must account for the changing context within which research occurs. The research is responsible for describing the changes that occur in the setting and how these changes affected the way the researcher approached the study.
- **Confirmability** (analogous to objectivity). Qualitative research assumes that each researcher brings a unique perspective to the study. Confirmability refers to the degree to which the results can be confirmed or corroborated by others. There are a number of strategies for enhancing confirmability, such as documenting the procedures for checking and rechecking the data throughout the study, and using several 'judges' of elements along the way. When the study is complete, a *data audit* can be conducted. This is an examination of the data collection and analysis procedures.

Types of qualitative research

As with quantitative methods, there is a range of possible methods within the qualitative approach. This variety arises, first, from the focus of the research, which can range from an examination of one's own experience to others' experiences examined through their speaking or writing, behaviours, or products. Secondly, there is variety in how data is collected, which can focus on the past or on the present, as in observation or introspection. Finally, there are different ways of analysing data from the highly structured repertory grid to forms that are viewed as more empathic, such as ethnography, phenomenology or grounded theory.

Ethnography

The ethnographic approach to qualitative research comes primarily from the field of anthropology. Anthropology is the study of people and their lives and cultures *in situ*, with a central concept being that of culture. This is interpreted as the evolved capacity to perceive the world symbolically, and to transform the world based on the perception of those symbols. Symbols are any material artefact of a culture, such as art, clothing, or even technology. The ethnographer strives to understand the cultural associations of symbols. Ethnographic research is *holistic*, believing that symbols cannot be understood in isolation but, instead, are elements of a whole. The emphasis in ethnography is on studying an entire culture, but using the symbols as the process of accessing the culture. This 'culture' concept may be tied to notions of ethnicity and geography, but is actually broader and includes any group or organisation. Macro-ethnography is the study of broadly defined cultural groupings, and micro-ethnography is the study of narrowly defined cultural groupings. The most common ethnographic approach is participant observation, in which the ethnographic researcher becomes immersed in the culture as an active participant and records extensive field notes. There are seminal examples of this approach in criminal psychology, such as Anne Campbell's *Girls in the Gang* (1992), which showed how female gangs were growing and were not necessarily an adjunct to male gangs, in which girls/women were the sexual property of gang members.

An ethnographer can adopt an emic or an etic perspective when studying the culture. An emic perspective is the study of the way the members of the given culture perceive their world and is usually the main focus of ethnography, whereas an etic perspective is the study of the way non-members perceive and interpret behaviours and phenomena associated with a given culture.

Phenomenology

Phenomenology is a philosophical perspective as well as an approach to qualitative methodology. It emphasises subjective experiences and interpretations of the world, so a phenomenologist sets out to understand how the world appears to others. However, there is an assumption that the researcher's own values and beliefs can be set aside, which is sometimes difficult to accept. Giorgi (1970) suggested that psychology approached from a phenomenological perspective provides an alternative paradigm to those found in an approach to psychology that follows methods of natural science. For example, Muetzelfeldt et al. (2008) used a phenomenological approach to determine the positive and negative effects of ketamine use, and concerns about the drug and its long-term effects, in users who were clean for three months. Two-thirds of their sample reported positive effects but coupled this with concerns for mental health and physical health issues. To that point, no research had determined the experience of using ketamine in recreational users.

Grounded theory

The purpose of grounded theory is to develop theory about phenomena of interest. However, this is not in an intangible, abstract form, but rooted, or grounded, in systematic observation. For example, Webster and Beech (2000) compared the empathy deficits in a group of sex offenders who were either extrafamilial or intrafamilial abusers. They asked participants to construct apology letters and subjected these to a grounded theory analysis. They found clear differences in the two groups: intrafamilial offenders used minimisation of their behaviour while exhibiting illicit power and control, and extrafamilial offenders directly blamed their victims and exhibited explicit offence details. This has implications for how sex offender treatment programmes implement the victim empathy components for different types of sex offender. In this analysis, the researchers approached the data with no preconceived ideas beyond the issues of type of offender, and various new categories emerged as they coded the data via a two-stage paradigm consisting of open and axial coding (Strauss & Corbin, 1990). This entails categorisation of data followed by a re-evaluation of the codes in terms of any dynamic relationships that are emerging. This was a clear employment of grounded theory's stated intent of allowing data to drive the discovery of meaning and theory.

Having decided on an approach to the research question, then next step is to decide on the method of data collection.

Data collection I: Experimental designs

There are many examples of experimental designs used in forensic studies, but let us look at two that show how we can use samples from both 'sides' of the justice system.

Studying the offenders

Beech et al. (2008) studied the attentional blink in convicted child sex offenders. The attentional blink is a robust phenomenon seen when two images are presented within 500 milliseconds of each other with the effect of errors induced on the perceptual report of the second image. The attentional blink increases when the first image has some salience to the viewer. This study examined the effects of using pictures of children as image 1 in the attentional blink in a sample of child molesters. A larger blink was recorded when the image was a picture of a child compared with when it was a picture of an animal. Beech et al. went on to propose that this task may be potentially used in the assessment of child molesters' level of interest in children.

Studying the scientists

Some studies in forensic psychology are carried out on the public, but others can examine the scientists who are involved in the investigation process themselves. Fingerprint analysis is a very technical and detailed process, requiring intense training in a series of competences. The expert must be able to recognise differences and similarities in friction ridge detail and explain this in court. The issue is thought to become problematic if the identification process becomes subjective. Some previous evaluations had suggested that subjectivity increases as the clarity of the print decreases, with an attendant increased vulnerability to external influences. In order to test this, Hall and Player (2008) carried out an experiment on 70 fingerprint experts to examine the effect of an emotional context on the judgement of an ambiguous or poor-quality print. The findings showed that the participants thought the emotional context was having an effect but no actual difference was observed between the high- and low-emotional contexts.

Data collection II: Correlational designs and surveys

Many questions in psychology cannot be investigated by experimentation. True experimentation involves the manipulation of variables, random assignment and control of extraneous factors in order to determine a causal relationship. Some variables that we might wish to define as our independent variables cannot be manipulated, such as sex of the participants. Some may lead to severe ethical implications if we did try to manipulate them, such as criminality. We can still carry out studies using such independent variables, though. One way is to use the quasi-experimental design, and the other is to use correlational designs.

A quasi-experimental design is one that looks like an experimental design but lacks key ingredients of manipulation and random assignment. Probably the most commonly used quasi-experimental design is the non-equivalent groups design. In its simplest form, it requires a pre-test and post-test for a treated and comparison group.

A correlational design is one in which the purpose is to discover relationships between variables through the use of correlational statistics – the correlation coefficient or 'r'. The square of a correlation coefficient yields the explained variance (r^2); in other words, what variability in the dependent variable can be attributed to its relationship with the independent variable. A correlational relationship between two variables is occasionally the result of an outside source, so we have to be careful and remember that correlation does not necessarily tell us about cause and effect. If a strong relationship is found between two variables, causality can be tested by using an experimental approach. The correlational method permits the researcher to analyse the relationships among a large number of variables in a single study. The correlation coefficient provides a measure of degree and direction of relationship.

These methods are often described as non-experimental, but this suggests that there is something lacking, or that they are a poor relation of the experiment. Common misuse of the term 'experiment' to mean any scientific study tends to lead to the conclusion that 'non-experimental' means non-scientific. This is not so. These methods do allow us to describe and examine behaviour scientifically. While they do not let us identify the causes or reasons for the behaviour, they are methods in their own right, and may even be thought of as more flexible, allowing us to get closer to real behaviour than experiments can. It is better perhaps to describe quantitative non-experimental designs in other ways – e.g. observational designs, correlational designs – rather than lumping them all together. Non-experimental methods do not let us explain why the behaviour occurs, but they do provide scientific data if we execute them correctly and interpret the data properly.

A major form of correlational design is the survey, an important aspect in psychological research. Psychologists conduct surveys to study many matters related to everyday life, opinions and attitudes. The word 'survey' is used most often to describe a method of gathering information from a sample of individuals who are usually part of the population being studied. Surveys can also be conducted in many different ways, including over the telephone, by mail, or in person, but should be carried out with the same attention to research rigour as any experiment. In other words, the selection of the sample is not haphazard, and information should be collected by means of standardised procedures so that every individual is asked the same questions. The survey's intent is not to describe the particular individuals who are part of the sample, but to obtain a composite profile of the population. The ethical considerations are also the same for surveys as for any other type of research, particularly anonymity, confidentiality and the safety of all concerned.

A major objective of surveys in psychology is to gather opinions and attitudes. One such well-known survey is the British Crime Survey, an annual survey carried out for the government in which people fill in questionnaires about incidents experienced in the previous 12 months. It gives a lot of information about levels of crime and public attitudes to crime in order to inform Home Office policy. The representative sample usually comprises over 50,000 people (Home Office, 2009), including, from 2009 onwards, 4,000 children aged 10–15. The major objectives of the survey are to provide information about levels of crime and public attitudes to, and worry about, crime in order to inform Home Office policy. Despite reported levels of crime falling, public perception still appears to be that there are high levels of crime nationally. Part of the survey targets attitudes towards crime and the criminal justice system with the expressed objective of measuring public perceptions of changing crime levels, worry about crime and public confidence. The designers of the questionnaire needed to take these objectives and transform them into questions. Without clear relationships between the objectives and questions the survey is useless.

Data collection III: Psychometrics

The purpose of psychological testing in forensic settings is usually concerned with the evaluation of strengths or weaknesses of individuals or evidence on several levels. However, the application of tests is dependent on whether rigorous research has been carried out in order to determine the validity of the test used in the relevant situations.

Psychological tests can be used in cases where a law enforcement agency or a court need to determine if someone is psychologically fit to be interviewed or interrogated, whether they understand what they are charged with, whether they are fit to stand trial, whether they are faking a mental illness or insanity (malingering), or what form of sentence is appropriate after conviction. If someone is sentenced to incarceration, a psychological evaluation may be needed as to their mental well-being and suicidal intentions, whether they would benefit from therapy or training while in prison or whether they are in a fit state to be released. In a civil hearing, the court may need an assessment of the outcome of a head injury on someone's employability or medical needs.

For example, one of the most widely used tests in mental health is the Minnesota Multiphasic Personality Inventory (MMPI) and its revisions. It was originally developed for use in the diagnosis of mental disorders and in screening for high-risk jobs, where psychological 'defects' would be problematic. The inventory ranges across scales for general health, affective neurological and motor symptoms; sexual, political and social attitudes; educational, occupational, family and marital questions; and neurotic or psychotic behaviour manifestations. It would seem ideal to apply it to forensic situations and, indeed, in its revised forms, the test has a good record of being used in forensic settings. As a forensic psychologist, you will need to be aware of the background to this in order to understand its applicability and validity in such cases. Take the question of malingering – the fabrication or exaggeration of the symptoms of mental illness – often done in order to avoid harsh sentences, even to the point of being declared not guilty due to insanity (see Chapter 18). Grossman and Wasyliw (1988) investigated the stereotype that defendants who claim insanity as a defence are actually malingering by analysing the proportions of insanity defendants who exaggerate psychopathology. They examined 49 defendants evaluated for fitness to stand trial and/or sanity at the time of the alleged crime and 52 subjects previously found not guilty by reason of insanity. They demonstrated that only a minority (14%) of defendants clearly malingered, whereas 39% showed evidence of *minimising* psychopathology. Eighty-one per cent of these subjects had MMPI profiles suggestive of psychosis, but relatively few showed evidence of primarily antisocial behaviour. Thus, the malingering stereotype may be applicable to only a minority of insanity defendants and is specifically inapplicable to a substantial proportion who minimised psychopathology or showed evidence of psychosis consistent with the claim of insanity.

This was also supported by Lewis, Simcox and Berry (2002), who used the MMPI-2 and the delightfully named Structured Inventory of Malingered Symptomatology (SIMS) screening and the Structured Interview of Reported Symptoms (SIRS) on 55 men undergoing pre-trial psychological evaluations for competency to stand trial or criminal responsibility in the US federal justice system. On the basis of results from the SIRS, 31 were classified as honest responders and 24 as feigning. This distinction was also found from the SIMS and MMPI-2 fake bad validity scales (fake bad scales or sub-scales are designed to detect malingering). So the MMPI has usefulness as screens for malingering when assessing defendants.

In addition to such screening benefits, tests such as the MMPI-2 can also measure the specific personality traits thought to be important in forensic research. For example, Sellbom, Ben-Porath and Stafford (2007) examined the convergent and discriminant validity of the MMPI-2 measures of psychopathy on two samples of participants evaluated at a criminal court clinic. Subscales for social deviance traits of psychopathy were found to have significantly greater convergent validity in predicting psychopathy than the previously used tests.

So, forensic practice and forensic research can use a variety of psychometric measures, dependent on the theoretical framework in which the researcher/practitioner falls. An understanding of the psychometric measurements and the underlying methodology of construction, validation and administration is therefore necessary in forensic psychology. It is also important to know that there are problems with some well-known tests. For example, the Psychopathy Checklist Revised (PCL-R) has been criticised for its psychometric properties – its internal consistency is not high, its convergent validity with other scales is not good. It also relies heavily on clinical judgement, which may be subjective in nature. Additionally, it suffers from the same issue for any test used in forensic settings: it is very much based on information that the suspect is giving the professional and that may not be the best source of reliable information. There are alternatives, such as Psychopathic Personality Inventory (PPI), a self-report measure developed by Lilienfeld and Andrews (1996), which was updated and revised in 2005 (PPI-R). The PPI-R is based on the personality-based approach of psychopathy and it aims to measure the core personality traits of psychopathy in criminal, clinical, non-criminal and non-clinical populations.

Given such inherent difficulties with tests and measurement, which should forensic psychologists use? There are several criteria to be met:

- The extensive documentation and review in the scientific literature
- A reliability coefficient of greater than 0.8 and high validity
- Remember that not using the full form of a test reduces its reliability and validity
- Relevance to the legal issue
- The context needs to be taken into account, such as having to test in a noisy environment
- Tests can only be used for the purpose for which they were developed (i.e. you should use an IQ test to infer competence for giving testimony)
- Appropriate norm reference groups are required for forensic populations

Usually, in a forensic setting, test results would be combined with various other pieces of information, such as that derived from a clinical interview. The use and interpretation of tests is covered in more detail in Sections 5 and 6.

Data collection IV: Qualitative designs

Qualitative research figures importantly in forensic psychology. Whilst quantitative research is designed to collect data from a large number of people, such as in the case of surveys, or to determine causal relationships between variables, qualitative research sets out to examine phenomena in detail and gather rich information about those phenomena. There are several matters to take into consideration when choosing to use a qualitative research methodology. First, such methods can be used to attempt to understand a phenomenon about which little is known because there is little previous research. Theory and data can emerge through the process of qualitative research, thus providing guidance towards knowledge of psychological events. Conversely, even when a great deal is known about items, a fresh perspective may be useful. This is where qualitative research also excels. In both these cases research questions are open-ended, leaving a lot of scope and freedom in choosing and designing the approach, but unfortunately not much guidance. In order to identify the approach and not leave researchers floundering in a mass of choices, there are several features that might lead down particular paths towards the best method.

Therefore, qualitative research means examination of phenomena *in situ*, and in rich detail, with an acknowledgement of the researcher's own perspective. It is important to stress the emergent nature of qualitative research design, as researchers seek to observe and interpret meanings in context. Due to this, it is often not possible, or indeed appropriate, to finalise a strategy for investigative process before data collection has begun. Many feel uncomfortable with this, but it is this very freedom that is also most attractive. The design of qualitative studies depends on the objectives, and judgements about usefulness and credibility are left to the researcher and the reader.

Sampling strategies

The most popular sampling technique is purposeful sampling, which can be contrasted to probability sampling in quantitative research. Purposeful sampling is an attempt to provide cases relevant to the research question that are rich in information and will give in-depth insight. There are several varieties of purposeful sampling, but perhaps the most useful, and most used, is maximum variation sampling. This strategy allows the capture and description of central themes or principal outcomes from the greatest variation of participants. Such variation can be seen as a problem, but if the intention is to gain maximum variation, then the sampling strategy is turning an apparent weakness into a strength. This is because common patterns that emerge from maximum variation will be those of interest in observing core, shared experiences and aspects of the sample (Patton, 1980).

Data collection techniques

Interviews with open-ended questions are the most popular way of gathering data since they are deemed to give insight into a participant's thoughts and feelings, but they can also be used in conjunction with other methods. For example, Dodge (2006) explored the use of juvenile police informants by interviewing police officers and examining known cases. There are several difficulties in the use of minors as informants, not least the ethical implications, but also the legality of the practice and the potential for harm to the informant. Dodge (2006) affirmed these concerns and addressed issues of harm to, and coercion of, minors.

The major questions to be answered when using qualitative methods are how to record data and how to transcribe it if it is a spoken record. This issue becomes even more evident when attempting to record data from observation. One way to overcome this is to use written data from the participants, but the act of writing can affect the data as it makes the participant focus on the issue and may prevent some points being made explicit. Other sources of data include other documents that have been produced by the population of interest, such as journals or diaries, official records, letters, newspapers, etc.

Analysis

As with design, psychological research can be analysed in several ways but the analytical technique will depend on the approach taken, the way in which the study was designed and the data collected.

Analysis of quantitative data

Quantitative designs can be roughly separated into two formats, those looking for differences in groups and those looking at relationships. Most experimental designs would be concerned with comparison and employ a calculation of difference. However, this is not as clear-cut as first appears. Take the Hall and Player (2008) study of fingerprint experts. Here, they tried to establish whether there was any difference in accuracy of analysis when the emotional context for the analysis was varied. Their findings showed that a test of association revealed no link between context and accuracy, rather than a difference between high and low emotional context. This finding, although it was determined using a test of association, does support their hypothesis of no difference, i.e. fingerprint analysts can maintain their professional accuracy no matter what the context. Hall and Player (2008) may be criticised for using a non-parametric statistical procedure, although their final analysis does meet the needs of the research question.

Tests of difference in groups include parametric tests such as the t-test and the analysis of covariance, which are covered in great depth in undergraduate psychology programmes. Alongside this, graduates will be familiar with tests of relationship, such as bivariate and partial correlation, and linear regression (simple and multiple). As such, analysing quantitative data is often considerably more straightforward than qualitative data analysis. Once the quantitative design is considered and the data collected, the analytical procedure is usually obvious, as described in Tables 2.1 and 2.2. However, there are several more complex pieces of analysis that blur the distinction between quantitative and qualitative analysis.

Analysis of complex quantitative data

A good deal of the data encountered in forensic and criminal psychology will be multi-level. For example, a criminal psychologist might need to compare different strategies to tackle violent crime. It would be of little value to simply compare numbers of incidents. The crime rate is dependent on a number of factors, and the likelihood of experiencing a violent crime might be correlated with that of burglary or sexual crimes. These correlations must be represented in the analysis for correct inferences to be drawn. There are several ways of analysing such complex data.

Cluster analysis is an exploratory data analysis tool for solving classification problems. It is used to organise cases (people, things, events, etc.) into groups (clusters) so that there is a strong association between members of the same cluster and a weak association between clusters. Each cluster describes the class to which its members belong, and this can be taken to describe general classes of cases. Cluster analysis is therefore used in purely exploratory terms to attempt to reveal structures in data that are not evident before analysis, but which make sense once seen. The results of cluster analysis can therefore contribute to a formal classification scheme, such as taxonomies of animals or plants or statistical models describing populations. It can also indicate rules for assigning new cases to classes.

For example, Spaans et al. (2009) examined MMPI profiles of men accused of serious crimes. They used a hierarchical cluster analysis with the MMPI-2's clinical scales as clustering variables, as previous studies had cast doubt on the suitability of this test in forensic settings. Their findings indicated distinctions between 'non-disturbed' and 'disturbed' profiles, with these clusters differing on age of first conviction, indicating a late onset of criminal activity for disturbed offenders. As such, this suggests that there is little distinction in personality profiles and that psychologists should advise that the MMPI-2 has restricted usefulness in the investigation of diverse and severe psychopathology and their linkage to serious crimes.

Multidimensional analysis
Analysis of qualitative data

Qualitative data analysis means organising it into meaningful and manageable units in order to search for patterns. This is the same as quantitative data analysis. Each set of numbers must be reduced and re-synthesised in the same way, but here we have a complex, rich and non-numerical set of data to be examined. Usually this process is inductive in qualitative research, meaning that the patterns or themes will emerge from the data. This is very challenging, and much more difficult than statistical analysis. Here we need to be creative and look at the whole set together in order to place it into meaningful categories – a daunting task with piles of interview transcripts or field notes.

The other point of paramount importance is making the process of analysis transparent in order to ensure its credibility to the reader. Naturalistic research assumes that there can be multiple realities, but this also means that the possibility of generalisation may be removed. This means that there is a lack of transferability of the results and conclusions.

The other issue with qualitative data is the lack of objectivity. This is not necessarily a bad thing if the researcher can acknowledge influences on the findings in some way, and even minimise this influence. Then the findings do not need to be seen as objective. Instead, Lincoln and Guba (1985) suggest it requires 'confirmability', which is how much neutrality can be seen in the interpretation of the data. Keeping notes of the process of analysis and induction, the ways in which several judges make sense of the data, and so on, can allow readers to confirm whether or not the findings are ones that others would have found by the same process.

Such process transparency is particularly needed in thematic analysis (TA), in which interview transcripts or other forms of text are subjected to a process of making explicit the structures and meanings that the participant or reader embodies in a text. TA is a complex process which will be necessarily inductive. Themes are not objects but expressions of phenomenological experience and therefore the process of discovering them cannot be wholly explicit. Data must be gathered in as open a way as possible, and analysed in conjunction with someone who did not necessarily share the same experience or perception of the research setting. This allows a check on accuracy of analysis and minimises the effect of bias. It is accepted and welcomed in qualitative analysis that subjective views will form part of a researcher's process, but that there is a responsibility to manage this influence. Assistance from another person not involved in the process is seen as a suitable measure towards reducing the input of bias (Mehra, 2002).

There are many examples in the forensic literature of the use of TA. For example, in the section on experimentation above, the input of subjectivity to fingerprint analysis was examined. Using a thematic analysis approach, Charlton, Fraser-Mackenzie and Dror (2010) investigated whether emotional and motivational factors were involved in fingerprint analysis, and whether this was different for day-to-day routine casework or more high-profile criminal investigations. They interviewed 13 experienced fingerprint examiners and found themes relating to job satisfaction and the use of skill. However, satisfaction related to catching criminals was a significantly recurring factor, with particular relevance in feeling a contribution was made to solving high-profile, serious or long-running cases. There were positive emotional effects when matching, coupled with fear of making errors. This might seem to contradict the experimental findings discussed above, as that study showed that subjectivity did not affect the accuracy. But in fact it supports it, and goes deeper, by showing that the analysts are emotional human beings, and yet this does not affect their professional stance.

Similarly, TA can be used when direct data from participants are not available. Studying paedophilia is a difficult topic due to the illegal nature and cultural abhorrence of child sex abuse associated with it. Convicted child sex offenders are not necessarily an accurate source of information either, as they are not necessarily primarily paedophiliac in nature (see Chapter 8), or may be in denial, or undergoing treatment, all of which will affect the data derived from them. To overcome this problem, textual analysis is a viable alternative. For example, in 2008 Lambert and O'Halloran examined a website for women with a sexual interest in children, pointing out that although the involvement of the Internet in sexual offending has received much attention, it has focused predominantly on male paedophiles. They found five main categories of discussion and information in the website, which they identified as cognitive distortions, recognition barriers, sexual motivation, the role of the Internet, and personal factors. They suggest that this demonstrates that 'women are using the Internet to express a sexual interest in children and that they display similar characteristics to male individuals engaged in the same processes' (2008: 284). This is a revealing and controversial finding in a period when female paedophilia and female child sex abusers are hardly discussed in the literature (Gavin, 2010).

An alternative form of qualitative/interpretive analysis, particularly of text, is discourse analysis (DA), which is concerned with the elements of language and the context in which they are placed. It was first used in connection with psychology by Potter and Wetherell (1987) to describe the study of linguistic and rhetorical devices rather than the behaviour of the language user. Definitions of discourse analysis vary and can be very ambiguous and confusing, but researchers generally agree on several points. First, that discourse analysis is concerned with language use beyond the boundaries of a sentence or utterance. Secondly, that it is concerned with the relationships between language and the wider context. Thirdly, that it is concerned with the interactive or dialogue properties of everyday communication.

One particular way that researchers apply discourse analysis is to examine the dynamics of the exchange and the relationships formed within it. The dynamics of the discourse mean that each participant has a role and function within the exchange that may go beyond the particular time and place of the conversation, but that are brought to bear within it. According to French and Raven (1960), power is always evident in interpersonal communication and there are various ways in which any differential possession of power can be expressed. In interpersonal discourse, the more inherent the power a contributor has (derived from his or her role or expertise), the more influential or 'in control' of the discourse he or she should be. Analysing discourse in terms of power and control exerted and the shifts they undergo is very valuable in understanding how different roles are handled and outcomes achieved.

Haworth (2006) carried out an analysis of the use of power and control in an interrogative interview between police officers and a murder suspect. The suspect was Dr Harold Shipman, who was convicted of the murder of 15 of his patients and implicated in the death of more than 260 patients over 27 years. The interview analysed by Haworth took place early in the investigation of the death of Kathleen Grundy, which was suspicious because Mrs Grundy was robust and healthy and she had recently changed her will in Shipman's favour. The will later proved to be a forgery. Haworth was ostensibly interested in the way in which the British police use power and control when interrogating/interviewing murder suspects. The control of the interview would seem to be in the hands of the police, as the officers control the setting and make decisions based on answers to questions. However, the interviewee has control over what s/he reveals and the objective of interviews is for the interviewer to gain information. Haworth also points out that although the police have a clearly defined institutional role to play, this *particular* interviewee has a powerful role in a different institution, and therefore the asymmetry may be of a different nature from the more regular interrogative setting. Haworth concentrated on the dynamics of power and control, and she identified four features that demonstrate these shifts: topic, question type, question-and-answer sequence, and references to institutional status. Throughout the interview, Shipman appears to be trying to exert control through his medical knowledge and the status this gives him, and it appears that the interviewer allows him to do so, but is in fact just letting him talk and implicate himself. Haworth's analysis shows this clearly.

ETHICAL CONSIDERATIONS FOR RESEARCH

Psychological research is regulated by professional bodies, funding agencies and agencies of access. In other words, there are several organisations to which researchers are responsible, to ensure not only that the work they carry out is of good quality, but that everyone involved is treated properly. Professional bodies such as the British Psychological Society or the American Psychological Association have developed codes of conduct for all professional practice as a psychologist, including researchers. These include aspects of research ethics in addition to practice ethics. Funding bodies, which can include research councils, universities, private companies or government agencies, all have a vested interest in making sure research is effective and carried out within legal and ethical guidelines. Agencies of access are those bodies to which a researcher must apply in order to gain access to the population and sample under examination. In terms of research carried out in forensic psychology, this usually includes prison governors, probation officers, and so on, but can also include school-teachers and GPs. It is the responsibility of a researcher (and his or her supervisor, if appropriate) to ensure all the relevant bodies are contacted and are fully aware of the research and its implications, and to ensure that any other checks are in place (such as a Criminal Records Bureau check) prior to applying for access to participant groups. There will also be various applications for ethical approval that will need to be made, and this is one of the checks that need to be in place in order to satisfy funding bodies and agencies of access.

In order to meet the approval needs of ethical panels, the research should be designed by taking into consideration the codes of conduct from the professional bodies.

How to design ethical research

When still learning about research and design, researchers should ensure that they have supervisors who are competent to aid the design of studies of this nature. The choice of methodology and design for the study should be appropriate to investigate the research question. While designing research, researchers should attempt to consider how participation in the study will be perceived from the participants' point of view. One way to do this might be for the researcher to carry out the procedure him- or herself, but this might not be possible in some studies, such as those designed to elicit responses from people who have experienced something specific, or who possess attributes that the researchers do not. Therefore advice should be sought from people who may be able to give an opinion about those specific issues.

DISSEMINATION

It may be possible to think of the performance of research as an end in itself, but knowledge does not progress without letting other people know what has been found out and allowing criticism and discussion of the findings. Any findings that have not been independently evaluated are of questionable value, so they are presented in the form of formal papers and published in journals. This means we must be familiar with this communication format in order to conduct research for two reasons: to understand what has been found in an area and also to communicate what we have found.

Research writing must be understandable and meaningful. There is little value in writing papers using language that is so obscure that it will confuse and complicate the issues. They should be designed to tell somebody something, not to show how many big words the writer knows.

SUMMARY

Research in forensic or criminological psychology is not easy. The questions posed are difficult because defining crime is problematic and subject to all sorts of bias. Consider the question of sexual offending. Historically, homosexuality was regarded as a crime, and still is in many cultures. It is no longer a crime in most of the Western world, but many people within society still vilify homosexuals and subject them to abuse. How then should we treat the question of alternative or varied sexualities? Or, considering that the age of sexual consent differs from 9 years old to 21 across the globe, how can we globally define child sexual molestation? Even the age at which someone is deemed legally responsible varies. In Scotland, an 8-year-old child is seen as criminally responsible, but in England and Wales the child would have to be at least 10 years old, and in Sweden, 15 years of age. Not only that, but the law and the legal system are not static entities; they evolve and shift depending on the time, public attitude and the needs of society.

Another problem is trying to determine the extent of crime when much of it goes unreported. For example, it is estimated that only 12–15% of women who are raped report the incident. The successful conviction rate of that proportion is approximately 6% (HMIC & HMPCSI, 2007), suggesting that the conviction rate for all rapes is somewhere in the region of less than one per hundred. Psychological input to understanding these figures – why so much of this crime is hidden and why the conviction rate is so poor – would be invaluable.

Outlined above are the basic forms of research that you need to understand in forensic psychology, but the professional discipline needs to also draw on the methodologies and research findings of other disciplines within psychology, so an understanding of other areas than crime is essential. For example, in order to understand delinquent behaviour, it would be helpful to draw on the research findings of developmental/lifespan psychology and individual differences – is it the result of parental separation, lack of discipline or personality disorders? Is it a genetic predisposition or the result of environmental factors?

Also, consider the question of how reliable eyewitness testimony might be. Memory research conducted by cognitive psychologists suggests that it may not always be as reliable as we might like to think. However, these researchers have also shown that it is possible to improve the quality of testimony through the use of the 'cognitive interview', a technique developed to improve memory recall.

Social psychology has a great deal to contribute to the understanding of criminal behaviour. The work on conformity helps to understand how peer pressure can influence behaviour, particularly in groups or gangs. Similarly, research on the phenomena of deindividuation helps us to understand how normally law-abiding people can become lawbreakers, e.g. in riots. Social psychologists have also studied bystander apathy, which explains why victims of crime, particularly street crime, do not always receive help from those who witness it.

The application of psychological research methods is an extremely important aspect of forensic psychology and an understanding of the techniques is crucial. An equally important aspect is the understanding of the context in which research findings are applied.

Journals in which research about forensic psychology can be found (not exhaustive)

Addictive Behaviors

Aggressive Behavior

American Journal of Drug and Alcohol Abuse

American Journal of Forensic Psychology

American Journal on Addictions

Annual Review of Clinical Psychology

Applied Psychology in Criminal Justice

Archives of Suicide Research

Behavioral Sciences & the Law

British Journal of Clinical Psychology

Child Abuse and Neglect

Criminal Justice and Behavior

Homicide Studies

International Journal of Forensic Mental Health

International Journal of Forensic Psychology

Journal of Aggression, Maltreatment and Trauma

Journal of Family Violence

Journal of Forensic Psychiatry and Psychology

Journal of Forensic Psychology Practice

Journal of Interpersonal Violence

Journal of Investigative Psychology and Offender Profiling

Journal of Personality Assessment

Journal of Personality Disorders

Law and Psychology Review

Legal and Criminological Psychology

Psychology of Addictive Behaviors

Psychology, Crime, & Law

Psychology, Public Policy, and Law

Sexual Abuse: a Journal of Research and
  Treatment
Substance Abuse
Substance Abuse Treatment, Prevention, and
  Policy
Substance Abuse: Research and
  Treatment

Substance Use and Misuse
Suicide and Life-Threatening Behavior: the
  Official Journal of the American Association
  of Suicidology
Trauma, Violence and Abuse: a Review
  Journal
Traumatology

Section 2

Psychological Explanations of Crime

This section explores the ways in which psychological theory can be used to explain crime and criminals. It is therefore related to the knowledge and research dimensions and Core Role 2 (research).

Chapter 3 provides an overview of psychological theories and Chapter 4 examines the psychology of the criminal mind, using two famous case studies (the Kray twins and Ted Bundy) to illustrate the two major perspectives of mental illness and personality disorders. Chapter 5 examines the juvenile criminal, relating this topic to the sad case of Jamie Bulger, killed by two 10-year-old boys. What makes some children behave in anti-social ways, sometimes in the most extreme ways?

Theoretical Explanations of Crime

3

Crime and the role of society	Crime and the role of biology	Crime and the role of individual differences	Crime and the role of social psychology	Rape: an application of theory
Strain	Genetics 47:XYY syndrome Twins	Intelligence	Biosocial factors	Medical models Rapists are sick
Social control	Biochemistry Androgens Serotonin Drugs and alcohol	Personality Psychodynamics and crime Psychopathy	Social learning	Evolutionary models Sex is a biological imperative
	Evolution Competitive behaviour is passed on			Feminist models Rape is a way of exerting power and control
	Neuropsychology Head injury			Social learning models Rape is a learned behaviour

KEY THEMES

- Biosocial theories of crime
- Social learning theory and crime
- Psychodynamic theories of crime
- Evolutionary models of crime
- Feminist models of crime

INTRODUCTION

In many sciences there are attempts being made to find a unified theory, so far, unsuccessfully. Even in a discipline such as physics, the concept of a unified theory has a seemingly insurmountable barrier to overcome in that two compellingly explanatory theories (general relativity and quantum theory) are totally incompatible. So, it is hardly surprising that the study of mind and behaviour is no exception to such a quest, or such difficulties. The study of crime is no stranger to this desire to discover a global explanation, but we remain with the position of several different perspectives attempting to provide understanding of criminal behaviour within existing psychological frameworks. Psychological explanations of crime suggest that individual differences may make it more likely that some people commit crimes than others. These differences may be due to personality characteristics, biological factors or social influences. There is therefore a hierarchical set of different perspectives, from the social to the individual, that are useful in understanding the nature of crime and the theories attempting to explain it.

Strain theory – social structures exert pressures which may lead an individual to commit crime.

CRIME AND THE ROLE OF SOCIETY

Social theories suggest that crime is an outcome of the breakdown in social structures. This can be either at a structural level, where societal processes affect members of society, or at an individual level, where the experiences of people as they seek ways to satisfy their needs are examined. The first major theorist in this area was Merton, whose 1938 analysis of the relationship between society and the values and behaviour of members of that society was pivotal in the sociological examination of crime. The resultant theoretical perspective, strain theory, is an attempt to explain crime via the pressures that society and societal goals can exert. Hence, unemployment, inequity, abuse of power and other macro-level issues are direct influences on crime and the causes of crime. Violence may occur as a result of harassment, stealing may be to resolve financial problems. Agnew (1992, 2009) updated the theory to account for different types of strain, such as that resulting from society preventing the achievement of goals, and the strain occurring when in receipt of negative or noxious stimuli, such as the theft of valued items, or anger against the individual. Strain then results from the failure to achieve goals that society demands, such as money, status and autonomy.

There are issues with this type of explanation, however. The first focuses on the difficulty in establishing any kind of empirical testing of the theoretical positions, despite Agnew's (2009) attempts to do so. Additionally, Langton and Piquero (2007) explored whether it could be applied to types of crime other than those mentioned in Merton's and Agnew's work. In particular, neither the original nor the revised theories extended to white-collar crime, defined as crimes committed by people of high socio-economic status within their occupations. Langton and Piquero attempted to apply the same criteria to offences such as fraud and embezzlement, and they concluded that the theory might be applicable, but that the factors that cause strain might be different. Other criticisms centre on the lack of explanation of individual differences in the theory, such as the disparity in rates of crimes attributed to different genders, ethnicities, and so on (Higgins et al., 2010).

An alternative to strain theory is drawn from social learning theory, famously highlighted by Bandura's experiments in children's imitative aggressive behaviour (Bandura et al., 1963). According to this viewpoint, people learn to engage in crime through association with people who are already criminals. Crime may bring reward, hence it is reinforced, and beliefs are learned that are conducive to crime. Social learning theory can incorporate the concept of differential reinforcement in that frequent reinforcement is available (reward from excitement or acquisition) accompanied by infrequent punishment (being caught). Society therefore acts as a social learning force as it is the provider of low levels of punishment, due to lower resources being applied to the detection of petty crime, a situation that zero-tolerance policing attempts to rectify (Reiner, 2010).

> Social learning theory – behaviour is learnt by imitation, and therefore criminal behaviour is the result of learning from criminal peer groups and is reinforced by reward and by not being caught.

Strain and social learning theories look at the factors that make people turn to crime. An additional viewpoint is to consider what prevents people from committing crimes; why do people conform to social norms? Control theory (see Hirschi & Gottfredson, 1995), accepts that there are needs and desires that the individual or a group have, and that these are often more easily satisfied by crime. Hence, if it is easier to obtain money by criminal means, then why work for it? Here working to achieve a goal is seen as the aberrant behaviour, and the behaviour is not a result of pressure because there is more social pressure when not engaging in criminal activities. Some people simply feel freer from social control than others and therefore are more able to commit crime. This is because they are less likely to encounter direct control, such as observation or monitoring, rule setting and censuring of behaviour than others, and have a lower stake in conformity. The latter means that if an individual has more to lose in social terms by not conforming to rules, then they are more likely to conform.

According to some theories of society's influence on crime, the more society attempts to control crime the less likely this strategy is to be successful. Labelling someone as 'criminal', such as the imposition of an antisocial behaviour order (ASBO), increases the likelihood of them participating in further crimes. Labelling someone as 'criminal' leads to lower job prospects, increasing the level of strain encountered, and lowering the stake they have in conforming to prosocial behaviour. The issues in labelling theory are well established and their links to crime are clearly described by Becker (1974).

However, even if broad societal issues affect crime, there are still influences that have a more focused effect. There is a community level in that people within one area of a larger population will form a mini-society. Each community acts on its own rules, predominantly within those of the large society, but some communities become problematic due to the localised impact of wider social harms. Some communities are therefore prone to crime; the social problems that exist are concentrated inside the area and, due to the propensity for criminals to operate in districts that are familiar to them, these problems become ones of crime. Social disorganisation theory, first proposed by Shaw and McKay (1969), seeks to explain differences in crime rates that appear to be due to locality. By identifying the characteristics of communities with high crime rates, it is thought possible to explain why these characteristics contribute to crime. Crime appears to be more prevalent in communities that suffer from factors contributing to social disorganisation, such as economic deprivation, overcrowding (high population density coupled with smaller housing units or multi-unit housing), high residential mobility and family disruption (high rates of divorce, single-parent families). The theory places these factors at the heart of the community members' lack of ability or willingness to affect social control, thereby failing to provide young people with adequate self-control.

Social disorganization theory – an explanation of why some communities are more prone to crime.

Such a simple theory does have its criticisms, of course, notably those described by Shoemaker (1996). He pointed out that social disorganisation ignores ethnic and cultural factors and assumes that 'inner-city' areas have the highest level of disorganisation. It also fails to take into account non-delinquency within areas of high delinquency.

Sociological explanations of crime are well established in the literature regarding these issues. All such societal explanations have their merit, but psychologists tend to be more concerned with identifying individual characteristics linked to criminal behaviour. This does not ignore the influence of society and its action, but provides an alternative emphasis. Psychological theories try to take account of the group and societal processes that impinge upon the person, but are naturally individualistic, at either the biological, personal or social level.

CRIME AND THE ROLE OF BIOL

Historically, there have been attempts to classify criminals as physically different from non-criminals. Lombroso (1876) compared the facial characteristics of criminals with non-criminals and claimed that criminals had more 'primitive' facial features and a lower sensitivity to pain. These theories have shaky methodological underpinning to say the least. His research groups were criminal samples containing large numbers of the mentally ill; his control groups were usually soldiers. The conclusions were also drawn on a correlational basis, that is, his criminal group shared many physical characteristics, but this does not mean that the physical appearance was indicative of criminality or had any causal effect. He also failed to take into account any social circumstances, such as poverty, which could have led to the physical anomalies he observed. He also declared that criminals had extra nipples, toes and fingers. Strangely, later studies have not supported these findings. The only finding that comes close to this is that 'unattractive' people tend to be seen as more criminal (Saladin et al., 1988), demonstrating that perhaps Lombroso was simply influenced by the same stereotypes as others. It is evident that there are more factors at play here than simply bodily characteristics offer.

Physiognomy – criminal types have different facial characteristics from non-criminal types.

Genetics

Other biological aspects of criminal behaviour, such as genetics and neurology, can be examined. Biology's 'magic bullet' of the twentieth and twenty-first centuries was the surge in understanding genetics and the increasing sophistication of DNA analysis (for definition of DNA, see Glossary). As such, the unlocking of the genetic code seemed to offer the possibility of identifying a criminal gene. For example, it has been noted that the overwhelming majority of crimes are perpetrated by men, at least those that are detected. Most people have 46 chromosomes, and a person's sex is determined by the X and Y chromosomes. Women usually have two X chromosomes and men have an XY pair. In a condition known as 47:XYY syndrome, occurring in around one in every 1,000 male births (Torniero et al., 2010), males have an additional Y chromosome, i.e. XYY, and this has led some to think that such men are 'extra-masculine' and more prone to sexual aggression (Schröder et al., 1981). This has been found not to be the case, but, according to Cohen and Shim (2007), men carrying the extra Y chromosome do tend to be taller and more muscular than average. Bishop et al. (2011) report that they are also more at risk of learning disabilities, hypotonia, involuntary movements, and behavioural and emotional difficulties, together with possible delays in the development of language and motor skills, with as many as 20% of 47:XYY syndrome individuals having autistic spectrum disorders.

47:XYY syndrome – men with two Y chromosomes, a very rare occurrence – were thought to be 'hypermasculine' and more likely to be violent and criminal.

Interest in the XYY anomaly, and other syndromes in which an extra sex chromosome is found, was triggered when it was found that there is a larger number of XYY men in prison than the population incidence would predict (Jones, 2006). The problem here is, of course, establishing a causal link, and such individuals are not necessarily linked to violent crime. XYY syndrome may provide the circumstances for aggressive behaviour, but it is more likely that social circumstances in combination with the anomaly determine how behaviour manifests itself.

Other genetic characteristics can be examined in terms of the transmission of criminality. Empirical studies of identical twins with identical genetic characteristics, or children within a family who are not biologically related, such as those adopted into the family, are an excellent way to provide evidence for the relationship between genes and criminality. In this way, biological identity or social and environmental influences can be investigated. It is clear that criminal children often come from criminal families; there is some form of familial transmission of criminality. However, family studies alone cannot help but isolate the social factors inherent in producing criminality, and the biological perspective can be gained from twin studies.

Monozygotic (identical) and dizygotic (fraternal) twin studies show that consistency between behavioural aspects of an individual is significantly higher in the identical twins. This is compelling evidence. However, it still does not rule out the social influences, because there is a high likelihood of similar familial and social environments with twins, particularly identical twins. A much more persuasive argument would be derived if identical twins reared apart demonstrated the same level of identical behaviour seen in those reared together. The rarity of this situation means using a case study approach. The largest study of this kind is the Minnesota Study of Twins Reared Apart (MISTRA), which began in 1979 (Bouchard et al., 1990). This intensive study determined that at least 70% of the variance in IQ was due to genetic factors. There was also a significant level of similarity in a wide range of other anthropometric and psychophysiological factors, and psychological and social behaviours, mirroring the similarity seen in monozygotic twins reared together. It has not been clearly established, however, whether this extends to criminal and offending behaviours.

The contrasting examination is of children who are genetically dissimilar but who were brought up in the same parental and familial environment. In the case of adopted children and criminal tendencies, the criminality of the biological parent is more likely to predict the child's criminal involvement than that in the adoptive parent.

Twin studies – twin studies attempt to separate the contribution of genetics from that of the environment, but still cannot determine the genetic influence on crime.

What implications would a genetic predisposition for criminality have for psychology and law? There have been several cases in which behavioural genetics have been at the heart of a criminal defence as grounds for mitigation.

Jeffrey Landrigan

If criminal tendencies are transmitted from criminal parents to children, and biology determines much of our psychology, then Billy Hill really had no chance whatsoever. Billy's father, whom he never met, died while awaiting execution for murder. His birth mother was addicted to drugs and alcohol, which she continued to use during her pregnancy; she abandoned him at a day-care centre when he was six months old. He was adopted by an Oklahoma couple named Landrigan, who renamed him Jeffrey. As Jeffrey grew up it was clear that he had many problems, including his own abuse of alcohol and drugs. He also had many behavioural problems and spent time in correctional facilities. In 1982, he stabbed a man he described as his best friend to death. Found guilty of first-degree murder, the conviction was overturned on appeal and he was sentenced to 20 years in prison. He was put on a minimum security work crew and escaped in November 1989. In December of that year he killed Chester Dyer, claiming he made sexual advances to him. On 28 June 1990, he was found guilty of first-degree murder, after a trial in which he had been uncooperative and disruptive.

In 2001, Landrigan appealed against the death sentence on the grounds that his legal defence team had been ineffective, as they had not presented any mitigating evidence. This mitigation would have been based on behavioural genetic evidence that he was unable to control his behaviour. The judge who sentenced him to death stated that she would have applied clemency if she had known about the difficult childhood he had experienced, the criminality in his biological family, the brain damage caused by the *in utero* and subsequent substance abuse. This plea was initially rejected on the grounds that a jury could find him genetically predisposed to be violent and that this would count as much against him as for him. The difficulty was enhanced by the fact that he had refused to have such evidence placed before the court at his initial trial. The appeal was overturned and Landrigan was executed by lethal injection of sodium thiopental (an anaesthetic), pancuronium bromide (a paralytic agent) and potassium chloride (a heart-attack-inducing agent) on 26 October 2010 (Guardian, 2010a).

The genetics of criminality provides a convincing line of reasoning, but is only a partial explanation. Genetic makeup determines not just physical and possibly psychological makeup; it also influences the internal state of the individual.

Biochemistry

Testosterone is an androgen, a hormone which is a major component in behaviour and is of interest due to its influence on violent and aggressive behaviour. In both males and females, testosterone is produced by the adrenal glands, with some being released from the ovaries in females, but the release is much slower than in males. In men, it is made by Leydig cells in the testes and is secreted into the bloodstream in spurts, which means that levels can change significantly within minutes. Testosterone has clear masculinising and anabolic effects in both sexes, but a high level in men appears to affect aggression, and is a possible reason for

Basal and reciprocal models of testosterone action – the attempt to understand the influence of testosterone on behaviour. 'Basal' suggests that testosterone is the causal factor; 'reciprocal' suggests that testosterone changes are led by behaviour.

the difference in level and type of aggression from each sex. Animal experiments demonstrate that castration reduces aggression in male mice, for example (Wagner et al., 1980), but does not eliminate it. Such findings lead to the conclusion that high levels of testosterone are necessary but not sufficient to trigger aggression. Castrated animals rated as non-aggressive before the removal of the testes cannot be made aggressive by injections of testosterone, whereas mice initially rated as aggressive do return to prior levels of aggression if given testosterone after castration.

As always, animal studies can be criticised for their limited application in humans. Human data is derived from non-experimental studies, which also have their problems due to the lack of direct observation. Studies on hormone levels in male and female prisoners do seem to suggest that testosterone does encourage social dominance, competitiveness and impulsiveness, all of which facilitate aggressive behaviour.

There are two hypotheses about the effect of testosterone. The basal model suggests that testosterone causes changes in dominance behaviour, whereas the reciprocal model posits the idea that testosterone changes as dominance changes. This clearly has implications for a biochemical model of aggression when sex differences are examined. If females are submissive and hence low in aggression due to a low ranking in hierarchies, then the basal model would suggest that it may be a result of a lack of testosterone or the lack of an ability to release it quickly into the blood stream at crucial moments. However, if individual women are raised in dominance, according to the reciprocal model, their testosterone levels should be rising too. No conclusive data has been found to suggest either model is correct, as injecting non-aggressive but ambitious women with testosterone is not the most ethical of studies.

In addition to endogenous hormones, the study of the influence of neurotransmitters on aggression also follows an animal model paradigm. Neurotransmitters are chemicals that allow the transmission of signals between neurones by their release into the synaptic cleft, the gap between neurones. The molecules can then bind to receptor proteins within the postsynaptic cell, which causes a change in its electrical state. This change in electrical state can either excite the cell, passing along the chemical message, or inhibit it. Excess molecules are taken back up by the presynaptic cell and reprocessed. One neurotransmitter of particular interest in aggression is serotonin (also called 5-hydroxytryptamine, or 5-HT). The neurones in the brain that release serotonin are found in small dense collections called Raphe nuclei, situated in the medulla, pons and midbrain. Serotonergic neurones have axons which project into many different parts of the brain; serotonin therefore affects many different behaviours. 5-HT receptors mediate both excitatory and inhibitory neurotransmission.

Serotonin or 5-hydroxytryptamine (5-HT) – raised levels of serotonin may reduce aggression.

Animal models show that increases in the availability of serotonin reduces aggression. This increase is facilitated by increasing the activity at neurotransmitter sites with drugs such as 5-HT agonists (drugs that stimulate the action). This has been shown to reduce several different types of aggression (Nelson & Trainor, 2007). There are several types of drugs that inhibit the 5-HT receptors. Inhibiting the re-uptake of serotonin allows higher levels to circulate in the system. The famous Prozac (fluoxetine) is one such drug that acts in this way. A second class of drugs are known as monoamine oxidase inhibitors or MOA inhibitors. Monoamine oxidase (MAO) is an enzyme that causes serotonin, dopamine and noradrenaline inactivation. MAO inhibitors prevent inactivation of monoamines within a neuron, causing excess neurotransmitter to diffuse into the synaptic space. Brunner et al. (1993) conducted a study on a large extended family, finding a mutation in the structural gene for MAO that appeared to be associated with aggressive behaviour among the males. They were reported to have selective MAO deficiency, again with an association with impulsive aggression, at least within circumstances of socio-emotional hypersensitivity (Eisenberger et al., 2007). There were no such deficiencies or aggressive behaviour reported in the female members of the family.

The final class of drugs are those that interfere with the ability of synaptic vesicles to store monoamines, again displacing serotonin. Such drugs include amphetamines. Animal experimentation shows clearly that 5-HT inhibitors do reduce some forms of aggression, or prevent its escalation (Takahashi et al., 2011), although de Boer and Koolhaas (2005) questioned the simple linkage between such serotonin increase and the reduction in all forms of aggression.

Extending these findings to humans is again not very clear, but it is known that there are reduced concentrations of 5-HT and 5-HIAA (a metabolite of 5-HT) in the brains of suicide victims, particularly those involving violent suicide methods, suggesting a link between suicidal and dominance/homicidal related behaviours. If this linkage appears tenuous, it may be illuminated by the findings of Dumais et al. (2005) that high levels of impulsive–aggressive behaviours are a clear marker of violent suicide.

Nelson and Trainor (2007) suggest that aggression is the result of impaired recognition of social cues and enhanced impulsivity, and that these are mediated by biological signals at the molecular level. This hypothesis is credible but difficult to test. Further findings make the issue even more complex. The release of the hormone prolactin from the pituitary gland is controlled by serotonin, and its levels in the bloodstream can be used to determine changes in serotonin levels. The action of the 5-HT agonists is to allow serotonin to be released, increasing the level of prolactin. However, there is no linear relationship between the dose of a drug and the amount of prolactin across individuals, showing a highly variable response to either the drug or the serotonin levels. Coccaro et al. (1989) showed that violent psychiatric patients, who were given fenfluramine (an anti-obesity drug that encourages the release of serotonin), showed negative correlation between measures of irritability and impulsive aggression (on the Buss–Durkee Hostility Inventory) and prolactin concentration. Those with high levels of aggression showed an attenuated response to fenfluramine, suggesting that they had reduced serotonergic activity, consistent with low serotonin activity being associated with increased aggressive and impulsive behaviours.

Other biochemical models are those linking ingested chemicals and their effects on the body and emotions. One of the world's most popular and widely available drugs is, of course, alcohol, which can increase aggression due to a disinhibitory effect. Most studies have concentrated on the effect of alcohol on aggression in men. However, when experimental studies do include female participants, it has been shown that the aggression-inducing effect of alcohol is less pronounced in women (Giancola et al., 2009). Light may be cast on this finding when the issue of physical size and the effect of alcohol on aggression is examined. DeWall et al. (2010) established that larger/heavier men were more likely to become aggressive after ingesting alcohol. They suggested that this is not necessarily a physical difference, but is more to do with a cognitive acceptance of larger men as being more aggressive anyway, and to be avoided when they are drunk. In other words, larger physical size permits men (but not women) to think that they can inflict costs on others if they find themselves in conflictive situations. This in turn increases the likelihood that they will escalate to aggression, together with a feeling of self-importance and entitlement to special treatment, which, when threatened, results in aggression. Support for this position comes from Vandello et al. (2009), who demonstrated that men misperceived aggression as more expected or socially desirable. In comparison to women, men consistently overestimated the aggression of peers and peer approval of aggression. Additionally, men perceive aggression as attractive to women. All of these misperceptions were highly correlated with lower self-esteem and weaker gender identification. The conclusion may be drawn that male aggression is a result of social inadequacies that have yet to be explored fully.

Ingested chemical – alcohol and some other drugs are implicated in raising aggression due to disinhibitory effects.

Genetics, and the possibility of inherited criminal behaviour, also provides another viewpoint, that of the evolutionary perspective, which is concerned with the behaviour necessary for the preservation of genetic material.

Evolution and crime

Psychological evolutionary theories work on the supposition that if elements such as physical characteristics can be inherited, so can behavioural characteristics and the psychological constituents that underlie them. As natural selection determines that the fittest, strongest or cleverest individuals will survive to pass on their genetic material to the next generation, so it follows that the behaviour that has facilitated this survival, and hence the psychological characteristics that have allowed this, will be passed on. Does this also apply to criminal behaviour and the psychology underlying it?

According to such theories, behaviour is passed to the next generation if it confers some evolutionary advantage. In other words, adaptations that allow survival will be inherited. The problem of applying such a point to the modern criminal is the difference between today and the ancient past, in which such behaviour must have arisen. However, it is the psychological tendency that is seated within the genes, not the acts. Therefore, it is the individual traits of criminal behaviour, such as impulsiveness, aggression and low empathy, that persist. Human

> Evolutionary psychology – attempts to explain behaviour as adaptions that have been successfully inherited via natural selection, and of particular (and controversial) application to sexualised violence.

behaviour is essentially social, in which cooperation is favoured by natural selection. However, this can create exploitative behaviour in those not predisposed to cooperation. There are numerous examples in animals where competition for resources and mates ensures current survival and a chance to pass on genetic material. Humans are not equipped with ready-made weapons of teeth or claws but they still need to compete; the human weapons are the brain and the mind and the ability to solve problems and plan for future events. Strategies designed to outwit others competing for resources and mates put humans in a unique cognitive position (Duntley & Shackleford, 2008) – they have the ability to *plan* how to inflict cost on rivals. While animals do inflict costs on rivals, i.e. physical injury or death, the human strategy is exploitation rather than injury. Those with psychopathic tendencies (see Chapter 4) are thought to be the result of evolutionary adaptations that allow a strategy of exploitation to be the natural form of interaction.

Lalumière et al. (2001) suggest that the strategy of exploiting others that is seen in psychopaths is a special adaptation that has evolved in order to achieve success in manipulating others for personal gain, whether sexual or monetary or otherwise.

Most evolutionary theories concentrate on reproductive strategies because reproductive success is, according to this perspective, the major imperative of all living things. Hence, it is suggested, violence, particularly sexual violence, can be explained by the necessity for maximising sexual activity. As may be imagined, this opinion is highly controversial and heavily criticised, particularly by feminist theorists. Evolutionary theories suggest that sexual violence is simply an aberrant strategy to attempt reproductive success, with the goal being the sexual activity. Feminist critics of this point out that a great deal of sexual violence is not about the sex; it is about violence and the attempt to control and humiliate the victims. Hence the underlying psychological characteristics of crimes are not fully explained by this biological imperative.

Neuropsychology and crime

Other scientific advances have been in the examination and understanding of brain function and how this can be affected by brain damage, illness or congenital or developmental problems. Linking this to criminal behaviour is still problematic. For example, there appears to be a higher rate of head injury in criminals compared with control groups (Farrer & Hedges, 2011). According to Williams et al. (2010), this is particularly noticeable in juvenile offenders. However, people who are involved in lots of violent incidents are more likely to suffer injuries, including head injuries, so this could be the result of the criminal behaviour, and not the other way round. Other neurological anomalies can be viewed with the same scepticism. Furthermore, the methodological limitations, such as constructing appropriate control groups and eliminating the effect of other factors, are clear. The social utility is also difficult to gauge, given that we cannot simply decide that anyone with a head injury or chromosomal abnormality is a potential criminal.

CRIMINAL BEHAVIOUR AND INTELLIGENCE

IQ – the measure of intellectual capacity/ability; it is controversially linked to crime through a weak correlation.

Associating crime with levels of intelligence has been an easy, but flawed, argument to make. The social factors that accompany low intelligence, such as poor educational attainment, high levels of unemployment, lack of basic social skills, and high likelihood of arrest, are clearly linked to crime rates. Examining research comparing the IQ of chronic offenders and non-offenders suggests that the offenders are generally eight points lower on the scale (Guay et al., 2005). However, the correlation between criminality and IQ is very weak, and no one would advocate the incarceration of everyone with low IQ scores. In addition, these findings suffer from the same criticism as any other research using IQ as a measurement, namely that the validity of IQ scales is questionable (Borsboom et al., 2004). Nevertheless, the differences are there, no matter what they may demonstrate, and, as Guay et al. (2005) showed, become wider when the offenders involved are violent or sexual offenders.

These differences persist even when economic and social factors, together with motivation to perform well on the tests, are taken into account. What does this mean for the aim of explaining criminality? Proulx et al. (2001) suggested that, for sexual offenders, low IQ is another facet of low impulse control, with certain characteristics of crime, and the criminal who is caught, contributing to the overall picture of the psychology of crime. Such a view coincides with one very influential theoretical perspective on crime that attempts to combine the individual (biology, IQ and personality) with the social (reward and punishment from others).

BIOSOCIAL THEORIES OF CRIME

Eysenck's theories of personality are highly influential and are readily applied to criminal behaviour (see Eysenck & Gudjonsson, 1989). Eysenck believed that personality was genetically and socially determined and that any individual personality comprises various combinations of extraversion, neuroticism and psychoticism, and the extent to which these can be acted on by reinforcers in the environment. Extraversion is linked to sociability, neuroticism to negative moods and low self-esteem, and psychoticism leads to aggression and antisocial behaviour. According to Eysenck, criminality indicates higher scores on these dimensions compared to the non-criminal population. For biosocial theories of this nature, social behaviour is produced by socialisation, a complex form of conditioning.

> Biosocial theory – an attempt to link biological characteristics and social influences; when applied to crime, it suggests that antisocial behaviour is the result of a biological predisposition to crime that has not had prosocial influences directed on to it.

Acceptable social behaviour results from a conditioning process in which social groups exert influence through rewards and punishments. When this process is deviant and aberrant behaviour becomes reinforced, antisocial behaviour will result. Eysenck's biosocial argument involves the view that extraversion indicates a central nervous system naturally requiring more stimulation, leading to difficulty in conditioning. Delays in conditioning would lead to delays in socialisation and can result in lack of reinforcement of acceptable behaviour. Such difficulties also apply to people scoring high on neuroticism, and the attendant high levels of emotionality. High levels of psychoticism, on the other hand, means a person has a poorer grasp of reality than others do, possibly to a delusional level. While this alone may be associated with criminal behaviour, psychotics also lack empathy and have high levels of impulsivity, characteristics that lend themselves to aggression and violence. Hence, for Eysenck, personality is a result of the interaction between individual biology and socialisation; a criminal personality is a genetic predisposition for the failure of acceptable social reinforcers.

Eysenck's theory is very attractive in its plausibility. Intuitively, it seems to make sense, but there is a lack of practical application. For example, the theory does not distinguish between different types of crime or criminal. It should also be relatively easy to test the link between the personality scores and criminality. However, most research has found a less than straightforward relationship, with neuroticism and psychoticism being correlated with criminality but not extraversion (Hare, 1982). It can be argued that the measurements of the personality components are flawed or that the elements of social influence are underrepresented by the Eysenckian theory.

SOCIAL LEARNING THEORY AND CRIME

Social learning theory can be viewed not only from the point of view of society's influence on the individual, but also from the individual perspective. Bandura (1977), when adapting the social learning theory to social cognition, suggested that there is interaction between the individual point of observation, understanding of the world and self-imposed understanding of consequences, environmental input and conditions determining behaviour. Criminal behaviour is no exception to this. Learning theories can be useful in trying to understand crime, particularly when the aspect of differential association theory (Sutherland, 1939) is added.

Differential association suggests that criminal behaviour occurs in a context of conflict and association with other criminals. Refining this by incorporating issues about learning, Burgess and Akers (1966) added the ideas of reinforcement to the differential association, and said that differential reinforcement of deviant behaviours is also required. Thus, we have the position of imitation as being the way in which criminals learn their behaviour, which in turn is more likely to happen in association with criminal people, and then this is being reinforced by rewards (not being caught, the thrill and the possession of items not usually available). This pattern of behaviour is then internalised (Siegel et al., 2006). There is some empirical work to support this position. For example, Rebellon (2006) used a vicarious reinforcement hypothesis to demonstrate that when delinquent behaviour is rewarded (by attention or other gratification), others will raise the level of their own delinquent behaviour. Thus there is a secondary effect of an individual's behaviour on another.

Social learning experiments demonstrate the way in which children will learn by imitation, that imitating acceptable behaviour is rewarded and that this extends to unacceptable (i.e. violent) behaviour. This certainly leads to the hypothesis that criminal behaviour can be learnt and subsequently reinforced. If the environment in which a child develops is deviant or criminal, then there is a high probability that the child will learn this behaviour and see it as normal. The main problem with this theory is in making a truly causal link between the environmental experience and later criminal acts, particularly as some children do not go on to become criminals, even though the home environment may have been violent or deviant. What is needed is a much more individual perspective.

A theory that gives more of an individual perspective is rational choice theory (Cornish & Clarke, 1998). 'Rational choice' is the term applied to the decision taken to commit crime after all consequences are considered in the light of rewards. Rational choice theory suggests that the choice to commit crime holds a specific purpose for the criminal, which varies with the type of crime (Guerrette, et al., 2005). In this perspective, individuals utilise a cost–reward decision-making process in choosing to commit a crime or not, and this process is related to the self-concept and moral code of each person. What this theory does not explain is how these internal positions of morality are reached.

PSYCHODYNAMIC THEORIES OF CRIME

Psychoanalytic or psychodynamic theories of behaviour were formulated by Freud and neo-Freudian theorists. Freud never applied his theories to the understanding of criminal behaviour directly, so the psychodynamic approach to criminality is an expansion of the original viewpoint. The most notable interpretation of psychoanalytical theory in terms of criminality was by Aichhorn (1925). In this, he proposed that criminality is a result of a strong id coupled to a weak superego – hence the demand for immediate gratification of urges is not inhibited. He also suggested that the contemporary treatment for delinquent youth, which involved harsh discipline, was ineffective for

> Psychodynamic theory – when applied to crime, psychodynamic theory suggests that the internal structure of personality, coupled with environmental influences, can lead to unconscious conflict that causes damage, resulting in a weakened superego.

several reasons: it simply encouraged physical violence as a response to the world. Weak development of the superego could lead to behaviour that we would term psychopathic, hence Freudian theory might be used to understand some forms of criminal behaviour. If there is id/ego/superego imbalance due to conflict with societal norms, then this should be painful and would be pushed into the unconscious (Shoemaker, 2005). This results in coping strategies (defence mechanisms) and problematic personality traits and problematic behaviours, such as deviant or criminal behaviour. Such a model means the criminal behaviour is the external manifestation of internal disease, a position with which many feel uncomfortable. This is further compounded by Erikson's (1994) 'identity crisis', which results from the inner imbalance. This is a very difficult concept to test empirically. As such, psychoanalytic theories are limited when trying to apply them to criminality.

Other facets of the theory are events such as resolution of the Oedipus complex – the notion that boys become (murderously) jealous of the father's sexual access to the mother. Boys can navigate and resolve this issue by identifying with the father (or equivalent) and thereby imitating the father's behaviour (Dimas et al., 2008). If this behaviour and the values associated with it are criminal, Freudian concepts mean that boys will assume them as their own. Therefore, as children go through the stages of psychosexual development, they also develop a moral sense, an internalised view of right and wrong.

A traumatic event, or deviant learning during this stage of development, might lead to underdevelopment of the superego. As McWilliams (1994) suggests, this could lead to difficulty with understanding issues of morality and possibly the development of a socio-pathic/psychopathic personality.

Psychopathy and criminality

Psychopathy is usually used to describe serious and violent criminality, although those with psychopathic personalities can be law-abiding. Setting aside the misconceptions about psychopathy, however, the manifestation of a personality disorder of this nature is seen to be associated with the most serious and persistent crimes. The DSM does not include psychopathy as a disorder in itself, but describes the antisocial personality disor-

Psychopathy – a set of personality characteristics that can lead to antisocial personality disorder but are not always associated with antisocial behaviour.

der (ASPD), which is discussed in more detail in Chapter 4 on the criminal mind. The theoretical position about ASPD is that it differs from other personality theories in terms of direct application to criminality, which neither biosocial theories not psychodynamic positions claim. Eysenckian theories do suggest that there is a link between lower cortical arousal levels and the ability to be conditioned by social norms. This can lead to the likelihood of delinquent behaviour, with possible personality traits such as higher extraversion and neuroticism being found in criminal subjects, but this link was tenuous at best. Even findings that introverts are more sensitive to punishment (Gray, 1970) did not lead to the conclusion that introverts were less likely to be criminal in nature.

The range of theoretical perspectives demonstrates that there are various approaches to explaining criminal personality and behaviour. Perhaps a more fruitful strategy would be to examine the ways in which psychology can be used to understand particular types of crime. The psychological examination of rape demonstrates how theoretical positions can be applied in practical ways.

RAPE: AN APPLICATION OF THEORY

Major approaches to rape include medical models, suggesting that rapists are mentally ill, evolutionary models, in which rape is seen as a strategy for perpetuation of genetic material, feminist theories, in which rape is viewed as male behaviour exerting power and dominance, and developmental studies, in which the rapist's childhood experiences and environment are examined.

Medical models of rape

A medical model means that the behaviour of an individual is accounted for by some form of pathology. If rapists are classified as mentally ill, then rape occurs as the result of uncontrollable sexual urges. A psychoanalytic explanation would fit into this model quite neatly, as rape would be seen as a conflict between the id and ego that the id has won. A weak superego cannot exert control over such a state. Some psychodynamicists, such as Abrahamson (1960), have even gone as far as to say that victims have some form of need to be raped and hence provoked the attack. Such notions are unpalatable to the general public and are easily contested. Very few rapes happen as unplanned events; rapists stalk victims and plan when they are going to carry out the attack. Also, the majority of rapists do not suffer from documented mental illness (Harrower, 1998). If there is a specific mental illness to be applied to this behaviour, it has yet to be found. However, certain issues do arise when examining the psychological status of rapists. As Dhawan and Marshall (1996) point out, many insist that they were sexually abused at some point in their lives. If sexual abuse leads to being abusive sexually, this might be a component of a mental illness with a particular manifestation in violent or coercive sex.

Evolutionary models of rape

Socio-biological or evolutionary theories explain behaviour in terms of the value it has in evolutionary significance. In order to perpetuate itself, a species needs to reproduce, and evolutionary psychology applies this drive to human behaviour, in particular sexual behaviour. The theory suggests that pregnant females are vulnerable and need protection from a strong and healthy mate. This in turn means that the mate's genetic material is being protected. Some males are not able to acquire mates in this acceptable way and need to force sex on a female. In addition, those men who are stronger and more powerful (but who lack sexual attraction for some reason) will have an advantage in this situation, and the genes for dominance in sex are therefore more likely to be passed on. Hence, rape is rewarded by evolutionary advantage.

The evidence that leads to this conclusion is somewhat tenuous. Rape victims do tend to be younger women who are of the age to reproduce, and rapists are often in socially disadvantaged positions (poor, low educational attainment, physically unattractive). Such a position, however, relies on the motivation for coercive or violent sex to be the chance to reproduce. It becomes difficult to see this as a full explanation when the fact that victims can be older women, children or men is considered, and also that sometimes the victim is killed or physically assaulted as well as raped. Feminist theory has an alternative position to offer.

Feminist models of rape

Some feminist theories were diametrically opposed to the evolutionary view and stated that, in a patriarchal society, men assert physical and economic dominance. Due to this, women assume a subservient role, and men are hence encouraged to see them as property and objects of sexual gratification. Rape, then, is a consequence of this imbalance in power, and all men are potential rapists, because here rape is not about the sex, but power, anger and the need to subjugate and humiliate. Some feminists even go as far as to say that, in such an imbalanced, patriarchal society, no woman can ever consent to sex, and all sex is rape. This is the most extreme form of the theoretical position. However, Scully (1990) points out that this explains rape's attendant issues such as violence, humiliation and degradation, and the forcing of victims into behaviours that have no outcomes of reproduction, such as anal or oral sex. There is also a level of evidence from convicted rapists that they tend to hold a particular view of women that is distrustful or hateful. The main criticism of a feminist view of rape is that it tends to be somewhat extreme and all-encompassing, but does not take into account individuality and environment.

Social learning models of rape

An alternative position is that rapists learn sexual aggression due to early exposure to such behaviour. This can be in terms of, for example, sexual abuse or viewing pornographic material in the media, thus providing an association between violence, pain and sex. This position has little evidence to support it; in fact, there is nothing to directly link pornography and rape. For men who rape, the highest-level use of pornography is at an earlier age than others, but this still does not indicate a causal link. According to research by Howitt and Cumberbatch (1990), the deviant thoughts and behaviour precede the use of pornography. There is also no correlation between the amount of pornography and liberal attitudes to its use and sexual offending in countries around the world.

These models and their relationship are summarised in Figure 3.1.

So, where does all this leave us in terms of explaining and, more importantly, understanding how to deal with rape, its victims and the perpetrators? In many fields of the study of crime, researchers and practitioners are advocating the integration of theory. Harrower's (1998) integrated theory of rape attempts to do just that – pointing out that men may have a biological need or drive for sex, but that societal and sexual signals that equate sex and aggression are confusing. In normal circumstances, socialisation means that men are able

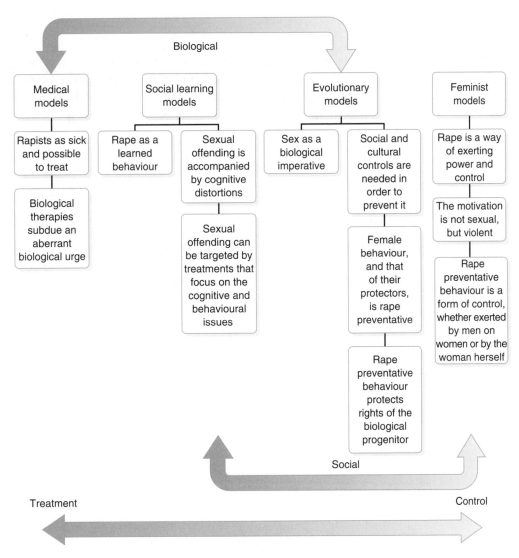

Figure 3.1   Connections between psychological theories about rape

to keep such tendencies under control, and not even realise they are there, but the deviant developmental environment some children inhabit leads to psychological issues that are compensated for by aggression, including in the sexual arena. Couple this to a society or culture in which women are devalued, and such tendencies are less likely to be seen as antisocial.

SUMMARY

There are many psychological perspectives and each can be used to explain crime. This may appear to be confusing and unclear at first, and this feeling can persist. In order to achieve some clarity the psychology of each type of crime and criminal should be examined. In the next few chapters, the psychological theory and research outlined above will be used to examine various crimes and criminals.

Who Commits Crime? The Criminal Mind

'You have a magnificent brain, Moriarty. I admire it. I admire it so much I'd like to present it, pickled in alcohol, to the London Medical Society.' So says Basil Rathbone as Sherlock Holmes in '*The Adventures of Sherlock Holmes*' (Twentieth Century Fox Film Corporation, 1939). As a detective, Conan Doyle's fictional character Sherlock Holmes is the consummate investigator, utilising methods of forensic science as well as crime scene analysis and even criminal profiling. But he also alludes to one side of the question about the criminal mind: is criminality centred in the brain or in society's influence on the individual?

This question – what is the criminal mind and what are its antecedents – has been one that has perplexed scholars throughout history. In the twenty-first century we are no nearer to determining the nature of the person who commits crimes, and distinguishing him/her from those of us who do not, but we have more information and better tools at our disposal to investigate the question. Additionally, we do not have to pickle any brains in order to examine them. When we look at some of the most infamous criminals, it would be tempting to think we can determine what the criminal brain is, as Sherlock Holmes seemed to think we can. Questions of paramount importance are whether there are personality disorders or mental illnesses that make people commit crime, or whether it is that some people are just plain evil. In other words, is there a criminal mind?

KEY THEMES

- Antisocial personality disorder
- Attachment failure
- Biological differences
- Psychopathology and crime
- Psychopathy and crime
- Psychopathy
- Sociopathy/psychopathy

The Kray twins – A twin study in crime

Reginald (Reggie) and Ronald (Ronnie) Kray were twins born ten minutes apart on 24 October 1933. They were devoted to their mother, Violet, and had promising boxing careers in their teens. Pearson (2010) describes how they were also the foremost perpetrators of organised crime in London's East End during the 1950s and 1960s. They ran legitimate businesses, such as nightclubs and gymnasiums, but as a front for other activities, including extortion and

Twin studies – research utilising examination of twins, usually monozygotic twins, to determine genetic and inherited characteristics and psychology.

drug running. They were convicted of the murder of Jack McVitie in 1969, Ronnie also being convicted of the murder of George Cornell (Metropolitan Police, 2012). Their older brother, Charlie, was also found guilty, with others, of being an accessory to the McVitie murder.

The Kray family is an intriguing case study, not just because we have twins and an older brother all involved in criminal and violent activities, but also because Ronnie was diagnosed schizophrenic. His life sentence for murder was spent in psychiatric hospitals. Ronnie was also openly gay in a period when male homosexuality had not yet been decriminalised. There are other recorded differences between the twins. Ronnie was clearly the more violent, possibly due to a loosened grip on reality. At one point he became a danger to the whole operation the brothers had set up, and it was Ronnie's final acts of violence that led to their imprisonment.

The Krays are a twin case study all of their own, and give us an opportunity to examine whether mental illness contributes to criminality. Whether it does or not is still an undecided issue, as there are several cases we can examine that show quite clearly that mental illness is not at play.

Ted Bundy – the homicidal psychopath

Theodore Robert Bundy was not mentally ill, but he was lots of other things. He was charming, handsome and charismatic. He was very intelligent and studied psychology at the University of Washington, and worked on Seattle's suicide hotline crisis centre. When he graduated in 1972 he enrolled in law school. He also killed at least 36 young women between 1974 and 1978, ensnaring them by asking for help while wearing a plaster cast on his arm or pretending to be a police officer. He may be responsible for more murders and kidnaps, but these were the only ones to which he confessed, and only after a spectacular and headline-grabbing trial. He sometimes revisited his dead victims, grooming and having sex with the corpses until the bodies decayed too much even for him (Michaud & Aynesworth, 2000). He decapitated at least twelve victims and kept the severed heads in his apartment as mementos. He was executed by electrocution on 24 January 1989.

Bundy's crimes are horrific, but what makes him just that bit more interesting to the forensic psychologist is what happened at his trial and the time leading up to his death. During his trial he sacked his defence team and represented himself, believing he could do a better job than them. It was a grandiose gesture that allowed him to take centre stage in the full glare of the media, as the trial was filmed. He was found guilty on all counts, with indisputable evidence, such as bite marks and eyewitness accounts, including from women he had failed to abduct. All the evidence confirmed his guilt of horrific crimes: abduction, sexual assault, rape, sodomy, blunt force bludgeoning, dismemberment of bodies and necrophilia. Nevertheless, while Carole Anne Boone was testifying as a character witness, he proposed marriage and she accepted. In October 1982, two and half years after Bundy was sentenced to death, Boone gave birth to a daughter, naming Bundy as the father. Conjugal visits were not allowed in the jail where Bundy was being held, so the paternity of the child is debatable (Rule, 2009).

There are several books about Bundy. Some, like Robert Keppel and William Birnes' *Signature Killers* (1997) and Stephen Michaud and Hugh Aynesworth's *Ted Bundy: Conversations with a Killer* (2000), are first-hand reports of Bundy's hubris and self-aggrandisement, but they are also definitive descriptions of his crimes. He loved talking to writers about himself, and even offered opinions to the FBI on how to go about investigating another case, the so-called 'Green River Killer' (Keppel et al., 2004). His need to be admired was very clear, but he also felt he could manipulate the system in terms of his own death. He stated that he was too precious to execute because he offered so much to the world in terms of insight into his mind. While all of these characteristics and behaviours seem odd, and we know they turned out to be fatal, they are not indicative of mental illness. Despite common public perception, psychopathy is not synonymous with violence or psychosis (Skeem et al., 2011). In contrast with psychosis, psychopathic individuals present as rational, non-delusional, oriented to their surrounding and situations, and they understand the consequences of their actions.

It appears Bundy knew right from wrong, but he did not care about the difference, and he thought it did not apply to him. His DNA profile has now been entered into the national US database to see if he can be linked to several unsolved murders of young women that occurred at around the same time.

Narcissistic, egotistical, manipulative, risk-taking, callous and a compulsive liar: Ted Bundy was all these, and this has led many to suggest he was a psychopath. This is not the rampaging slavering monster beloved of Hollywood, but a personality disorder that has had what might be described as a pretty bad press.

PSYCHOPATHY

Psychopathy is usually defined as a collection of affective, interpersonal and behavioural characteristics, including egocentricity, impulsivity, irresponsibility, shallow emotions, lack of empathy, guilt or remorse, pathological lying, manipulativeness, and the persistent violation of social norms and expectations (Cleckley, 1976; Hare, 2000). None of these is related in any way to criminal behaviour, but the issues inherent in many of these characteristics do appear to be connected to the ability and willingness to commit crime. In particular, the lack of empathy and high levels of manipulativeness would seem to be a specification for a confidence trickster or fraudulent criminal (see Chapter 11). Psychopathy is not a diagnostic category in either the *Diagnostic and Statistical Manual of Mental Disorders* (DSM) (American Psychiatric Association, 2013) or the *International Classification of Diseases* (ICD). However, there is a disorder in each of these manuals that includes many of the characteristics that Hare and Cleckley have given as definitions of psychopathy.

Antisocial/dissocial personality disorder

The DSM includes a category of personality disorder termed 'antisocial personality disorder' (ASPD); in the ICD, it is termed 'dissocial personality disorder' (DPD). The essential features of a personality disorder are impairments in personality (self and interpersonal) functioning and the presence of pathological personality traits. This is not necessarily synonymous with mental illness (Kendell, 2002) as it does not have the disabling effect associated with psychopathological conditions. The DSM-V (American Psychiatric Association, 2013), it is proposed, should include an updated reformulation of this definition. In both texts (the DSM and the ICD) there are a high number of similarities, including failure to conform to social norms, impulsivity and lack of remorse or disregard for others. In addition, diagnostic criteria include the need to exclude the possibility of other personality disorders, such as conduct or emotional disorders.

The diagnosis of ASPD has long been controversial, but is also the subject of ongoing research. Such research indicates that it is much more likely that men will exhibit ASPD than women, with the most recent figures being a 1–6.8% occurrence rate in men and a 0–1.3% occurrence rate in women (see Swanson et al., 1996; Coid et al., 2009). Such ranges and disparities reflect the difficulty in diagnosing and understanding this disorder, as well as the ranges of methodology used and the countries in which the study takes place. In addition, Yang and Coid (2007) suggest that people with ASPD are more likely to require the attention of forensic services and that women in this situation have more severe problems, such as comorbidity of mental disorders. There is naturally, given the range of behaviour contributing to ASPD, a higher proportion of people with the disorder in the prison setting (Fazel & Danesh, 2002), with as many as 49% of male and 31% of female prisoners meeting diagnostic criteria. ASPD is regarded as inherently linked to criminal behaviour, but many regard it as a category of diagnosis that occurs when no other diagnosis is possible. In addition, it is not synonymous with psychopathy since the incidence of high scorers on measures of psychopathy is much lower, suggesting that ASPD is only a behavioural subset of psychopathy. Kosson et al. (2006) suggest that ASPD and psychopathy are separate disorders that have high levels of comorbidity, and that ASPD, with and without psychopathy, represent two distinct but related syndromes in those with criminal tendencies.

Psychopaths

According to the main proponents of a taxonomy of this concept, such as Cleckley (1976) and Hare (1999), psychopathy includes problems within the individual that lead to a personality that is deeply dissocial. Cleckley originally distinguished between the primary psychopath, in whom the disorder is the principal issue, and the secondary psychopath, who presents with an aspect of another disorder. Primary psychopathy, then, is that which contains items that are identified as Factor 1 from the reviewed Psychopathy Checklist (see below). These are the traits of arrogance, callousness, manipulativeness, lying. The Factor 2 traits, which are seen in secondary psychopaths, are impulsivity, a proneness to boredom, irresponsibility and displaying a lack of long-term goals (Lykken, 1995). In criminal situations, this distinction is thought to manifest itself in the lack of planning in secondary psychopaths. Things are not straightforward, however, as Mealey suggests that primary psychopathy is biological in origin and secondary psychopathy is a result of genetics and environment. In other words, psychopaths are born, sociopaths are socialised.

Cleckley's original description includes superficial charm, grandiosity, pathological lying, manipulativeness, lack of remorse or guilt, shallow affect, callousness, lack of empathy, parasitic lifestyle, poor behavioural controls, promiscuity, lack of goals or the motivation to follow through on them. Each of these characteristics alone would be a problem, but when found in clusters in the individual can lead to a delinquent lifestyle.

There are various examinations of how these characteristics manifest themselves. The psychopathic personality has wide prevalence across societies and across time. Many people throughout history can be identified as exhibiting the characteristics, and it is not limited to any one society or level of society. This stability has led to speculation that there is a biological or genetic cause for psychopathy in addition to simply socio-cultural or developmental causes (Pitchford, 2001). In addition, evolutionary positions are presenting viable explanations for psychopathy in that predatory behaviour, including social predation, is a suitable adaptation that natural selection will sustain (Quinsey, 2002). This does not suggest that antisocial behaviour is acceptable, but that it perpetuates in the same way as the tendency for lions to kill gazelles persists. The psychopath often gets what he or she wants. Mealey and Kinner (1996) suggested that there was a benefit to be gained from certain antisocial behaviours, such as cheating. Sexual cheating avoids much of the cost of courtship, marriage and childrearing that non-cheating men must 'endure', meaning that those who cheat have better reproductive success because they are having sex with a larger number of women. As such, cheating is a genetically mandated behaviour. Extending this behaviour to other forms of cheating is tenuous, but it does represent a certain validity to the evolutionary position of psychopathy being a genetically inherited characteristic and behaviour.

If psychopathy is, in fact, a reproductive strategy, can we extend this to other characteristics found in this cluster of personality traits? It is well established that psychopaths do not experience social emotions (shame, embarrassment, guilt, empathy and love) to as high a degree as others do. This is a consistent psychological and behavioural finding, supported by neurological findings. Social emotions provide clues about the interactions we have and the relationships we form, and are distinct from what might be defined as more primary emotions, such as anger and happiness. They are clearly associated with cortical and limbic system function, particularly the amygdala, and override impulses that would lead to behaviours successful in the short term (such as cheating) and to allow us to consider long-term strategies for success (such as bonding). The weaker these signals are, the less likely we are to inhibit behaviour that allows manipulation of others for our own gain. Social emotions are also those that allow us to detect the cheats among us, but they in turn will develop mechanisms to become better at hiding their behaviour. However, the latest pieces of neurological research are showing ways in which the psychopath and the non-psychopath can be distinguished, perhaps making Sherlock Holmes more accurate than Conan Doyle might have imagined. For example, Rilling et al. (2007) examined fMRI scans while participants were playing a game called Prisoner's Dilemma. Those scoring high on psychopathy, particularly male participants with high scores, were more likely to betray their hypothetical partner, but also demonstrated weaker activation in the orbitofrontal cortex when choosing to cooperate and showed weaker activation within the dorsolateral prefrontal and rostral anterior cingulate cortex when choosing to defect. According to Blair (2003), the amygdala is involved in aversive conditioning and instrumental learning, particularly in terms of punishment, as it is activated in fear repsonses. Overall, there is weaker amygdala activation in those with high psychopathy scores than lower scorers, suggesting high scores are linked to weaker aversive conditioning. They conclude that high psychopathy scorers have an emotional bias towards betrayal and defection that, due to its neurological basis, can only be negated with effort.

The Prisoner's Dilemma: Two men are arrested, but the police do not possess enough information for a conviction. Following the separation of the two men, the police offer both a similar deal to betray his partner to his advantage if the other man remains silent, as the betrayer will go free. If both remain silent, they would both be convicted, but of a lesser charge. If both betray, they will both be convicted of the original charge. Each prisoner must choose to betray or not.

So, is psychopathy a result of biology or society? While genetics, evolution and neurobiology play a large part, the differential manifestation in people such as successful businessmen and murdering brutes must be a result of circumstances. Although psychopathy cannot be understood solely in terms of antisocial childrearing or impaired development, it is certainly a developmental disorder, as identified by Frick et al. (1994). It can be recognised in children, even if it is not named as such. However, Blair et al. (1997) determined that the supposed developmental causes of criminality, such as child abuse, would not lead to the reduced emotional responsiveness seen in psychopathy.

Neither position can be completely correct. Some people with psychopathic personalities never commit a truly criminal act in their lives, and certainly not violent ones. Babiak and Hare (2007) coined the phrase 'corporate psychopath' to describe someone who is manipulative, callous, impulsive and unreliable, but within a non-criminal framework. These are colleagues who take credit for others' work but blame others if it goes wrong. Babiak and Hare suggest that they are social predators, hunting power, prestige and money. In some industries these characteristics are praised and even desired. Someone who is charismatic and highly socially skilled but completely ruthless can be very valuable in businesses that require little empathy but high remorselessness in pursuing a goal where there is no social advantage, such as hostile takeovers and asset stripping. However, it is not the successful, ruthless businessperson who may be a singlulary unattractive personality but who acts within the law that interests the forensic psychologist. It is the psychopath who takes behaviour one step further and commits crimes. Hence the criminal psychopath has been the focus of a great deal of psychological research.

Measurement of psychopathy

The measurement of psychopathy is, in itself, controversial. Hare's PCL-R (1999a) is based on Cleckley's 16-item checklist, and is designed only to be used in clinical settings and accompanied by a clinical interview. Diagnosing someone as psychopathic can have severe consequences, and the potential for harm is considerable if the PCL-R is used incorrectly, so it should only be used by experienced and qualified personnel who are familiar with the literature and the use of tests of this nature.

The PCL-R items can be reduced to two stable factors. Factor 1 comprises the affective and interpersonal style of the individual, and Factor 2 comprises the more behavioural aspects of psychopathy, that is, those items that describe impulsive, antisocial lifestyles and characteristics of APSD (see Table 4.1). There are also several items that do not load on either factor.

Although there are other instruments that have been developed to measure psychopathy, the PCL-R is perhaps the most well-known instrument, as Hare's work has a large impact

Table 4.1   PCL-R items (Hare, 1999a)

Factor 1 (Affect and interpersonal style)	Factor 2 (Behavioural, especially anti-social lifestyle)	Not loading on factor
Glibness/superficial charm	Need for stimulation/ proneness to boredom	Promiscuous sexual behaviour
Grandiose sense of self-worth	Parasitic lifestyle	Many short-term marital relationships
Pathological lying	Poor behavioural controls	Criminal versatility
Conning/manipulative	Early behavioural problems	
Lack of remorse or guilt	Lack of realistic, long-term goals	
Shallow affect	Impulsivity	
Callous/lack of empathy	Irresponsibility	
Failure to accept responsibility for own actions	Juvenile delinquency	
	Revocation of conditional release	

in the study of psychopathy. A respected alternative measurement is the Psychopathic Personality Inventory (PPI/PPI-R), a 154-item self-report measure of both global psychopathy and the component traits of psychopathy. It is designed to detect response styles relevant to psychopathy and does not focus exclusively on antisocial or criminal behaviours, but measures the continuum of psychopathic personality traits present in a large range of populations and can be used in both clinical and nonclinical settings.

Why measure?

Although it is clear that there are psychopathic individuals who will never carry out an antisocial or criminal act, psychopathy is implicated in a disproportionate amount of serious repetitive crime and violence. A reliable measurement instrument is therefore an important tool. Criminal psychopaths are more likely to have taken part in criminal activities throughout their lifespan than other offenders, and it is more likely that those behaviours are violent. There is also evidence that high scorers on psychopathy measures are more likely to be recidivist. But it is still evident that even psychopathic criminals are high functioning and are not mentally ill.

MENTAL ILLNESS AND CRIME

Ronnie Kray's mental illness certainly affected the way in which he and his twin brother ran their 'firm', the name given to their organised crime network and activities. Ronnie was diagnosed schizophrenic, but many agree that his symptoms show he had a particular form of the illness – paranoid schizophrenia. Schizophrenia is characterised by a breakdown of thought processes and by poor emotional responsiveness. Paranoid schizophrenia is a recognised subtype, the defining feature of which is delusional thoughts, which are coherent and consistent over time. There may be increasing paranoia and difficulties in relationships as the individual ages, but paranoid schizophrenia does not mean that the person cannot function. Indeed, the person's thinking and behaviour is less disordered than found in other subtypes.

Ronnie was imprisoned for a serious assault on a rival gang member that took place between 1955 and 1959, and it was during this period he was first diagnosed as mentally ill. Reggie, on the other hand, was beginning to make good money as a legitimate businessman, with a bar and gym that attracted the celebrities of the day. He was working with his older brother, Charlie, to expand and manage the business very successfully. When Ronnie was released from prison, after a stint in a lunatic asylum (as it was called then), he tried to work within these businesses, but it became clear his violent nature was a real embarrassment to Reggie and Charlie. It appears that, in the following years, Ronnie steadily lost his grip on reality and only his brothers prevented him from going completely insane. However, the escalating use of violence was unstoppable, and Reggie, inconsolable at the suicide of his first wife, erupted into a cycle of murder that was finally stopped only by their arrest and the trial for McVitie's death, which resulted in a life sentence for the twins.

What does the Kray twins' story reveal to psychology? First, we have a clear picture of what it meant to grow up in poverty in the East End of London, and to attempt to make money by legitimate and criminal means. It is clear that the social structure had a lot to do with how the Kray twins lived their lives. However, the difference between them tells us a good deal about mental illness and the effect it can have on personality and behaviour. Ronnie clearly was the more violent of the two, with Reggie managing to behave, to a certain degree, in non-criminal and non-violent ways when removed from his brother's influence. Does it tell us that mental illness is related to crime? No, but it may indicate that mental illness, in the social structure of places like 1960s London, was conducive to antisocial behaviour. Within the twins' circle this kind of violence was not unusual, and was even expected. Ronnie's mental illness did mean he was probably lacking in control and had high levels of disinhibition. Did this mean he was destined to be criminal? No, there were many factors that contributed to the ways in which the Krays lived their lives, but undoubtedly Ronnie's illness added a psychological dimension to the combination of social, financial and genetic factors that made them the most talked about crime lords of mid-twentieth-century England.

Mental illness does not mean someone is necessarily going to be violent, but some forms of illness may disrupt a person's thinking, feeling, moods and ability to relate to others. If that person is not then equipped with skills or the therapeutic means to overcome such disruptions, this can result in antisocial behaviour. However, the inability to relate to the world may mean that someone with mental illness may not be able to manipulate a crime scene sufficiently to evade capture. So it is unlikely that serial offenders have serious mental health problems beyond the personality disorders described above.

SUMMARY

Is there a criminal mind? Mental illness quite often precludes the likelihood of a criminal life without other factors being present. In the case of the Kray twins, the social circumstances in which they were born and the 'firm' they constructed allowed Ronnie to participate in and even initiate criminal activities. Nevertheless, the violent nature of their life cannot have helped Ronnie's grip on reality and violence fatally erupted. Schizophrenia did not mean the violence was inevitable – their lifestyle was partly responsible for that – but it did not help. The study of mental disorder in the prison system may cast more light on this and it is discussed in more detail in Chapter 19.

A more serious candidate for the criminal mind is psychopathy, but the link between that and crime is not clear-cut at all. Psychopathy may be useful to society outside the criminal arena, in that our most successful industry and political leaders are totally without remorse and the goal in sight, whether that is economic growth or winning a war, becomes society's goal.

Where does that leave us in trying to define the criminal mind? It leaves us in need of more research and more work trying to understand those who carry out antisocial and criminal acts. Over the next few chapters we will encounter some of those acts and the psychological explanations for them.

Discussion point: What is the value of twin studies in crime research?

Twin studies are invaluable in the debate about nature and nurture, i.e. what contributions do genetics and the environment make to psychological issues? Can they be used in any way when studying criminal and antisocial behaviour? The Kray twins are a fascinating addition to this debate, but this case study is not completely decisive. The papers below give an outline of how twin studies can be used in forensic and criminal psychology.

Barnes, J. & Jacobs, B. (2012) Genetic risk for violent behavior and environmental exposure to disadvantage and violent crime: the case for gene–environment interaction. *Journal of Interpersonal Violence* [online], first published on 24 July.

Beaver, K. (2012) The familial concentration and transmission of crime. *Criminal Justice and Behavior* [online], first published on 27 June. (This paper attempts to bring the two strands of nature and nurture together.)

Forsman, M. & Långström, N. (2012) Child maltreatment and adult violent offending: population-based twin study addressing the 'cycle of violence' hypothesis. *Psychological Medicine*, **42**(9): 1977–1983.

Juvenile Criminals

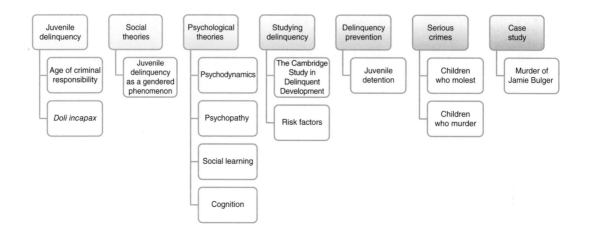

Juvenile delinquency
- Age of criminal responsibility
- *Doli incapax*

Social theories
- Juvenile delinquency as a gendered phenomenon

Psychological theories
- Psychodynamics
- Psychopathy
- Social learning
- Cognition

Studying delinquency
- The Cambridge Study in Delinquent Development
- Risk factors

Delinquency prevention
- Juvenile detention

Serious crimes
- Children who molest
- Children who murder

Case study
- Murder of Jamie Bulger

Jamie Bulger was almost 3 years old when he wandered away from his mother on 12 February 1993. His mother quickly realised he had gone and looked for him anxiously, but by that time it was too late. Jamie was missing. His body was found the next day alongside the nearby railway line, battered, sexually assaulted, his body severed by a train. The immediate thought was that he had been taken by a predatory paedophilic adult, but CCTV footage from the shopping centre was to reveal something that was even more chilling, if that were possible. He was seen being led out of the shopping centre by two 10-year-old boys, Jon Venables and Robert Thompson. The boys were charged on 20 February 1993 with Jamie's abduction and murder, and found guilty on 24 November, making them, at that time, the youngest children to be convicted of murder in the UK.

KEY THEMES

- Age of criminal responsibility
- Delinquency prevention
- *Doli incapax*
- Juvenile delinquency
- Juvenile detention

The Bulger case is a landmark in British criminal history, both in legal and psychological terms. It is still unclear why the two boys kidnapped and killed Jamie. They were tried as adults in open and public court, but they did not speak. Two psychiatrists had examined the boys and testified that they knew right from wrong. The moral indignation caused by the thought that two young children could kill was evident in the British press, which suggested that this was a breakdown in lawful society and family life, and in the large numbers of protesters outside the court. This righteous anger revived when it was clear that the boys, now young men, might be released on licence in 2001 (Guardian, 2000). There was little recognition of the fact that in other European countries these boys would never have been charged with the crime at all. In the Norwegian city of Trondheim, in October 1994, 5-year-old Silje Raedergard was attacked by two 6-year-old boys, who left her to die in the snow. The names of her killers have never been revealed and neither boy was prosecuted. In 1999, the European Court of Human Rights ruled that the Venables and Thompson trial had not been fair due to the age of the defendants and that fact that they were tried in public in an open, adult court (Wolff & McCall Smith, 2000).

Although the legal age of responsibility in England is 10, in Belgium it is 18, while it is 12 in Holland, 13 in France, 14 in Italy, 15 in Norway

Doli incapax – deemed incapable of forming the intent to commit a crime or tort, especially by reason of age (under 10 years old).

and 16 in Spain. However, in Scotland it is 8 years, and many American states do not have a minimum age. The idea of a minimum age at which children can be seen to be culpable for their criminal acts is a modern one, and rests on the principle of *doli incapax*. This is a presumption in law that some people are not capable of a crime because they do not understand that the behaviour is a crime. If a prosecutor wishes to prove otherwise, this must be contested in court. In the Bulger case, the prosecutor rebutted *doli incapax* and the boys were deemed to have understood that what they had done was a crime. They had carried on assaulting Jamie in the full knowledge that this was a crime. In 1998, *doli incapax* was abolished in England and Wales, raising concerns about the treatment of children and other vulnerable people in legal situations and about compliance with international human rights standards. Hence, the question of youth and crime is a vexed and difficult one, ranging from the moral panic of the Bulger case to the policy of juvenile detention. The psychological issues are no less problematic. Theories that attempt to explain delinquency and criminal behaviour in general, from the social to the neurological, are not necessarily applicable to juvenile delinquency.

JUVENILE DELINQUENCY

A juvenile is a person under the age of majority, or a minor. This term is defined in some very inconsistent ways around the world, and varies both in terms of the age referred to and the status accorded to the juvenile. For example, in the UK the age of majority is 18. This is when someone is deemed to be an adult and is accorded all the rights of an adult, with some minor exceptions. However, there are differing ages for some issues; in the UK, for example, people can work part-time at age 13, join the armed forces, consent to sex and get married at age 16, and learn to drive a car and hold a driving licence at age 17, but not vote in elections or buy alcohol until they are 18 years old. This variation in legality of ages becomes even more diverse when considering responsibility for crimes. In England, the age of responsibility (i.e. the age at which a person can be found guilty of a crime) is 10 years, which was why Venables and Thompson were prosecuted, but to be found guilty of rape or other sexual crimes a child must be 13 years old.

The furore resulting from crimes such as the Bulger murder and other instances of youth crime have been termed a 'moral panic' (Cohen, 1973), a situation in which a community expresses severe concern over an issue that appears to be a threat to social order. Juvenile delinquency is the term often used for criminal acts carried out by juveniles, but it is also used to refer to a social problem that requires examination and policy development. Most jurisdictions have specific processes for dealing with those juveniles who commit crimes and for addressing the social issues perceived to be attendant on the problem. As such, it is a subject worthy of criminological and psycholegal theory and research separate from the examination of criminal behaviour carried out by adults. The 2003 UN World Report on

Youth details several causative factors for youth crime and delinquency, including problems with social and economic development at a national level, urbanisation and migration, family issues, the media, peer influences and delinquent identities (such as gang membership) (United Nations, 2003).

SOCIAL THEORIES OF JUVENILE CRIME

If the cause of a crime lies within the criminal rather than the external environment in which they exist, then the individual is regarded as making a rational choice to commit crime. Rational choice theory, also called rational action theory, posits that people compare the advantages and disadvantages of committing a crime and will do so when the advantages are greater (Clarke & Felson, 1993). It therefore explains *when* someone will commit a crime, but not *why*. Nor does it explain differences between individuals and groups in terms of the likelihood to commit crime, or the influence of peers, or the ability to understand the consequences of actions or any other circumstances outside the decision point (Walklate, 2003a). It also does not take into account any ability that a child or children may or may not have to take all of these elements into consideration. Laying blame for a child's criminality solely on his or her capacity for making rational decisions is not a position most judicial systems would find appropriate. An alternative position is that of social disorganisation theory (also called social ecology theory), in which crime is said to be the result of the breakdown of traditional values and norms. This is thought to happen because urban areas have high levels of transient populations and migration, leading to the breakdown of community. Such disintegration and disorganisation would have a greater effect on the developing child than adults.

If crime and the associated levels of juvenile crime are the result of community breakdown or social disintegration, then strain theory would suggest that the disintegration could lead to social difficulties, such as poverty, and therefore individuals need to achieve their socially valued goals by illegitimate means (Agnew, 2009). Hence the position of assuming criminality is due to the children of low-income families having no means by which to gratify their needs. Strain theory is a compellingly convincing explanation, but the difficulty here lies in explaining why children of poor families would necessarily be poorly educated, particularly in societies that have publicly funded education, such as the UK. It also fails to address the issue that much of youth crime does not have an economic motivation, but is essentially thrill-seeking and/or violent in nature. It is also geared towards the attainment of socially valued status and goals as opposed to goods of high economic value. Brezina et al. (2009) suggest that underlying motivations may be linked more to a lack of a sense of any meaningful future, that is, if young people fail to anticipate a good future for themselves and that includes the probability of an early death, they see little point in delaying gratification or obeying societal rules. The difficulty in achieving any goals leads to young people forming what is viewed as delinquent subcultures (Eadie & Morley, 2003), which again are focused upon non-economic crimes. Gang culture is an example of subcultural theory in practice, in which young people, predominantly young men, reject societal norms for the attainment of goals (Decker, 2004).

While gang culture is worthy of study in itself, the group context is interesting simply from a juvenile delinquency point of view. Differential association suggests that groups of young people are subjected to peer pressure, leading to a new focus for the study of motivation to commit crime. What is unclear in social theories of juvenile crime is whether economic or social pressure force young people to form groups which become delinquent or whether the existence of the group means that delinquent behaviour will result. There is also the issue of the social perception of groups of young people. Once an individual or group has been labelled as delinquent, they are much more likely to offend or reoffend (Eadie & Morley, 2003). Labelling theory is clear that boys from poor families are more likely to be labelled deviant than those from higher income families, and suggests that this is why higher numbers of delinquents are found within lower income brackets than in higher ones (Walklate, 2003b).

Social theories of delinquency do have currency in assuming society's responsibility for juvenile delinquency and crime. However, this does not take into account the fact that delinquency is not a solely modern problem, but is one that has been considered for hundreds of years (Clement & Hess, 1990). If society has changed but the problem has not, it is probable that the issue should be considered at a more individual level. However, if the problem is changing, perhaps societal-level explanations still have value. One facet of juvenile delinquency that has not remained constant highlights this question quite clearly. Female juvenile delinquency is on the rise; it does not seem to follow the downward trend observed in other areas.

Juvenile delinquency as a gendered phenomenon

An interesting point raised in the social theories is that of male delinquency being easily labelled. All figures suggest that boys are much more likely to commit crimes than girls. This may be a result of the need to establish a developing masculinity and the need to appear powerful. If there are no legitimate means by which to express this, then young men may act out their manhood in criminal ways. This position has both biological and psychological factors to support it. Both research literature (Dodge et al., 2006) and policy reports (United Nations, 2003) have established that more delinquent and criminal acts are carried out by boys than by girls.

More recently, however, this apparent gender gap in offending is shrinking. This may be because women and girls are becoming more aggressive in their offending behaviour and/ or that female offending is becoming more frequently reported (J. Schwartz et al., 2009). What remains unclear is the aetiology of female juvenile delinquency, and whether it is the same as for boys. Research suggests that delinquency occurs more often in the context of a relationship for girls than for boys (Odgers & Moretti, 2002) and that these relationships are likely to be adversarial in regard to parents and romantic partners (National Mental Health Association, 2005). Given that romantic relationships can start as early as 13 years of age for girls, and that this is a normal part of adolescent psychological and sexual development (Savin-Williams & Diamond, 2004), it would seem reasonable to suggest that these are a salient factor in delinquency as well as everything else. Teenage girls also typically date older boys (Carver et al., 2003), and this has been suggested as a higher risk factor for involvement in delinquent behaviours for girls (Meeus et al., 2004) as they are more likely than boys to be strongly influenced by a romantic partner (Haynie et al., 2005). This element also interacts with the parent–teen relationship, as, according to Meeus et al. (2004), parental influence on adolescent offending is higher when there is no romantic partner in the mix. This is still very unclear and research is lacking into what influences these might be and whether a paternal or maternal influence is stronger or if it is a combination of the two. It seems important, then, to examine female juvenile delinquency in the context of the relationships found in that group, but this still regards the female offender as secondary to any male offenders within the social grouping.

Emerging research is moving from this perspective to that of examining the female offender as an entity in her own right. If, as suggested, the rates of female offending are growing, then to what is this attributed? J. Schwartz et al. (2009) suggests that the perceived change in offences and arrest rates are an artefact of policy changes that reflect cultural changes in the perception of gender roles and gendered behaviour. There is still an overwhelming difference in the number of incidents attributed to men/boys and women/girls, but the growth of female delinquency does bear scrutiny. It is particularly important to address this issue in the light of the falling off in the rate of male-perpetrated violent crime, which is attributed to policies targeting this behaviour. This would tend to suggest that female aggression needs a different focus in research and practice from that addressing male behaviour. There is evidence to suggest that, while parental aggression, antisocial peers and academic problems can be associated with delinquent (particularly aggressive) behaviour in youths of both sexes, there are considerable differences in social and psychological factors when relating offending to girls. These include levels of mental illness and physical or sexual victimisation (Leschied et al., 2000). Further distinguishing factors may be due to differences in impulsivity or the readiness to take risk (Campbell and Muncer, 2009).

No matter what the reason for female delinquency being on the rise, it clearly is not simply poorly expressed imitative behaviour of male counterparts and should be treated as criminal behaviour in its own right. Therefore, consideration of the risk factors inherent in juvenile delinquency must take into account both male and female perspectives. Social theories point to the breakdown in social groupings being responsible for juvenile delinquency. Psychological theories range from the psychoanalytical to the cognitive, but concentrate on the individual, while taking into account the environment in which the individual develops.

PSYCHOLOGICAL THEORIES OF JUVENILE DELINQUENCY

Social commentators suggest that although the breakdown in society is a root cause of juvenile delinquency, there are still issues within the individuals themselves. The psychology of juvenile crime ranges from the aberrant personality of a weak superego to the maladaptation of internalised knowledge.

Psychodynamics of juvenile crime

Psychoanalytical/psychodynamic theories suggest that criminality is associated with a weak superego and that the id operates without control. As such, if an individual gives in to the urges, Freudian positions suggest that deviant behaviour or violence and/or sexual crimes are more likely to be committed because there is no restraint. A weak superego means an individual is unable to act outside his or her own interest. This will have resulted from fixation during development through the psychosexual stages due to inappropriate stimulation. The resultant criminal behaviour is indicative of the stage of fixation. There are, however, likely to be internal conflicts that are psychologically painful to the individual, so they are repressed (Shoemaker, 2005), resulting in defence mechanisms, leading to problematic personality traits and behaviours. Hence, psychodynamically, delinquent behaviour is the external manifestation of an internal disease. Later psychodynamic theorists suggest that delinquency is an 'identity crisis' perpetuated by the inner conflicts. This is, of course, impossible to verify empirically, and psychoanalytic/psychodynamic theories are always criticised for their circular nature. The fact cannot be denied, however, that psychoanalytical approaches to problems do help when attempting to build effective treatment; whether this works as well with delinquency problems is yet to be established.

Personality approaches to juvenile crime

Other personality-based theories centre on issues concerned with psychopathy, as outlined in Chapter 4. Vizard et al. (2007) examined the cases of a large number of juveniles presenting with sexually abusive behaviour. They concluded that early onset (which they defined as between 5 and 11 years of age) of sexually abusive behaviour was indicative of higher levels of psychosocial adversity and early childhood antisocial behaviour. This in turn was associated with the existence of distinct developmental trajectories of emergent severe personality disorder. Support for this comes from Chabrol et al. (2009), who found that in 625 French high-school students psychopathic and sadistic traits were independent predictors of delinquent behaviours in boys. Such findings serve to consolidate the notion that there is a delinquent personality type.

Social learning

An alternative position comes from social learning theories. Sarason and Sarason (1981) suggested that maladaptations manifest because individuals fail to formulate behavioural patterns appropriate for everyday situations. They sought to readdress this issue with social skill training. Participants in their studies who received the special training were able to think of more adaptive ways of approaching problematic situations and performed more effectively in a self-presentational situation. They concluded that those labelled delinquent were less able to think of alternatives before acting and that they were less 'future' or 'present' oriented. So, appropriate role model training leads to the internalisation of a different set of behavioural patterns. This was supported by theoretical and empirical positions on deviant behaviour that argue that delinquents lack appropriate social skills to deal with problem situations. Welsh and Farrington (2006) contend that such interventions as social skills training and cognitive behavioural approaches are indispensable in crime prevention. Further issues base the problems in either the family or the individual's moral development. These theories emphasise the learnt nature of the understanding of the principles of respect for justice and the rights of others. This alludes to the concept of theory of mind being important for the ability to apply morals in socially desirable ways (Lane et al., 2010), and that children who commit crimes are somehow lacking in the ability to apply their own experiences to another.

Script theory

A position using a more cognitively based approach is script theory, first developed by Schank and Abelson (1977). Script theory outlines ways in which processes of understanding during a situation or event can be examined as it suggests that all memory is encoded episodically, that is, in order to be retained, everything must be related in some way to personal experiences. However, there are distinctions, as personal scripts about personal experience are accompanied by more generalised scripts that have been learnt in order to deal with both experienced and novel events. For example, an individual may have a general script for meeting a new teacher, even though personal experience has not been encoded. Scripts are used to guide behaviour because the script provides the holder with a set of expectations about what will happen during the unfolding of an event, thus offering a way of predicting the outcome and aiding the individual to act accordingly. Eifler (2007) demonstrated ways in which scripts could be applied to deviant behaviour by presenting participants with verbal and visual vignettes of mild deviant behaviour and asking them what they would do. Participants tended to choose the criminal response, even though they identified the behaviour as deviant. This research was carried out using non-offenders, so Gavin and Hockey (2010) applied the same method to an offender population – young men (aged 16–21) with one or more convictions in their history. They discovered that there was definitely understanding of socially desirable responses, but that offenders will overwhelmingly choose the deviant response as 'it's everyone for themselves in this world, innit!' (Gavin & Hockey,

2010: 402). The ways in which this behaviour has been learnt depend on the environmental stimuli for deviant behaviour and its reinforcement, outweighing the reinforcement of socially acceptable behaviour.

STUDYING DELINQUENCY

One of the most useful research methods for studying juvenile delinquency is the longitudinal prospective study. In 1961, Professor David Farrington of the University of Cambridge set up *The Cambridge Study in Delinquent Development*. This is a longitudinal interview-based survey of 411 boys from south London who were all aged 8 at the start of the study. The boys, and then subsequently men of course, were measured extensively over the period up to age 32 and then follow-up measurements were taken up to the age of 46. Over this period, the study has documented various patterns of offending and antisocial behaviour, its onset and duration, and the risk and protective factors predicting both the behaviour and the association between that and factors such as age and intergenerational transmission. The final measurements were taken to investigate whether antisocial behaviour could be predicted by any individual, family, socio-economic, educational and any other variables from earlier measurements. Of the cohort, 41% had convictions, but 7% of the boys accounted for over half of convictions, with high average numbers of total convictions in this small minority. Boys convicted at an early age were those who then went on to have the longest criminal careers (Farrington, 1996), so early detection and punishment had no deterrent effect. Farrington further reports that the study has identified important childhood predictors of antisocial behaviour that would persist into adulthood, such as impulsivity, low educational attainment, a family history of criminal behaviour, poverty and unsupported parental childrearing. A major difficulty with this research is that there was no inclusion of female subjects of the same age as the boys in the study. While this may not have been seen as important in 1961, as it became clear in later years that female delinquency was becoming a comparable issue, it may have been possible to include female subjects at a later date, but they were not. However, what this study has highlighted is that it is important to understand risk factors associated with juvenile delinquency.

Risk factors

The Cambridge longitudinal study, and similar research, identifies psychological and behavioural factors that are closely associated with offending behaviour in childhood. These include intelligence and/or lack of opportunity for educational attainment, impulsivity and the inability to delay gratification, and high levels of aggressive behaviour both within the family and the environment and the individual. Performing poorly at school is also linked to truancy, a further identified risk factor. None of these factors is, by itself, conclusive, for example, poor educational attainment is closely linked to the inability to earn high incomes, and strain theory would suggest that being excluded from wealth leads to crime. Furthermore, boys are more likely to be impulsive and misunderstand the consequences of their actions. In certain circumstances this could be offending behaviour. Farrington (2002) posits that this might be indicative of a dysexecutive syndrome, a neurological problem, but this is still unclear.

Williams et al. (2010) point out that adolescence is not only a risk period for offending, but also for traumatic brain injury, due to the higher likelihood of being involved in reckless behaviour or abusing drugs and alcohol. They examined the level of injury in a sample of convicted young men: 46% of the sample reported head injuries with a loss of consciousness, with a number of incidents being correlated with the number of convictions, particularly for violent offences. There is a clear association between violence and neuropsychological dysfunction. For example, Serin et al. (1994) reported a significant difference between violent offenders and controls in several cognitive tests of frontal lobe functions, including control and impulsivity. In addition, Barker et al. (2007) report a clear differential relationship between neurocognitive function and violence and theft, with the latter being more likely to be associated with neurocognitive dysfunction that was not related to a frontal lobe problem.

Neurological issues, then, are clearly associated with delinquent, if not criminal, behaviour in young men. No such study has been carried out on young women, which is again a problem for reporting on full results of research.

One factor that did emerge from the studies above is that of a familial environment. Learning theory, in particular, suggests the environment in which the individual develops is important in the genesis of a delinquent mind and attendant behaviour. The family environment includes the level and type of parental supervision and discipline, intrafamilial conflict, criminality in the family, abuse or neglect, and the quality of relationships. Farrington et al. (2009), using the Cambridge longitudinal study, clearly describe the ways in which criminality is transmitted through the generations of a family, but also how this can be mediated by outside factors. However, this research again suffers from a lack of contemporary female control groups, even though the criminality of mothers and daughters of the study sample is taken into account in terms of intergenerational transmission. This is interesting when one particular family configuration is considered, that of the single-parent family – overwhelmingly, the single parent is the mother (Office for National Statistics, 2011).

There has been much made of the single-parent family, as if it were solely a modern phenomenon, which it clearly is not (Yarber & Sharp, 2010). Graham and Bowling's (1995) large-scale study of young people and crime showed that those in families with both natural parents present are less likely to offend than those in lone parent or step-families. But they then went on to examine what effect parent–child conflict might have, together with parental supervision and poverty experienced by single-parented households. They concluded that, taking this into account, the difference in offending behaviour disappeared. Hence, it is not the family structure that is the problem, but the social pressures attendant to having only one parent. When parents do not provide appropriate supervision to their children, they are more likely to offend, and this is clearly more difficult to maintain without the support of a spouse/partner. Thus children will truant and possibly associate other criminal juveniles, both factors being highly associated with delinquency, and they are also less likely to confide in adults, including the parent.

DELINQUENCY PREVENTION

'Delinquency prevention' is the broad term for all efforts aimed at preventing youth from becoming involved in criminal or other antisocial activity. Increasingly, governments are recognising the importance of allocating resources for the prevention of delinquency. Because it is often difficult for states to provide the fiscal resources necessary for good prevention, organisations, communities and governments are working more in collaboration with each other to prevent juvenile delinquency.

With the development of delinquency in youth being influenced by numerous factors, prevention efforts are comprehensive in scope. Prevention services include activities such as substance abuse education and treatment, family counselling, youth mentoring, parenting education, educational support, and youth sheltering.

SERIOUS CRIMES

Children who molest

Children are sexual beings, and many adults find this particularly difficult to accept. There are, however, sexual behaviours that are part of normal sexual development and there are deviant behaviours. Parents and carers and child care professionals need to be aware of what is and is not deviant. Child safeguarding agencies, such as the National Society for the Prevention of Cruelty to Children (NSPCC) in the UK, produce excellent literature describing age-appropriate behaviour in relation to developing sexuality. Essentially, such behaviour should be non-intrusive, should not be hurtful to either child, and will become more sexualised as children grow. Sexual behaviour problems tend to be seen in children from homes in which they have experienced inconsistent parenting, violence, abuse or neglect (Kellogg, 2009). According to Bladon et al. (2005), adolescents and children who sexually molest also show psychosocial and psychiatric vulnerabilities, including severe conduct disorder, post-traumatic stress disorder (PTSD) and paraphilias, along with a high prevalence of sexual and physical abuse. The fact that children who are abused go on to become abusing adults is well established, with both intergenerational transmission within the family (Egeland et al., 2002) and outside (Haywood et al., 1996). What is less clear is that those who are abused may offend against younger children while they themselves are still adolescent, or even younger. Moreover, as Masson et al. (2013) have found, this can happen with both abused boys and girls who then go on to perpetrate sexual offences. In their sample of girls who have been referred to community-based services for issues including sexual offending, Masson et al. found girls as young as 8 years old. The majority had been in neglectful and abusive families, echoing the findings from similar samples of boys. Johnson's (1988) sample of boys between the ages of 4 and 13 who had molested children all had a history of sexual and physical abuse in the family. And more recently, Slotboom et al. (2011), contrasting male and female juvenile sex offenders, found that, for all of the boys, a history of sexual victimisation was the main predictor of their own behaviour.

However, young people with problem or offending sexual behaviours do not always come from abusive and chaotic backgrounds. This is much more likely to be seen in those who kill.

Children who kill

The case of Jamie Bulger was extremely shocking on several levels: the ease with which the child was abducted, the seriousness of the assault, and the fact that two 10-year-olds were charged and convicted of murder. Children who kill are rare in comparison to adults, but homicides and the reasons for them fall into several categories. Children or adolescents most frequently kill within their own family, but there are cases of murder outside these confines.

Children who kill within their own family usually kill parents (Seller & Heide, 2012). According to Hart and Helms (2003), there are several reasons why this happens: the child is mentally ill, antisocial or abused. Mental illness in these cases tends to result in delusional states or hallucinations (Heide, 1992). They may have a history of treatment but lack understanding of their psychiatric state. The murders they commit are likely to involve multiple victims and even dismemberment. As with adults who murder, mental illness may mean that a police case is not pursued against the child, but it is also possible that young people are found fit to plead despite an obvious disorder. Such children may be unaware of what they have done or that they have done anything wrong (see Chapter 16 on the mind of the defendant).

West and Feldsher (2010) and Sellers and Heide (2012) also point out that there are gender distinctions in the killing of a parent. Sons who kill are more likely to be diagnosed as having a psychotic illness, usually schizophrenia, whereas daughters are less likely to be seen as psychotic, unless they kill overbearing mothers with excessive force. A different form of disorder leading to violence is a conduct disorder. The DSM describes adolescents with conduct disorder as aggressive, destructive, deceitful and who tend to violate the rights of others with little or no remorse. This is essentially a precursor to the adult antisocial personality disorder, with psychopathy its underlying problem. Juveniles with this issue may exhibit antisocial behaviour due to family problems, but may also have a mental disorder that is being masked by the behaviour (Ewing, 1997). It is also possible that this may be masking child abuse too. The severely abused child is the most likely to kill his or her parents. Abuse throughout childhood is a clear indicator of someone who may kill. Adolescents who kill abusive parents just reach that point sooner. There may be mitigation for a child who kills his/her abusive parent as they have little way of escaping the abuse; an adult who has been abused as a child has at least survived it and can use alternative ways of coping with the parent, such as distancing (Gavin, 2011). A child suffering from abuse who then kills often raises the questions as to why she/he did not seek help or run away. These are the same questions faced by women who claim 'battered wife syndrome' as a defence against the murder of an abusive spouse.

These issues are pertinent here because the victim of abuse develops a sense of helplessness (Goodwin, 1996). In addition to this, children become hypervigilant to any sign of the abuser's behaviour that signals abuse. In these circumstances, self-defence would be a reasonable defence to any charges of murder, but this is difficult to prove (see Chapter 15 on psychology in the court room). The original definition of battered child syndrome was given by Kempe and colleagues (1962), but has been broadened, allowing more cases to be viewed as self-defence (Smarty, 2009). It is still difficult in many cases to reconcile the murder and the abusive state. There have also been some very infamous cases of defendants attempting to use the abused child defence in some very tenuous ways, such as the Menendez brothers, who killed their parents in 1989.

In December 1968, 10-year-old Mary Bell was found guilty of murdering two boys, aged 3 and 4. Mary's mother was an alcoholic prostitute who tried to kill her with sleeping tablets, and then sold Mary (to men who wanted to have sex with the child) from the age of 4 onwards. Such mental and physical torture echoes children who kill abusive parents, but there are several cases of children who kill who do not come into the abused child category, particularly those who kill outside the family.

In October 2009, 15-year-old Alyssa Bustamente stabbed 9-year-old Elizabeth Olten to death because she wanted to know what it felt like to kill someone. The deaths of Jamie Bulger and Silje Raedergard have already been mentioned. Reponses around the world to children who kill can be varied, dependent partly on the legal system that prevails in the nation. If the legal age of responsibility is low, then children who kill, or indeed offend in other ways, can be treated harshly, as in the case of Venables and Thompson. These boys were locked up at 10 years of age and released at age 18 into a world they did not understand and that did not want them. One is currently back inside prison.

JUVENILE DETENTION

Historically, there was little distinction between children and adults in terms of how they were treated by the criminal justice system. Until children were recognised as a different legal category, they were tried as adults and subjected to the same punishments or incarceration. In the UK, in 1895, the Gladstone committee resolved to separate children from adults within the prison population and the first prison designed for boys was opened in a village called Borstal in England in 1902. Youth prison became a national institution and was formalised in the Prevention of Crime Act 1908. All such prisons were known colloquially as Borstals, and boys and young men (under age 23) were sentenced to borstal training. The system was extended to girls and young women in 1908. Borstals were for education, not punishment. A highly regulated regime was implemented, focused on routine, discipline and authority. Despite the popular image of the borstal, corporal punishment was seldom used (Osborough, 1975). However, there were alternative institutions for 'delinquent boys' up to the age of 19, called approved schools, in which authority was often imposed by caning (Franklin Report, 1951). The Borstals were abolished by the Criminal Justice Act 1982. They were replaced by young offenders' institutions, housing offenders between age 18 and 20, although some house younger offenders.

In the USA a youth detention center, also known as a juvenile detention center or juvenile hall, is a secure residential facility for young people prior to court hearings and/or placement in long-term care facilities and programmes. Secure detention for juveniles is used if they are considered a threat to public safety or the court process. However, the USA incarcerates more young people than any other country in the world, a reflection of the larger trends in incarceration practices in the USA (US Bureau of Justice Statistics, 2009).

Questions that arise around juvenile detention are concerned with why juveniles are incarcerated – and incarcerated away from adults – and what effect does imprisonment have on them and any reoffending behaviour? Cécile and Born (2009) reviewed programmes designed to intervene in juvenile delinquency. The concluded, not surprisingly, that grouping adolescents together who have the same problems and the same behavioural issues was more likely to result in reinforcing that behaviour. They concluded that the best programmes for youths were those that did not require placement into detention, but they did not seem to address the other issues of incarceration, such as public safety. Wolff and McCall Smith (2000) point out that in addition to rehabilitation, education and social integration of the offender, the objectives of sentencing should include the protection of society, and that the two are impossible to disentangle.

SUMMARY

The question of why criminal behaviour develops in young people is a complicated one that is no more easily answered than any other issue in criminal psychology. Psychological approaches can be used to theorise, but interventions are of paramount importance. The effectiveness of those interventions is something that will continue to be examined for some time.

Discussion point: How should we treat young people who have committed crimes?

The Bulger case highlights the dilemma the criminal justice system faces when children commit crimes. Society demands those who commit crimes, particularly the ones it views as the most heinous, such as murder and sexual assault, are punished, but there is disagreement about when the youngest of perpetrators are culpable. If *doli incapax* does not apply, then we must try children as adults, and then we must deal with them as adults when they are convicted. What should we do with them when they are convicted, and what effect will those decisions have?

Dmitrieva, J., Monahan, K., Cauffman, E. & Steinberg, L. (2012) Arrested development: the effects of incarceration on the development of psychosocial maturity. *Development and Psychopathology*, **24**: 1073–1090.

Gold, J., Sullivan, M. & Lewis, M. (2012) The relation between abuse and violent delinquency: the conversion of shame to blame in juvenile offenders. *Child Abuse & Neglect*, **35**(7): 459–467.

Section 3

Psychological Explanations of Specific Crime Types

This section examines specific types of crime and the psychological explanations for each. These chapters therefore relate to the knowledge and research dimensions in terms of underlying psychological theory and the research issues supporting them. Core Role 2 is represented here.

Chapter 6 looks at homicide and the different forms it can take, using some infamous adult killers to illustrate the points being discussed.

Chapter 7 moves into more international territory, considering terrorism and the psychology of the terrorist and how people can kill for a cause, including, sometimes, themselves. What are the forces acting on the minds of people who commit the most extreme forms of political or social violence?

Chapter 8 examines crimes of a sexual nature – rape and sexual assault – in which sex is used as a weapon to dominate and control. Child sexual abuse is also considered, along with atypical sexual choices.

Chapter 9 looks at why people commit arson, and examines the strange case of Bruce Lee, who changed his name to that of his film idol. Fire is a dominant force in humanity's development, an essential component of development as humans. Here we see what happens when someone's relationship with it becomes problematic.

Chapter 10 examines stealing, including the acts of shoplifting, mugging and burglary, and Chapter 11 takes this further by looking at stealing on a large scale in white-collar crimes.

The Psychology of Homicide

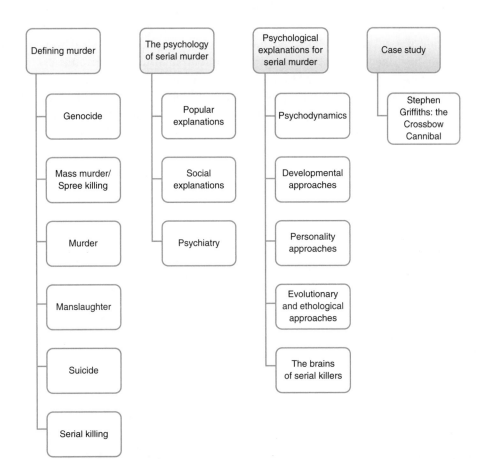

Defining murder
- Genocide
- Mass murder/ Spree killing
- Murder
- Manslaughter
- Suicide
- Serial killing

The psychology of serial murder
- Popular explanations
- Social explanations
- Psychiatry

Psychological explanations for serial murder
- Psychodynamics
- Developmental approaches
- Personality approaches
- Evolutionary and ethological approaches
- The brains of serial killers

Case study
- Stephen Griffiths: the Crossbow Cannibal

Stephen Griffiths always attracted quite a lot of attention. A psychology graduate, who had registered for a part-time PhD in criminology, Griffiths had pet lizards that he walked on a lead, was often seen dressed in a long leather coat and wore sunglasses even at night. The 40-year-old man lived alone in his flat in a converted stone mill near Bradford's red light district and was considered friendly but eccentric, or possibly weird, by his neighbours. In May 2010, according *The Guardian* newspaper (Guardian, 2010b), the caretaker at the flats was checking CCTV footage from the weekend and saw the missing sex worker Suzanne Blamires running from a flat, pursued by Griffiths, before he knocked her to the floor. Moments later he returned to view and shot the unconscious woman with a crossbow bolt through her head, and then, acknowledging the camera with a gesture, he dragged her body out of shot. The caretaker, pausing only to contact a tabloid newspaper to sell the story, telephoned the police and Griffiths was arrested on 24 May. Suzanne's dismembered remains were found floating in the River Aire, her head in a rucksack with a crossbow bolt and broken knife embedded in it. When all of her body was recovered it was in 81 pieces. Other tissue found in the river belonged to another sex worker called Shelley Armitage. Griffiths confessed to killing Suzanne and cutting her up, and then confessed to killing Susan Rushworth, who had disappeared on 22 June 2009, and Shelley Armitage on 26 April 2010. With three murders attributed to him, Griffiths was officially a serial killer.

Griffiths was a former public school boy and university graduate. He had been brought up by his mother along with his brother and sister, in some hardship, but nevertheless in relative social comfort. No one regarded him as violent or dangerous. How and why did this man arrive at the stage where he murdered a woman in front of a camera? The topic of killing people and the psychological theories that try to explain murder fascinate us, but do they explain why Griffiths did this?

KEY THEMES

- Definition of murder
- Forms of homicide
- Genocide
- Mass murder
- Spree murder
- Serial murder
- Single murder
- Manslaughtes
- Suicide

DEFINING MURDER

Murder is when a man* of sound memory, and of the age of discretion, unlawfully killeth within any country of the realm any reasonable creature in rerum natura** under the king's peace, with malice aforethought, either expressed by the party or implied by law, so as the party wounded, or hurt die of the wound or hurt within a year and a day after the same.

Sir Edward Coke (1552–1634), British jurist and politician whose defence of the supremacy of the common law had a profound influence on the development of the English legal system.

*person   **a creature born that has taken breath

Edward Coke's definition of murder, arcane language aside, still holds the essential elements of the legal status of the charge of murder. Some issues have moved on, of course, such as the time limit. Without the 'year and a day' rule, a person who wounded someone would remain under threat of prosecution for their murder for ever. Since we are all going to die, murder is in fact simply an acceleration of death. What matters is whether the wound inflicted by an attacker caused the death and the courts system of the seventeenth century felt that it would not be possible to show such links after more than a year and a day had elapsed. In the twenty-first century, life can be prolonged by medical technology and the rule was removed by the Law Reform (Year and a Day Rule) Act 1996.

The other issue related to the charge of murder is that the attacker must be shown to have intended to kill, the state known as 'malice aforethought'. In other words, it must be shown that the attacker acted knowing that the action would lead to the death of the person attacked, or intended to cause grievous bodily harm. If such considerations are not present, then manslaughter, rather than murder, would apply.

So, when is it murder and when is it not? It may be helpful to examine the different forms of killing that can take place and what psychology has to offer in explaining them.

FORMS OF HOMICIDE

Genocide

The 1948 United Nations Convention on the Prevention and Punishment of the Crime of Genocide defined genocide as:

any of a number of acts committed with the intent to destroy, in whole or in part, a national, ethnic, racial or religious group: killing members of the group; causing serious bodily or mental harm to members of the group; deliberately inflicting on the group conditions of life calculated to bring about its physical destruction in whole or in part; imposing measures intended to prevent births within the group, and forcibly transferring children of the group to another group

(United Nations, 1948)

The nature of these acts distinguishes genocide from terrorism, which is not necessarily directed at only one national or ethnic group, but against an agency of the state (Post, 2007). Genocide is also distinguished from ethnic cleansing, although genocidal acts may happen during the forcible removal of an ethnic group (Winton & Unlu, 2007).

Genocide – the killing of a group in order to eradicate that group's identity, ethnicity, race or religion.

Various psychological explanations of genocide are available, but none seems able to encompass all of the issues. Monroe (2008) suggests that there are three levels of consideration when building theoretical models of genocide. These are macro-phenomena, such as war, structural-political factors, such as oppression, and personal-psychological factors. For the latter, Monroe goes on to describe the ways in which perpetrators of genocide rationalise their behaviour in terms of distancing themselves from their victims, who are originally, in many cases, neighbours and friends. A more detailed and influential psychological model is described in Waller's (2007) book on the development of evil in ordinary people, in which he proposes three elements that can lead to genocide. These are termed ancestral drives (ethnocentrism, xenophobia and social dominance), perpetrator identity components (cultural beliefs, moral disengagement and self-interest) and contexts or cultures of cruelty (socialisation, group influences and role/person merger). Hence identity and self-concept are central to the psychology of genocide. While genocide is clearly a description of deliberate mass killing, it can also be the act of undermining the biological, social or cultural integrity of the victim group.

One element of genocide that is difficult to reconcile is that it is often accompanied by mass rape, the victims of which are then killed. The rape of female members of the victim population is well documented, even in the relatively recent conflicts in Nanking, Rwanda and Bosnia (Dutton, 2007). Theories of rape are covered in detail in Chapter 8, but the psychological explanations for single or serial rape do not seem pertinent to the mass rape and killing appearing in incidents of genocide. Dutton (2007) suggests that this is not rape for sexual needs, but an example of the extraordinary brutality that accompanies genocidal killing, and is another example of behaviours such as torture, killing children in front of their parents, and sexual humiliation of the living and the dead. Such behaviour, it is suggested, is similar to that found in the sexual sadism of some serial killers (Marshall & Kennedy, 2003).

Examples of genocide can be found throughout history and, sadly, in more recent records. For example, 10 million Ukrainians died in the 1932 Holomodor, Stalin's forced annexation of crops from, and subsequent starvation of, independent farmers. Six million Jewish people died in the Holocaust, the Nazi exterminations of the Second World War. Unknown millions lie buried in the killing fields of Cambodia, the victims of the Khmer Rouge's attempt to annihilate intellectuals and other sources of dissent in the late 1970s. During 1994, at least three-quarters of the Tutsi minority were exterminated by the Hutu in Rwanda. Rwanda houses three ethnic groups, the Tutsi, the Hutu, and the marginalised Hwa, who are probably the indigenous group and are classified as a pygmy race. The Tutsi were favoured when the country was colonised by Germany, then Belgium. The Tutsi have a more 'European' appearance (taller, with paler skins) than the other ethnic groups and the colonisers assumed they were the dominant ethnicity. They allowed only the Tutsi to be educated and placed them in government positions. This naturally caused tensions between the groups and there have been many instances recorded of murderous acts committed by both sides of this ethnic divide. The racial tensions became particularly deadly after the colonists withdrew, culminating in a civil war (1990–94) and the final attempt to eliminate the Tutsi. Accounts record that the killing was not the only aim of the attack on the Tutsi people; the men were to be killed, but the women were to be raped before their own deaths. The raping was as important as the killing, with the militia wielding rape and sexual humiliation, and subsequent sexual mutilation of bodies, as weapons (DesForges, 1999). Genocide is an atrocity that the world condemns; at some point it is always exposed to global scrutiny due to its political consequences.

Mass murder

Multiple murders committed on one occasion or very close together, and outside the arena of war or civil conflict, are termed mass murders (Aggrawal, 2005). They have a different motivation from the genocidal acts described above. Mass murders by individuals are also sometimes referred to as 'spree killings', although there are distinctions; spree kill-

Mass murder – multiple murders taking place at the same time and location.
Spree killing – multiple murders taking place within the same time frame but at differing locations.

ings take place in different locations and mass murder in only one location. One notable case that would definitely qualify as a spree killing is the fatal shooting in Hungerford, England, of 16 people and the wounding of 15 others by 27-year-old Michael Ryan on 19 August 1987. This is still known as the Hungerford massacre. It ended with Ryan shooting himself – a common element of the spree killer or mass murderer (Knoll, 2010b). Perhaps some of the most distressing examples of mass murders are school shootings, such as the Columbine High School (Colorado, USA) massacre, in which Eric Harris and Dylan Klebold killed 12 pupils and a teacher, and the murder of 16 children and a teacher at Dunblane Primary School, Scotland, by Thomas Hamilton. After incidents of this nature there is a clamour to know why this happened.

The major difficulty with the psychological examination of mass murderers is that, as Palermo and Ross (1999) note, a large proportion of incidents end with the murderer(s) committing suicide. Knoll (2010a) terms this the 'pseudocommando' phenomenon, an individual, or sometimes a pair of killers, acting publicly in daylight and demonstrating planning and the gathering of weaponry. Planning does not extend to escape; the pseudocommando is prepared to die in the execution of his acts, either by his own hand or by the police or similar agencies. Such people have strong feelings of anger, persecution or mistreatment, and the 'spree' is therefore an act of revenge.

Murder

The salient components of a common law definition of a murder are that it is the unlawful and intended killing of a human by another human, outside certain boundaries such as war, and not including the killing of an unborn child. Also, suicide is no longer considered to be murder in law, even though it may be considered such in religious thought.

Intent to kill includes the intention to cause grievous bodily harm when those actions lead to death and the reckless endangerment of life or indifference to the risk of death.

Some jurisdictions have several divisions of murder, particularly those seen in the American judicial system. Intent to kill forms the definition of second degree murder and first degree murder, including issues of aggravation (such as premeditation and deliberation). Therefore a major issue in the legal and psychological position of murder is intention. The question arises as to whether a suspect intended to act knowing that it was probable these actions would kill or cause serious injury. This does not take into account any extenuating circumstances surrounding the actions. The amendment in UK law that allows the courts to take such circumstances into account was the Homicide Act 1957, introduced after the outcry against the hanging of Ruth Ellis in 1955. Ellis killed her lover in a fit of jealous rage and was charged without legal representation. Many prominent people were horrified at the death sentence and the reform allowed someone to be convicted of manslaughter if provocation could be shown.

Murder – the unlawful and intentional killing of one person by another or others.

Manslaughter

Manslaughter is homicide without intent to kill and is distinguished from justifiable homicide (killing someone in self-defence or the defence of another person). There are also distinctions between voluntary, involuntary and reckless manslaughter, causing death by dangerous driving or while intoxicated. The main difference between them is that voluntary manslaughter requires intent to kill or cause serious bodily harm, but which is not premeditated, while involuntary manslaughter does not.

Voluntary manslaughter is an intentional killing that is accompanied by additional circumstances that mitigate, but do not excuse, the killing. Such mitigations might be provocation, as seen in several cases of a person who is the recipient of extreme domestic violence who then kills the abusive partner.

Involuntary manslaughter does not involve intent to kill or harm. Such deaths might occur as a result of negligence or a failure to act.

Manslaughter – killing without intent to kill.
> Involuntary – killing with no intent to harm.
> Voluntary – unpremeditated intent to harm but not to kill.

Familial homicide (UK) – joint criminal liability of all adults involved in the death of a child.

Vehicular manslaughter (USA) – killing by driving (often including 'while intoxicated').

Corporate manslaughter – the culpability of a corporation for behaviour that results in a person's death. This is separate from but linked to:

Negligent homicide – death resulting from the negligence of another person or corporation.

Suicide

Suicide is not strictly a form of homicide but several categories of suicide do blur the line between the legal definitions. There are about 20 million suicide attempts each year across the world, according to Perper and Cina (2010), and around 1 million of these attempts are successful. People take their own lives for many different reasons. In some cases, an individual may need assistance, such as in the circumstances of debilitating and degenerative illnesses. While physician-assisted suicide is illegal in many countries, and any person who aids the suicide may have charges brought against him or her, it is also true that several nations do not currently have such restrictions. As Dees et al. (2010) suggest, this is a controversial issue and the subject of heated debate.

A particular form of suicide is of interest here, that of the murder-suicide. This is carried out by individuals who either kill themselves immediately after committing murder, kill with the intent of being shot by police officers responding to the crime, or as a means of receiving the death penalty (van Wormer & Odiah, 1999). Such behaviour is usually

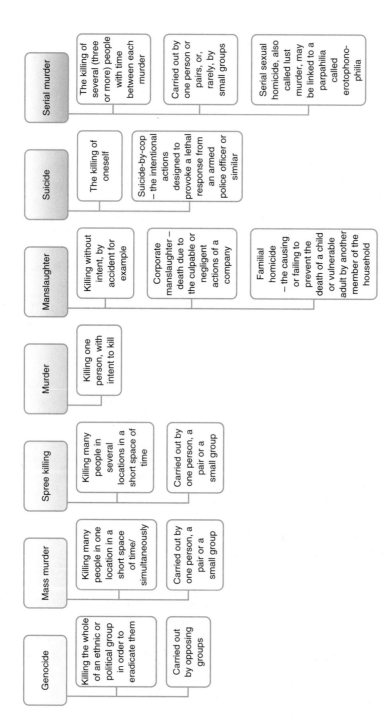

Figure 6.1 Type of murder

interpreted psychoanalytically as conflicted expressions of the death instinct. However, there are other explanations, such as mental illness (Eliason, 2009).

Having considered the legal standing of the act of murder, there is a multitude of questions concerning the urge to kill. Where does it come from and why is it so powerful? If we all experienced this urge, would we be able to resist? Is it genetic, hormonal, biological or cultural conditioning? Do killers have any control over their desires? We all experience rage and sometimes even inappropriate sexual instincts, yet we have some sort of internal monitor that keeps our inner monsters locked up. Why do some people let loose the monster? These questions are best answered by considering the case of one particular type of murder, that perpetrated by the serial killer. A large body of work in the research on murder refers to the serial killer; he (or she) is a popular subject for both the media and the psychologist. Due to the nature of the serial murderer, we have the dubious luxury of being able to explore the crimes over a period of time, examining the minds and behaviour of some of the most notorious people in history.

Murder-suicide – the act in which an individual kills one or more other persons before, or at the same time as, killing him- or herself. It is related to but distinct from:

Suicide-by-cop – the act in which a suicidal individual deliberately acts in a threatening way, with the goal of provoking a lethal response from a law enforcement officer or other legitimately armed individual.

THE PSYCHOLOGY OF SERIAL MURDER: THE MIND OF A MONSTER?

One of the most influential definitions of serial murder is that given by Egger (1984). Serial murder is defined as several (three or more) killings, separated by time and location and carried out by the same person(s). The murders may be motivated by compulsive fantasies. In addition, the selection of the victim appears to be random at first, and the connection between them is made by deduction, not by other similarities, such as familial relationship.

It is tempting to suppose that serial killers are a modern phenomenon because the first time this term was used was in the 1930s. Ernst Genet, a German police officer who worked on several infamous cases, used the term 'Serienmörder' to describe the men who killed many people, often with gruesome methods. The first English use of the term is attributed to Robert Ressler of the FBI in the 1970s (Ressler & Schachtman, 1993). However, simply because they were not named as such does not suggest that serial murderers have not been with us for some time, they may have just not been subject to the same scientific attention as now. Widespread literacy did not

Serial murder – the act of killing several people (usually three or more) with a cooling-off period in between.

happen until relatively recently, but the descriptions of murder and mayhem found in folk tales, passed on orally, still appear to be stories about serial killers, albeit supernatural in nature. Werewolves and vampires delight in multiple murder, but they probably represent creatures that are all too human in nature (Tatar, 1998).

Serial killers choose victims weaker than themselves, often members of vulnerable populations, such as prostitutes, runaways and young people. Many criminologists suggest that victims may hold some form of symbolic meaning for the killer.

Popular explanations

Serial killers have been operating throughout history. Before the modern understanding of crime, people have attempted to explain serial murder in various ways, demonic possession being only one of these. During the nineteenth century, scientific advances meant that there was the possibility of applying biological and psychological explanations. Such developments include theories of physiognomy and phrenology: criminologists Cesare Lombroso and Max Nordau believed that they could identify violent men because they had 'primitive' faces with heavy jaws and low foreheads. Franz Josef Gall promoted 'phrenology', the idea that by feeling the bumps on a person's head, their character and level of intelligence could be predicted. Herman Mudgett (aka Dr Henry Howard Holmes) was hanged in 1896 for murdering at least nine guests at his boarding house in Chicago. After his execution, a map was made of his head and Schechter (1994) describes how people clamoured to see if the bumps spelled 'murderer'.

However, science does move on and modern explanations are sought elsewhere.

Childhood

One of first places our society looks to for an explanation is the serial killer's upbringing. In some cases of serial killers, the childhood can be described as barbaric, with physical, sexual and emotional abuse beyond most imaginings. It seems impossible that a child subjected to the cruelty described by killers such as Albert de Salvo would not develop into some sort of monster. De Salvo (the 'Boston Strangler') was sold as a slave by his father in return for money to buy alcohol (Philbin & Philbin, 2009). He went on to murder 13 women between the ages of 19 and 85, gaining access to their homes with little trouble.

Many murderers describe their childhood as abusive, but it must be remembered that not all survivors of abuse develop into sadistic serial killers. Many girls are victimised as children, but very few grow up to be sadistically violent towards strangers. In addition, some may view stories of horrific abuse as a way to mitigate their crimes and gain sympathy. After all, if there is a high level of psychopathy among serial killers, then manipulating sympathy by exaggeration of abuse would certainly be a tactic employed. However, some cases are corroborated, and even families that appear healthy on the outside may harbour a sadistic parent or two. Childhood abuse may not be the sole excuse for serial killers, but it is an undeniable factor in many of their backgrounds. Are the parents to blame?

Mothering is a difficult task even in the best of circumstances. The mothers of those who turn out to be serial killers are easy targets to blame for the sins of their children, not least because some of them end up as their child's victim, and hence cannot defend themselves. Henry Lee Lucas started murdering by killing Viola, his abusive mother (Wright & Hensley, 2003). Viola Lucas was a prostitute who forced him to watch her with clients and beat him, frequently to the point of unconsciousness. He was convicted of 11 murders, but is linked with around 600. Lucas was brought up in abject poverty, abuse and neglect. The Appalachian hills of Virginia in the 1930s suffered badly in the American depression, subsistence farms failing and families moving out. The Lucas family was no exception, and the parents brewed and drank moonshine, a lethal and illegal distilled spirit. Both parents were violent alcoholics and had little time for young Henry Lee. It appears he was also subjected to emotional abuse, such as being made to dress like a girl, and physical beatings. He confessed to 600 murders, but it is still unclear how many he and Otis Toole, his partner in crime, actually committed.

Our mothers are important central figures in our lives, but when she is in fact a monster, the child has little recourse to help. She is also a ready-made excuse – mother blaming (McBride-Chang et al., 1992) is still prevalent in research and society. It is also true that examining the upbringing of many of the most infamous serial killers indicates that there is a fatal link between mother and murder – whether she is too strict or too immoral, either way, she cannot win.

Freudian psychology suggests that repression of one's sexual nature can result in a reassignment of that energy into other activities (Freud, 1961). Mothers who impose subjugation of a developing sexuality in their children are often motivated by religious fanaticism, which may or may not be accompanied by sexual sadism (LaBrode, 2007). For example, Ed Gein's mother, a highly religious woman, taught her sons that women were vessels of sin and caused disease. Gein's father died in 1940, and his brother in 1944. His mother followed in 1945. Three deaths happening very shortly after each other, and finding himself alone, must have affected Gein – no one is immune from grief. However, Gein's reaction is certainly not the usual response to bereavement. He sealed off the upstairs of the farmhouse where they had all lived, and remained in one bedroom and the kitchen. He then began to exhume bodies from the cemetery, moving on to killing several older women in order to fashion cereal bowls from their skulls.

Ed Kemper's mother, Clarnell, was a tyrannical shrew who appeared to hate her son. When he reached puberty, he started to grow, reaching 6 feet and 9 inches; his mother thought he would molest his two younger sisters and locked him in the basement. This may have been prompted by other strange behaviour by Ed, of course, such as the dismemberment of the family's cats. Clarnell decided she couldn't cope with him and he was packed off to his estranged father, but Ed ran away. He was then sent to his paternal grandparents on a remote Californian farm. Ed, a very bright young man, was bored. He killed his grandparents simply to see what it would be like. He was then committed to the Atascadero State Mental Hospital for the criminally insane. He was released at the age of 21 and sent to live with his mother, who had asked for him to be released into her custody. Unfortunately, she began subjecting him to emotional abuse again. There is speculation that she was mentally ill (Lawson, 2002), but Kemper went on to kill six young women and became known as the 'Co-ed killer' (White et al., 2011). Finally, he beheaded his mother, put her vocal cords in the garbage disposal unit, and allegedly used her head as a dartboard (Damio, 1974).

In contrast to the strict mother, some serial killers blame their sexually uninhibited mothers. Exposure of children to inappropriate sexual behaviour is clearly implicated in later behavioural problems, including sexual dysfunction (Silovsky, 2002). Serial killers whose murders involve a sexual element are an extreme version of this. For example, LaBrode (2007) describes several killers who killed susbtitues for significant females in their lives. For example, Bobby Joe Long killed prostitutes or women he perceived as such, because they reminded him of his mother. He was born with an extra X chromosome (XXY), which caused several developmental problems, including pubescent gynaecomastia. It is easy to imagine how much teasing and bullying he was subjected to because of his breasts and how much distress this must have caused. He also suffered multiple head injuries as a child (Giannangelo, 1996). His relationship with his mother was also strange, as he slept in her bed until he was a teenager, only leaving it when she had sex with other men. It could be speculated that this perpetuated several quasi-oedipal issues in the developing teenager. Long was finally convicted of abducting, sexually assaulting and killing ten women in Florida during 1984.

Gynaecomastia – the abnormal development of large mammary glands in males resulting in breast enlargement. It can be caused by hormone imbalance, medication, drug or alcohol abuse, illness or Klinefelter's syndrome.

Mothers appear to be clearly implicated as the abuser in many serial killers' childhoods. However, fathers, or father figures, are no less likely to abuse their children, particularly in physical or sexual terms. Father–daughter incest is reported as the most common form of intrafamilial sexual abuse (Celbis et al., 2006). However, this rarely leads to female murderers, still less female serial sexual murderers, but when it does, the result is spectacular. Probably the most famous female serial killer is Aileen Wuornos, who never met her father because he was in prison for the rape and attempted murder of an 8-year-old boy when she was born (Kennedy, 1994) and he hanged himself in 1969. When Aileen was almost 4 years old, her mother abandoned her children, leaving them with their maternal grandparents. Wuornos claimed that she was sexually assaulted and beaten as a child by her grandfather. It is known that she engaged in sex from a very early age, and she became pregnant at 13, claiming rape by an unknown man. Her child was placed for adoption and a few months later her grandmother died. When she was

15, her grandfather threw her out of the house and she began supporting herself by prostitution. It is speculated that her grandfather sexually abused her, but it is definitely established that he was physically abusive, beating her for little reason (Cluff et al., 1997). Wuornos killed seven men to whom she had offered paid sex, claiming that each had tried to rape her. During her time on Death Row, she repeatedly said that she should be executed, that she was worthless (Kester & Gottlieb, 2012). This appears to be a clear indication of low self-worth, which can be the result of accumulated negative experience in childhood (Gavin, 2011), although again, such feelings do not necessarily lead to murder.

Sadistic disciplinarian fathers (or father substitutes as in Wuornos's case) feature most prominently, but there is also the emotionally distant father to consider. Not all serial killers were beaten or sexually abused as children, but some abuse does not make visible bruises. Jeffery Dahmer killed at least 17 men during 1978–91, with the killings involving rape and torture, dismemberment, necrophilia and cannibalism (Purcell & Arrigo, 2006). To the outside world, Dahmer's upbringing was normal, but according to Lionel, his father, Jeffery's mother was mentally ill, exacerbated by a difficult pregnancy. In *A Father's Story*, Lionel Dahmer (1994) describes her as a biological contaminant and himself as a destructive influence but pays little attention to his own level of emotional detachment and lack of affection and what this may have contributed to his son's strangeness. As Tithecott (1997) points out, a father who takes little part in childrearing due to a lack of understanding of children's need for affection must take some of the blame if the child turns out to be odd.

Childhood is a crucial time for all of us; our psychological well-being in adulthood is dependent on our experiences as children (Gavin, 2011). It is tempting to suggest, then, that the childhood of serial killers must be littered with poor experiences. There are things other than abuse, however, that may contribute to difficulties in the developing years.

Adoption studies are important in psychology as they give a potential basis for studying the effects of nature in comparison with nurture. In the study of the serial killer, two questions arise: what deviant genes may the biological parents have bequeathed to their offspring, and what effect does the environment of a, presumably, loving new environment have on a child whose biology may be problematic? There are further question here, though, as, according to Grotevant (1997), the discovery that one is adopted may affect the developing sense of identity and make the child prone to fantasising an identity of his 'true' parents, either good or bad.

This sense of rejection can have profound consequences on an already unstable psyche. If the child meets his/her biological parent and is again rejected, the damage is worse. Of course, adoption does not create serial killers. At worst, it may dislodge a child's self-identity. But that does not mean that finding oneself involved in multiple murder is the only option available to adopted children. However, studying cases of murderers who were adopted gives some insight into the nature–nurture debate that holds just as well for violent crimes as it does for any other psychological or behavioural issue. For example, Jeffery Landrigan, whose case is discussed in Chapter 3, was adopted when still a baby, but tried to use the brain damage he suffered from fetal alcohol syndrome and other substance abuse issues as mitigation for his actions. Adoption for Jeffery was not only inevitable, but may have been the best thing for him. Sadly, the psychological and neurological damage was already done, and he committed horrific crimes despite being taken into a family who could care for him.

Some murderers claim that exposure to violent events triggered their violence. Andrei Chikatilo, the 'Butcher of Rostov', killed 22 boys, 14 girls and 19 women between 1978 and 1992 in Ukraine (Egger, 2002). His first murder set the scene for the others. Nine-year-old Yelena Zakotnova was lured to his house and he attempted to rape her. Failing to achieve an erection and angered by her struggling, he choked her to death and stabbed her corpse, ejaculating in the process. As Cullen (1993) describes, after Yelena Zakotnova's murder, Chikatilo was only able to achieve sexual arousal and orgasm through stabbing and slashing women and children to death. He attributed the sadistic treatment of his victims to hearing frightening childhood stories. Many of us have encountered the stories collected by the Grimm brothers but we do not go on to brutalise, rape, torture and murder victims, removing the eyes for souvenirs. Chikatilo reportedly ate the uteruses of his female victims (Hickey, 2002). It is difficult to imagine what kind of childhood tale would awaken that kind of desire.

Juvenile delinquency

Other childhood experiences appear in the backgrounds of some serial killers quite frequently. Juvenile detention does, of course, signal juvenile delinquency; children are not incarcerated without a great deal of thought from the justice system and, presumably, a great deal of nuisance being experienced by the community. It is also clear that there many mental health issues to be dealt with in the incarcerated population, and this is also true of juvenile detention (Fazel et al., 2008). Adult prison can be a brutalising place (de Viggiani, 2007), and juvenile detention was little different until quite recently. Some killers describe how the treatment they received in detention aggravated an already fragile hold on temper, rage or reality. At the age of 5, Albert Fish was already a regular in juvenile detention. He claimed that he was tied up and beaten with a board on his buttocks throughout his child and teen years, eventually learning to enjoy the pain. He later kidnapped children, beat them with a board, and then killed and ate them. His obsession with pain led him to poke large needles into his pelvic region for excitement (Lassieur, 2000).

Detention is an extreme form of social isolation in which a child receives little warmth from others, or positive role modelling. Other forms of isolation, although not as visibly brutal, do have an effect. Peer rejection is a form of social bullying, and several killers have experienced it. Kenneth Bianchi, one of the pair known as the 'Hillside Stranglers', sexually assaulted and murdered ten young women with his cousin, Angelo Buono, and killed two others on his own. Bianchi was a difficult child. He was born to a prostitute and adopted, and he had several medical problems. One of these was involuntary urination, which his mother dealt with by making him wear sanitary napkins. He also had tics and behavioural problems (Schwarz, 2001). None of these things made him attractive to other children as a potential friend. Such social isolation can make children retreat to a fantasy world, and if this becomes centred on violence, the damage is already done to the developing psyche (Zara & Farrington, 2009).

However compelling theories and examples of poor upbringing are in our search for explanations, no child or family stands in isolation from the community in which it finds itself. Societal explanations for crime, as introduced in Chapter 3, must also have a contribution to make.

Social explanations

Merton (1938) sees social ends and the means to achieve those ends as learnt. Some people have high aspirations; others do not. However, if cultural goals exceed structural opportunities, then this strain is overcome by the use of illegitimate means to obtain legitimate goals. In Western society, personal fulfilment is deemed to be a socially approved goal. In the absence of the ability to obtain such fulfilment by normal means (i.e. sex with a consenting partner), it may be that the serial murderer resorts to illegitimate means to achieve this socially approved goal (i.e. s/he feels justified in 'taking' if blocked from 'earning'). A predisposition to resort to illegitimate means to obtain social goals may explain why 60% of serial murderers have previous criminal convictions (Myers et al., 1993).

An alternative social theory is seen in the writings of Sutherland (1939), who asserts that criminal behaviour is learned in primary group relationships rather than through secondary sources, such as television, etc. This theory is an attractive one in relation to serial murder, as many offenders are incarcerated prior to their first murder, and it may well be that they learn techniques from others in this way.

Other theories suggest that it is the breakdown in the structure of society and its bonds and constraints that allow the serial killer to emerge. Danto (1982) provides some support for this theory in suggesting that, as 67% of murderers have a childhood history of violence, it may be that sexual serial killers are exposed to sexual violence in particular. This does not explain why some killers do not have experiences of violence in their backgrounds.

One position that tries to bring development issues and social problems together as an explanation for serial murder is one focusing on inadequate socialisation. Reinhardt (1962) examined a set of case studies of mass and serial murderers, and demonstrated that there was evidence to suggest that normal social communication was missing as a factor in the development of social or personal frames of reference. Many other researchers, such as Hazlewood and Douglas (1980), have pointed to lack of socialisation as an aetiological factor in both murder and serial murder, stating that the lack of a proper nurturing environment is an important issue. Even if the absence of love does not mean a child has been abused and neglected, it is a source of conflict and leads to the possibility of inability to develop and use adequate coping devices (Gavin, 2011). It must be reiterated, though, that not everyone growing up in an environment of abuse or neglect becomes a serial murderer, and such studies suffer from any adequate control groups. It is likely that the effect of socialisation relies upon complex interaction between social and psychological factors and biological predispositions. One of those biological predispositions seems to be being male. There are very few female serial killers.

Gender roles

There are so few female serial killers that it would seem easy to overlook them but for the fact that the world is fascinated with them (Gavin, 2010). Most female multiple murderers are healthcare poisoners, such as Beverly Allitt, or are viewed as being subservient to men in offending partnerships, thus being less blameworthy than their male partners. Other female serial killers are described as being of the comfort type (Kennedy, 1992). It is unusual to find female killers who are predatory in nature. Why are predatory serial killers predominantly male? Feminist theory suggests that the problem of violence against women is one of misuse of power by men who have been socialised into believing that they have a right to control the women in their lives, even through violent means (Walker, 1990).The predominance of female victims fits with such an analysis. Sexual murder is seen as an act of violence exercised to override not only a woman's sexual choices, as in rape, but also her choice over life or death. This links with the notion of serial murder as a patriarchal act of 'sexual terrorism' (Caputi, 1989). The different forms of socialisation that boys and girls encounter (Farrington, 2005) within the family or peer groups or via the media may then lead to differences in the way boys and girls are exposed to and demonstrate violent behaviour. Such hypotheses remain under-researched, with the growth in violent crime perpetrated by women only recently being addressed (Farrington et al., 2010).

A further element in the gender role issue of serial murder is the concept of the serial sexual killer. Sexual homicide, often term 'lust murder' (see Purcell & Arrigo, 2006; McLellan, 2010), may be linked to a paraphilia (see Chapter 8). Erotophonophilia is a deviant form of sexual behaviour in which the killer uses sexually sadistic and murderous actions in order to achieve arousal and even climax. For example, Andrei Chikatilo, mentioned above, claimed to have achieved orgasm while stabbing his victims. Erotophonophilia can also include elements of necrophilia, as seen in the cases of Ted Bundy and Jeffery Dahmer (McLellan, 2010). Very few lust murders are carried out by women, at least outside pairings such as Ian Brady and Myra Hindley, and Fred and Rosemary West (Gavin, 2013). The gendered nature of serial murder may therefore not be simply socially determined, but also biologically, and be linked to the dimorphic nature of human sexuality and psychological problems linked to sexual behaviour.

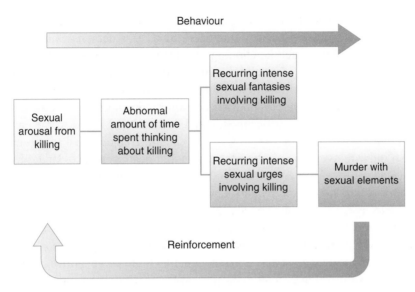

Figure 6.2 Erotophonophilia: Sexual murder, but with the primary goal sexual arousal

The place of psychiatry in explaining serial murder

Medical models of crime, and particularly murder, have been a persistent view in attempting to explain motives for violent behaviour. The heinous crimes we encounter when studying murderers would suggest that the individuals responsible must be insane, but, as we will see in Chapter 16, this is not the case, and is probably a view that has dangerous consequences. There is little to support the idea that murderers are mentally ill and, more pertinently, to perpetuate the idea that mentally ill people are violent and dangerous. However, psychotic illness, particularly that including auditory and visual hallucinations and delusions, particularly of a persecutory, grandiose, religious, suspicious and aggressive nature, has been shown by several killers.

David Berkowitz ('Son of Sam') claimed to have been told to commit his crimes by a 6,000-year-old man who spoke through his neighbours' dog. Berkowitz confessed to eight shootings in New York between 1976 and 1977, in which six people died and several others were wounded. Berkowitz also claimed he had joined a religious cult (Terry, 1987) where he was introduced to drug use, sadistic pornography and violent crime. In most cases the debilitating effects of serious psychotic illness would not allow someone to think through the complex actions of several murders and evasion from capture over time.

However, one psychiatric condition and its connection to violent crimes has attracted quite a bit of interest. Multiple personality disorder (MPD) or dissociative identity disorder has been used as a defence by a number of serial murderers, most notably in the case of Kenneth Bianchi, one of the 'Hillside Stranglers'. In MPD, a person exhibits two or more disassociated personalities, each functioning as a distinct entity. There has been very little evidence to suggest that this is a valid disorder, and Casey (2001) notes that there have been fewer than 300 cases ever reported. Although incorporated in both the DSM (the third edition) and the ICD-10, many psychiatrists are still sceptical about the disorder. Bianchi and his cousin, Angelo Buono, kidnapped, raped, tortured and killed women and girls in the hills above Los Angeles in 1977–78. When caught, Bianchi tried to present as having MPD in order to avoid prosecution for a potential death sentence. Under hypnosis, a personality called Steve Walker emerged and admitted the killings, and implicated Buono. The psychiatrist conducting the hypnosis believed him, and diagnosed MPD. However, one of the detectives noticed an anomaly in that 'Steve' always referred to himself in the third person. He called for a second expert, who also diagnosed MPD, but a third disagreed. Finally, Dr Martin Orne suggested to Bianchi that multiple personalities usually involve more than just two personas. Sure enough, two more personalities emerged. These inconsistencies in clinical presentation meant that Bianchi failed to convince experts that he suffered from MPD. However, this does not mean that it is never going to be a valid diagnosis, even in a serial murderer. Egger and Doney (1990) note that dissociation (the lack of integration of thoughts, feelings and experiences into consciousness) is often seen in serial killers, but this might be the result of psychopathy (Giannangelo, 1996) as there is little evidence of the DSM description of MPD as symptoms of fugue, amnesia, depersonalisation or post-traumatic stress.

Other psychiatric diagnoses have also been suggested for the actions of serial murder. Possibly a more credible psychiatric hypothesis for violent crime, including serial murder, is that of psychopathy, or the more correctly termed anti-social personality disorder (the two are not totally synonymous). In the DSM, antisocial personality disorder (ASPD) is a persistent disorder or disability of mind resulting in abnormally aggressive or irresponsible behaviour that is not the product of psychosis or other illness (see Chapter 4 for more details on the disorder). A large proportion of serial killers (and other criminals) show aspects of the personality disorder, but as Skeem and Cooke (2010) point out, this does not necessarily mean that criminality is a core element of psychopathy, simply that it is a correlate. This also means there is no hypothesis of causality to be made either. Is there any link between psychopathy and serial murder? Some of the elements of the psychopathic personality do appear within some serial killers. For example, Skrapec (1996) suggests that serial sexual murderers may experience the anhedonic boredom that is a characteristic, and the 'thrill' of murder is one way of counteracting it. Psychopathy is likely to play a role in the internal justification of criminal behaviour, including murder, and may be an aetiological component of serial crimes, as guilt would preclude a repetition of a killing. However, there are also elements of psychopathy that do not correlate with serial murder, such as planning and the lack of deep emotion. Egger (1984) suggests that psychopath is an easy diagnosis to make to explain the crimes we do not understand.

It appears there is more to this issue than simply a diagnosis of antisocial behaviour, particularly for the most antisocial behaviours of all.

Ressler et al. (1988) identified a wide range of sexual behaviour as components of serial murder. For example, they found that 81% of sexual offenders used pornography as a major sexual interest. While the use of pornography is not an unusual finding in both straight and gay males (McKee, 2007), within sexual offenders the pornography is often of a type that represents the forms of paraphiliac behaviour seen in sexual murders, i.e. necrophilia, sadism, exhibitionism, transvestism, voyeurism, frotteurism (rubbing against another person for sexual arousal.), compulsive masturbation, piquerism (sexual excitement from stabbing/bloodletting), coprophilia (use of faeces in sex) and zoophilia (sexual activity with animals). Briken et al. (2010) found that there was an average of 3.2 paraphiliac disorders within a group of serial sexual murderers, a statistically significant difference compared with other offenders, and a similarly significant difference was found for schizoid, antisocial and sadistic personality disorders. If this can be generalised to the wider population of serial killers, then it is clear that there is a paraphiliac tendency within most serial murders, and that there is likely to be a high incidence of fantasy being used in the life of the killer. This also leads to a hypothesis that the psychological disturbance may also contain elements of sexual dysfunction. There are few studies that demonstrate such a link. However, there may be confusion between what appears to be paraphiliac behaviours and sexual dysfunction (Myers et al., 2006). This may mean that behaviour that appears deviant may be necessary for an individual to achieve 'normal' sexual intercourse.

Substance abuse

Substance abuse refers to the harmful or hazardous use of psychoactive substances, including alcohol, illicit drugs and various other chemicals (World Health Organisation, 2011). Dependence on the chemical being abused can easily follow its abuse. Dependence syndrome is a cluster of behavioural, cognitive and physiological phenomena that develop after repeated substance use, including persisting in its use despite harmful consequences, to the detriment of other activities and obligations, increased tolerance and sometimes a physical withdrawal state. A high lifetime prevalence of substance abuse is found in serial killers (Hill et al., 2007). Disorders of substance abuse may not only affect the cognitive state, but also the social status. While alcohol and other drugs are almost certainly facilitators of offences, any connection is spurious.

So if psychiatry does not offer us a full explanation, where does that leave us? Psychology needs to look wider than a medical model to explain these crimes.

Psychological explanations

If psychiatry's models are based on illness, then psychology's models are based upon essentially 'normal' behaviour. Comparison between typical and atypical behaviour can aid the construction of a serial killer's psychology, but each must be applied with caution.

Psychodynamic theories

The Freudian concepts of unresolved sexual conflict, infantilisation and maternal over-protection or rejection would seem to be ready-made explanations for serial murder. If the components of the mind, the id and superego, are in conflict due to unresolved childhood issues, it is suggested that the result may be violent. A particularly compelling view is the frustration/aggression hypothesis, in which the Freudian hydraulic model of aggressive energy build-up needs a cathartic release before the pressure becomes dangerous. This cathartic release is reportedly found in many serial murderers' reports of their own behaviour (Abrahamsen, 1985). Again, this is not a full explanation of serial murder, as many people can act cathartically without violence. The frustration/aggression hypothesis advocates an increased likelihood of aggressive behaviour with increasing frustration, rather than simple causality. Additionally, Carlsmith et al. (2008) demonstrated that 'getting even' does not in reality serve to repair mood; indeed, it prolongs frustration and anger. Getting revenge does not provide the pleasurable feelings that might be predicted, and alternative coping strategies might be more appropriate and helpful. If serial murderers, for example, are more likely to choose the aggressive route to frustration dissipation than others, due to inadequate socialisation or lack of coping responses, then this will only serve to perpetuate the emotions and actions. The hypothesis is thus a hybrid one, borrowing from sociology, psychodynamics and developmental approaches.

Developmental approaches

In spite of the widely recognised difficulties with psychodynamic explanations, the debate does lead on to a fairly consistent finding of serial killer research: the presence of the 'MacDonald Triad' in serial killers. MacDonald (1963) found early childhood behaviours such as enuresis (bed-wetting), firesetting and torturing animals to be common in the background histories of multiple sadistic killers. Commenting on this, Hellman and Blackman (1966) suggested bed-wetting is a form of sadistic and hostile rebellion towards parents (by damaging bed and sheets and causing parental concern). Bed-wetting is the most personal of these 'triad' symptoms, and is less likely to be divulged. However, some estimates suggest that 60% of multiple murderers wet their beds past adolescence.

Firesetting is clearly associated with violence and is found in high incidence in the serial killer population, possibly with pseudo-sexual elements. Pyromaniacs are often sexually stimulated by fire. The dramatic destruction of property feeds the same perverse need to destroy another human. If serial killers do not see other humans as anything other than objects, the leap between setting fires and killing people is easy to make.

Zoosadism refers to the pleasure, often sexual pleasure, gained from cruelty to animals. The third element of the MacDonald Triad is a clear indicator of later sadistic behaviour. Torturing animals is interpreted as a further form of rebellion against the norm of keeping pets as cherished friends and is definitely a disturbing danger sign. The torturing and killing of animals is often seen as some sort of macabre practice-run for killing humans. Ed Kemper would bury animals, including the family pet cat, alive, and then dig them up for further torture. This is not a universal trait, though. Dennis Nilsen (aka the 'Muswell Hill Killer') killed at least 15 men and boys between 1978 and 1983, and reportedly kept the corpses for sex. He was caught because he tried to dispose of parts of the bodies into the drains, which then blocked. He had difficulty initiating social contact with people, but loved his faithful companion, Bleep, a mongrel bitch. After his arrest, he was very concerned for her welfare, as she was taken to the police station too (Masters, 1993).

Although the MacDonald Triad may represent a repeated finding, care is needed to avoid overrepresenting its importance. A full retrospective study, one that would allow us to examine the prevalence of the MacDonald Triad in a population of children that have grown up to become normal adults compared to serial killers, has never been carried out. This would need to be linked to other issues of psychological makeup.

Personality approaches

In addition to the high levels of psychopathic personality disorders, other personality variables have been identified as contributing to homicidal behaviour, and serial homicidal behaviour in particular. Daly and Wilson (1994) suggest that the tendency for violent aggression is a personality variable which leads to the distinction by some researchers, such as Berkowitz (1993), between instrumental aggression and emotionally reactive aggression, identified in theories of aggression (see Chapter 3). However, it is now thought that serial killers exhibit instrumental aggression in an emotionally reactive capacity.

Intelligence is another variable that many, such as Ressler et al. (1988), have attributed to serial killers and their success in evading capture, together with a heightened use of fantasy. Rhue and Lynn (1987) showed that fantasy-prone adults reported more physical abuse in childhood than non-fantasy-prone individuals, together with a greater frequency and severity of physical punishment and a higher likelihood to have used fantasy to block the pain of punishment. However, they never suggested any link to crime. The idea that some individuals need to retreat into a separate world is one that bears further scrutiny, with the attendant hypotheses around substance abuse and subsequent addiction.

The frustration/aggression hypothesis, with discomfort/tension between offences being alleviated by the aggressive 'fix', lends itself to immediate comparison with addictive behaviour such as alcoholism and other substance abuses (Skrapec, 1996). As with addiction to any form of behaviour that reduces a tension, so the 'rush' of killing may be the addiction for the serial murderer. This analogy is interesting but research has yet to identify any factors that maintain this addiction.

The addiction approach to serial murder acknowledges the role of operant conditioning. The murder is the reward, or the feelings gained from it, providing positive reinforcement, and hence the likelihood of repeating the crime. Reward and lack of punishment (non-detection) may also be linked to the use of fantasy.

Fantasy is also an inherent component in considering the cognitive aspects of serial murder. Seminal research carried out by the FBI suggests common attitudes and beliefs within serial murderers, such as devaluation of people, views of the world as unjust, obsession with domination via aggression, autoerotic preference, and an inability to distinguish fantasy from reality (Federal Bureau of Investigation, 1985). Gresswell and Hollin (1994) suggest that a lack of an inhibitory belief system (or developing the means to overcome such a system) is an integral part of the cognitive process of serial murder. This has yet to be fully established and there may be simpler and more testable explanations.

However, we may not need to look for complicated reasons to explain the serial killer's aggression. Some theories suggest that human aggression that is emotional in nature is a result of negative affect; this is termed 'aversively stimulated aggression' (Berkowitz, 1988). This theory holds that the escalation of behaviour to aggression may result from an unpleasant or aversive state. Such a state may be exposure to unpleasantly high temperatures, noxious smells or disturbing pictures (Berkowitz, 1993). Theoretically, these resultant emotions of anger and stress can trigger a network activating further mood-congruent cognitions. If such connections are strong, even though aberrant to normal responses and coupled to a lack of inhibitory control, the behaviour may escalate to aggression and even murder.

So, we reach a position in which a person's childhood and the society into which s/he develops is at the root of how an individual reaches a point at which s/he will murder. However, we are still missing some parts of the puzzle. While animal studies are criticised for making too many anthropomorphic comparisons, there might still be something to gain from the positions that have grown out of comparative psychology.

Evolutionary and ethological approaches

Darwinism identifies the process of sexual selection in animals as the source of competition between males for access to fertile females, leading to highly specific forms of aggression. Extrapolating from this position has led to the hypothesis that this explains men's violence against women (see Chapter 8 on crimes of a sexual nature). This seems to be an insecure position, as animal studies identify male-to-male violence, and it is unclear why this explains between-gender violence. It also seems precarious to apply these explanations to serial murder, again as a great many examples are of male killers exhibiting violent and sadistic behaviour towards female victims. A further objection to this position is that there is little exchange of genetic material in serial murder, and, even in sexualised murder involving rape, little likelihood of fathering children if the recipient is dead. Therefore serial murder cannot be explained by any issue of evolutionary survival.

However, a secondary purpose of animal aggression appears to be the desire for dominance allied with, but not central to, the struggle for resources. This may explain the serial killing of potential mates, which would otherwise contradict an evolutionary position. There is an obvious sex difference in the capacity for the use of physical means of violence. The majority of serial killers are male, and the sex difference is a clear underlying reason for this finding. This difference has evolved for particular reasons, and, despite the societal constraints against violence, the capacity for violence remains. However, a thorough ethological examination of serial murder has yet to be carried out. This suggests that such an explanation might not be as compelling as some, as the controversy surrounding evolutionary biology and psychology would not be enough to deter theorists, particularly when other contentious questions are examined. For example, the issue of race and serial murder has been examined, because there are questions as to why ethnic minorities seem to be underrepresented in this type of crime, particularly in comparison to other crimes. There are very few black (Afro-Caribbean/African-American) serial killers in societies in which the predominant ethnicity is white. Researchers such as Whitney (1990) suggest that other crimes see an overrepresentation of Afro-Caribbean people, and that this indicates a genetic difference between racial groups. This may be an unpopular stance, and does not take into account any social or environmental explanations for the difference, yet it is apparently true that this overrepresentation does not hold for serial murder. This may be due to serial killing having little economic value, and therefore the economic factors that lead to crime in economically depressed sectors do not lead to murder that does not have economic reward. However, even this anomaly does not bear full scrutiny, for, as Walsh (2005) points out, the underrepresentation of African-American people in the serial killer population is actually a misperception. He notes that of all the serial killers recorded in the USA up to 2004, over 20% were African-American men. However, the percentage of African-American males within the general American population is approximately 10%, suggesting that the number of murderers is out of proportion. As we have no figures for the different races of serial killers within countries in which white is the numerically minority ethnicity, it is difficult to see what implications can be derived from this disproportionate figure, but it is likely that race is not a determining factor in explaining serial murder.

If neither evolution nor racial differences can explain serial murder, is there any biological underpinning for this crime? Delving into the case study-based research indicates there are some much more individual characteristics to be taken into account in explaining serial killers.

The brains of serial killers

Some offenders have histories of neurological abnormality, in particular that related to head trauma and anomalous neuropsychological test results. It has been reported that aggression can be related to neurological abnormalities. A seminal piece of research was carried out by Williams (1969), who took a sample of 333 violent prisoners and separated them into habitual aggressors and those who had only perpetrated one incident. The habitually aggressive group had almost three times the amount of EEG abnormalities than the other group. Having excluded from the habitually violent group anyone who was likely to have had organic brain damage (those who had suffered a major head injury, anyone with epilepsy, etc.), Williams then found that the proportion of the abnormality increased. He concluded that this meant that if there is a single incidence of violence, the cause is within the environment, and that habitual aggressors are more likely to have brain abnormalities, particularly in the limbic system.

The difficulty with using such findings and those that have followed is that extrapolating from this to a wider population is spurious. A great deal of the neuropsychological literature is based on case study research. Williams' study is of groups, but nevertheless its conclusions are based on a very small sample of people whose characteristics are highly distinctive, making it almost impossible to determine if the proportion of habitually aggressive people with brain abnormality would be generally found. The case study approach and the experimental research on anomalous groups are undoubtedly a valuable source of information, but extrapolation from them must be carried out with caution.

Neuropsychological research in aggression has focused on various structures, including, but not limited to, the thalamus and hypothalamus, which are closely associated with the evaluative aspects of emotion. Abnormalities here might explain the inability to form close bonds or exhibit empathy seen in serial killers (Kiehl et al., 2001). The thalamus is also involved in activation in response to aversive stimuli and sexual functions; abnormalities can suggest anomalous activation confusing the pleasurable feelings of sexual activation with the aversive stimuli of fear or anger.

It is clear from research over the last few decades that brain abnormalities are found in a high proportion within the serial killer population, or at least the captured and incarcerated portion. The causes of the abnormality can range from severe head trauma to genetic disorders or exposure to drugs or toxins (Norris, 1988). In a review of brain imaging studies in antisocial behaviour, Raine (2008) painstakingly draws the parallel between the psychological problem associated with brain damage in a specific location and its antisocial correlate. For example, lesions in the amygdala are associated with problems with fear association, moral emotion and social-emotional judgements, with antisocial expression as misinterpretation of others' feelings and a non-compliance with societal rules.

Some abnormalities can be as a result of a congenital, genetic or developmental problem. However, it is difficult to distinguish one from the other without examining genetic issues as a whole, and taking into account the environmental factors and attendant developmental problems. A more productive approach may be to consider the electrochemical activity of the brain, instead of its structural elements.

Some studies in neurotransmitter action clearly show that their actions on cortical and subcortical regions are implicated in the control of aggression and violence. A metabolic by-product of serotonin, 5-hydroxyindoleacetic acid (5-HIAA), is sometimes seen in abnormally low levels in persistently aggressive and antisocial people. If this means that serotonin is in low concentrations in those likely to commit violent acts, this could be controlled by the application of drugs such as selective serotonin reuptake inhibitors (SSRIs). Could it be that the simple application of Prozac is all that is needed to stop murder? This has not been tested as there is little to suggest a causal link here, never mind in which direction it might be.

In addition to the neurotransmittor questions, there is clear involvement of hormones in violent behaviour, particularly androgens such as testosterone. Women exposed to excess androgenic activity show increased aggression (Mehta & Beer, 2010), with evidence of reduced activity in the medial orbitofrontal cortex, an area responsible for impulse control and decision making. Again, can we extrapolate this to our serial killer population? This is difficult as no studies comparing testosterone levels in serial killers to controls have been carried out.

Other hypotheses about biochemical difference have been posited to explain aggression, with an extrapolation to serial killers, but none is conclusive. They are bound up with questions about neurological abnormalities and developmental experiences. We do not therefore have one approach that gives a clear picture of why serial killers kill, and kill again and again. Perhaps it would be profitable to examine case studies in depth and consider how each of the approaches outlined above can explain the behaviour of killers one by one.

A SERIAL KILLER AND HOW THEORY HELPS UNDERSTAND HIM

Stephen Griffiths confessed to killing Suzanne Blamires and cutting her up. The second murder to which he confessed, Shelley Armitage, 31, had been recorded on his mobile phone, which he later accidentally left on a train. The person who found it sold it on before police retrieved it, but the film was intact. The woman is seen bound, with the words 'My Sex Slave' written on her back. She is then filmed dead in Griffiths' bathtub. He recites a commentary, claiming to be a persona named Ven Pariah. Parts of Shelley's spine were recovered from the river, along with a suitcase containing knives and saws. Griffiths was also charged and convicted of a third murder, that of Susan Rushworth, in the previous year. Griffiths told police about her death, but no remains were ever found. He also claimed to have killed other women. What made a man such as Griffiths into a murderer?

Griffiths' parents split up when he was young and he lived with his mother and siblings in Wakefield, Yorkshire. The family was clearly estranged from the father, but his mother managed to save enough to afford to send Stephen to a private school, coincidentally the same one John Haigh (the 'acid bath vampire') attended on a scholarship. Perhaps this made an impression on Griffiths – Haigh was extremely infamous in his day. Was Griffiths affected by his parents' split or the lack of a father figure? Was he then adversely affected by a connection to an infamous murderer?

Griffiths used social networking sites, using the identity he called 'Ven Pariah'. This persona became increasingly more bizarre, quoting from the Bible, and describing himself as a misanthrope. The day before Suzanne's murder, Griffiths clearly expressed the idea that he thought he was the Ven Pariah character, and that Griffiths was merely a body Ven Pariah was using to allow 'him' to emerge into the world (Guardian, 2010b). Is this an indication of mental illness? Many people use the Internet to create alternative personalities but not all for reasons that are sinister. While there are many recorded cases of nefarious uses of the Internet for activities such as paedophilic child grooming and other sexual offences (Boer et al., 2011), it must be recognised that much of the interpersonal communication carried out over the Internet is harmless, even when the human users are adopting virtual personas that are not like them. However, it is also recognised that when evaluating a patient in terms of impairment, credibility and dangerousness or risk, the patient's Internet presence may help to confirm, corroborate, refute or elaborate on the clinical impression being gained (Recupero, 2010). So, it may be productive to examine Griffiths' online activity as well as his face-to-face interactions with police officers and other evidence.

David Wilson, a well-known criminologist, whose books Griffiths had apparently read, has examined the Griffiths' case and has been given access to various materials such as interview tapes. He suggests that Griffiths is a misogynist, with a narcissistic personality disorder. He *wanted* to be a serial killer, setting out to kill at least three people so he could be recorded as one. He had several relationships with women, but when they ended the affair he blamed them, a behaviour called neutralisation that is very common among abusers (Roche et al., 2011). According to Wilson, Griffiths talked about himself with powerful language. He aimed to dominate the conversation, for example, by claiming that he had eaten portions of the women he killed. Wilson also states that Griffiths was very aware forensically, and took steps to destroy DNA evidence on the bodies of his victims. He also attempted to influence and control the media, as typified by his behaviour in his court hearing on 29 May 2010 when he attended to enter a plea: when asked to give his name, he stated clearly and loudly 'The Crossbow Cannibal'. This stunned those in the court room, including the families of the victims (Times, 2010). A few days later, another murderer hit the headlines. Derek Bird had gone on a shooting rampage in Cumbria, killing several people in one day. Wilson suggests that Griffiths would have been annoyed at his few minutes of fame being eclipsed by the new news. He made a suicide attempt in his cell, tying a plastic bag over his face, but was seen in the guard's video link and suffered no lasting damage (Daily Mail, 2010). He did, however, reappear on the front pages of the newspapers.

On 21 December 2010, Griffiths pleaded guilty to the murder of Susan Rushworth, Shelley Armitage and Suzanne Blamires and was sentenced to life imprisonment.

How does Griffiths' case equate to our theoretical explanations above? Griffiths does not seem to have had an abusive childhood, although his father went out of his life at an early age. His mother worked hard, and to his benefit, so it appears that at least his financial and educational welfare was of concern, if not his emotional needs. He had siblings, so probably did not experience social isolation in the home, but was described by family members as more withdrawn than his brother and sister, even as a 'loner' (Daily Mail, 2010).

There is nothing to suggest that Griffiths has any neurological problems, or head trauma, or that he has any developmental or genetic disorder. It might appear from some of his behaviour that he was mentally ill; he projected a persona by which he claims he felt subsumed or possessed, perhaps suggesting a dissociative identity disorder. However, there is no evidence to suggest that this was ever considered as a possible psychiatric diagnosis. Indeed Griffiths' defence never entered any claim for insanity. He made at least one attempt to commit suicide, which may have been an expression of depression. Suicidal ideation accompanied by depression is common among prisoners, hence the vigilance around prisoners at risk (Sarchiapone et al., 2009). In the prison which housed Griffiths, Harold Shipman had killed himself and Ian Huntley had taken drug overdoses on two occasions. However, David Wilson dismisses this suicide attempt as attention-seeking behaviour to regain some of the notice he was getting from the national and international press. Wilson claims that Griffiths must have read diligently during his studies, and had simply set out to become notorious as a serial killer, as demonstrated by his naming himself as the Crossbow Cannibal. Perhaps Stephen Griffiths is simply a highly unfortunate product of the world's fascination with murder.

SUMMARY

There are several different ways in which people can kill each other, from the national atrocity of genocide to the infamy of the serial killer. Social science has produced several models that can be considered when trying to explain murder, from the societal, such as strain theory, to the biological, such as neurological models of dysfunction. Psychology adds to these models by providing a psychological perspective on each level of explanation, such as the effect that social strain has on the individual, or the psychological effect of brain damage. However, the application of such theories to case studies of particular murderers is not as clear-cut as each model would suggest, and the integration of theory would appear to be a way forward.

Discussion point: Is the Macdonald Triad still a viable account of serial killer childhood?

Three behaviours – bed-wetting, firesetting and cruelty to animals – known as the MacDonald Triad, were first described by J.M. MacDonald (1963) as possible indicators, if occurring together over time during childhood, of future episodic aggressive behaviour, and it was noted that such behaviours appeared frequently in the childhood histories of serial killers. Is this still a credible linkage?

(Continued)

(Continued)

Kori, R. (2009) The MacDonald Triad: predictor of violence or urban myth? Unpublished graduate thesis, California State University, Fresno, CA.

Overton, J., Hensley, C. & Tallichet, S. (2012) Examining the relationship between childhood animal cruelty motives and recurrent adult violent crimes toward humans. *Journal of Interpersonal Violence*, **27**(5): 899–915.

Schwartz, R., Fremouw, W., Schenk, A. & Ragatz, L. (2009) Psychological profiles of male and female animal abusers. *Journal of Interpersonal Violence*, **27**(5): 846–861.

The Psychology of Terrorism

7

Typologies

Psychological theories of terrorism

Individual models

Profiling terrorists and terrorism

Case study

Psychoanalytic and personality theories

Psychopathology and psychopathy of terrorism

In-group/out-group

Samson syndrome

Vulnerability and radicalisation

Predictive software

Profiling fallacies and counter-terrorism

Contribution to counter-terrorism

9/11 and the war on terror

On 11 September 2001 the world watched in horror as two hijacked planes flew into the twin towers of the World Trade Center in New York City. Another airliner was flown into the Pentagon building (the headquarters of the United States Department of Defense) in Virginia, and a fourth, intended for the White House (the official residence and workplace of the US President), crashed in Pennsylvania after passengers attempted to retake control. Everyone on board the aircraft died. Almost 3,000 people died in the attacks in total, many of them emergency response personnel. The film of the acts of destruction of people and property flashed around the world instantly and caused global outrage. The 19 male hijackers were quickly identified, as they had made no attempt to hide their identities, and their links to a terrorist organisation known as al-Qaeda were discovered. On 20 September 2001, US President George W. Bush declared that America was fighting a 'war on terror'.

Al-Qaeda was also linked to the London bombings on 7 July 2005, in which 56 people died and over 700 were injured. The four bombers all died in the blasts, making this the first suicide attack on mainland Britain (Eggen & Wilson, 2005). The bombers all had homes and families in Britain, three in Leeds in West Yorkshire, and were previously unknown to the authorities (Hansard, 2005). International condemnation of the attacks swiftly followed, with renewed efforts to investigate and eradicate terrorism. A positive outcome was the joint efforts of American, British and Pakistani authorities to avert a further airliner bombing in 2006 (Hoffman, 2009). A less positive outcome is the resurgence in racism experienced by South Asian and Arabic people around the world (Hussain & Bagguley, 2013)

The study and identification of the terrorist, together with intelligence-gathering activities, are therefore of global concern, both in the eradication of terrorist violence and in the protection of those unwittingly caught up in it.

KEY THEMES

- Typologies
- Psychopathology
- Suicide by terrorism

TYPOLOGIES

There is no single definition of terrorism, as there are various actions that come within the framework of terrorist deeds. However, there is agreement on a fairly broad description that it encompasses acts of violence intentionally perpetrated on non-combatants with the aim of furthering ideological, religious or political objectives (Borum, 2004).

The psychological purposes of the act are to publicise a political or religious cause and to intimidate or coerce a target into accepting the terrorist group's demands. In addition, Pearlman (2002) suggests that terrorism results from envy and humiliation, and is a re-enactment of trauma. Post et al. (2002) classified types of terrorist groups, as follows:

- Nationalist-separatist
- Religious fundamentalist
- New religions
- Religious extremists, including millennium cults
- Social revolutionary
- Right wing

Such classifications are helpful in identifying groups that may be moving towards violent action. Husain (2006) also detailed the configuration of certain types of terrorist groups, pointing out that this is not a set of categories based on geographic location, race or culture. In this classification we see that the majority of terrorists and terrorist organisations are ethnic, religious or nationalist groups. These groups represent those that are deprived of power and who need to use violence to gain or regain rights. Revolutionary groups, with either extreme left-wing or extreme right-wing orientation, tend to be volatile and have disagreements with themselves, even though they espouse a common aim. In contrast, anarchist groups do not have a specific political agenda; they simply represent opposition to any governmental control. This seems close to the next group, pathological individuals or organisations. This type of terrorist does not have a distinct political goal but indulges in violence for the sake of it, although is not necessarily linked to any specific psychopathology.

Kfir (2002) expanded on the religious fundamentalist grouping, as this undoubtedly includes extreme Muslim fundamentalists. Since the 9/11 attacks in the USA and the 7/7 bombings in London, these groups are now synonymous in the minds of the West with reli-gious terrorism. However, many attacks perpetrated by these groups of terrorists are carried out in their own homeland, with the aim of oppressing domestic targets, destabilising the existing government and reinstituting traditional values. A further set of terrorist actions is seen in suicide terrorism, where the terrorist agent intends to kill him/herself along with other members of the target group. Conversely to the avowed act of suicide heroism, Kfir (2002) points out that these acts are actually aimed at the domestic groups and can be seen as an individual (or group) expression of their own oppression. Being prepared to die for a cause is something many find difficult to understand, making the psychological effect pro-found (Patkin, 2004). Such acts have ancient roots. Yousafzai and Siddiqul (2007) report that the Jewish revolutionary group known as the Zealots were using suicide terrorism as early as the first century AD against the Roman occupiers of Judea. The use of suicide terrorism as both physical and psychological warfare is very effective (Hoffman, 2003). Suicide bomb-ers are even viewed as cost-effective: there is no need to build in escape plans; the damage

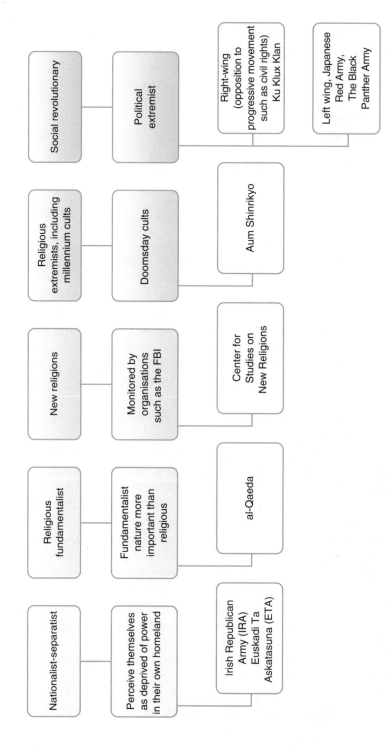

Figure 7.1   Typologies of terrorist groups

caused, both physically and psychologically, is high; there is high media attention; and there is little residual intelligence to be gained from examining them (Bloom, 2007).

The majority of these 'martyrs' have been male, but the use of women has increased. Bloom (2011) reports that the trend to use women as suicide bombers is increasing within the 17 terrorist groups known to use this tactic. Women draw less suspicion than men in areas that are subject to military or security personnel scrutiny; in cultures where women are not allowed to disrobe in the presence of men, it is easier for women to pass through check-points. It is difficult to imagine why anyone would turn themselves into a human explosive device, and an examination of the female demographics does not help. They are young, with an average age of 22 years, but of varying marital status and some are pregnant. It is suggested that suicide bombers are recruited due to levels of innocence, personal distress and thirst for revenge (Schweitzer, 2003). However, some intelligence agencies suggest that women who become suicide bombers are essentially victims of trafficking into the terrorist organisation, and subsequently drugged or brainwashed into killing themselves in this way, or raped and blackmailed if they do not participate (Bloom, 2005). A further suggestion is that there is an overwhelming desperation or negative life experience that leads the individual to a position where there is complete absence of hope, which obviously reflects suicidal ideation generally, but which is channelled by those around them into grandiose and paranoid delusions, leading to the final act of annihilation (Salib, 2003).

Others believe the bombers are highly motivated, with high levels of patriotism and religious fervour (Zoroya, 2003), with religion offering a justification for murderous and/or suicidal behaviour. For example, devout Muslims believe that martyrs, male and female, are greeted in heaven by a number of *houri-al-ayn* (non-gendered inhabitants of heaven) who wipe away sins and provide the pleasures of paradise (Nydell, 2005). Hence, to enter heaven having killed and died for one's cause is to receive the desired rewards in the service of God. There is also evidence that suicide bombers may be offered rewards in this life too, in both financial gain and enhanced reputation. Murder and suicide in the service of an ideology, then, is an act that the perpetrator thinks will return great rewards. However, this is clearly not the only reason that people commit acts of terrorism.

PSYCHOLOGICAL THEORIES OF TERRORISM

The wide range of definitions of terrorism has a complicated theoretical development, and psychology is no exception to this. Theories have pondered whether the explanation is at the individual or group level, which tends to lead to a distinction between psychopathological factors and social psychological issues. There is a third set of theoretical positions which suggest that there is a combination of the two – the individual within the group.

As with many theories of violent acts, psychoanalytical theories have been examined as a possible explanation for the willingness to commit violence in the name of a cause, and even for acts of self-violence. Such theories lead to the question of the personality of the terrorist and personality theories that can be applied to explaining the capacity for violence.

Psychoanalytic and personality theories

Early work on the psychology of terrorism was based on psychoanalytical approaches, even though Freudian psychology was never intended to apply to crime or criminal behaviour. This was first proposed by Post (1984), who suggested that there is an illness or personality defect underlying the dysfunction leading to terrorist violence. Post outlined two different forms of dysfunction: first, the anarchic-ideologue individual whose early abuse leads to an extremist ideology that is a displacement of their hostility: and secondly, the nationalist-secessionist, who is avenging wrongs done to his family (in its broadest sense) by the state. Post (1984) suggested that the most salient psychoanalytic feature of a terrorist is projection, what he terms as an 'infantile' defence mechanism attributing inner feelings that are painful or problematic on to an exterior object (the group being attacked). A damaged self-concept idealises the self that is pleasant and acceptable and separates off the less favoured or bad self. The bad self becomes the other, via projection, and the act of terrorism is truly an act of self-hatred. There is then only one more step to becoming a suicide terrorist.

Basic components of psychodynamics suggest that the motives for terrorism are unconscious and are a product of hostility towards parental figures and early trauma and abuse (Casoni & Brunet, 2002) This is given credibility by the fact that many terrorists do seem to have suffered abusive family conflict or other early trauma (De Mause, 2002). However, as stated many times, not all abused children turn into killers, of whatever nature, and a more fruitful application of psychodynamics appears to be in the trait theory to which it leads, particularly in respect of narcissism. Again, terrorism studies saw an early linkage with this from Morf (1970), with more recent attempts by researchers such as Martens (2004). If terrorism is the product of a damaged sense of self, then pathological narcissism would seem to be the culprit. If an overvaluation of self and a devaluing of others is present, along with the satisfaction of allying the self to a 'perfect' cause, then violence in the name of that perfection could result. This perfection could be derived from aligning with a charismatic leader or a cause that is perceived as 'higher' and 'fighting' a perceived injustice. The violence that results is termed a 'narcissistic rage', which is akin to that seen in antisocial personality disorder (ASPD) (see below). It is proposed that this rage evolves from early childhood experiences that are abusive and/or humiliating, making fear and vulnerability integral to the personal self. Elimination of the fear creates a more palatable self-concept.

Psychopathology and psychopathy of terrorism

Is there a psychopathology of terrorism? Research on links between mental illness and the committing of terrorist acts is inconclusive, but there is general agreement that, in terrorists who are incarcerated, there is no higher risk of mental illness or psychopathic personality disorders than in the general population (Horgan, 2005). Psychopathy would actually seem to rule terrorism out, as a psychopath would find it difficult to make the connections to principles or ideology that is necessary for espousal of the possibility of carrying out acts in the name of that ideology. A psychopath would also be unlikely to kill him-/herself for a cause. Kruglanski and Fishman (2006) suggest that viewing terrorism as a 'syndrome' is counter-productive to understanding the root causes, whether psychological, economic or political. It is better to view it as a 'tool', as a means to an end that motivates the individual or the group to act in specific ways. This is an application of the cognitive theory of utility, as it is thought that the expected utility of the act is a function of the value of its expected outcome, which is higher than that achieved by other means. There are other means available to political activists, such as diplomacy, political leverage and media manipulation, and such a utility-driven psychological aspect would mean that violence is seen as having a more productive outcome. This suggests that terrorism is a chosen pathway to a particular goal, and that there is no function of individual personality or psychopathology to be considered.

On the other hand, a personality disorder that is close to psychopathy would be anti-social (or dissocial) personality disorder. Martens (2004) suggests that many terrorists exhibit several of the traits of ASPD (or possibly narcissistic or paranoid personality disorders) but without necessarily having the clinical disorders as recognised in either the DSM or the ICD. This may, according to Martens (2004), indicate a specific category of interest: the terrorist with ASPD, individuals who share several characteristics including social alienation, disturbed socialisation, aggressiveness, hostility, impulsivity, low self-esteem, a tendency to escalate into violence, moral disengagement and a lack of self-criticism. The suggestion is that the considerable overall presence of these, and more, means there is a subcategory of terrorist that could be diagnosed with ASPD or have some characteristics of psychopathy. This may then mean that terrorism has at its roots causal elements such as disregard for authority due to early unresolved Oedipal issues and a tendency to revolt against rules, societal issues and individuals perceived as being unjustly privileged. Martens recognises this potion as speculative and suggests further research that could be carried out.

Studies attempting to identify a personality-based theory of terrorism have also been unconvincing in their findings. As Horgan (2009) suggests, there is no common set of personality characteristics to be found in the terrorist that can be examined, and this would also not be a very satisfying way of examining terrorists. A more productive way forward might be to examine vulnerability or risk factors for terrorism, or espousal of extremist ideologies.

If terrorists are not psychologically ill and do not have personality disorders, there must be other factors that lead to someone being willing use violence, lethal and self-lethal, to further their causes. Other psychological perspectives are therefore likely to be more fruitful in trying to understand these acts and the people who commit them.

INDIVIDUAL MODELS

Absolute moral thinking has been proposed as a possible explanation for terrorism. Lifton (2000), in examining cult psychology, reports that some groups espouse mass destruction as a route to an apocalypse that will usher in a new world. Here an absolute moral mind-set motivates terrorist acts in people with weak ego identities, as the cult leads them to positions of isolation and numbed affect. This theory-driven position is not strongly supported, as there is little empirical support, but a related perspective is found in what Canter (2006) calls the Samson syndrome. Samson is a biblical figure who was granted supernatural strength by God in order to become a hero and deliver the Israelites from the Philistines. He dies by pulling down the pillars, to which he is chained, of a temple filled with Philistines. Samson is therefore a figure of self-destructive rage, and the Samson syndrome illustrates suicide bombers and their psychology.

First, according to Canter (2006), the terrorist makes a very clear distinction between the in-group, with whom they identify, and the out-group, all others, who are characterised as sub-human. The second aspect is a belief that the out-group does not alter in any way, including their membership (all others) and that they deny the in-group its identity. This is, as Victoroff (2005) suggests, indicative of a basic attribution error in that those with weak identities who join this in-group attribute only evil motivations to the out-group, who are characterised as oppressors and do not consider the possibility of motives other than those of oppression. This cognitive inflexibility is linked to a need for attention-seeking behaviour that spirals into more and more destruction which fails to achieve the desired end of political or social change.

Such psychological positions are attractive as explanations for individual terrorists but fail to explain another group within the terrorist organisations – the leaders. It has been suggested that within some organisations there may be a high proportion of authoritarian personalities and it is these that become the leaders. Lester et al. (2004) also suggest that this is a form of cognitive inflexibility, but that the desire for revenge overrides any possibility of submitting to what is viewed as an authority that is unpalatable as an occupying force. Hence the leaders of a terrorist group are simply a stronger expression of the same people who are their followers or subordinate within the organisation. However, all are vulnerable in terms of their likelihood to identify with the values and people of a group.

Vulnerability means that a person is more open to engagement with something than others are. This can be positive or negative and, in the case of terrorists, it seems that there is a greater vulnerability to negative connections. This is not necessarily problematic unless the vulnerability is exploited in some way. There are three regularly occurring vulnerabilities observed in terrorism and potential terrorists: a perceived injustice or humiliation, a need for identity and a need for belonging. If an individual possesses such vulnerabilities, there is a possibility of becoming radicalised, which can lead to violent extremism. According to McCauley and Moskalenko (2008), political radicalisation is defined as being prepared for and committed to intergroup conflict through changes in beliefs and behaviours that increasingly lead to the justification of violence and sacrifice. However, as Mandel (2010) points out, radicalised thinking may mean there is a higher potential for violent action; it does not necessitate it, and radicalised individuals may never exhibit such behaviour. Hence there is an increasing use of the term 'violent radicalisation' to describe the process by which radical thinking becomes terrorism.

There are several mechanisms by which people or groups can become radicalised. These include:

- personal victimisation
- political grievance
- joining a radical group
- a shift to extremism in similar groups
- extreme cohesion
- competition with state power
- competition between groups
- competition within group
- violent political ideologies
- hate
- a capability for martyrdom

According to Moghaddam (2005), the process of becoming a terrorist is not a simple one, and it is something that builds. Many people feel discontented with the way they are treated by other people, the government or the corporate world, but few take the next step to doing something to express that discontent violently. Some will resolve feelings of frustration and aggression by displacing them on to the (perceived) cause of them and will join groups that advocate violence against the agent. This is the frustration-aggression hypothesis that grows out of psychodynamic positions applied to the attempt to understand the terrorist. It is clear that there is something missing because many people within society are frustrated by many things – poverty, injustice, inequality – but not all take the violent means of terrorism to express and alleviate their frustration. In addition, some terrorists do not belong to those groups in which it might be reasonable to suppose the high levels of frustration would exist (Victoroff, 2005). Such groups and the individuals within them become radicalised, a process that McCauley and Moskalenko (2008) define as an escalating commitment for intergroup conflict via changes in beliefs, feelings and behaviours that justify violence and personal sacrifice in pursuit of that goal.

An examination of routes to terrorism and individual motivations for such acts can be helpful, but there are other tools within psychology that might be useful, such as the investigative processes of profiling.

PROFILING TERRORISTS AND TERRORISM

Chapter 12 deals with processes within profiling and contrasts various forms of this tool. The possibility of using such a method to investigate terrorism is relatively new. Dean (2007) outlined the ways in which profiling could be applied to the examination of terrorism. He did this with caution, of course, as profiling itself is beset with definitional problems (see Chapter 12), which means the application contact moving from criminal to terrorist brings with it the problems of what the instrument actually is.

The debate over definitions of profiling is covered in Chapter 12 so need not be repeated here, except to reiterate that an instrument based on sound principles is what is required in a real-life application, which seems to mean the statistically based approaches. Such approaches have resulted in various pieces of predictive software, such as the Multistate Anti-Terrorism Information Exchange or MATRIX packages used in some parts of the USA after 9/11. This combines records and data from intelligence agencies and other sources, including criminal history records, drivers' licence information and motor vehicle registration information. These are analysed in order to provide a high terrorist factor (HTF) to individuals who show a statistical likelihood of committing terrorist acts or of being terrorists (Krouse, 2004). It is difficult to imagine the leap between driving records and terrorist profiling, and the MATRIX project was shut down amid concern for the privacy of US citizens (US Department of Defense, 2004).

Leaving the aborted attempts to produce statistical packages to predict the emergence of terrorist individuals, profiling has a different contribution to make. When used in criminal cases, profiling often centres on the psychological disturbance that may be evident in the behaviour of an individual. The things left at a crime scene, for example, or the ritualistic behaviour of a criminal may lead to a wider consideration of his/her psychological makeup, with particular reference to any psychological disturbance s/he may have. In general, it has been noted that terrorists do not tend to exhibit the same significant behaviour as other criminals do (Townshend, 2002). As such, it is thought that this process would not lend itself to examining terrorists. If it is pursued, then those carrying out the profiling may fall foul of the very things criminal profiling attempts to avoid, such as profiling on the basis of personal characteristics rather than statistically determined ones.

For example, racial profiling is carried out on the basis that an ethnic or racial group is more likely to carry out certain acts than others. Ellman (2003) suggests that the two most likely targets for such a process would be Arab and Muslim groups, and that this would be discriminatory and foolish. Being Arabic is not synonymous with being Muslim, and neither is synonymous with terrorism. The membership of al-Qaeda, the group identified as being responsible for 9/11 and other attacks, is not limited to either an Arabic or Muslim individual. As Rae (2012) points out, the majority of attacks on mainland America have been carried out by white Republican dissidents, not Arabic people. Using other characteristics, such as gender, lead to fallacies in pinpointing individuals who carry out terrorist acts, as women have been as active as men in terrorist groups, including carrying out the violence (Graham, 2008). Similarly, there is no age profile to be made of terrorists: although the perception is that they are usually in their twenties, the average age is possibly lower, with those in the upper hierarchies being much older (Benmelech & Berrebi, 2007).

Therefore, there is little mileage in profiling on the basis of personal characteristics or psychological disturbance. There is very little probability that there is a terrorist personality or a profile to be made on the basis of the terrorists' characteristics because, as with any other organisation, terrorist groups recruit a variety of personalities in order to carry out a range of activities. It may be fruitful, therefore, to consider the roles that the organisation's members carry out – such as those actually performing the acts of violence, those supplying them with the means to do so (financial and product based), those managing the organisational or management functions and those issuing propaganda, among other types of functions (Post, 1998).

Most commentators now agree that although profiling appeared to be a useful tool in the detection and investigation of terrorism, it is probably not conducive to producing a useful profile of the terrorist individual, but it may be useful in determining the circumstances necessary to produce terrorists (Rae, 2012).

Contribution to counter-terrorism

The aim of psychological research is to lead to a better understanding of the processes being investigated. The psychology of terrorism is no exception to this; some psychological research has been commissioned and/or examined by the organisations employed to stop terrorism and apprehend individuals and groups who are engaged in it. Horgan (2008) describes the need to identify the common factor within terrorist organisations and actions in order to advise counter-terrorism initiatives. He says that the focus on the process by which people become radicalised and/or terrorists is the most fruitful course of action. However, it may be that instead of concentrating on the reasons why people become dissatisfied with the current state of their lives (living in an occupied state, the need for revenge, etc.), we need to focus instead on the ways in which the terrorist organisation offers an answer to those dissatisfactions. It is the ways in which those organisations can be discredited and individuals led to an understanding that this is not the answer that is a more productive form of counter-terrorism, and, as such, might have more impact on those in the early stages of involvement.

SUMMARY

Definitions of terrorists are difficult to pin down due to the multifaceted nature of the act. The psychology of terrorism covers views of those employing violence in the pursuit of political or social ends as being mentally ill or as being goal-directed. What is clear is that we can only consider the psychology of those terrorists who are captured; there are many more who have died in their cause or who have not been caught.

Discussion point: Is radicalisation a valid perspective when investigating terrorism?

The theory that vulnerable individuals can become radicalised by extremist groups leads to the position that terrorist acts are the result of this radicalisation. This process is regarded as psychological in nature, which may be linked to psychopathology within individuals. However, some have criticised this approach as pathologising not just the individuals, but the groups to which they belong, and, by implication, the wider communities in which they are located. Is this approach, then, simply a xenophobic view of groups other than our own?

Hörnqvista, M. & Flygheda, J. (2012) Exclusion or culture? The rise and the ambiguity of the radicalisation debate. *Critical Studies on Terrorism*, [online], 6 September.
Kundnani, A. (2012) Radicalisation: the journey of a concept. *Race & Class*, **54**(2): 3–25.

Crimes of a Sexual Nature

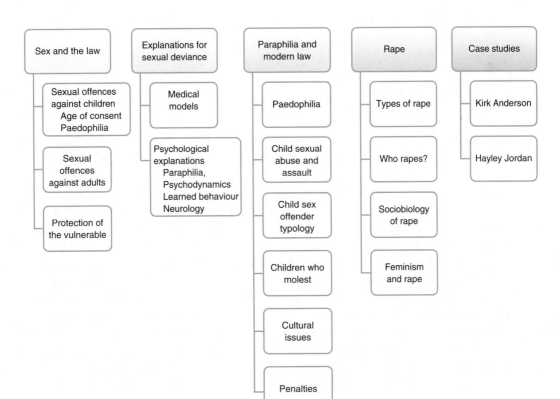

Sex and the law
- Sexual offences against children
  Age of consent
  Paedophilia
- Sexual offences against adults
- Protection of the vulnerable

Explanations for sexual deviance
- Medical models
- Psychological explanations
  Paraphilia, Psychodynamics
  Learned behaviour
  Neurology

Paraphilia and modern law
- Paedophilia
- Child sexual abuse and assault
- Child sex offender typology
- Children who molest
- Cultural issues
- Penalties

Rape
- Types of rape
- Who rapes?
- Sociobiology of rape
- Feminism and rape

Case studies
- Kirk Anderson
- Hayley Jordan

In some countries, it is legal for a man to have sex with a 12-year-old girl, as long as he does not pay her for it. In some countries, it is illegal to have sex unless the couple are married to each other. In some countries, it is illegal to have sex with someone of the same sex. In some countries, a man can force his wife to have sex with him and he will not be charged with any crime (MacKay, 2001). Given this diversity of cultural attitudes to sexual behaviour, what constitutes a sex crime? This chapter examines the background to our private and public views on sexual behaviour, its acceptability or otherwise, and legal positions with respect to sex. It outlines some of the ways in which sexual behaviour is governed by the law and provides a history of the development of what is perceived as acceptable sexual behaviour and what is considered as deviant. The various models of sexual deviance are outlined, and the psychological theories that underpin these models are explored, together with psychological attempts to explain the ways in which deviant sexual behaviour manifests itself. The applications of the psychological models in several sexual crimes are then explored.

KEY THEMES

- Child sex abuse/molestation
- Paedophilia
- Rape
- Sex offenders
- Sexual(ised) legislation
- Sexual violence

The perception of what is sexually perverted or the definition of which sexual acts are legal shifts depending on who is talking about it. A person's profession, gender, age, race, proclivities, education, nation and even which century they live in, have all affected the viewpoint on sex and sexual perversions. For example, homosexuality has long been stigmatised as sexually perverted (and remains so among some portions of society), but psychological and medical professionals no longer consider it pathological. Even the term 'perversion' is controversial. Psychologists generally refer to unconventional sexual behaviour as sexual deviation or, in cases where the specific object of arousal is unusual, as paraphilia. There are a number of clinically recognised disorders of sexual or paraphiliac function. Many of these behaviours are punishable by law. Additionally, although rape is not classified as a paraphilia, it is a serious sexual offence and is perhaps the most highly reviled form of sexual gratification, alongside child sexual abuse. Such sexual behaviour often comes to the attention of forensic psychology as distinct from clinical psychology. In clinical psychology, the distress that can be the result of having unusual sexual desires is the important aspect of sexual deviance. For forensic psychology, the issue of sexual deviancy only becomes important when behaviours are illegal.

SEX AND THE LAW

Forensic psychologists should ensure they acquire and maintain knowledge about legislation surrounding sexual behaviour. The most recent sex legislation in the UK as a whole is the Sexual Offences Act 2003, implemented in 2004, which updated and expanded the definitions of and punishments for crimes of a sexual nature (OPSI, 2003). Due to the fact that the UK comprises several smaller juris-

Sexual Offences Act 2003 – An Act making provision about sexual offences, their prevention and the protection of children from harm from other sexual acts and for connected purposes.

dictions, there are several minor variants on the sexual offences legislation. In Northern Ireland, a new set of laws to protect children from sexual offences and to clarify the situation of teenagers engaging in consensual sex was introduced in 2008. In Scotland, the Sexual Offences Act was amended in 2009 to bring the definitions of the offences in line with other legislations.

In the USA, the legislative position is much less clear as each state has its own legal definition and legal position on sexual offences. The best source of information about laws in the USA is the publications and website of the US government, which holds a record of all laws and amendments.

Legislation regarding sexual behaviour refers to the issue of consent as it is generally accepted that unless sexual activity is carried out between consenting partners there will be elements of illegality in the behaviour. There are laws relating to the age of consent and inappropriate sexual activity with a child (including grooming), coercion/force (rape or sexual assault), prostitution, homosexual behaviour, indecent exposure, non-consensual deliberate displays or illicit watching of sexual activity, harm to animals, acts involving dead people, harassment, nuisance, fear, injury, and pornography.

Sexual offences against children

In a great many jurisdictions, the age at which it is legal to have sex is around late puberty, for example, 16 years of age in the UK. There are some areas in which the restrictions appear to be at odds with European or Northern American practice (see Figure 8.1). This geographical variation would suggest that the age of consent, and possibly other sexual issues, is influenced by cultural aspects of life. As a result, even psychologists practising in those areas with a relatively late age of consent should be aware that other cultures differ and that migrants carry their home culture with them. Of particular note are areas in which there is either no law on age of consent (such as Saudi Arabia) or where the law fixes consent at a seemingly very low age, such as 9 years, as in Yemen, but also stipulates that the partners must be married.

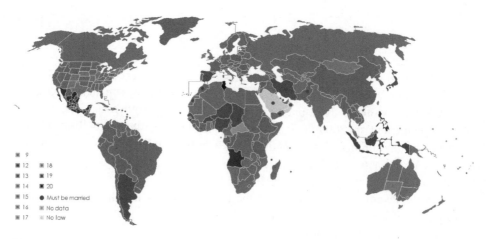

Figure 8.1   Legal age of consent (for heterosexual sex) in various countries

Another point to note is that laws stipulating the age of consent do not eradicate under-age sex. This is evidenced by the high proportions of teenage pregnancy seen in the UK (Allen et al., 2007) and the USA (Chandra et al., 2008). Where laws exist, sex between two children of similar ages is often not regarded as illegal. Many legal systems also distinguish between children of various ages, for example, in the UK, any sex act with someone under the age of 13 is defined as rape, and sexual activity with 13–15-year-olds where the other person is over 18 is considered an offence. Such activities include sexual penetration or sexual touching, causing or inciting a child to engage in sexual activity, sexual activity in the presence of a child, and meeting a child following sexual grooming.

For 16-and 17-year-olds, UK legislation also covers offences such as a family member engaging in sex with minors and people in positions of authority or trust, such as teachers and youth leaders, doing the same.

Sexual abuse of children should be distinguished from paedophilia, although the two terms are often used interchangeably. As discussed below, paedophilia is the sexual attraction of adults to children, but not all paedophiles will abuse children and not all child sex abusers are paedophiles. In various legislatures around the world, the term 'paedophilia' is never used, and the crimes are referred to as sexual abuse or molestation, reserving the paraphilia description for medical usage (Arnaldo, 2001).

Sexual offences against adults

In addition to the offences against children, the legislation also includes specific crimes of a sexual nature committed against adults.

Rape is the intentional penetration with the penis of the vagina, anus or mouth of another person without that person's consent. The Sexual Offences Act 2003 has a subsection here devoted to the question of reasonable belief in consent. Assault by penetration differs from this in that it covers intentional penetration of the vagina or anus of another person by something other than the penis of the offender. This excludes legal intimate searches and medical procedures. Sexual assault is the intentional sexual touching without that person's consent. This offence covers a wide range of behaviour, including, for example, rubbing up against someone's private parts through the person's clothes for sexual gratification.

A major subsection of the Act affords protection to people with a mental disorder. Mental disorder here is defined as a condition impeding choice, which could be an intellectual impairment, for example, or a mental illness that leads to an individual being unable to give consent. In the UK, this category of vulnerable people is further defined in the Mental Capacity Act 2005, which defines conditions that may determine lack of capacity and how this can be identified. Lack of capacity to make choices about consenting to sexual activity, for example, should be determined by an approved mental health professional or similar clinician. Doyle (2010) describes how such protection is not straightforward as there is a tension between the individual's right to enjoy sexual relationships and the right to protection from unwanted sexual attention. The difficulty arises in the need to have objective clinical assessments of the capacity to consent (Lyden, 2007), and in the experience of victims of sexual crimes of the criminal justice system's inadequacy to support them (McLeod et al., 2010). Such assessments are not necessarily made as a matter of course, and may not be applied until the questions of whether a sexual assault has been perpetrated arise.

Can people with mental incapacity truly consent to sex? The case of MG

Anderson (2010) describes the case of MG, a 17-year-old woman in New Jersey, USA, who had a measurable IQ of 64. She participated in sexual acts with a group of eight young men, most of which she attested that she carried out without being forced. The co-defendants were charged variously with crimes under the New Jersey code of first degree aggravated sexual assault, sexual penetration of a mentally defective person, sexual penetration using physical force or coercion, and aggravated criminal sexual contact. Several charges were dropped, those for one defendant were dismissed, and some charges were reduced to endangering the welfare of an incompetent person. At trial, the defendants were acquitted of some charges, but the sexual assault charges were upheld for several of the defendants. The court's deliberations centred on the nature and applicability of the tests of IQ, mental age and understanding the nature of sexual acts. According to Anderson, these are problematic in that the victims, or indeed defendants, in such cases may understand the nature of sexual acts but they may not be able to communicate this to the court's satisfaction.

Hence, judgements could be based on the incorrect elements of the incapacity. Due to these difficulties and the need for a methodical process of assessment, the use of a set of algorithms for determining capacity in an emergency medical situation is advocated, and McLeod et al. (2010) propose improvement of training and other support mechanisms for these cases.

Protecting the vulnerable

Despite such legal protection, throughout human history and in some cases in contemporary societies, there were/are large numbers of people left unprotected even against the most brutal forms of sexual assault. It is a relatively recent innovation that vulnerable members of society have been protected against abuse. The basis of just about every legal system has been religious laws, and the earliest known sex laws were no exception to this rule. Originally, there was no difference between sin and crime, and punishment was by divine order. The presented an invaluable excuse for the control of the behaviour of a populace, or parts of it, such as women.

A comparison of the attempts throughout history at sex legislation shows they have at least one thing in common – they all covered both social and religious offences. Sexual behaviour was punished not only when it caused harm to other human beings, but also when it expressed disbelief in God. Thus, sexual non-conformists could never claim to be socially harmless. Even if they endangered nobody in particular, they still posed an indirect threat to the community and an insult to God. Thus, the laws encouraged marital coitus at the expense of all other sexual activity and prohibited various forms of non-reproductive sex. Rape, adultery and illegitimate pregnancies violated the rights of individual men, who regarded their wives and daughters as their personal property and who demanded compensation for any 'damage'. Homosexual behaviour and sexual contact with animals were associated with the worship of foreign gods, being signs of idolatry or abominations, and were punished much more harshly.

Naturally, in the course of time, certain specific sex laws were modified and others were reinterpreted in the light of changing circumstances. Generally speaking, the ecclesiastical attitude towards sex was prohibitive, with even coitus between husband and wife being restricted. Religious standards eventually gave way to the secular, but the state simply adopted the traditional moral standards and enforced them with all its might. However, it did mean, among other things, that the sex laws could no longer be directly copied from the holy books, but had to be based on rational and empirical grounds. As a result, many sexual acts that once had been crimes were now found to be permissible (Gavin & Bent, 2010). In recent years, the views have become more sophisticated, and thus humanity is beginning to understand that sexual freedom is as much a human right as religious freedom and freedom of speech. So we move from a moral stance to a legal and/or medical one. The Western psychological and medical views are obviously coloured by this, but by no means constrained.

EXPLANATIONS FOR SEXUAL DEVIANCE

The medical model of sexuality and sexual deviance

A medical model is based on the assumption that any problem can be explained as a disease. Physical diseases have traditionally been divided into three major categories, according to their causes:

- Infectious diseases, i.e. diseases caused by some germ or virus, for example, a cold or syphilis
- Systemic diseases, i.e. diseases caused by some physical breakdown or malfunction, for example, a hardening of the arteries, an enlargement of the prostate or diabetes
- Traumatic diseases, i.e. diseases caused by some external agent or influence on the body, for example, food poisoning, a broken limb, a cut or a burn.

Grubin (2008) points out that a clinical approach to sexual deviance and sexual offending must necessarily be problematic. For doctors, including psychiatrists, the focus of any approach to sex crimes is one of the offender as patient and that any disorder that has led to the aberrant behaviour can be treated. Hence, social needs of consideration of crime and control are irrelevant to a medical model. There is also the issue of the medicalisation of mental disorders. As Widiger and Trull (2007) argue, this approach has not proved to be very useful with regard to sexual deviance and offending. The traditional medical categories have often led to confusing and contradictory propositions. For example, when homosexuality was viewed as deviant, it was linked to each or all of three different kinds of medicalised causes. Specifically, under the strictly medical model, the following 'causes' of homosexuality would be proposed:

- People are homosexual because they were seduced by other, mostly older homosexuals. Therefore, homosexuals must be kept away from young people. (In this view, homosexuality is an infectious disease.)
- People are homosexual because they were born with a certain 'weak personality' because they have become senile or because their 'character has disintegrated'. (In this view, homosexuality is a systemic disease.)
- People are homosexual because neurotic parents or traumatic early sexual encounters have prevented their normal sexual development. (In this view, homosexuality is a traumatic disease.)

The assumption of a medical explanation further implies that sexual deviants are medical patients, with a medical diagnosis, that should (and can) be corrected by a doctor. It is now seen as unproductive to make a direct relationship between mental and physical diseases in this way. For such examinations to make sense, and for treatment, we need to turn from a strictly medical model to psychological ones. Such models take into account not only the deviation, but also the underlying cause and development and the social context in which the deviance occurs.

Psychological explanations of sexual deviance

Psychological models of sexual deviance focus on various aspects that refer to alternatives to consensual adult heterosexual sexual behaviour in terms of psychosexual development, learned behaviour, or mental disorder. Each of these models can refer to sexual deviance as 'paraphilia', a term that refers to sexual arousal in response to objects or situations that may interfere with the capacity for reciprocal affectionate sexual activity. Paraphilia is also used to imply non-mainstream sexual practices without necessarily implying dysfunction or deviance. In addition, it may describe sexual feelings towards otherwise non-sexual objects. A paraphiliac interest is not normally considered clinically important unless it is also causing suffering of some kind, or strongly inhibiting a 'normal' sex life (according to the subjective standards of the culture and times). Paraphilia or more pejorative synonyms are sometimes used by laypeople in a more judgemental or prejudicial sense, to categorise sexual desires or activities lying well outside the societal norm. Many sexual activities now considered harmless have been viewed as perversions or psychosexual disorders in various societies, and how to regard these behaviours has been, and continues at times to be, a controversial matter. What is considered to be perversion or deviation varies from society to society and some specific paraphilias have been or are currently crimes in some jurisdictions. The field of psychology has attempted to characterise paraphilias in terms of their aetiology and in the ways they change the functioning of individuals in social situations.

Due to the somewhat subjective nature of their definition, the specific acts included under the umbrella of paraphilia vary, and successive editions of the relevant texts, such as the *Diagnostic and Statistical Manual of Mental Disorders* (DSM), are updated accordingly. The current version of the DSM (the fifth edition; American Psychiatric Association, 2013) discusses eight major paraphilias individually. According to the DSM, the activity must be the sole means of sexual gratification for a period of six months and cause marked distress or interpersonal difficulty to be considered such.

The recognised paraphilias are described in Figure 8.2a, while Figures 8.2b and 8.2c describe other paraphilias not yet included in the DSM.

The next edition of the DSM – DSM-V – is due to be published May 2013. There are currently no revisions proposed to change the list of paraphilias to be included, although some sexual disorders may be added or aggregated (American Psychiatric Association, 2013). The DSM-V Paraphilias Subworkgroup has also suggested that a paraphilia alone is not necessarily a psychiatric disorder, and that there is a distinction between paraphilias and paraphilic disorders. A paraphilic disorder is observed when a paraphilia causes distress

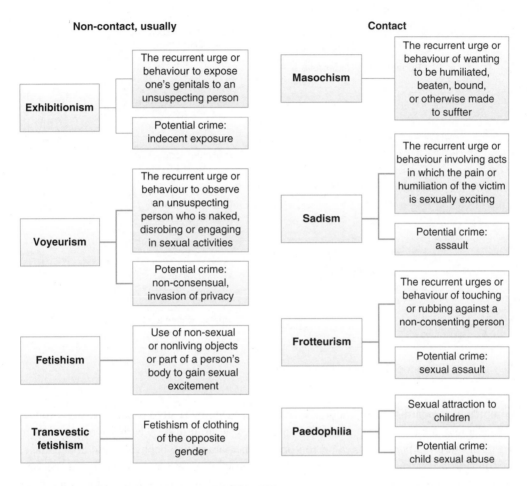

Figure 8.2a   Paraphilias recognised in DSM-V-TR

or impairment to the individual or harm to others. In this way, the DSM-V will distinguish between normative and non-normative sexual behaviour, but does not label non-normative sexual behaviour as psychopathological (American Psychiatric Association, 2013).

There are also examples of how changes in culture and law affect the views of sexual behaviour previously regarded as non-normative. Homosexuality was declassified as a paraphilia by the time of the publication of the DSM-III in 1980, consistent with the change of attitude and legislation. There is still a disorder related to homosexuality, but this refers to clinical distress caused by the repression of homosexuality.

It seems that anything can, in theory, become sexualised, given the right circumstances, and that therefore paraphilias can encompass almost any imaginable subject. Clinicians distinguish between optional, preferred and exclusive paraphilias, though the terminology is not

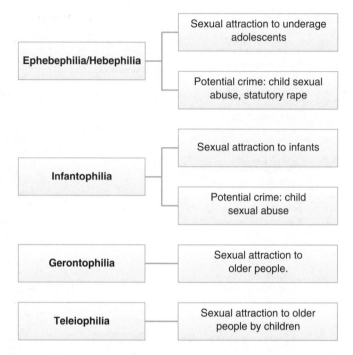

Figure 8.2b   Chronophilias other than paedophilia

completely standardised. An 'optional' paraphilia is an alternative route to sexual arousal. For example, a man might sometimes enhance sexual arousal by wearing women's underwear. In preferred paraphilias, a person prefers the paraphiliac behaviour but also engages in conventional sexual activities. In exclusive paraphilias, a person is unable to become sexually aroused in the absence of the paraphiliac content. Optional paraphilias are more common than preferred paraphilias, which are more common than exclusive paraphilias.

Psychological theories of sexual deviance and paraphilia

Normal biological processes may sometimes manifest themselves in idiosyncratic ways. Behavioural theory suggests that, in at least some of the paraphilias, these unusual manifestations are frequently associated with unusual and/or traumatic events associated with early sexual experience. They appear to be caused by imprinting, that is, a sexual stimulus has been associated with stimuli and situations that do not typically result in sexual response, and are then perpetuated through operant conditioning, with the sexual response being its own reward or positive reinforcement (Darcangelo, 2007). Hence, if sexual imprinting is the process by which a young animal learns the characteristics of a desirable mate, and this is somehow linked to deviant behaviour, the object of desire becomes unusual. Money (1986)

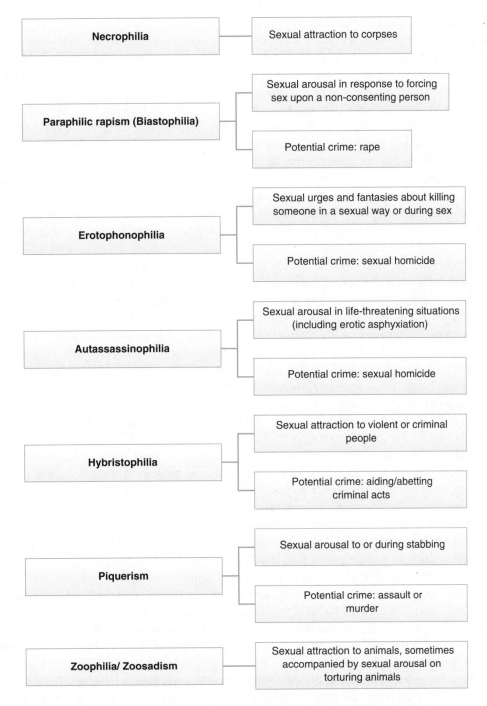

Figure 8.2c   Paraphilias classed as 'Not otherwise specified' (diagnostic code 302.9)

called the sexual imprint the 'lovemap' in an attempt to assist discussion of why people like what they enjoy sexually and erotically. According to Money, it is a developmental representation or template in the mind and brain depicting the idealised lover and the idealised programme of sexual activity. A lovemap can be shaped by both positive and negative factors, things that attract or repel the person whose sexual preferences are being mapped. A lovemap can be shaped by environmental factors that facilitate the formation of a sexual bond, or that enhance or diminish sexual response. Money suggests that paraphilia arises because the lovemap has become distorted. A vandalised lovemap occurs when the lovemapping process involves trauma, for example, being exposed at a young age to paraphiliac parents, or involvement in a paedophilic or incestuous relationship. Paraphiliac lovemaps develop when sexual arousal is attached to fantasies and practices that are socially forbidden, disapproved of, ridiculed or penalised. Sexual imprinting on inanimate or non-sexual objects is a popular developmental theory for sexual fetishism, and this imprinting can take many forms, objects, behaviours or fantasies.

As already mentioned, it is clear that a great deal of sexual behaviour is, or has been at some time, viewed negatively by various religions or other cultural agencies. What is unclear is how such behaviour is detected; if the people know the behaviour is prohibited and/or illegal, they are unlikely to practise it openly (Gavin & Bent, 2010). However, some aspects of non-sexual life, such as extreme religious observances, may have become distorted into sexual behaviours, explaining, to some extent, the development of atypical desires. For example, flagellants were bands of people who wandered from place to place whipping themselves in public self-humiliation. It could be supposed that for many of them the practice had sexual connotations, particularly when it is compared to the use of flagellation in eighteenth- and nineteenth-century English brothels. Customers paid large fees to be whipped by prostitutes, and a preference for sexual whippings became known as 'the English vice' (Gibson, 1978).

Another strange juxtaposition of religion and sex can be seen in the witch hunts of the pre-eighteenth-century period in Europe and North America. Purkiss (1996) suggests that an examination of the historical documentation reveals strong sexual undertones in the witch craze. Apart from a morbid interest in sexual matters, the authors also reveal an obsessive hatred of women, emphasising that a woman is more likely to be a witch than a man, and that 'all witchcraft comes from carnal lust, which in women is insatiable' (Goldenburg, 2007). Hence, the extermination of witches was not simply to protect against the influence of witchcraft, but also the threat to the safety and sexual health of the community. Confessions were obtained under torture or the threat of torture, and the court records were kept by the inquisitors, not by their victims, or anyone acting as advocate for the victim. The bizarre sexual fantasies or 'hallucinations' ascribed to witches therefore said less about them and more about their accusers.

The subjugation of sexual desire into religious ecstasy has been a recurrent theme in the evolution of some religions, such as Catholic Christianity. So, repression of sexuality under religious strictures may be, in and of itself, a deviant view of sexuality. Repression is, of course, an underlying concept in Freudian theory, which suggests that the three constructs of the psyche (id, ego and superego) are in constant turmoil over energy (Kimmel, 2007). Some theorists suggest that sexual deviants or offenders have very weak superegos (morals) and very powerful ids (sexual impulses, libido). It must be stressed that Freudian psychology never purported to be applicable to the study of any crime, including sexual offending.

Such psychodynamic positions are, of course, subject to much criticism in terms of evidence, accessibility of its components and applicability to understanding the mind. Feminist critics, for example, argue that psychoanalytical positions ignore or minimise the role of the female in sexual behaviour. Freudian psychology presents the male as norm and female sexual needs as deviant from this norm (Buikema & Smelik, 1995). For Freud, the female sexual identity is the result of a castration complex, and the sexual development of women is based on a lack of male organs rather than as an identity in its own right. Whether this is an underlying contributor to sexual deviance is unclear. Feminist theorists also suggest that neo-Freudian psychologists' focus on the role of the maternal relationship in the deviant development of sexuality is problematic, particularly in sexual homicides (Meloy, 2000). Additionally, the unconscious nature of this theoretical and practitioner position means it is inaccessible, which also presents a problem for the scientific examination of psychological, including sexual, issues.

In contrast, cognitive and behavioural theories suggest that irrational beliefs and cognitive distortions help to initiate sexual deviancy. If an individual becomes conditioned to negative sexual stimuli, with orgasm being the reinforcer, the constructs combine to create persistent patterns of how the person behaves as well as views the world. The secrecy needed also becomes part of the conditioned response and perpetuates the deviancy. Learning theory is also a significant component of this approach. It is thought that children who are sexually abused learn sex through inappropriate means, and if exposed enough, children may internalise this learned behaviour. Sex offenders, as opposed to non-criminal deviants, do appear to view the world differently from 'normal' people; they perceive people, sex and arousal in qualitatively different ways (Gavin & Bent, 2010). Learning theory would suggest that an offender has somehow learned the sexual deviancy from his or her environment. This theory also incorporates modelling, the process of learning behaviour from observation (Almond et al., 2006). Studies, which have inherent difficulties in quantifying such information, suggest that 30% to 80% of offenders have been sexually abused themselves in the past. This information may offer credible evidence to support this theory, although the variation is problematic. However, there are many offenders who report that they have never been sexually abused and have never witnessed sexual abuse in the past. Survivors of sexual abuse also point out that many do not go on to abuse, so the aetiological pathway is very complex. Many offenders do appear to be continually learning and advancing in their sexual deviancy, particularly in refinement of behaviour and learning how not to be caught.

While it does seem to be clear that sexual deviancy has a learned element, other theories suggest different underlying mechanisms. Evolutionary theory posits that behaviour, including sexual aggression, develops and is inherited if it contributes to the successful mating and passing on of genetic material (Thornhill & Palmer, 2000). Hence, men have learned to become more aggressive and dominant towards women, or others weaker than themselves, even in the absence of a mating scenario. If more sexually aggressive males mate much more frequently than passive males, then those genes would be kept in the evolutionary pool. The learned aspect is the domination during the sex act. Although our brains are more advanced than those of our prehistoric ancestors, the inherent drive to reproduce is not. While this theory may partially account for rape, it still fails to address child molestation, paraphilias and sexual aggression in women. A more tangible position might be drawn from neurological studies.

Neurological hypotheses of paraphilia suggest that sexual deviance is associated with frontal and/or temporal lobe damage (Joyal et al., 2007). Frontotemporal dysfunctions have been reported among sexual offenders, but there is no clear link to sexual offending behaviour specifically rather than general criminality and delinquency. However, some dysexecutive symptoms and verbal deficits are found in sexual offenders, even when reasoning and cognitive flexibility are intact. This would suggest basal frontotemporal anomalies. There is also a distinction between child sex molesters and rapists, with more neurological impairment seen in the former.

Both cortical and subcortical structures are important for normal sexual functioning, particularly those in the anterior parts of the brain (Schiltz et al., 2007). While the frontal and temporal cortices are believed to be involved in the modulation of drive, initiation and sexual activation, subcortical structures, including the hippocampus, the amygdala and the hypothalamus, are implicated in the modulation of sexual behaviours and genital responses. Neuroimaging studies confirm the involvement of frontal, temporal, cingulate and subcortical structures in the regulation of sexual arousal. Damage to one of these neural nodes is hypothesised to be involved in sexual deviance, including hypersexuality, although the more common outcome of brain injury is a reduction, not an increase, of the drive. If there is malfunction in both right and left medial temporal lobes, then a patient may develop Klüver–Bucy syndrome, which includes the symptoms of docility, dietary changes (such as eating inappropriate objects and/or overeating coupled with hyperorality, a compulsion to examine objects by mouth) and altered sexuality (Devinsky et al., 2010). It can be characterised by a heightened sex drive or a tendency to seek sexual stimulation from unusual or inappropriate objects, which in itself could be deemed deviant sexual behaviour (Absher et al., 2000).

In contradiction, it has been found that sadistic sexual offenders performed significantly better in neuropsychological testing than the non-sadistic sexual offenders, which makes for a difficult interpretation. The same group of researchers measured different brain areas in paedophiles, incest offenders, aggressive sexual assaulters and non-violent non-sexual offenders to find smaller left frontal and temporal areas in sexual offenders. Left hemispheric asymmetry (a smaller left than right hemisphere) was also observed exclusively among the child sex offenders. Overall, there is a possible, but weak, association between frontal and temporal lobe anomaly and sexual offences. The physical contact/non-contact distinction might also be clinically significant, at least from the neuropsychological perspective.

Psychological theories do present alternative approaches to understanding sexual deviance and offending, and may also offer a path to treatment and rehabilitation. This will be discussed in more detail in Section 6.

PARAPHILIA AND MODERN LAW

In legal and lay terms, there are few pieces of behaviour that cause as much outrage as those which sexualise or sexually harm children. The group of paraphilias of sexual attraction to specific age groups is termed chronophilia and includes the attraction to older people as well as to children. A primary attraction to children is termed paedophilia, although this specifically refers to pre-pubescent children. Discussion about what categories of attraction to different ages of children to include in the DSM-V suggest that we also adopt specific terminology to describe attraction to young adolescents (11–14 years) as hebephilia, and to late adolescents (15–19) as ephebephilia (Blanchard et al., 2008). However, for clarity, this section uses the term paedophilia to describe the sexual attraction to all children below the legal age of sexual consent.

Paedophilia

In contrast to the generally accepted medical definition, the term 'paedophile' is also used colloquially to denote significantly older adults who are sexually attracted to adolescents below the local age of consent, as well as those who have sexually abused a child. It is the definition of 'child' that causes problems here. In the 1860s, the age of consent in Britain was 12 years old. Campaigners concerned about young girls being sold to brothels (and other aspects of the white slave trade) petitioned to raise this age. In 1875, a partial success came when Parliament raised the age of consent to 13. This was, of course, not satisfactory and further campaigns exposed the increase in child procurement and prostitution. In 1885, the Criminal Law Amendment Act raised the age of consent to 16, strengthened existing legislation against prostitution, but also had the unfortunate effect of proscribing all male homosexual relations.

The term 'paedophilia erotica' was coined in 1886 by the Vienna psychiatrist Richard von Krafft-Ebbing. He gave the following characteristics:

- The sexual interest is towards children, either prepubescent or at the beginning of puberty
- The sexual interest is the primary one, that is, exclusively or mainly towards children
- The sexual interest remains over time

Strictly speaking, this definition would include many adolescents and prepubescents, for whom such an interest might be normal. Thus, some experts add the criterion that the interest must be towards children at least five years younger than the subject.

The DSM-IV-TR gives the following as its 'diagnostic criteria for 302.2 Paedophilia':

- Over a period of at least 6 months, recurrent, intense sexually arousing fantasies, sexual urges, or behaviours involving sexual activity with a prepubescent child or children (generally age 13 years or younger).
- The person has acted on these urges, or the sexual urges or fantasies cause marked distress or interpersonal difficulty.
- The person is at least age 16 years and at least 5 years older than the child or children in Criterion A.
- Do not include an individual in late adolescence involved in an on-going sexual relationship with a 12- or 13-year-old.

The actual boundaries between childhood and adolescence may vary in different countries or cultures and are difficult to define in rigid terms of age. The World Health Organisation (2013), for instance, defines adolescence as the period of life between 10 and 19 years of age, although it is most often defined as between 13 and 18.

The American Psychiatric Association (APA) diagnostic criteria do not require actual sexual activity with a child. The diagnosis can therefore be made based on the presence of fantasies or sexual urges alone, provided the subject meets the remaining criteria. In a legal sense, however, being a paedophile is not an issue unless sexual or related activity has taken place.

The extent to which paedophilia occurs is not known with any certainty. Some studies have concluded that a large proportion of all adult men may have some feelings of sexual arousal in connection with children, perhaps as many as 25%. This may seem to be a shockingly high figure, however, Briere and Runtz (1989) conducted a study on male undergraduate students, in which 21% acknowledged sexual attraction to children; 9% reported sexual fantasies involving children; 5% admitted masturbating to these fantasies; and 7% conceded some probability of actually having sex with a child if they could avoid detection and punishment. These sexual interests were associated with negative early sexual experiences, masturbation to pornography, self-reported likelihood of raping a woman, frequent sex partners, and attitudes supportive of sexual dominance over women. The authors also noted that it was highly possible that the results were affected by the inclination to give socially desirable answers, meaning the rates were, in fact, higher.

A perpetrator of child sexual abuse is, despite all medical definitions, commonly referred to as a paedophile. However, there may be other motivations for the crime (such as stress, marital problems, or the unavailability of an adult partner), much as adult rape can have non-sexual reasons. Thus, child sexual abuse alone may or may not be an indicator that its perpetrator is a paedophile; most perpetrators are not primarily interested in children.

Those who have committed sexual crimes against children but who do not meet the normal diagnostic criteria for paedophilia are referred to as situational, opportunistic or regressed offenders, whereas offenders primarily attracted towards children are called structured, preferential or fixated paedophiles, as their orientation is fixed – this is their primary desire. Estimates of the number of child sexual abuse perpetrators that meet criteria for paedophilia vary between 2% and 10% (Groth, 1979).

Forensic psychological research in paedophilia is beginning to unearth some explanations for such a socially objectionable desire. Bancroft (2009) suggests that there is an androgen-sensitive neurophysiological substrate of sexual desire. The exploration of a brain-wave measure, the contingent negative variation (CNV), which is an increasing negative shift of the cortical electrical potentials associated with an anticipated response to an expected stimulus, supports this. The CNV is an electrical event that is indicative of a state of readiness or expectancy. As a group, paedophilic child sex offenders showed undifferentiated CNV responses to adult and child stimuli, unlike non-paedophilic child sex offenders and controls, who showed larger CNVs to adult rather than to child stimuli. These results suggest that CNV may be usefully developed as an adjunct to penile plethysmographic (PPG) assessment of deviant sexual interests in offenders.

Paedophilia is regarded as resistant to psychological intervention, as reported success rates of modern treatment on paedophiles are very low. Treatment strategies for paedophilia include those that parallel addiction therapy, although such systems are thought to be the least efficacious method of treatment. Other approaches are derived from cognitive-behavioural therapy or medical therapies. The latter are those utilising anti-androgenic medications such as Depo Provera, which may be used to lower testosterone levels, and are often used in conjunction with the non-medical approaches above. This is commonly referred to as 'chemical castration'. Other programmes induce an association of illegal behaviour with pain by means of the more controversial aversion therapy. Convicted sex offenders, including many paedophiles and homosexuals, have been treated by psychosurgical procedures, including lobotomies. This is very controversial, and has low success rates. Thalamotomy is an alternative surgical treatment of sex offenders used since the 1980s, when it was increasingly hailed as an 'effective therapy' for sex offenders, as well as for some children suffering from symptoms of child sexual abuse. However, irreversible psychosurgical interventions of this nature are not likely to be employed when other therapies are readily available.

There is a certain amount of moral pressure put upon sex offenders, such as offering them amnesty in return for therapies such as surgery, which (according to Sigusch, 2001) leads to subdued states or increases in violent behaviour. Others criticise neurosurgery used on sex offenders as a 'sedative' strategy where a patient is made quiet and manageable by an operation. However, these conclusions are in conflict with those of other researchers, who have found that paedophiles can comorbidly exhibit many psychiatric features not directly associated with the deviant sexual desire. The research and medical evidence surrounding paedophilia is unclear, and it may be better for forensic psychology to concentrate on the legal rather than clinical aspects of the behaviour.

Child sexual abuse and assault

Child sexual abuse is the sexual assault of a minor or sexual activity between a minor and an older person in which the dominant position of the (presumed) adult is used to coerce or exploit the younger. As stated above, this adult is not necessarily a paedophile, despite the general interchangeable usage of the term. The danger of conflating the two terms is that a large category of child abuser, the non-paedophiliac, is either ignored or assumed to fall under the heading of having a diagnosable disorder (Sanghara & Wilson, 2006).

Those who have committed sexual crimes against children but who do not meet the normal diagnosis criteria for paedophilia are referred to as situational, opportunistic or regressed offenders, whereas offenders primarily attracted towards children are called structured, preferential or fixated paedophiles, as their orientation is fixed by the structure of their personality. It was first estimated that only 2% to 10% of child sexual abuse perpetrators meet the regular criteria for paedophilia (Groth, 1979). Later research is even less clear. A 2001 FBI report suggested that there was a high proportion of child sex offenders who were primarily paedophiles (Lanning, 2001), and British research demonstrates that a high number of child abuse cases are within the family, sometimes with a parent, whose primary sexual attraction is to adults (Glasser et al., 2001).

Child sexual abuse is illegal in all countries about which information is available. The term also includes the commercial sexual exploitation of children, defined by the International Labour Organisation (ILO) in the text of the Worst Forms of Child Labour Convention (Dennis, 1999).

Child sexual abuse is generally viewed as inherently harmful to minors. A wide range of psychological, emotional, physical and social effects has been attributed to child sexual abuse, including anxiety, depression, obsession, compulsion, grief, post-traumatic stress disorder (PTSD) symptoms such as flashbacks, emotional numbing, pseudo-maturity symptoms, and other more general dysfunctions, such as sexual dysfunction, social dysfunction, dysfunction of relationships, poor education and employment records, eating disorders, self-mutilation, and a range of physical symptoms common to some other forms of PTSD (Molnar et al., 2001). Additionally, adolescent female victims of abuse may become pregnant, with all the attendant psychological, social and physical problems associated with underage motherhood (Leeners et al., 2006). There is also the risk of contracting sexually transmitted illnesses (STIs), as in other forms of sexual offences. Some studies have shown that some of the negative effects associated with child sex abuse are caused by the negative family environment that is often also present for children who are abused. Those studies also concluded that the negative effects of child sex abuse were smaller and that some groups of children were not negatively affected by being abused (Rind et al., 1998), a finding that was heavily criticised for being methodologically unsound and seeming to advocate child sex abuse (Dallam, 2001).

Wakefield and Underwager (1991) suggested that there is a difference between child sex abuse experiences of males and females, where more males than females report the experience as neutral or positive, hypothesising that, while women/girls perceive their experience as sexual violation, men/boys regard it as 'sexual initiation'. A review by Rind et al. (1998) showed that this difference was present in 59 studies on the issue, showing that males who claimed that their abuse was consensual were not significantly less well adjusted than the norm. Dracker (1996) and Gavin (2010) contested these findings, arguing that sexual abuse of both boys and girls has similar effects, or can be even more traumatic in boys as they are not believed. Sexual initiation forms part of the myth that males are always the initiators of sex and therefore cannot be abused. Perceptions such as this, along with the view that child molestation is the province of the male stranger, are not supported by the findings about offenders in both research and practice literature.

Child sex offender typology

Offenders are more likely to be relatives or acquaintances of their victim than strangers. Most reported offenders are male; the percentage of incidents of sexual abuse by female perpetrators is usually reported to be between 5% and 20%, although some studies have identified higher rates (e.g. Gannon & Rose, 2008). Several recent cases have brought the topic of female child sex abusers to the attention of the public, with high levels of shock and disbelief. For example, Vanessa George, an employee at a Plymouth day care centre, pleaded guilty in 2009 to sexually abusing children in her care, and distributing indecent photographs to two other people (one woman and one man) she met via the Internet. All three received prison sentences but there was an interesting level of public outrage and disgust expressed in comparison to similar cases of child sex abuse involving male perpetrators (Gavin, 2010).

Offenders are typically classified by their motivation assessed by reviewing their offence characteristics or phallometric test results. Groth et al. (1982) proposed a simple system that classed offenders as either regressed or fixated. However, some add a third, but rare, category – sadistic offenders (see Figure 8.3 for details).

Children who molest

Children who molest children are usually deemed to be acting out their own sexual victimisation. According to Hershkowitz (2011), some children who molest not only have a history of sexual abuse, but may also have experienced physical and emotional abuse. However, it is by no means a straightforward correlation between sexual abuse victimisation and later sexual offending behaviour, as not all abused children go on to abuse, especially while still in childhood. What is clear is that when a child has been sexually used, abused or overly exposed to adult sexuality, disruptions in multiple areas of the child's sexual development may occur (Cavanagh Johnson & Friend, 1995). The behaviour of concern is distinguished from normal sexual exploration and parents, carers and health professionals need to be educated in the differences. The problem here is that many adults are unwilling to accept that there is such a thing as normal sexual exploration in children. It is expected that 40–75%

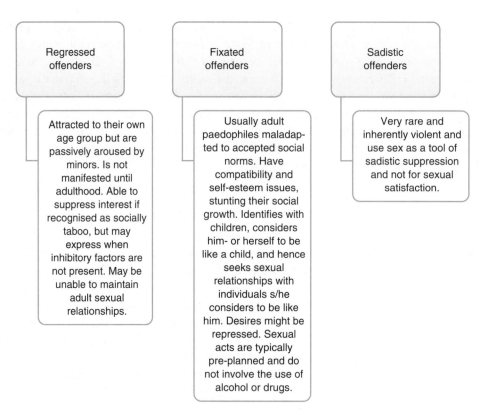

Figure 8.3   Groth's typology of child sex abusers

of children will engage in some sort of sexual behaviour before reaching 13 years of age (Cavanagh Johnson & Friend, 1995). In these situations, children are exploring each other's bodies while also exploring gender roles and behaviours; it does not mean that these children are child sex offenders.

According to Friedrich et al. (1998), a wide range of sexualised behaviours can be observed in children when there is no reason to suspect sexual abuse. Agencies such as the NSPCC (2010) publish excellent literature for parents and professionals to recognise sexualised behaviour in children, as opposed to sexual exploration. According to their research, sexually abusive behaviour will involve children of significantly different ages or developmental stages. The behaviour is out of balance with other aspects of curiosity, continues despite requests to stop, and has adverse effects on other children. It progresses in frequency, intensity or intrusiveness over time and is associated with fear, anxiety, deep shame or intense guilt or anger. None of this is seen in normal sexual exploration, such as the interest a 5-year-old child will show in others' bodies or in an adolescent discussing sexual acts with friends.

Variation in cultural practices, norms and research findings

Green (2002) notes that sexual interactions between adults and children are commonplace and accepted in a variety of cultures. Cultural differences in the view of children and their sexuality mean that it is difficult to universally legislate for child sexual abuse. In different cultures, the practices sanctioned by cultural norms involve male and female circumcision, castration, infibulation, and sexual relationships between adolescent boys and adult men sanctioned by the state and sanctified by religion (in ancient Greece in particular). In Japan, sexual relationships between adolescent boys and adult monks in feudal Japan were tolerated, indeed, encouraged. Again, child prostitution is somewhat tolerated in poor societies as a way for children to support their families. Forensic psychologists need to be aware of the varying cultural practices that migrants may carry with them that are at odds with the society in the adopted country.

Penalties

There is a range of penalties for child sexual abuse crimes, including imprisonment, as well as post-release conditions, such as parole supervision and registration as a sex offender. Paedophilia and child sex abuse are reviled and heavily punished in Western society. It does seem to be a universally censured behaviour, even given the variation in age of consent across the world. However, those who hold quite vehemently negative views about child sex abuse do not necessarily condemn the sexual abuse of adults in quite the same way.

RAPE

Historically, rape was seen in most cultures not as a crime against an individual, but as a crime against the property of the head of the household or against the concept of chastity. As a consequence, the rape of a virgin was viewed as a more serious crime than of a non-virgin, even a wife or widow, and the rape of a prostitute or other unchaste woman was, in some laws, not a crime because her chastity could not be harmed. The penalty for rape was often a fine, payable to the father or the husband whose 'goods' were 'damaged'. That position was later replaced in many cultures by the view that the woman, as well as her lord, should share the fine equally.

In some laws the woman might marry the rapist instead of his receiving the legal penalty. This was especially prevalent in laws where the crime of rape did not include, as a necessary part, that it be against the woman's will, thus dividing the crime in the current meaning of rape, and as a means for a couple to force their families to permit marriage. This should be distinguished from marriage by capture, which is the rape of an abducted woman who is then forced into marriage.

Rape in the course of warfare also dates back to antiquity, and is ancient enough to have been mentioned in the Bible (e.g. Deuteronomy 21:10–14). It is now recognised as an instrumental action rather than a by-product of territorial aggression (Buss, 2009).

In the common law of the United Kingdom, Australia and the United States, rape traditionally describes the act of a man who forces a woman to have sexual intercourse with him. Until the late twentieth century, a husband forcing sex on his wife or a wife forcing sex on her husband was not considered 'rape', since the woman or man (for certain purposes) was not considered a separate legal person with the right of refusal, or sometimes was deemed to have given advance consent to a life-long sexual relationship through the wedding vows. However, most Western common-law countries, as well as civil-law countries, have now legislated against this exception. They now include spousal rape (vaginal intercourse) and acts of sexual violence, such as forced anal intercourse, which were traditionally barred under sodomy laws, in their definitions of 'rape'.

There is a clear *mens rea* element in the law regarding rape, in that the accused must be aware that the victim is not consenting or might not be consenting. However, different jurisdictions vary in how they place the burden of proof with regards to belief of consent. Under English law, until May 2005, a 'genuine' belief that the victim was consenting, even if unreasonable, was sufficient. The law was changed so that belief of consent is now only a defence if the belief is both genuine and reasonable. Under the Sexual Offences Act 2003, rape in England and Wales was redefined from non-consensual vaginal or anal intercourse, and is now defined as non-consensual penile penetration of the vagina, anus or mouth. The maximum sentence of life imprisonment was maintained under the new Act. It also altered the requirements of the defence of mistaken belief in consent so that one's belief must be now both genuine and reasonable, and this cannot be the case when violence is used or feared, the complainant is unconscious, restrained, drugged, or is by reason of disability unable to communicate a lack of consent. Any consent of the complainant is of no relevance if he or she is under the age of 13.

Many people are surprised when women are found to be perpetrators of sexual offences. A woman who forces a man to have sex can now also be prosecuted, as can a woman assisting a man to commit rape, child molestation or sexual assault. A woman can also be prosecuted for causing a man to engage in sexual activity without his consent under section 4 of the 2003 Act, a crime that also carries a maximum life sentence if it involves penetration of the mouth, anus or vagina. Section 2 of the 2003 Act introduces a new sexual offence, 'assault by penetration', with the same punishment as rape. It is committed when someone sexually penetrates the anus or vagina with a part of his or her body, or with an object, without that person's consent. The policy of the 2003 Act is to make offences gender-neutral. However, research demonstrates that there is still a difference in the perception of the typical sex offender (see Gavin, 2005, 2010; Gannon et al., 2008).

Statutory rape

For the rape of children by adults see above. National and/or regional governments treat any sexual contact with a young person below the age of consent as an offence, even if he or she agrees to the sexual activity. The offence is often based on a presumption that people under the age of consent (variously defined) do not have the capacity to give informed consent. Sex that violates age-of-consent law, but is neither violent nor physically coerced, is sometimes described as 'statutory rape', a legally recognised category in several countries, including the United States and Scotland. Several high-profile cases involving celebrities who appear to have committed statutory rape have been discussed at length in the media (see the cases of Roman Polanski, Rob Lowe and Elvis Presley).

Acquaintance ('date') rape

The term, 'acquaintance rape' or 'date rape' refers to rape or non-consensual sexual activity between people who are already acquainted, or who know each other socially. The vast majority of rapes are committed by people who already know the victim. If two people are regularly sexually intimate, in many countries it is not a crime for one partner to have sex with their sleeping or drunk partner even though that partner did not give express consent.

Spousal rape

Also known as marital rape, wife rape, partner rape or intimate partner rape, spousal rape is rape between a married or cohabiting couple. Spousal rape first became a crime in the United States in the state of South Dakota in 1975. It took another 16 years for the idea that women agree to sex on marriage to be changed in the UK (23 October 1991) and it was only applied to all US states in 1993.

It is often assumed that spousal rape is less traumatic than that by a stranger. Research reveals that victims of marital/partner rape suffer longer lasting trauma than victims of stranger rape, possibly because of a lack of social validation that prevents a victim from getting access to support, and the sense of betrayal of an intimate relationship. This is further complicated as the rape often takes place within the wider context of domestic violence (Martin et al., 2007).

Gang rape

Group rape (also known as 'gang' or 'pack' rape) occurs when a group of people participate in the rape of a single victim. Of reported rapes, 10–20% involve more than one attacker. It is thought to be far more damaging to the victim and in some jurisdictions is punished more severely than rape by a single person (Ullman, 2007). Group rape is usually carried out by adolescent or young adult male offenders who see the practice as recreational (Rothman et al., 2008).

Male rape

The fact that men can be raped is often treated with surprise or disbelief, particularly those who are raped by females. Such a response to rape victims is common. The exact number of victims of any form of rape is difficult to ascertain as various agencies estimate that large numbers do not report the attack (HMIC & HMCPSI, 2007). It is thought that this is particularly true for male rape victims, due to higher levels of fear of humiliation and the feeling that they will not be believed.

Rape of males by males

Male-on-male rape is common in incest and other situations (such as in prisons) where men and boys are dependent on elder males and/or are unable to escape stronger males. There are, however, few reliable statistics on male-on-male rape.

Male victims suffer rape-related trauma similar to that seen in female victims. In addition, due to male socialisation to consider all male–male sexual contact to be shameful and to reject victimhood, many male survivors of rape choose not to disclose and report the crime. Rape of male children by adult men in responsible roles is an especially traumatic form of sexual crime that has gained widespread attention, for example in the various Roman Catholic priests' sex abuse cases. Male-on-male rape often does deep damage to or destroys the survivor's image of himself as a man and may cause him to feel helpless and alone among other men.

Rape of males by females

Women also can commit an act of rape or sexual assault by penetration with force or deception to make a man (or adolescent) engage in a non-consensual penetrative sexual act. Rape of males by females is widely, but incorrectly, considered impossible because male erectile response is seen as voluntary, when, in fact, it is involuntary, as can be the case of sexual arousal/response in female victims too (Levin & van Berlo, 2004). Women commit about 2% of all sexual offences (Porter, 2010), although there does not seem to be any distinction in these statistics as to how many of the offences were rape.

Kirk Anderson

In 1977, Kirk Anderson, a Mormon missionary, went missing, disappearing from the steps of his church. A few days later Anderson reappeared and told police he had been abducted and imprisoned, chained to a bed and that Joyce McKinney had raped him. The media attention was wide and salacious, centring on the belief that Anderson must have consented and enjoyed the experience. This disbelief and prurient interest was still apparent 30 years after the case first hit the headlines (see O'Neill, 2008). McKinney could not even be charged with rape, as female rape of men was not recognised as criminal in the 1970s (Gordon, 2008). McKinney was a very slight woman, and it was difficult for the public to see how she could have overcome Anderson, although she is alleged to have had an accomplice, Keith

May. She denied the charges of indecent assault and claimed that Anderson had gone with her willingly and that chaining him up was simply part of sex play. She fled from the UK before the trial and was sentenced to a year in prison in her absence.

The source of disbelief in male victims of rape is the lack of understanding of sexual arousal. Male erectile response is involuntary (Krahé et al., 2003) and therefore does not prevent illegal penetration. Female-on-male rape is often perceived as consensual sex when, in fact, the female sexual predator usually uses covert psychological or emotional coercion to commit the crime (Gavin, 2010). In many countries, male rape is legally classified under a different law or name.

It must be noted that there are some excellent support services available to both male and female victims, for example, within the UK, the Rape Crisis Centres (www.rapecrisis.org. uk) often have facilities to help male victims in addition to those available for women and girls. In addition, Mpower is devoted to male victims (www.male-rape.org.uk).

Drug facilitated rape

Various drugs are used by rapists to render their victims unconscious; some also cause memory loss. Date rape drugs are substances that render a victim unconscious or compliant and able to be easily raped or sexually assaulted. The drug may also be used to allow a victim to be robbed. In cases of sexual assault, in most jurisdictions, the victim's inability to consent to sex may legally constitute rape.

Some commonly known date rape drugs are GHB, ketamine and flunitrazepam (Rohypnol). Despite widespread media hysteria, these drugs are used in only a small minority of rapes. Hypnotic agents such as flunitrazepam (Rohypnol) and gamma-hydroxybutyrate (GHB) have been used by rapists to render victims unconscious, although there is an additional negative outcome in that they can produce anterograde amnesia. However, ketamine, an anaesthetic, and MDMA (Ecstasy), an empathogenic phenylethylamine, both of which are at times referred to as potential date rape drugs, are unlikely to actually be put to this purpose.

Victims may not be aware that they ingested a drug at all. Many drugs are invisible when dissolved and are odourless. Rohypnol can incapacitate victims and prevent them from resisting sexual assault. It can produce specific anterograde amnesia.

There is one drug, however, that is easily, legally and cheaply obtainable, and has been used for centuries to lower inhibition. It also renders people insensible and hence can be put to the rapist's use.

Hayley Jordan

On a sunny afternoon in August 2005, Hayley Jordan and her two young sons attended a barbecue party in the garden of her neighbour (BBC News, 2007). She is reported to have drunk two bottles of wine (approximately 12 units of alcohol; the recommended limit for women is 14 units in a week). There is a great deal of speculation about whether she drank that much knowingly, given that she had her children with her. Whatever the circumstances, she felt ill, so three neighbours, Adam Sorrenti, David Hedges and Kyle Scott, escorted her home. There, clearly under the influence of a great deal of alcohol, she became unconscious. The men stripped her naked and sexually assaulted her in front of her children, filming the attack on a mobile phone.

In the days after the party, Hayley remained oblivious to what had happened, and was only concerned that her 5-year-old son, Daniel, seemed quiet and withdrawn. Meanwhile, the film of the assault, in which Daniel can be heard very clearly crying and pleading with them to stop, was being passed around the neighbourhood. One horrified viewer contacted police, who traced Hayley, and she was shown the tape and interviewed. The consequences of this attack were devastating for Hayley. First, there was the trauma of learning she had been sexually assaulted, and the fact that her memory was faulty, thereby probably supplying horrific embellishment. Secondly, the shame of her neighbours having viewed her degradation and humiliation must also have figured in her dismay. Finally, she was judged to be an unfit mother and her children were taken into care. She committed suicide by an overdose of antidepressants in June 2006.

Two of the men pleaded guilty and were sentenced accordingly, but the third, Scott, pleaded not guilty. This meant that a jury, and Hayley's family, were subjected to the viewing of the tape and hearing Hayley's police interview. The three men were all convicted of sexual assault and sentenced to several years in prison. The case has brought once more to the fore the questions of negligent behaviour by women who drink and fuelled the debate about culpability. The UK's Criminal Injuries Compensation Authority undertakes to evaluate cases to determine compensation for physical or mental injury (CICAS, 2012). In several cases where rape or sexual assault has been proven, the female victims have had their compensation reduced because they had been consuming alcohol before the incident.

Who rapes?

Rape and other sexual offences have been the subject of attempts to profile the crimes in terms of perpetrators and, less frequently, victims. Chapter 14 considers profiling as a form of crime investigation and prevention, with its attendant criticisms. Here, the outcomes of these attempts are discussed with respect to rapists.

Male rapist profiles

Groth described four types of deliberate rapists, based on their motivations and behaviour patterns (see Figure 8.4). Since the data on rape is predominantly based on crimes perpetrated by men, it is thought that these are more applicable to male rapists.

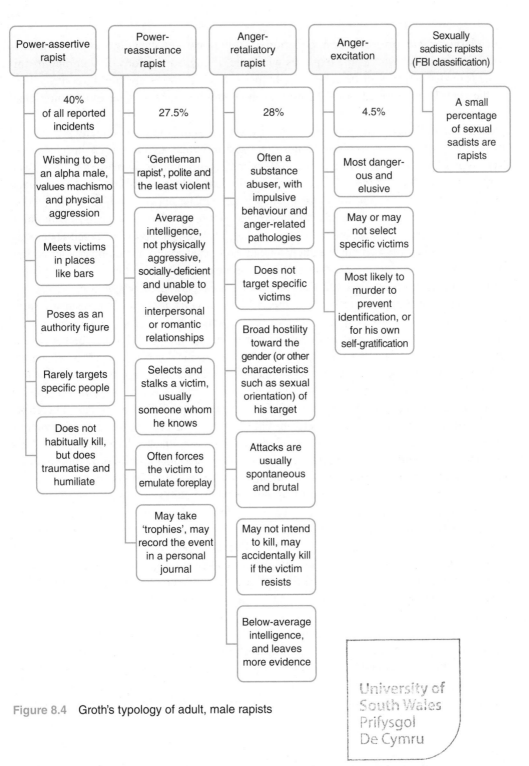

Figure 8.4   Groth's typology of adult, male rapists

Sociobiological/evolutionary theories of rape

Sociobiological theories are the appellation of evolutionary explanations to human behaviour. The sociobiology of rape explores what role, if any, adaptations play in rape in animals (or what appears to be rape) and humans. Such theories are highly controversial as they can be interpreted as explaining, even condoning, rape as a necessary biological response.

Some sociobiologists suggest that our ability to understand rape, and thereby prevent and treat it, is severely compromised because its basis in human evolution has been ignored. They argue that rape is a reproductive strategy that is encountered in many animals; it is a way for males who lack the ability to persuade the female by non-violent means to engage in sex and provide an opportunity pass on their genetic material (Thornhill & Palmer, 2000). It is clear that some animals *appear* to show behaviour resembling rape, such as combining sexual intercourse with force and/or violent assault. These observations of forced sex among animals are not questioned but the interpretation and extension to human behaviour is. It is because rape can result in reproduction that sociobiologists theorise that it may be genetically advantageous for rapists, and thus prospers as a psychological adaptation.

Thornhill and Palmer's argument is that all human behaviours are the result of some evolutionary adaptation. They note that since the human brain and all its capabilities for controlling behaviour evolved from natural selection, the only question is whether rape is only a by-product of another adaptation (such as aggression) or if rape itself is an adaptation favoured because it increases the number of descendants of rapists. They assert that the underlying motivations of rapists evolved because they were at one time conducive to reproduction, and that the majority of rape victims are of childbearing age. Therefore, childbearing ability is the major factor in choice of victims. They also state that victims of childbearing age suffer more emotional trauma from rape than older women, citing this as evidence supporting their theory. They go on to say that they are not providing biological excuses for rape, but rather are examining ways that rape can be eliminated by raising awareness of its evolutionary origins (Thornhill & Palmer, 2000).

Thornhill and Palmer further argue that rape is primarily driven by sexual desire, which is again contrary to the evidence that sexual offending is motivated by power, aggression and a range of negative emotional states (Prentky & Knight, 2000). Thornhill and Palmer (2000) suggest that the predominance of rape attacks on women of childbearing age supports the notion that rapists desire to reproduce through sex. A fundamental flaw with this idea is the lack of explanation for male victims of male rapists, or female victims who are too young or too old to conceive.

There are other scientific criticisms of this theoretical position. In order to determine behaviour as a result of evolutionary processes it must meet certain criteria: first, that it is influenced by genetics and, secondly, that it has an effect on reproductive success. It has been argued that every human behaviour, including sex, is the result of evolution. To demonstrate this would mean identifying genes or group of genes that influence each behaviour.

Tang-Martinez and Mechanic (2001) point out that no study to date has demonstrated a genetic basis for rape in humans, that rape has a very low level of reproductive success, and that there is little empirical data to support the reproductive motivation for rape. They also refer to the spurious discussion of emotional distress as a function of reproductive age, as this does not seem to be less in victims who do not have anxiety over conception.

Other sociobiological theories of rape

There are other sociobiological theories of rape, which support, to an extent, those of Thornhill and Palmer (2000). Human children remain dependent upon their parents for many years. Therefore, mothers must invest significant time and bodily resources in pregnancy in order to reproduce and raise their offspring, whereas males can biologically father considerably more offspring with much less of a bodily investment. Many sociobiologists, such as Buss and Schmitt (1993), argue that this causes females to be more likely to scrutinise their mates, whereas males are more likely to be motivated simply to have many mates. In this view, rape is a male attempt to remove the female's decision-making power regarding reproduction. Proponents of this theory have also stated that during the most fertile part of the female menstrual cycle, women are more likely to pursue potential mates (Johnston et al., 2001) while simultaneously avoiding situations conducive to the possibility of rape (Guéguen, 2012). However, there is contradictory evidence to this, such as reports that appear to show a higher incidence of rape occurring during the less fertile points in the menstrual cycle of the victim, with one exception. Women using birth control medication do not report rape with any bias towards a specific period of their cycles and birth control inhibits ovulation. There is also evidence to suggest that rape is more likely to lead to pregnancy than casual sex, although this is open to many challenges, not least that women do not report one night stands to the police. According to these theories, males who attempt rape are more desperate to mate, and hence misinterpret sexual signals. However, there are behaviours that are indicative of rape-preventative measures to take into account. Women tend to be more cautious about rape in young adulthood. They are also more likely to resist rape, or resist more forcefully, during young adulthood, but, of course, younger women tend to be physically stronger or quicker than older women or children, and more able to resist attack and/or run away.

Sociobiological explanations of rape base their argument on two possible hypotheses. First, rape is a specific adaptation promoted by natural selection in favour of dominant males who rape. Secondly, it is a by-product of evolution in that there is no direct selection for rape, but it is has arisen out of selection for male aggression and indiscriminate mating. The by-product premise is not sound; nor is it refutable, as anything could be said to be a result of another development. For example, language may have developed because it was an evolutionary advantage to be able to warn your relatives of danger, but sarcasm has no clear evolutionary advantage, so it is a by-product of speech development. To suggest that rape is a by-product of male aggression is specious and unhelpful. Therefore, we are left with the adaptive hypothesis. Hagen (2005) states that there is no clear evidence for the hypothesis that rape is adaptive. Moving further than this, some critics argue that it is difficult to determine to what extent the idea of rape can be extended to intercourse in other animal species, as the defining attribute of rape in humans is the lack of informed consent. As such, any attempt to extend this concept to animals is both anthropomorphic and scientifically unsound. Others claim that forced sex in animals is ineffective as a means of reproduction; males will attack other males, or groups of males will attack lone females, killing them in the process. Tang-Martinez and Mechanic (2001) also point out that forced copulation rarely leads to reproductive success. It is evident that rape can be viewed as a strategy linked to female sexuality and reproduction, although most would see these as being culturally conditioned rather than as a product of evolution.

Feminist theory

Feminist theories of sexual coercion hold that all men use rape as a process of intimidation in order to keep all women in a state of fear. Historically, rape and sexual coercion have hindered women's rights to choice and opportunities, sexually and otherwise. With the finding that high proportions of women will be victims of forced sexual acts at least once (HMIC & HMCPSI, 2007), the feminist movement has focused on rape as one of its main issues (Brownmiller, 1975; Malamuth, 1996).

Brownmiller was one of the first researchers to use feminism to explain sexual coercion. She asserts that a key interspecies difference in motivation to engage in sexual activity is the lack of an oestrous cycle in human females. Humans do not have a directly observable oestrus, unlike other primates, and are hypothetically fertile every day of every month. Without a clear biological mating signal, a male can engage in sexual behaviour with a female in a way that is not dependent on biological cycles, and therefore can rape. Brownmiller contends that at some point in our biological history, human males realised they could rape and proceeded to do so.

Most feminists believe sexual coercion is motivated by a desire to exert control over women and not due to lust. Rape, according to feminist theorists, is not necessarily a sexual act but is an act of violence. Violence asserts power, and men use this power to dominate women. This theory views rape as emerging from a social framework that emphasises group conflict. Since men have constructed a patriarchal society in which they are holders of wealth and power, they engage in behaviours that maintain this control, whether consciously or unconsciously. Physically, men are stronger and have sexual anatomy that makes rape possible. Throughout history, men learned that women could be controlled and traumatised by dominating them using sex (Brownmiller, 1975; Malamuth, 1996). Sex and gender roles variously reinforce this, in that girls are taught to be passive and submissive, and boys/men are socialised to devalue women and develop masculine self-concepts, including hostility towards women and sexual arousal from domination. Additionally, disparities in size and strength make women vulnerable to sexual coercion and control. Convicted rapists have been found to hold more violent attitudes towards women, and to be physiologically aroused to the same degree by non-consensual and consensual sexual behaviour (Gannon et al., 2008). Research also suggests that rape is related to sociopolitical and economic disparities by suggesting that rape actually increases with less disparity between the genders, upholding the theory that men rape to maintain an existing hierarchy (Ellis, 1989).

In direct contrast to sociobiological theories, feminist theory asserts that any woman may be a victim of rape, irrespective of her appearance, age and status. Feminist theory also accounts for one of the main criticisms of the evolutionary perceptive, namely that women outside the range of reproductive age and men can be raped. If rape is an expression of aggression, violence and power, then the biological murder to procreate is not a significant factor in the criminal acts.

According to Harrower (1998), further theories of rape include the purely psychological models, in which rapists are themselves victims of abuse or trauma during childhood, leading to deviant values being learnt, and the medical or disease models, in that rapists suffer from a mental illness and are not responsible for their crimes.

Effects of rape and its aftermath

The effects of rape can be physical, psychological, or both. Physical consequences often include injuries, sometimes pregnancy or sexually transmitted disease. Several kinds of psychological results may be experienced over both the short and long term, particularly in child victims, who commonly suffer lasting psychological harm into adulthood. Rape victims often undergo painful social difficulties due to blame for the incident from family, friends or professionals, and frequently fail to report sexual assault because of these and other fears. Due to the intimate nature of sex crimes, psychological effects are commonplace, with immediate and longer lasting symptoms including unpredictable and intense emotions, intrusive thoughts about the assault, nightmares, insomnia and difficulty concentrating. Feelings of self-blame (i.e. personal responsibility for the attack) and feelings of dirtiness are also commonly experienced (Dearing et al., 2005).

Self-blame

Self-blame is among the most common of both short- and long-term effects. It is an avoidance coping skill that inhibits the healing process. It is primarily caused by illogical (or counterfactual) thinking and falls into two main types. Behavioural self-blame means the victim thinks s/he should have done something differently, and the failure to do so leads to feelings of being at fault. Victims who experience characterological self-blame feel there is something inherently wrong with them and hence they deserved to be assaulted (Frazier et al., 2005).

Characterological self-blame is a serious barrier to healing because of the feeling of shame, which promotes withdrawal, lack of motivation to seek care, lack of empathy, disconnection from other people, anger and aggression (Tangney et al., 2005). This can be associated with eating disorders, substance abuse, anxiety and depression.

Secondary victimisation

Rape victims are more likely to be stigmatised in cultures with strong customs and taboos regarding sex and sexuality. For example, a rape victim (especially one who was previously a virgin) may be viewed by society as being 'damaged'. Victims in these cultures may suffer isolation, be disowned by friends and family, be prohibited from marrying or even killed. This phenomenon is known as secondary victimisation, the re-traumatising of the victim through the responses of individuals and institutions. Types of secondary victimisation include victim-blaming and inappropriate post-assault behaviour or language by medical personnel or other organisations with which the victim has contact (Campbell & Raja, 1999). Secondary victimisation is particularly seen in cases of drug-facilitated, acquaintance and statutory rape. Kennedy (1993) suggested that the forms of secondary victimisation can extend to the court room because the mythology surrounding rape serves in the same way as legal precedent, that the ruling in a prior case is applied in the present one. Such myths include the idea that rape is only commited by strangers, at night, with a weapon or means of force, that the victim is always injured because they will always resist, that victims, particularly women, put themselves at risk of rape by 'provocative' clothing or other behaviour, that lack of prompt reporting means the rape was not 'real' and that everyone behaves the same way after being raped (RapeCrisis, 2012).

In addition to any physical trauma, the victim is usually subjected to intimate questions and medical examination, and this can be difficult for female victims in societies that do not accord equal civil rights to both sexes, but is often a problem for any victim. In societies where denial, sexual stereotyping and pervasive double standards exist, any victim of rape can suffer secondary victimisation when they seek support from legal, medical and psychological professionals.

Victim-blaming

The term victim-blaming refers to holding the victim of a crime to be responsible for that crime, either in whole or in part. In the context of rape, it refers to the attitude that certain victim behaviours (such as flirting or wearing sexually provocative clothing) may have encouraged the assault. In most Western countries, the defence of provocation is not accepted as a mitigation for rape, but it is unclear to what extent such views might be present in juries or law professionals. It has been proposed that one cause of victim-blaming is the 'just world' hypothesis. People who believe that the world is intrinsically fair may find it difficult or impossible to accept a situation in which a person is badly hurt for no reason. This leads to a sense that victim must have behaved in a way that indicates they deserved their injury.

SUMMARY

What all of the things discussed so far tell us is that sexual deviance or violence is a multi-dimensional concept and our understanding of it is incomplete. Public perception of sexual non-conformity is coloured by the stereotypes, culture, religion and even media representation of sex. There do appear to be some significant research advances in understanding clinical characteristics of various types of sexual offence. However, even research issues are clouded by the researchers' own values and beliefs. Whether one is a Freudian psychodynamicist or a neurological reductionist can depend as much on one's own nature as on the compelling (or not) nature of the theoretical positions. There is no single cause of sex offending just as there are no typical sex offenders. It is therefore practical to draw on a variety of ideas when researching sexual offences or treating individual offenders.

Discussion point: How do we view female child sex offenders?

Female sex offenders are often viewed in terms of their relationship with a male offender, either as being coerced by a male sexual predator into helping him or as being a willing participant in male-initiated crime. Increasingly, however, women are seen as acting as sexual predators themselves. This is slowly being recognised by law enforcement and the criminal justice system. Why has it taken so long to recognise that the sexual abuse of children by women is one of the most under-reported crimes? The papers below investigate views of female sexual offending and can be used to start a discussion about the public and professional opinion of this under-recognised group.

Gannon, T.A. & Rose, M.R. (2008) Female child sexual offenders: towards integrating theory and practice. *Aggression and Violent Behavior*, **13**(6): 442–461.

Gavin, H. (2010) 'Mummy wouldn't do that': the perception and construction of the female child sex abuser. In M. Barrett and T. Porter (eds), *Grotesque Femininities: Evil, Women and the Feminine*. Global Interdisciplinary Research Studies Series. Oxford: The Inter-Disciplinary Press, pp. 61–78.

The Psychology of Firesetting

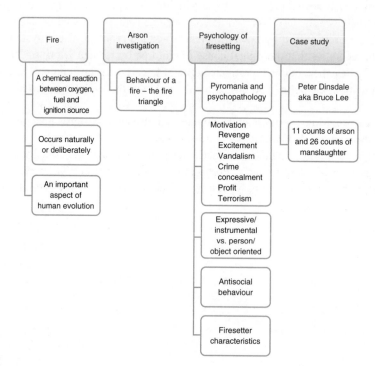

Fire	Arson investigation	Psychology of firesetting	Case study
A chemical reaction between oxygen, fuel and ignition source	Behaviour of a fire – the fire triangle	Pyromania and psychopathology	Peter Dinsdale aka Bruce Lee
Occurs naturally or deliberately		Motivation Revenge Excitement Vandalism Crime concealment Profit Terrorism	11 counts of arson and 26 counts of manslaughter
An important aspect of human evolution		Expressive/ instrumental vs. person/ object oriented	
		Antisocial behaviour	
		Firesetter characteristics	

Peter Dinsdale worshipped the martial arts movie star Bruce Lee and changed his name to that of his idol. The son of a prostitute, Peter/Bruce had epileptic fits, congenital spastic hemiplegia[1] in his right limbs, and was a homosexual child sex predator known to his community as 'Daft Peter'. He is also Britain's most prolific serial fatal arsonist, admitting to setting more than 30 fires, and has been convicted of the manslaughter of 26 victims. He is reported as saying that at least one fire was started because he had a grudge against the family, but the others were simply for the pleasure derived from fire.

KEY THEMES

- Defining arson
- Typology
- Firesetting
- Functional analytical model
- Mental disorder
- Psychodynamic models

Fire is a chemical reaction between atmospheric oxygen and a fuel substance (wood, petrol, etc.) that is started due to some ignition source bringing these two components to ignition temperature. This ignition can be a natural force, such as lightning, or from a more controlled source, such as a match. Hence fire can be a natural occurrence or it can be accidentally or deliberately started by the action or inaction of one or more people. The problem with fire is that these chemical reactions are self-perpetuating as long as there is sufficient oxygen and fuel. In other words, fire spreads.

Fire is a major factor in humanity's development. Every culture has myths surrounding the discovery of fire or how it was gifted by mythical creatures. In Ancient Greek mythology, fire is given to humans by Prometheus, the god of Forethought. To punish Prometheus, Zeus, the chief of the gods, chained him to a rock where a vulture would peck out his liver all day. As Prometheus is a god and immortal, the liver grows back in the night and he must suffer the ordeal every day for eternity. This story shows how ancient societies regarded fire as something potent; they viewed it as something that the gods wished to withhold from them. It is hardly surprising, then, that some humans have developed a strange relationship with it.

Fire allows us to cook food and affords warmth and protection. It also means that early humans could extend activity into the hours of nightfall. Controlling fire has major implications for human evolution both physically and culturally; taking fire from

---

[1]A neuromuscular condition of spasticity that results in the muscles on one side of the body being in a constant state of contraction.

a natural source, such as volcanic eruptions or lightning strikes, led to the ability to control it for specific uses, resulting in a fire-adapted species able to produce fire (Medler, 2011). Fire-specific adaptations include different dentition and digestion due to cooking food. Anthropological evidence suggests that such changes in digestion (e.g. a shorter intestine is needed to digest cooked food), is synchronous with the development of a larger skull, housing the much bigger brain of the modern *Homo sapiens* (Wrangham, 2009). There are several hotly debated suggestions about when all this happened, given that the uncontacted people of the Andaman Islands, who live in complete isolation, appear not to have developed the use or control of fire, but do have the larger cranium seen in modern humans. However, this is not important to psychology; it is clear that our physical evolution owes much to fire and its control was an important aspect, whenever it happened.

What about our psychological development? Has fire affected the way that our psychological evolution has progressed? If, as Wrangham (2009) suggests, the change in digestion was paralleled with the growth in cranium size and, by implication, brain size, then there must have been some profound neuropsychological changes going on too. Controlled fire suggests that not only was cooking happening, but also communication and social grouping. Evolutionary psychologists suggest that this was the start of the large groupings now observed in every human society. Even Freudian psychology has something to say about it: that flames appear to be phallic symbols and putting out the flames with a stream of urine satisfies some infantile pleasure. The person who was able to suppress this urge and to take fire away with him [sic] was the first to understand that there are uses other than its destructive force (Freud, 1930). Freud does not consider the possibility that the first person to do this – to not extinguish fire with a stream of urine, thereby declaring this masculine ability – might just have been a woman.

Undoubtedly, the ability to use fire, to control and fashion it, was part of our evolution in terms of our food, our living arrangements and even exploration outside our own world. With this power has come the threat of fire that gets out of control, the burning of our environment, our habitat, and even ourselves. This means fire can be used in criminal ways. 'Arson', also called 'deliberate firesetting', is the crime of setting a fire with intent to cause damage. The definition of arson was originally limited to setting fire to buildings, but was later expanded to include other objects, such as bridges and vehicles. In the UK, of all criminal damage offences reported to the police, arson forms 4%, with almost 35,000 incidents in 2009 (Home Office, 2010). Arson is the single main cause of fires, with an estimated annual cost to property of over £2 billion in the UK alone (Arson Prevention Bureau, 2010), with inestimable cost to lives.

Arson – the act of deliberately and maliciously setting a fire with intent to cause damage.

Arsonist – someone who commits this act.

Firesetting – the intentional setting of a fire but not necessarily with the malicious intent to cause damage. **Firesetting** is the preferred term clinically, with arson being the legal term of firesetting with intent to cause damage.

ARSON INVESTIGATION

The forensic examination of arson starts when the fire is ended. It must therefore involve the reconstruction of the incident and the investigator needs an in-depth knowledge of the chemistry and behaviour of a fire. According to Daeid (2005), the basic behavioural nature of a fire is usually described as the 'arson triangle' or 'fire triangle' – fuel source, oxidant and energy – although a fourth factor is also involved – the self-sustaining chemical reaction that ensures fire will endure (see Figure 9.1).

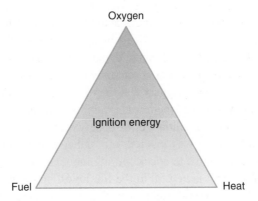

Figure 9.1   The fire triangle (Daeid, 2005)

Arson means that one or more of these factors has been manipulated, such as increasing the level of fuel or adding accelerant material (such as petrol, alcohol or similar), or adding oxygen by opening windows. Fire follows the elements of the triangle. For example, fire burns upwards in a V pattern, and opening a window on the upper floor of a building will cause a fire to drive upwards more rapidly. As it get hotter, it travels upwards more quickly, and the presence of combustible materials will accelerate the process, increasing the temperature and thus the speed of the fire. The path of the fire will be influenced by air currents and the presence of walls and stairways. A wall will prevent fire, or at least delay it; a stairwell is open and will allow fire to move. The actions of fire-fighters will also have an influence on the course of a fire. If they need to open doors to rescue people, for example, the fire will spread in a different pattern than if the doors remain closed. The understanding of the behaviour of a fire is essential to investigators. Being able to understand the investigators' process of analysis of this behaviour can aid understanding of the psychology of firesetters, in terms of whether a fire was deliberately set, and whether it was set for revenge or profit, for example.

Understanding the behaviour of a fire in this way is a basic skill for a fire investigator. Observations from fire-fighters can aid the investigator, as they too are trained to note the fire's behaviour in order to maintain their safety and facilitate the extinguishing of the fire. They can also note if there has been any manipulation that could not be done by accident or nature. For example, in addition to igniting a fire, a lightning strike would cause damage that would be absent if the ignition was by an artificially introduced source. The fire-fighter, then, becomes the first witness to be interviewed; in this way, any damage to evidence caused by fire-fighter actions can be identified and fire-fighters' first impressions of the position and track of the fire can be gained. Other witnesses will also be interviewed and give impressions of how the fire progressed and any other evidence they may have observed. For example, colour of the flames and smoke can give clues to the material burning.

In addition to the behaviour of the fire, other observations made by fire-fighters and other people present in an official capacity (police officers, etc.) can be helpful. For example, noting familiar or unfamiliar faces watching the fire can be revealing. If the fire-fighters regularly see someone who does not belong in the area but has appeared at several fires, this could be an indication that there is serial arsonist to blame. Secondly, fire-fighters can observe within the building while the fire is still going, depending on the need for safety and rescue, of course. Any items unusually present or absent may indicate a suspicious fire; for example, the absence of valuable items may suggest that they have been removed prior to the fire to prevent their loss, so whoever moved them was aware of their intent.

An investigation following this initial set of observations will examine motives for the fire, such as whether a building was insured, etc. Other experts may be included at this stage, such as forensic accountants to check for any monetary motive for a fire. This is the point when psychological input is helpful to the fire investigator, as forensic psychology is more concerned with why the fire was set than with how it progressed. The consideration of psychological factors in a fire and its setting will range from understanding any pathological influences to the psychology of fraud.

Arson is a relatively easy crime to commit, and the perpetrators can usually leave before the fire starts or comes to any attention, hence arsonists are difficult to apprehend and convict. In addition, the fire-fighters are concerned with fighting the blaze, not protecting evidence, and can destroy much of what is needed to investigate the cause of the fire.

THE PSYCHOLOGY OF FIRESETTING

The psychology of arson or firesetting and its investigation must first consider whether the behaviour is the result of a pathological condition. There is a psychological illness that can result in arson, but pyromania (from Greek *pyre*, meaning fire, and *mania*, meaning loss of reason) is diagnosed extremely rarely.

Pyromania (compulsive firesetting)

Pyromania is a rare mental disorder in which the firesetter has an uncontrollable impulse to burn things and may even derive sexual satisfaction from watching the flames consume something. Pyromania is classified in the *Diagnostic and Statistical Manual of Mental*

Disorders as an impulse control disorder, other examples of which are obsessive–compulsive disorder and alcoholism (American Psychiatric Association, 2013). These disorders have various things in common, including a build-up of tension to irresistible levels before engaging in the behaviour and a feeling of relief or pleasure afterwards. The treatment of all of these disorders is either difficult or not well evaluated.

Pyromania is either an impulse or a compulsion to set fires. A compulsion requires more planning than an impulse, and as setting a fire requires forethought, it is therefore likely that it is a compulsive issue. The diagnostic criteria include the requirement that the person has set more than one destructive fire and that the impulse control disorder sequence of strong arousal before and pleasure or tension reduction after the act must be present. There must also not be any other external motive for setting the fire. Profit-motivated arson is rarely carried out by people with pyromania, although it would seem to be a perfect choice of profession! However, pyromania is often associated with poor learning skills and emotional difficulties, making behavioural interventions sometimes helpful. If pyromania is diagnosed in childhood, then treatment can be very effective, but adults can be resistant.

According to the DSM-V, the symptoms of pyromania are:

- deliberate and purposeful firesetting on more than one occasion
- tension or affective arousal before the act
- fascination with, interest in, curiosity about, or attraction to fire and its situational contexts (e.g. paraphernalia, uses, consequences)
- pleasure, gratification or relief when setting fires, or when witnessing or participating in their aftermath
- the firesetting is not done for monetary gain, as an expression of socio-political ideology, to conceal criminal activity, to express anger or vengeance, to improve one's living circumstances, in response to a delusion or hallucination, or as a result of impaired judgement (e.g. in dementia, mental retardation, substance intoxication)
- the firesetting is not better accounted for by Conduct Disorder, a Manic Episode, or Anti-Social Personality Disorder (American Psychiatric Association, 2013)

It would seem that a true pyromaniac just likes fire. There are other mental disorders associated with firesetting, and pyromania is rarely diagnosed. However, firesetters often come to the attention of mental health professionals due to other forms of illness being present, which may or may not be the reason for the firesetting behaviour. One of the first systematic analyses of the mental disorders found in firesetters was carried out by Harris and Rice (1996). They examined 243 male patients in a maximum security hospital; the sample included 208 firesetters. They obtained measurements from clinical files, which included information from police reports, families, other institutions in which the patients had been housed and the patients directly. The measurements were on items such as childhood and adult aggression, IQ and number of fires set. A cluster analysis revealed subsets of firesetters. These categories were associated with dimensions that the researchers identified as psychotics, unassertive, multiple firesetters and criminals. Each of these groups was distinguished from the others by firesetting behaviour and levels of violence. The multiple firesetters also had a distinction between the time their higher number of fires was set, childhood or adulthood. An analysis of fire types, instead of firesetter type, showed a distinction between fires in which damage and injury was low or high. Unfortunately, there was no association between the firesetter and type of fire, which would have been useful as a profiling aid for fire investigators.

The subtype 'psychotics' were of particular interest to psychology, of course. Here the illness was largely delusional and the firesetting was not linked to criminal or aggressive behaviour, or any history of substance abuse. However, they were likely to carry on setting fires unless treated. The group Harris and Rice (1996) called unassertives, on the other hand, had little history of aggression, or much criminality, were of higher IQ, and many gave motivations for firesetting as anger or revenge, as their lack of assertiveness led to them being unable to express the emotion in socially acceptable ways. Multiple firesetters were likely to come from unstable homes which had led to poor academic performance, and they had histories of institutionalisation as children and later, but no history of psychosis. They were also unassertive, however, leading to the expression of negative emotion through setting fires. The smallest subset comprised the criminals, who had extensive criminal history, were likely to come from abusive childhood households, and a large proportion of them exhibited personality disordered behaviour.

Harris and Rice had found a basic typology of firesetters which, although it did not correlate with fire type, has proved a useful basis on which to perform other research. For example, Geller (2008) examined the typology from this and other research to examine types of firesetting that are the most destructive. He centred on motivation as well as the type of firesetter, and concluded that the crime of arson appears as 'mysterious' due to the difficulty in apprehending the firesetter, and that research is needed to aid the investigative process.

Concentrating on the firesetter rather than the fire has proved more fruitful for psychology, however, in that Fritzon et al. (2011) proposed a model of firesetting based on the functions of the behaviour, using previous literature as a starting point, but incorporating empirical narrative data from firesetters' accounts of themselves. This model, they hoped, would be applicable in treatment processes for firesetters. Focusing on mentally disordered offenders, Tyler and Gannon (2012) concluded that, despite the research that had been called for many times, the literature was still showing little understanding of why mentally disordered people set fires. They discovered there was little research examining firesetters in comparison to other mentally disordered offenders. Mental illness is one factor to explain the reasons for firesetting, but it is a significant one and it remains relatively unexplored.

A related but different issue in the psychopathology of firesetting is the sexual arousal and gratification that can be derived from the setting of fires, including the planning of the act, the firesetting itself and the watching of the fire burn. This is a little known condition that is separate from pyromania, called pyrophilia, or the love of fire. This can entail completely separate behaviours from those found in pyromania, although there is obviously good deal of overlap too. The condition is not universally accepted; indeed, the scientific literature is much more likely to describe pyrophiliac plants or beetles than humans. It is also sometimes referred to as pyrolagnia, due to the release of tensions associated with urinating on a fire (Horley & Bowlby, 2011).

However, most people who set fires do not meet these diagnostic criteria of either pyromania or psychotic illness, and research needs to examine the characteristics of arsonists outside the problems of mental illness. There is a clear distinction between those who set fires due to mental disorder, such as pyromania, and those who do so for more concrete purposes. The two categories are not necessarily mutually exclusive.

Motivations for firesetting

According to the FBI classification manual (Douglas et al., 2006), arson/firesetting as an action can be classified in terms of the motivation for the crime. The figures for prevalence of motivations are from nationally compiled statistics that the FBI researchers have drawn on (see Figure 9.2).

Revenge, comprising 41% of the reasons for firesetting, is retaliation for some real or imagined wrong by destruction of property or even by putting lives at risk through fire. The attack is focused on what might be characterised as individuals but this is a broad range of targets, such as an individual person, or specific businesses or even schools, especially in juveniles. All the targets will have some connection with the offender, possibly an acrimonious association, indicating interpersonal or professional conflict. It is this group that contains the largest number of female arsonists too. Koenraadt (2010) discovered that of the number of arsonists examined, only 11% are female, but that the predominant motivation for firesetting was revenge, and the likely target was something of significance to the victim, such as cars or houses. The fire may be quite small and confined, and contained to clothing or bedding. This is coupled to a high level of personality disorders and low self-esteem, and this person is more likely to set fires near his or her home, which is usually where the target of their revenge is, of course. However, male arsonists tend to travel longer distances from home, especially if their motivation is revenge. They also burn more than the female arsonist and use excessive amounts of accelerant and/or incendiary material, which the female arsonist does not tend to use. They will typically be of low educational attainment and have problems with authority, and are likely to have a history of nuisance calls to the police.

Fire is destructive, it is noisy and it is bright. On a more modern note, fire engines are large, noisy and bright. This is all exciting to someone with little understanding that lives are at risk. Excitement as a motivation forms around 30% of the fires the FBI researchers examined, with precipitating factors such as boredom, thrill cycles (including sexual thrills) and the need for attention. Fires are set in public areas, usually outdoors, so the offender can watch the ensuing reactions from panicked bystanders to the arrival of the large fire engine and the heroic fire-fighters. The firesetter will use material at the scene, but will sometimes bring items with them, particularly incendiary devices. If the excitement motivation is linked to sexual excitement, then investigators will often find biological material, such as ejaculate or faeces, at the scene. There may also be evidence of substance abuse, as the older excitement arsonist may have a history of alcoholism or drug use. S/he will also tend to stay and watch the result of the fire.

Vandalism, the motivating drive for 7% of the fires, is deliberate damage to or destruction of property, and is more likely to be carried out by juveniles (see Chapter 5). Vandalism is often seen as a form of attention seeking, but this seems to be a minimisation of the destructive force of vandalism, particularly that which has firesetting as its main behavioural outcome. Fire, even as vandalism, is well beyond the nuisance behaviour of juveniles acting out. Kolko and Kazdin (1994) found that firesetters who were adolescent had high levels of other antisocial behaviours in their repertoire and higher levels of aggression than other youth or other firesetters. They also engage in other forms of property destruction, and there is often a history of crimes against both property and people (fighting, sexual assault, etc.). Due to the nature of the more aggressive crimes, little attention is placed on vandalism, including firesetting. However, attention-seeking behaviours are often found in the juvenile firesetter, who may be manipulating the environment in order to get a reaction from parents and authorities. Schwartzman et al. (1994) suggested that the function of the attention-seeking behaviour is both provocation and to receive any reaction, even if that was negative reinforcement or punishment, and that this was more likely to happen in households that would be regarded as neglectful of a child's needs (Luby et al., 1995).

Setting fire to a house with a murder victim in it seems to some killers an appropriate way to deal with the body. Crime concealment forms 10% of the motivations for arson. Other crimes can also be concealed by fire, such as theft and burglary, or it can be used to destroy documents, so the arson is a secondary criminal activity. Concealment of a murder attempts to obliterate the evidence that homicide has taken place, or to conceal the victim's identity, or the evidence identifying and linking the offender to the homicides. An autopsy would determine if any bodies found in the aftermath of a fire died before or after the fire was started, as living victims would breathe in smoke, etc. However, there is also the use of fire as a murder weapon to consider. Several victims grouped together would also lead to suspicion that the fire was deliberately lethal or was used to conceal other activity. Fire investigators often note excessive use of accelerant material, possibly an attempt to ensure the fire obliterates whatever is being concealed. An interesting point that the FBI manual suggests is that in order to conceal a sexual assault, the victims will often have what is term a 'DNA torch' – a concentration of burns around the genital area, indicating that the perpetrator understands that bodily fluids can be used to provide DNA matches.

Setting fire to insured properties is a major insurance fraud. In addition, setting fire to a competitor's place of business would gain the firesetter more trade. Profit-motivated arson is the least emotion-laden of all reasons for setting fires, and is likely to be well planned and methodical. The crimes scene is organised and may show that the offender has some knowledge of forensic investigation techniques. Items of value may be removed prior to the fire, along with personal items, indicating that the firesetter could be the owner of the arson

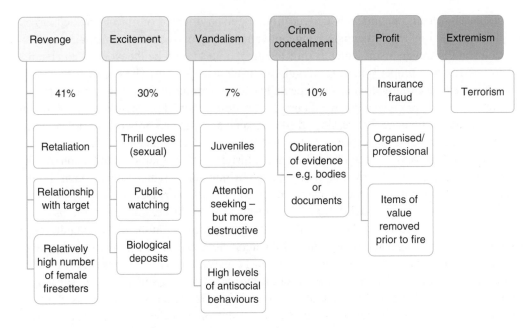

Figure 9.2   Motivations for firesetting

target. The means for setting a fire for profit tend to be more sophisticated than other forms of arson, and the offender is older, on average. There is also the 'arson for hire' element, in which someone will burn a property on behalf of someone else, removing the emotional link even further. Business properties that are burnt are often failing, and the fire is an attempt to recoup lost revenue by making an insurance claim.

The final motivation for arson is that of extremism or terrorism, which is covered in Chapter 7.

These motivations relate to the outcome of the fire, and are not really indicative of the firesetter. While some characteristics of the offender can be linked to each motivation, it has been noted that these overlap and confuse the move, the firesetter characteristics and the cause of firesetting behaviour (Prins, 1994). The end product of arson, for whatever reason it was set, is destruction, and the knowledge of the motivation may aid investigation but does little to aid understanding of the firesetter. More understanding could lead to preventative measures as well as legal and rehabilitative ones.

Canter and Fritzon (1998) suggested a different classification, one which is less linear and addresses the issue of overlap. They studied 175 case files of arson across England and tested a hypothesis related to the forms of motivation and targets. They suggest that arson can be clearly seen not simply as an act of destruction, but as a set of interactions with the world that follows a process from source of motivation to the form of destruction. In this framework, there are four classifications which demonstrate an interaction between these two facets. The first facet is whether the arson is derived from a person-oriented or object-oriented target, and the second is whether the underlying motivation is expressive or instrumental. Hence an instrumentally driven arson which is directed at an object could be the work of an arsonist who sets fire to a property in order to gain the insurance pay-out. The object is the house or factory etc., the motivation is instrumentally driven in order to gain money. Similarly, an expressive object-oriented arson would involve the destruction of property but for emotional reasons, such as revenge. Expressive person-oriented arson is probably the most dangerous form, whether to another person or to the arsonist, as suicide by arson would suggest that the emotional distress has been turned inwards. Instrumental person-oriented arson, on the other hand, is a reaction to frustration engendered by interaction with another person and the action is revenge, but in a focused manner directed towards the person.

Such classifications are helpful, and also result in more discussion about the psychology of firesetting. However, there is still a lack of consensus about the underlying drives to setting fires. There appears to be difficulty distinguishing the firesetter from other types of offender, perhaps because, as Soothill et al. (2004) suggest, for many arson is simply another offence among others. This approach considers the pathways to arson that those detected of it have taken. Here we see two distinctions being made again, but with the focus being on the firesetter and his/her mentality rather than the outcome of the fire. This distinction is between those who set fires due to an overall tendency towards antisocial behaviours, and those who do so because they are attracted to fire.

Antisocial behaviour and arson

Antisocial behaviour linked to arson is seen in both adolescents and adults. There is a prevalence in this group for the traits related to an anti-social personality disorder (ASPD, see Chapter 4) or conduct disorders (see Chapter 5). The antisocial firesetter is also likely to display a range of behaviours typical of the individual with ASPD, such as truancy, stealing and vandalism, and could be linked to the developmental issue noted in this general classification (Vaughn et al., 2010). With respect to linkages between firesetting and other antisocial behaviour, such as suggested by the MacDonald Triad (1963; see Chapter 6), there is little to suggest that there is a link between firesetting, bedwetting and cruelty to animals, despite psychoanalytical examination of extreme violence (Overton et al., 2012).

There is a difficulty with this characterisation of firesetters, as many detected arsonists do not come from developmentally adverse background, and some do not exhibit the range of antisocial behaviour or the traits associated with the personality disorder. However, it is clear that antisocial behaviour is predictive of firesetting, particularly in adolescents (MacKay et al., 2006). Although many fires are profit-motivated, and most other motivations are those most likely to be true of adults, research shows that the number of child firesetters is on the rise. A large proportion of those arrested for arson are under the age of 18, which may reflect the possibility they are simply not sophisticated or mature enough to hide the evidence rather than that higher numbers of children are setting fires. In addition, firesetting by both adults and children can be the result of pathological behaviours.

Arson as a pathological fascination with fire

MacKay et al. (2006) also suggested that, in addition to antisocial behaviour, an interest in fire can be predictive of arson. Here they noted that heightened arousal, indicative of excitement around fire, predicts the likelihood of setting fires simply for the 'rush' that the experience provides. Such excitement can be indicative of the potential for firesetting and this can be, in some cases, in exclusion to any other criminal or antisocial behaviours. This may be where the pyromaniac firesetter is located, but due to the criteria of pyromania as a disorder (see above), the interest in fire itself is not enough to attract a diagnosis. Pyromania is a diagnostic category of exclusion in terms of other antisocial behaviours, substance abuse and psychoses, and therefore could exist alongside these exclusionary characteristics, but would be diagnosed as such.

Classifications of arson, then, tend to rest either with the reason for setting the fire or the pathological or otherwise status of the firesetting individual. What do these examinations of firesetters tell us about the psychology of this antisocial and criminal act?

THE PSYCHOLOGY OF ARSON

Psychological research on arson tends to concentrate in two main areas. The first is the characteristics of people who set fires, beyond that occurring in pyromania, and examines motivations and attempts to create typologies based on the features of those motivations. The second approach, under the heading of psychodynamics, examines what has been termed a functional analytical model, that is, attempts to understand why people engage in certain behaviours and how they might be prevented.

Firesetter characteristics

Some research into the types of people who are involved in arson has evolved from offender profiling (see Chapter 12). For arson investigators, the important elements are the fire scene itself, but these do not necessarily lead to an understanding of the arsonist. Starting with a deduced motivation for the fire, profiling attempts to classify arsonists on the basis of this reason for setting the fire and the potential outcome for the firesetter. Profiling studies and applications have tended to focus on serial murder and serial rape, but Kocsis (2004) attempted to demonstrate that psychological profiles could be used in arson investigations. He used a simulated profiling exercise with professional profilers (people who had been consulted in this capacity by the police), fire service arson investigators and police officers, and students as a control group. Utilising a solved serial arson case, in which all the pertinent factors were already established but were unfamiliar to the participants, a case package containing all the information available to the real investigators, up to the point of arrest, was compiled. The participants were given this and a multiple choice questionnaire. Using a solved case meant the answers could be evaluated against the proven facts of the case. Fire service personnel who investigate fires are focused on determination of the cause and origin of fires and police officers concentrate on investigating suspects, hence they are a good comparison to profilers who are tasked with constructing the characteristics of the person who may be responsible. The findings indicated that the profilers were significantly more accurate in predicting the miscreants than the other groups. This accuracy extended to physical characteristics, social history and habits of the offender. This can be interpreted as showing that profiling can be an important tool in the investigation of arson, particularly if there is cause to examine the cognitive processes operating in the offender or behaviours at the crime scene. These results are only representative of the very small sample used in this study and lack the inherent anxieties of a real case, which may heighten the need for moving quickly to decisions about investigative tactics. It does seem to suggest, however, that profiling techniques are a fruitful way of understanding arsonists – who they are and why they set fires.

A second major theoretical position about the attraction of fire is the psychodynamic approach, first applied by Freud himself in 1932. Freud suggested that there was a sexual element to fire, and hence firesetting, and that the urge to put out fire with a stream of urine (by males) was homosexual in nature. Coupled to this is that the ability to control the urge is a major development in human nature. Freudian psychology has moved on somewhat since then, of course. It even allows for the inclusion of the female perspective, rather missing in the stream of urine hypothesis. Modern psychoanalytical approaches, whether or not they can explain delinquent behaviours such as firesetting, do seem to be an effective mode of treatment. Psychosexual stages of development can be used as a basis for a classification system for firesetters, which leads to a set of behaviour indicators, providing treatment strategies. Each psychosexual stage is linked to a set of firesetting psychological factors representative of other repressed and fixated behaviours seen in that stage. Treatment strategies linked to the stage are most effective (Taylor et al., 2004). Thus linkage and the treatment focus has not been examined with clear replicable research, although this can be levelled at any psychodynamic approach. However, it does seem to work. The first major attempt to apply this theory was when Lewis and Yarnell (1951) arrived at a number of subgroups within a large sample of pathologic firesetters. Excluding the for-profit arsonist, they classified the subgroups as motivated firesetters, pyromaniacs, volunteer firemen/would-be-heroes, vagrants, those with related sexual activity, and psychotics. Their motivated firesetters included those who set fires for revenge, jealousy and attempted suicide. However, the study is very descriptive and gives little theoretical background to the classification.

SUMMARY

Research on arson and arsonists is very sparse. As late as 2007, Canter and Almond were recommending large research projects into the extent of the problem and the characteristics and motivations of arsonists, particularly adults arsonists, as most work has concentrated on children. The difficulty of working with arsonists can be highlighted when trying to apply any theories to case studies. Bruce Lee/Peter Dinsdale, for example, typifies the low intellect and problematic sexuality of the arsonists in the psychodynamic approach, but does not fit glibly into any one category. 'Daft Peter' loved fires, but was also motivated by revenge. Any examination of arson must include the caveat that we know very little about deliberately set fires and the people who set them.

Discussion point: How can psychology contribute to identifying serial arson and serial arsonists?

Serial arsonists or firesetters are people who, according to the FBI (Douglas et al., 2006), set three or more fires, with a significant period between them. This does not include the profit-motivated arsonist, but refers to firesetters who exhibit the pattern associated with revenge, excitement or extremism. There is evidence of organisation, particularly when the offender has got away with previous firesetting episodes. There is therefore use of an accelerant, but the arsonist may also simply use what is to hand at the scene. The main problem encountered by the fire investigator is linkage of the crimes in order to identify them as a series committed by the same offender(s) and identification of the type of person they are seeking, as there is a range of motivations for firesetting. How might psychology and its techniques be of value when investigating arson and identifying it as serial arson, and then identifying the serial arsonist?

Ellingwood, H., Mugford, R., Bennell, C., Melnyk, T. & Fritzon, K. (2012) Examining the role of similarity coefficients and the value of behavioural themes in attempts to link serial arson offences. *Journal of Investigative Psychology and Offender Profiling*, **10** (1): 1–27.
Icove, D.J. & Horbert, P.R. (1990) Serial arsonists: an introduction. *Police Chief*, **57**(12): 3.

The Psychology of Theft, Robbery and Burglary

10

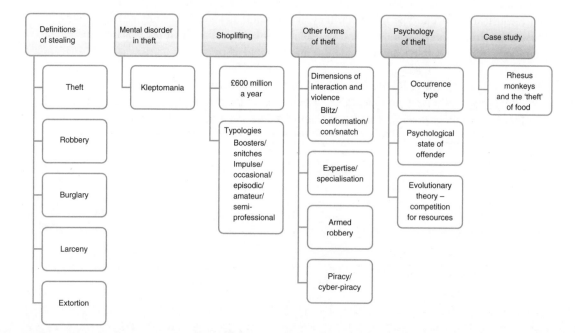

Definitions of stealing	Mental disorder in theft	Shoplifting	Other forms of theft	Psychology of theft	Case study
Theft	Kleptomania	£600 million a year	Dimensions of interaction and violence Blitz/ conformation/ con/snatch	Occurrence type	Rhesus monkeys and the 'theft' of food
Robbery		Typologies Boosters/ snitches Impulse/ occasional/ episodic/ amateur/ semi-professional	Expertise/ specialisation	Psychological state of offender	
Burglary			Armed robbery	Evolutionary theory – competition for resources	
Larceny			Piracy/ cyber-piracy		
Extortion					

In 2005, Flombaum and Santos carried out a set of experiments on rhesus monkeys, in which they observed their behaviour when competing for food (a grape) with a human. The monkeys consistently optimised their success in acquiring grapes by taking them from positions where the human could not see in preference to one in which the human was visually aware. As the researchers described it, the monkeys were stealing, and minimising the chances of being caught doing so, by making sure they pinched the grapes when it appeared the human wasn't watching. The monkeys observed the direction of the human's gaze and also acted when the gaze was averted in ways they did not when they could be observed.

Carefully avoiding any danger of anthropomorphism, the researchers concluded that the monkeys demonstrated theory of mind, that is, that they had the capacity to reason about what others think and were attributing a capacity to think to others. It also raises some other questions. Does this mean that the monkeys knew it is wrong to steal or simply that they had learnt they would be more successful when they were not being watched? It is an interesting concept and it demonstrates the differentiation between the *actus reus* and *mens rea* (see Chapter 16 for a more detailed discussion of these concepts) of stealing. While taking something which does not belong is not just limited to humans, the understanding that this is dishonest probably is. What the monkeys' behaviour demonstrates is their awareness of when best to do it, that is, when there is a lower chance of being seen. And, of course, it shows that they really like grapes.

KEY THEMES

- Theft
- Stealing
- Robbery/armed robbery
- Burglary
- Kleptomania
- Shoplifting
- Impulse control disorder

One of the most common crimes is theft, stealing something that does not belong to the person taking it, and in the full knowledge that it does not belong to that person and that this is wrong. Stealing can range from the petty theft of paper clips from an office stationery cupboard, to the armed robbery of a bank, or the embezzlement of millions from multinational companies. Such behaviour is regarded as universal and not culturally bound, and, as we see above, is even observed in non-humans. An evolutionary perspective would therefore suggest that theft has some survival benefit, if acquisition of required resources through legitimate means is not always possible. Alternatively, social theories are also viable explanations for theft. General strain theory, for example, would suggest that aversive circumstances, increasing the likelihood of criminal behaviour, would be most likely to have an effect on the decision whether or not to steal (Broidy & Agnew, 1997). An obvious motivation for stealing is impoverishment, and property crime does increase in times of economic crisis, although so do other types of crime (Malby & Davis, 2012).

DEFINITIONS OF STEALING

Theft – taking someone's property without their consent in the full knowledge that it does not belong to you. Within this overall umbrella term there are variations, as follows.

Robbery – theft of someone's property from their person, often with violence or threats of violence and/or intimidation.

Burglary – entering a structure (home, etc.) with the intent to steal.

Larceny – the taking of another person's property, but not necessarily from within a structure (such as a car parked in a road).

Extortion – forcing someone to hand over goods or money in order to prevent future damage or violence, such as in blackmail.

Each form of theft requires slightly different investigative processes. For example, the investigation of burglary, which is unlikely to be witnessed due to its stealthy nature, concentrates on points and manner of ingress to the dwelling, but robbery will focus on the descriptions of the offender(s). The psychology of theft, in addition to the consideration of theories of crime in general, concentrates on motivations for stealing, mental disorder and the outcomes of the behaviour on the victims. Mental disorders involved in stealing are highlighted in the study of a particular form of theft, shoplifting, in which many assume psychopathology to be the main determinant of the behaviour.

MENTAL DISORDER IN THEFT

The most obvious mental disorder associated with theft is an impulse control disorder called kleptomania – the compulsion to steal. The items stolen are not needed for monetary value, there is no economic aspect to kleptomania, and often sufferers do not need the items they steal.

Kleptomania is quite rare and is usually not present in people who steal for gain or because they have no regard for legality (this would be anti-social personality disorder or a conduct disorder in children) or because there is a real need for the items or money stolen. Sometimes the items stolen have very little intrinsic value. Kleptomania, as well as not being stealing for gain, is also an ego dystonic disorder. Those with kleptomania are usually otherwise law-abiding and may feel guilt or anxiety about stealing. Grant et al. (2007) examined 15 women with a primary diagnosis of kleptomania, who had a history of an average of 1.7 events of stealing per week. They found no deficits in neuropsychological functioning, but a below average performance in executive functioning tests, correlated with kleptomania severity. Grant et al. (2009) also discovered that comorbidity with depression, substance abuse and other impulse control disorders was common. They also found in their sample of those arrested that some 20% were then convicted and incarcerated, leading them to suggest that the psychiatric diagnoses were not having an impact on the legal consequences of their behaviour. Sung and Kim (2011), in an extensive review of the literature, concluded that the negative impact of kleptomania on social and occupational functioning is significant and that mental health professionals need more training in being able to recognise it. On the other hand, Lenz and MagShamhrain (2012) claim that kleptomania is an invented disease, dreamt up by society as a reaction to the increasing modernity of the early twentieth century, to pathologise women and exert social control over the potential users of the modern artefact, the department store. It is true that women are more likely to be diagnosed than men. It is also true that some forms of theft are portrayed in gendered ways. For example, shoplifting is seen as an almost exclusively female occupation, but this is not supported by crime statistics (Lamontagne et al., 2000).

The DSM-V classifies kleptomania as:

- Recurrent failure to resist impulses to steal objects that are not needed for personal use or their monetary value.
- Increasing sense of tension immediately before committing the theft.
- Pleasure or relief at the time of committing the theft.
- Stealing is not committed to express anger or vengeance and is not in response to a delusion or hallucination.
- The stealing is not better accounted for by Conduct Disorder, a Manic Episode, or Antisocial Personality Disorder. (American Psychiatric Association, 2013)

SHOPLIFTING

According to Tonglet (2002), revenue of more than £600 million a year in the UK is lost to shoplifting, the theft of goods from a retail outlet while it is open. There are several ways in which this behaviour is examined by psychology. One of these is identifying psychological predictors of shoplifting and shoplifting incidences. Day et al. (2000) discovered that self-esteem, stress and coping strategies were all factors that may precipitate specific shoplifting episodes, together with a propensity to use shoplifting in that way. They examined how these things might work together in predicting shoplifting behaviour, and discovered that they were mediated by an attitude that betrayed negative attitudes about 'the system' (that shops were overpricing goods and that stolen items would not be missed) and a perception that there would be few consequences to the behaviour.

Shoplifters' own testimony suggests that there is widespread use of cognitive distortions found in other crimes (Egan & Taylor, 2010). Neutralisation, for example, is a technique where people rationalise either before or after the act that the behaviour has a neutral effect (e.g. that it has no victim). It is commonly seen in the ways that shoplifters justify their actions. Other studies, such as that by Tonglet (2002), suggest that thieves have belief systems that contain rational intentions to steal, influenced by social factors and opportunities for theft. Still others are connected to the concept of sensation-seeking linked to risk-taking. A further exploration of psychopathology in the act of stealing, particularly shoplifting, links it to both depression and the issues associated with eating disorders, in which episodes of shoplifting were closely associated with low self-esteem, elevated depression and purging behaviours (Goldner et al., 2000). Depression also features in shoplifters in general. While the incidence of mental illness is not high, it is almost invariably depression that is diagnosed in those who do exhibit mental health problems (Freedman et al., 1996), with stress and anxiety being the alternative diagnoses (Tibbets & Hertz, 1996).

However, as stated, the linkage between shoplifting and mental disorder is somewhat tenuous and of low incidence. While this may explain some behaviour, and those with such problems need to have them addressed, concentrating on low numbers of cases does not lead to a more generally applicable explanation. Examining shoplifting and other forms of petty theft is important because, as Taylor et al. (2001) identified, this is often a gateway crime to other offences, particularly for juveniles. Young people who commit serious acts of theft and robbery reveal developmental histories that include petty acts of crime, including shoplifting (van Lier et al., 2009). However, there is a disparity that appears to be linked to the age of onset of antisocial behaviour. Boys who in later life move into aggressive and violent crime and substance abuse are more likely to have started exhibiting antisocial behaviour, including shoplifting, before the age of 10, whereas those who have adolescent onset are less likely to engage in high levels of violent crime later on. There is no gender disparity. Taylor et al.'s (2001) description of juvenile shoplifters suggests that this is linked to early childhood problems, including family issues such as marital discord and uninvolved parenting, psychiatric disorders such as conduct disorder, attention deficit hyperactivity disorder and childhood depression, particularly in girls. Hence shoplifting is seen as a gateway crime, which, if unmonitored and unpunished, leads to more serious crimes, with seriousness being a factor dependent on age at the initial shoplifting incident. As Lopez (2008) contends, theft by adolescents is a significant crime, particularly in countries such as the USA, and shoplifting is still the crime for which adolescents are more likely to be arrested.

The systematic examination of shoplifting and shoplifters is a quite recent phenomenon. Cameron (1964) carried out a study using a large sample of people stopped for shoplifting in Chicago and identified what appears to be the first typology. Cameron classified people into 'boosters' – those who carry it out in order to sell goods for profit (10% of the sample) – and 'snitches' – those who exhibit chronic pilfering, have no other criminal activity in their profiles and who do not resell the goods. The snitches also appear to have different motivations from the boosters, but they are not stealing from desperation/poverty and are not necessarily neurotic or kleptomaniacs. There are various criticisms to be made of this study, such as assumptions made about criminal activity outside the shoplifting, and there was no objective measure of personality or psychopathology made, but it represented a clear contribution to discussion of this topic.

For example, Cameron's typology was extended by Moore (1984), who attempted to determine patterns in shoplifting. Using a sample of 300 shoplifters who completed questionnaires and psychological evaluations, Moore suggested that there were five dimensions to shoplifting: (a) frequency; (b) primary precipitating factor(s); (c) attitude towards shoplifting as a crime; (d) use of stolen goods; and (e) reaction to detection, prosecution, and conviction. This resulted in five classifications. The 'impulse shoplifter' (15.4% of the sample) has limited shoplifting activity, did not plan and did not typically steal expensive items. When stopped they exhibited an intense emotional reaction of embarrassment, guilt and shame. The detection usually resulted in no further episodes of theft. The 'occasional shoplifter' (15% of the sample) may steal between three and 10 times a year, often as a result of peer pressure. Again, detection leads to mild embarrassment, but there is a lower likelihood of reoffending. The 'episodic shoplifter' (1.7% of the sample) steals specific goods, sometimes as part of bizarre rituals satisfying needs of self-punishment. This group is likely to exhibit severe psychological problems, including depression. Episodes of shoplifting occurred after psychosocial stressor triggers. Compliant, they are most likely to respond to psychotherapeutic intervention. 'Amateur shoplifters' represented 56.2% of the sample. They had regular patterns of shoplifting, which they found profitable, and they made conscious decisions to steal, taking small items that were easy to conceal. On detection, they claim little or no involvement in other or prior criminal activities and attempted to avoid punishment as much as possible. The conclusion was that this group of shoplifters would carry on doing so until caught. The remaining 11.7% of the sample were what Moore called 'semi-professional shoplifters'. Shoplifting was part of their lifestyle, they were very skilled at it, they engaged in reselling, and economic reasons were the primary motivational factors. They saved money, indulged in luxuries and perceived themselves as treated unfairly by society and having a right to these goods. Moore suggested that most acts of shoplifting were committed by those with at least some traits of anti-social personality disorder. Psychological or emotional problems in the sample were also equally distributed across both men and women, although more women than men cited psychosocial stressors as triggers to the episodes.

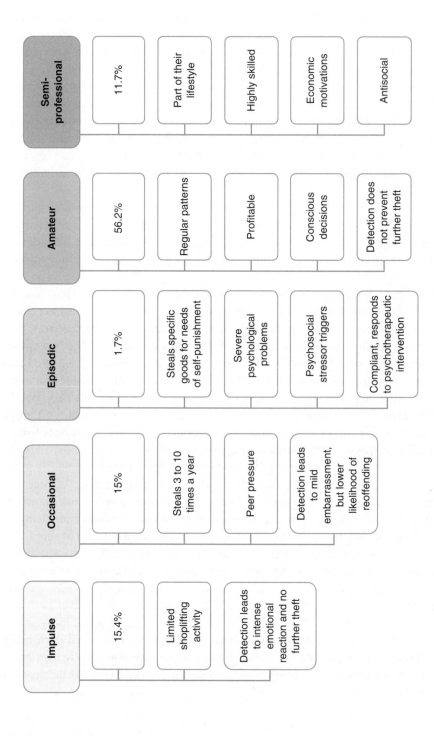

Figure 10.1 Shoplifters, Moore's typology (Moore, 1984)

Since these early attempts to classify shoplifters and build typologies, there have been several other attempts to describe shoplifters in this way. For example, Schleuter et al. (1989) suggested there was a distinction between rational and non-rational shoplifting, with rational shoplifting describing theft with a particular goal in mind and non-rational shoplifting appearing to have little motivation to need or desire. Other pieces of research simply extend or clarify Cameron's early work. However, it is clear that shoplifters are not a homogeneous group, and at the very least can be distinguished into those motivated by monetary needs and those motivated by other things. The term 'kleptomania' has come to be associated with shoplifters who have psychological needs that are to some degree satisfied by stealing, but it is generally accepted that the majority of this behaviour does not meet the clinical definition of kleptomania (Goldman, 1989). There are other factors that may be taken into account, such as substance abuse or addictions and eating disorders (see above).

Individual differences in the shoplifters, beyond the issues of kleptomania or other pathological concerns underlying the offending, centre on the personality and attitudes of those apprehended. They found distinct correlational patterns between shoplifting, unethical consumer behaviour and personality. The structural equation model that illustrates this pattern suggests that the likelihood of shoplifting is associated with age (active shoplifters are younger, suggesting it is something some people mature out of), lower levels of agreeableness and conscientiousness, and higher extraversion. They also discovered that contrary to popular belief, shoplifters are more likely to be male, or at least those who are caught are. In addition, Hoertel et al. (2012) found that male shoplifters are much more likely to have a comorbid anxiety disorder than are female offenders, who exhibit more substance abuse behaviour and antisocial personality correlates than male offenders. They speculate that this differentiates shoplifters on the basis of gender, with the behaviour in women being part of a larger impulse control disorder, and men exhibiting an internalising spectrum disorder.

> Unethical consumer behaviour – behaviour in a retail setting that exhibits a misuse of goods. For example, deshopping is the returning of goods after they have fulfilled a purpose, such as buying a suit for an interview and returning it after use. Other examples might be eating food that is sold by weight before it is weighed.

Other types of research into shoplifting have attempted to identify personality profiles as opposed to the behavioural profiles discussed above. MMPI profiles of shoplifters suggest high scores in psychopathic deviancy and mania. For those with only one instance of shoplifting, other factors appear to be relevant, such as hypochondriasis and paranoia. Ray et al. (1983), with a sample of 94 first offenders, found that there were high MMPI scores in psychopathic deviance schizoid tendencies, depression and anxiety, although this was also linked to economic stresses, social stresses and depression. Klemke (1992) also found poor coping strategies for stress in large portions of shoplifters, but also those who can be classified as antisocial show little remorse or guilt. It is concluded that most shoplifters fall somewhere between the two.

Treatment for shoplifting behaviour that is pathological seems to be somewhat effective. First, the shock of being apprehended often means shoplifters will not want to reoffend. However, for some, further intervention is needed. Such interventions are either punitive or offer global psychosocial assistance, and/or are specific to shoplifting behaviour. In the USA, a thorough, shoplifting-specific treatment, the Shoplifters Anonymous program, is educational and supportive in nature, and evaluations suggest that it is highly effective (Krasnovsky & Lane, 1998).

OTHER FORMS OF THEFT

While shoplifting is the form of stealing that has received the most research interest, there is a history of some studies in other forms of theft. For example, Riddle (1927) examined the aggressiveness of different forms of stealing and discovered that as the aggressiveness increased, so did the age of those committing the crime. He conjectured that the crimes could therefore also be arranged in some form of scale in terms of mental maturity and intelligence. This was one of the first systematic examinations of the linkage between IQ and crime and crime severity.

Robbery from the person

Later studies examined robbery from the person. A particularly useful study, commissioned by the UK Home Office, was conducted by Smith (2003). It proposed a typology of Blitz, Snatch, Confrontation and Con, which was categorised in terms of interaction between the offender and victim and by the level of violence involved. Goodwill et al. (2012) tested the structure of Smith's typology on 72 male offenders convicted of street robbery. Their multidimensional scaling analysis confirms the existence of the four types of robbery style (Blitz, Snatch, Confrontation and Con) and latent dimensions of interaction and violence, and provides a quantitative support for Smith's qualitatively defined typology (see Figure 10.2).

Blitz robberies involve high levels of physical force in order to control the victim, high levels of surprise and violence but little interaction, whereas Snatch means that there is a quick grab for visible property with the same low level of interaction. Blitz robbers are more likely to be substance abusers (48.6%), including at the time of the robbery, and this forms a common motivation for the crime. Hence there is a need to obtain money or goods quickly, and that the violence is often due to the level of verbal and physical resistance encountered from the victim and the need to overcome this. This can involve multiple acts of violence and aggressive behaviour. Snatch robbers will follow the victim without

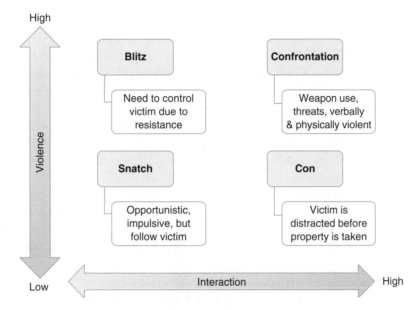

Figure 10.2   Robbery, Goodwill et al.'s (2012) analysis of Smith's (2003) typology

interacting until the circumstances are conducive to success. They commit only one act of violence (if any), quickly, and take easily identifiable and accessible property. This is both impulsive and opportunistic in nature. Despite following the victim there is little planning, but the violence is often used to stun the victim rather than as any interactive element. High interaction characterises Confrontations, which involve a demand to hand over property, with or without threat, and Cons, in which the victim is distracted in some way before their property is taken. Confrontations often involve the use of weapons as threats in order to persuade the victim to cooperate and comply with instructions to hand over their goods or money, with the interactions being verbally and sometimes physically violent. Cons are the least frequent form of street robbery, and this involves the most planning and interaction, possibly explaining its lower occurrence due to high cognitive demand. The offender waits for the victim and spends time on planning and interacting with the victim, often using an amicable approach in order to provide a level of comfort in which the victim will be more compliant or unguarded.

The level of interaction and violence and the interplay between the two have been identified as important in the psychology of crimes against the person, such as stranger rape (Canter et al., 2003) and homicide (Salfati, 2003), but this analysis of these dimensions has added a useful tool in the investigative process in street robbery. Smith's (2003) original typology was speculative, although derived from extensive reviews of literature and data on robbery. Goodwill et al.'s (2012) analysis of the structure forms the basis of a classification based on both the theoretical and empirical observations of street robbery.

Burglary

According to the European Institute for Crime Prevention and Control (see Harendorf et al., 2010), one of the most common crimes people in the developed world experience as a victim is burglary – the entering of a building by force and with stealth in order to steal goods. The highest rates are in Australia and New Zealand, closely followed by North America and West and Central Europe. However, the rate is declining, unlike for other crimes, particularly in the use of force or violence, although the FBI reports that there was an increase of 7.2% between 2000 and 2009, and that burglary accounts for almost 24% of all property crimes. It is therefore still an important issue for law enforcement agencies across the world, particularly in the developed countries.

Nee and Meenaghan (2006) interviewed five convicted burglars, all of whom had committed at least 20 offences. Experts rely on internalised automatic processes to speed up their performance and make it more accurate (Gavin, 1998) and the burglars were no exception. They described the process of choosing and searching properties as automatic, allowing them to focus on other aspects, such as returning householders, etc. Therefore, one of the aspects of theft that needs to be factored into an investigation is the expertise of the thief. With all learned behaviour, how to steal is something that evolves and reacts to the environment. Garcia-Retamero and Dhami (2009) compared experienced and novice burglars in terms of their decision-making processes when choosing properties to break into. Clear heuristic strategies were seen in the experts but were absent in the novices. These strategies involved eight cues that were thought to maximise success, namely what the garden was like in the property (hedges, fences etc.), signs of care, type of property, light in the property, the letter box (is it stuffed with post?), location, access and security (burglar alarms, etc.). The interesting point here was that police officers who were set the same tasks made decisions with the same heuristic efficiency, but based these decisions on different cues from the experienced burglars. This has clear implications for training officers to aid with burglary prevention.

In addition, the psychology of burglary and the application of its statistical methods will aid in the production of investigative techniques. Tonkin et al. (2012) showed that behavioural analysis can distinguish between burglary that is part of a serial offender's activity rather than a single incident. The behavioural elements of a crime, such as the distance between them (geographical proximity), the temporal proximity (how far apart they are in time), the actions of the burglar at the scene (how they gained entry to the building, for example) and characteristics of the property, all relate to each other, and when they exhibit a high level of similarity, it is likely that the offenders are the same in each instance of burglary (Markson et al., 2010). The knowledge that an offence has been carried out by the same offender as a previous burglary assists in the apprehension of serial offenders because evidence can be pooled from each linked crime, which also aids in the prosecution once someone is apprehended. Such analysis also exposes characteristics about the burglar, as identifying the behavioural elements of the crime scene – the method of operation of the offender (*modus operandi*, see Chapter 12) – reveals the level of expertise used.

This element of specialisation supports Yakota and Canter's (2004) finding that there were distinct themes within expertise and specialisation of burglars, and that these themes do not necessarily correspond to the categorisation in police reporting. For example, Yakota and Canter suggest that there is a similarity in shop and office burglaries in terms of property type, but these are classified differently in official records. The psychological meaning for the burglar, however, is consistent. This extends from property type (commercial) to element of risk, that is, that the property may be unoccupied during the night time period whereas residential properties are more likely to be unoccupied during the day. This has implications for investigation, as moving from strictly factual classification to psychological themes may provide more information. Hence if shop burglaries and office burglaries are all happening in the same area, police may conclude that these are carried out by different people, but, as they have the same psychological themes inherent within them, they may actually be the work of one person or a single group of people.

Yakota and Canter (2004) describe several themes related to property type, but also related factors about offenders that are important to consider. These factors are linked to the experience of the offender, as experienced burglars understand issues such as the level of risk inherent in entering certain property types, and the reward to be secured in the riskier ventures. However, the rewards may not be as high as perceived. With confidential and unique access to data from the British Bankers' Association, Reilly et al. (2012) discovered that the average theft from banks in armed robberies is around £20,000, a not insignificant amount but it would not make anyone rich, considering that the theft is often carried out by groups of people.

The risk associated with offences increases in proportion to the level of interaction with the victim(s) and violence involved. One of the most violent forms of theft is armed robbery.

Armed robbery

According to the Serious Organised Crime Agency (SOCA) in the UK, there were more than 3,500 incidences of robbery involving firearms in England and Wales in 2008–09, although this represented a downward trend of around 10%. The most likely theft was of cash, although other items of value can be stolen, especially from retail outlets. The majority of these offences are opportunistic with the offender acting alone, targeting cash for immediate needs. However, a significant proportion of armed robberies are highly sophisticated and organised, requiring the resources of a large, experienced group. There is a good deal of planning and expertise involved in perpetrating these crimes, including intelligence gathering, bribery and coercion prior to the actual robbery. Such robberies include the following:

- Cash-in-transit – security personnel are targeted as they transfer cash from one location to another
- Road freight – targeting easily disposable high value loads in transit on the road system (or, less frequently, rail system)

- Bank or similar robbery – blitz attacks during opening hours, often involving other crimes such as abduction of bank employees prior to the offence itself. (SOCA, 2013)

Piracy and Cyber-piracy

Armed robbery is akin to another crime, one which has ancient antecedents. Piracy is a set of specific crimes defined by customary international law, outlawed globally since 1648, but it has existed as long as there has been commercial maritime trading. The earliest documented cases of piracy date back to the fourteenth century BC. In addition, the International Maritime Organisation (IMO, 2013) reports maritime piracy has recently increased in both extent and severity, and is spreading from the originally identified 'hotspots' of the South China Sea and the Straits of Malacca and Singapore to areas such as the coast of Somalia, in the Gulf of Aden, and the wider Indian Ocean. The definition of piracy includes the same elements as landside armed robbery, namely illegal acts of violence in order to gain valuables.

Recently, however, the term 'piracy' has also been used to describe something which involves very little person-to-person interaction – the computerised forms of theft which are often called cyber-piracy. The use of electronic means to steal money, goods and even someone's identity is becoming a global problem with the widespread use of the Internet and the electronic facilitation of monetary transactions. Additionally, the use of the Internet to market pornography, infiltrate government and corporate computer systems (sometimes referred to as cyber-terrorism) and commit fraud has been termed a global epidemic (Fagbaibi et al., 2012). Such attacks are difficult to investigate due to the sheer volume of information to be examined, and the fact that crimes can happen across and within national borders. Of interest to the forensic psychologist, beyond the issue of victimology and the psychology of 'faceless' crimes, is the use of techniques known as data mining. This involves the process of using correlational analysis in ways similar to offender profiling in order to determine patterns in data to aid identification of the movement of data, property and people.

THE PSYCHOLOGY OF THEFT

The psychology of theft therefore focuses on the offence type, the factors associated with identifying it as such and the psychological state of the offender. With the exception of kleptomania, there are few cases in which the offender is unaware of the illegal nature of his or her offences, but the possibility of mental illness as a reason for theft is unclear. Another fruitful pathway for research might be the evolutionary perspectives in crime. Beyond the issues of immediate need and sheer greed, evolutionary theory extends the possibility of theft being due to competition for resources (Duntley & Shackleford, 2008). Observing both primate groups and humans leads to conclusions that both individuals and groups will encroach upon property and territory in order to misappropriate and exploit resources. However, it also makes the victim vulnerable to other attacks as they are seen as easily exploited. Hence properties in areas where one house has been successfully burgled may be seen as more vulnerable to attack, exposing the householder to many risks, such as the need for security and an increase in insurance premiums. As a result, crimes such as theft are seen in evolutionary terms as recurrent conflicts between individuals, which lead to successful natural selection strategies in competition for resources (Buss & Duntley, 2006).

SUMMARY

Theft is clearly not a uniform category of crime. Within it there are many gradations in severity, violence and criminal type. The psychology of stealing things centres on various perspectives, such as psychological disorders, the understanding of the crime by the criminal and the concept of the criminal career. There may also be evolutionary perspectives to consider too, given that primates apparently steal as well as humans. These perspectives are also applicable to other forms of theft seen in commercial crimes, such as those commonly known as white-collar crimes, which are considered in the next chapter.

Discussion point: How can we study successful thieves if they don't get caught?

Studying thieves, as with many types of criminal, is difficult due to the stealthy nature of the behaviour. In particular, burglary research relies on studying those whose success is measured by the number of convictions, but it could be argued that these do not represent the most successful criminals. How would it be possible to study those who do not get caught?

The criminal career paradigm is becoming more prominent in the study of crime. Gottfredson and Hirschi (1986) suggested that it is not a valid approach and does not merit such attention, but Blumstein et al. (1988) argued that it does. They contend that the concept of a criminal career, while not a full accepted one, together with the study of the frequency with which people participate in criminal activity, do have considerable utility. More recently, De Lisi and Piquero (2011) summarised the research that has been performed since this debate, concluding that it will expand as an approach to studying crime and successful criminals.

(Continued)

(Continued)

Using these three papers as a starting point, examine the way in which the more successful criminals can be studied in order to gain an insight into the psychological perspectives of these who do not caught, with a view to enhancing investigative processes.

Blumstein, A., Cohen, J. & Farrington, D. (1988) Criminal career research: its value for criminology. *Criminology*, 26: 1–35.

De Lisi, M. & Piquero, B. (2011) New frontiers in criminal careers research, 2000–2011: a state-of-the-art review. *Journal of Criminal Justice*, 39(4): 289–301.

Gottfredson, M. & Hirschi, T. (1986) The true value of lambda would appear to be zero: an essay on career criminals, criminal careers, selective incapacitation, cohort studies, and related topics. *Criminology*, 24(2): 213–234.

The Psychology of Economic Crime

11

White-collar crimes	The psychology of white-collar crime	Detection of fraud	Theoretical positions
The Fraud Triangle	The Fraud Diamond	Tips	Strain theory
The Madoff scandal	Selecting for honesty	Managerial reviews/audits	Power and the ego challenge
The Libor scandal		Accidental	The corporate psychopath/ antisocial personality
			Rationalisation/ neutralisation
			Cyber-fraud and the faceless victim

Charles Ponzi was an Italian living in the USA in the 1920s. He ran various suspect businesses, including an investment scheme in which he promised clients a 50% profit within 45 days, or 100% profit within 90 days. In reality, he was making no effort to generate legitimate income, and he was paying early investors with the money from later investors. He was charged with 86 counts of mail fraud, pleading guilty at the behest of his wife (Sobel, 1968). He was sentenced to five years in prison, was released after three, and was then indicted of 22 cases of larceny by the state of Massachusetts. He thought he had made a deal with federal authorities for immunity against state charges, but the Supreme Court disagreed and he faced court again, being sentenced to seven years in prison. He was released on bail while appealing this conviction, and fled to Florida, where he started selling land, promising a 200% return in 60 days. In reality, he was selling worthless swamp land and he was again charged with fraud (Zuckoff, 2005). Trying to flee the country, he was caught and sent back to Massachusetts to serve seven more years in prison, after which he was deported, as he had never applied for US citizenship. It is estimated that investors lost about $20 million in total, a huge sum in the 1920s.

Ponzi was nothing if not persistent. He has the dubious honour of having this type of swindle named after him, as it is now known as a 'Ponzi scheme' even though he was not the first to use such a money-making swindle. Such a system always collapses because earnings are less than payments to investors. The more investors it attracts, the more it is likely to attract the attention of financial regulators or to collapse under its own weight. While most of us would never consider defrauding in quite the spectacular way that Ponzi did, or other high-profile cases, the psychology behind behaviour that is sometimes called 'white-collar crime' is something we might all relate to.

KEY THEMES

- Acquisitive crime
- Fraud
- Embezzlement
- Money laundering
- Bribery/corrupting public officials
- Insider trading
- Fraud Triangle
- Fraud Diamond
- Ponzi scheme
- Madoff scandal
- Libor scandal
- Corporate psychopath

WHITE-COLLAR CRIMES

'White-collar crime' is now an outdated term, but was first used by Sutherland (1939) to refer to acquisitive crimes of a non-violent nature. This includes fraud (intentional deception in order to gain goods), embezzlement (the diversion of assests with which one has been entrusted), money laundering (the concealment of the source of money obtained by illicit means), tax evasion, bribery (the payment of money or goods in order to corrupt another) and insider trading (trading in a company's stock or securities when one has access to non-public information). His hypothesis was that these types of crime were different in both motives and characteristics from other forms of crime for monetary gain (such as theft, see Chapter 10). As such, these crimes are those committed against an organisation by people of high social standing within it, the organisation being anything from a social club to society in general.

Sutherland (1939) was working on this idea as the USA was coming out of the Great Depression and the economy and industry went through a very large growth in a very short time. He noted that people of high social class formed a very small proportion of those in prison and that they were more likely to commit the kinds of crimes he was describing, hence there was a relationship between money status and the likelihood of imprisonment for those crimes. He also suggested that the 'white-collar' crimes are crimes of opportunity, in which the criminals have learned to take advantage of the circumstances that have afforded them access to jobs in which they have engendered trust and have access to financial gain.

The discussion was taken further in a seminal paper by Cressey (1953), in which he examined embezzlement. He introduced the theoretical viewpoint of the Fraud Triangle framework, capturing the large number of factors working together in order for fraud to be successful. The triangle concerns three elements: motivation, opportunity and rationalisation (see Figure 11.1). The value of this framework is that endogenous factors (i.e. those relating to the person) are considered in the same model as exogenous factors, such as opportunity. However, it is clear, examining this from a psychological point of view rather than from one of forensic accounting, that it is the psychology that drives the factors within the triangle. Motivational factors such as incentives and pressure are clearly part of the characteristics of someone who decides to achieve the fulfilment of needs and reduction of pressure via criminal means. Rationalisation of such behaviour is a form of cognitive dissonance, and the perception of risk and opportunity is an inherent skill, albeit an undesirable one, in this setting.

More modern definitions of the issues that Sutherland (1939) and Cressey (1953) identified do not include the term 'white-collar', but rather categorise them via several characteristics, namely offence type, offender type and organisational type.

The type of offences include property crime, economic crime and corporate crimes such as environmental and health and safety law violations. Some of these crimes require the participation of senior members of organisations, for example, the movement of large sums of

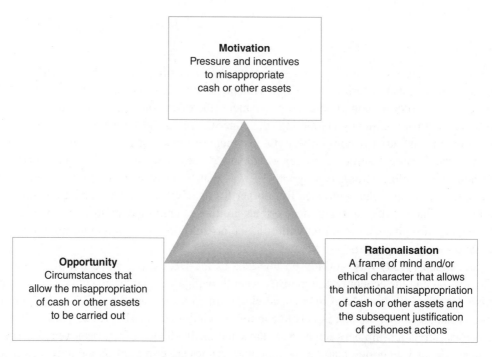

Figure 11.1   The Fraud Triangle (after Cressey, 1953)

money can only be accomplished by senior officers of a bank. In addition, the FBI suggests that the offences are carried out without threat or actual physical violence, but instead involve deceit and/or violation of trust (Federal Bureau of Investigation, 1989). By its very nature, such crime is difficult to detect, and the true extent and cost is unknown (Friedrichs, 2007). However, a report by the Association for Certified Fraud Examiners (ACFE) (2012), based on a survey of organisations experiencing fraud in the USA, suggest that there is a typical loss of 5% of a company's revenue to fraud. Extrapolating this to the gross world product translates to a global loss in excess of $3.5 billion or £2.2 billion or €2.7 million.

Due to the requirement for these crimes to be committed by a person in a position of trust, the offender can be classified by social class, socio-economic status or academic qualification. Almost all perpetrators of white-collar crimes are distinguished from other criminals by privilege. According to Appelbaum and Chambliss (1997), there are also occupational and organisational factors in these types of crime, often termed exogenous factors (the factors pertaining to the person are termed endogenous factors). Occupational factors mean that the crime is committed for personal interests, such as embezzlement or fraudulent business practices, where funds go to the individual(s). Organisational crimes are those committed by senior personnel to the benefit of the company, such as price fixing or overcharging. The Ponzi scheme is a good example of the former, but Ponzi's own fraudulent income is tiny in comparison to some people who have carried out the same type of scam.

The Madoff scandal

Bernard Madoff was sentenced to 150 years in jail and restitution of $170 billion for what is thought to be the biggest Ponzi scheme in history (Stewart, 2011). As of November 2008, he had 4,800 clients, half of whom lost no funds in accordance with the Ponzi scheme's operation, where early investors are paid funds from later investors' input. Federal authorities estimate the fraud to be in the region of $64.8 billion, according to the funds in the clients' accounts (Reuters, 2009b). The scheme started to come apart when the economic downturn accelerated around the end of 2008, although some investigations had already begun in early 2008. In December of that year, Madoff suggested to his sons, Andrew and Mark, that the firm, Madoff Securities, should pay out employee bonuses early, a sum totalling $170 million. At that time the firm apparently had assets of $200 million, but these bonus payments meant investors could not be paid. Madoff's sons were naturally concerned and, when confronted, Madoff admitted to them that he had been running an elaborate Ponzi scheme. Andrew and Mark Madoff then asked advice from a friend who was a lawyer, who then contacted the Federal Bureau of Investigation (FBI) on their behalf. The FBI investigators arrested Madoff on 11 December 2008, at which point he agreed that there was no innocent explanation for the way the firm had been handling investments. He pleaded guilty in 2009 to all 11 federal charges of securities fraud, investment adviser fraud, mail fraud, wire fraud, three counts of money laundering, false statements, perjury, making false filings with the US Securities and Exchange Commission (SEC), and theft from an employee benefit plan (US Department of Justice, 2009).

Madoff's legacy

Fraud such as Madoff's depends on the trust placed by investors in someone who is actually using their funds in a corrupt manner. According to Drew and Drew (2010), since the Madoff scandal broke, there have been at least a further 32 Ponzi schemes identified by the US Commodity Futures Trading Commission (a leading US financial regulator), a phenomenon termed 'rampant Ponzimonium' by the Commission. Other schemes have been under investigation by, for example, the UK Serious Fraud Office, South African police, and regulators and police forces in several other countries. Drew and Drew (2010) suggest that the reason for this proliferation is jointly that legitimate investment schemes have been hit badly by the global recession, and there is a general starvation of cash. Investors in legal investment schemes have withdrawn money from them, creating an investor panic in which it is estimated that over $100 billion US have been withdrawn from hedge funds in the USA alone (Grant, 2011). So investors have been seeking other places in which to invest their funds that appear to be safe while guaranteeing returns. A riskier exposure but one that guarantees returns, as Ponzi schemes are perceived to do from an external investor's point of view, would seem attractive.

The scale of the fraud being perpetrated within Ponzi schemes is quite unprecedented, and illustrates the widespread monetary risk that people are willing to take. Keeping your money in a box under the mattress has never seemed safer, as even long-established banking organisations with enviable reputations are not immune from fraud.

The Libor scandal

Fraud perpetrated by individuals or groups of people have reached huge proportions, but this is somewhat dwarfed by the fraud being carried out by organisations within a corporate culture. In June 2012, the UK bank Barclays paid fines in excess of $450 million to bank regulators in the UK and the USA in settlement of charges that the bank had manipulated the London Interbank Offered Rate (Libor). It is expected that other banks will be implicated in due course. The Libor is the rate at which banks lend unsecured funds to each other, and is an average of rates submitted daily to the British Bankers' Association (BBA), with major banks submitting their cost of borrowing unsecured funds for 15 periods of time in 10 currencies. It is calculated across a range of currencies because it is linked to international trading, being used worldwide as the basis for setting interest rates in both consumer and corporate financial dealings. There are over $800 trillion in securities and loans, including mortgages, loans and securities trading, linked to the Libor.

Barclays' alleged manipulation allowed its traders to make unfair profits via distortion of the marketplace in moving money around. Lowering the rate artificially also meant that Barclays looked more secure and less of a risk. When this behaviour was exposed, the chairman and chief executive of Barclays lost their jobs, as did another five senior employees, a further 13 were disciplined (Treanor, 2012). The scandal also destroyed a good deal of trust between financial institutions, and undermined investor confidence, with Barclays withdrawing from its tax advisory business and other areas of commodity trading (Treanor, 2012). Many high-profile bankers outside Barclays were investigated, resigned or were sacked due to the scandal, and global banks have, perhaps somewhat belatedly, put more regulatory procedures in place. It appears that the only reason these financial swindles were brought to light is that someone within this culture became a 'whistleblower' and agreed to give information about the practice and those carrying it out in exchange for immunity from prosecution (Financial Times, 2012).

One of the difficulties in detecting these sorts of crimes is that the employees can incorporate their criminal behaviour into legitimate business practices. In addition, it is difficult to identify a specific victim, as these crimes do not use physical violence or force, and companies naturally employ a culture of corporate confidentiality.

THE PSYCHOLOGY OF WHITE-COLLAR CRIME

At first glance the motivation for fraudulent crimes appears simple – greed. But greed is not illegal. Many large businesses make huge profits legitimately, although many people

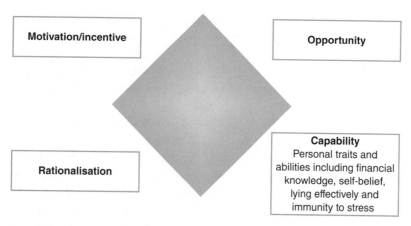

Figure 11.2   The Fraud Diamond (Wolfe & Hermanson, 2004)

would contest the definition of legitimate here! Individuals can also be naturally acquisitive without breaking the law. So greed itself is not an explanation for white-collar crime, and regarding greed as the only motivation oversimplifies the fact. In order for financial crimes to take place, Krambia-Kapardis (2001) suggested there need to be several things in place: motivated offenders, who have the ability to rationalise the crime, suitable targets and a lack of guardianship over money. This clearly refers back to the Fraud Triangle (see Figure 11.1).

What can be noted from the triangle is that it needs not just the financial atmosphere to be conducive to perpetrating fraud, but also various psychological elements to be present too. These are termed exogenous and endogenous factors, respectively. Endogenous, psychological factors, such as motivation to commit the crime and a personality capable of carrying out the crimes, and exogenous, situational factors, such as the opportunity to misappropriate assets and a lack of regulatory guards, are of paramount importance in fraudulent practices. However, motivation cannot exist alone; the opportunity needs to arise, and rationalisation will only occur once the crime is considered and carried out. Opportunity can exist without the motivation, so the motivation must be understood in order to investigate and then prevent the crime.

Later theories suggest that the triangle, although a useful tool in understanding the risk of fraud, is not the whole picture. A Fraud Diamond has been proposed (Wolfe & Hermanson, 2004) in which the element of capability has been added to motivation (or incentive) opportunity and rationalisation (see Figure 11.2).

Capability, Wolfe and Hermanson (2004) suggest, is the personal traits and abilities that determine whether or not that person will commit fraud when the other three elements are present. They point out that most frauds, and in particular the large ones seen recently, would not occur without the central person with certain skills being present. In other words, opportunity means the fraud can happen, incentive and rationalisation draw the fraudster into the position in which it can happen, but if s/he does not have the skills, then it will not escalate into crime, and particularly not into the spectacular frauds committed by people like Madoff. The Fraud Diamond, then, places into the equation what has been missing in the Fraud Triangle – the person.

The psychology of the individual is still needed even when examining the behaviour of the corporation. The fraudulent person needs to be in a position of trust, authority and, preferably, power with respect to the money and its security. If someone is not in a position to be able to exploit and divert the flow of money in some way, then they do not have access. This holds as well for the person selling fake jewellery from a street corner to the chief financial officer of a bank. Secondly, the fraudster needs to be clever. If they cannot understand the ways in which money moves and are not able to exploit the weaknesses in the system, or other people, then they cannot effectively defraud anything. Thirdly, the fraudster needs to believe in himself or herself; they need to have the confidence to carry off the fraud, particularly on a person-to-person level. This also means that during a cost–benefit analysis the egotistical nature of the fraudster will lead him or her to believe his/her abilities are such that the risk is acceptable. S/he also needs to be able to charm, coerce and to lie, and to be almost immune to stress because keeping up the appearance of normality for a long time is bound to cause stress.

The psychology here is complex, and remains unclear, but studying those who carry out these crimes does lead us to the possibility of determining what distinguishes them from other criminals and the rest of the law-abiding population. Ones, Viswesvaran and Schmidt (1993) suggested that honesty in employees can be measured, pinpointing those predisposed to criminally fraudulent behaviour. The MMPI (or MMPI-2), for example, is used extensively in both public and private sectors to screen out undesirable applicants, particularly those with whatever the company decides are undesirable personality traits and which they have linked to fraud (Goldstein & Epstein, 2008). Whether such measurement is valid is debatable, and certainly would not be useful in the case of the fraudster who acts outside a corporate structure, or who constructs it himself, such as Bernie Madoff. The report by the Association of Certified Fraud Examiners (2012) indicates that the major way in which law enforcement agencies or financial regulators find out about fraudulent behaviour within organisations is via a tip, as in the case of Madoff. Reassuringly, the next most frequent way of uncovering crimes is via managerial reviews and internal audits, but the fact that 7% of organisational fraud is detected by accident is somewhat worrying.

Fraud is big business, and big businesses therefore appear to need monitoring, particularly when the people committing fraud appear to be in positions of trust and power. Why do some people abuse their positions in this way? The answer lies in the same reasons that explain other types of crime, particularly acquisitive ones, but it seems something of a stretch to attempt to apply theories such as strain theory here. However, it is not impossible that people who are relatively well off experience economic strain; there are still comparisons to be made with neighbours, and issues such as gambling losses etc., that may impact on the rich as well as the poor. The desire to possess what one cannot afford is no different in the rich, and the threat of loss is probably greater when power and status is added to the equation. Fraudulent behaviour, then, may seem to be a solution (Nettler, 1982).

A further psychological aspect to this is the satisfaction to be financed by wielding any power that the fraudster possesses. Stotland (1977) referred to this as an 'ego challenge' because the challenge of carrying out a complex fraudulent scheme provides excitement and a sense of mastery over others or over systems. There is another aspect to power too: that wealth leads to status and power, and the power over others granted by high position may make fraud an attractive form of life due to the power that comes from manipulation of and contempt for others.

Fraudulent behaviour may of course be a short-term solution to a problem of lack of funds, but the lifestyle choices being made are not without impact. In addition, it is clear that there is a certain personality type that would find the lifestyle of power, money and contempt for others very attractive. The incidence of high scores on psychopathy scales of some successful business people is just beginning to be investigated. Examining candidates selected by a variety of companies for management programmes in the USA with the PCL-R, Babiak et al. (2010) found much higher scores of psychopathy traits than in community samples. This was consistent with the ratings of the candidates on dimensions of charisma, communication skills and creativity, and negatively correlated with ratings of being a team player and possessing management skills. There is no suggestion that these 'corporate psychopaths' ever behaved fraudulently, or that they harboured any criminal thoughts, but if this personality type exists in high numbers among those rising within corporate structures, it seems reasonable to speculate that the fraudster is among them (Smith & Lilienfeld, 2012).

A further explanation may simply lie in personality traits that are consistently found in fraudulent individuals, such as narcissism and the inability to empathise with others. These seem to be quite familiar to anyone looking at the diagnostic criteria for antisocial personality disorder, but these antisocial behaviours are inherently non-violent and would not necessarily attract the attention of mental health professionals. Wallang and Taylor (2012) suggest that there are several psychiatric conditions that can be associated with fraud offending, but that the consistently non-violent nature of the offences means that recognising them as such is difficult, and it is even more difficult to determine the efficacy of treatment.

Added to this is the rationalisation that we all make for undesirable behaviour, which appears to be included in criminal acts. This reduces or neutralises inhibition, and includes thoughts such as there is no real (identifiable) victim. It is linked to motivation, but is not the same. Offenders, according to Krambia-Kapardis (2001), use rationalisations and extenuating circumstances that they manufacture in order to adjust and remove the perception of criminality from their acts. Fraud against large companies, for example, is rationalised with the idea that the company can afford it. Other rationalisations attempt to blame the victim, or trivialise the crime to the extent that there is no victim. In other types of fraud, Blum (1972) suggests, the criminal will insist that victims were inherently greedy. This is borne out by the fact that most of these schemes were attractive to the victim as a get rich quick plan. Blum also noted that the fraudster or conman was essentially misanthropic, suggesting that a certain element of psychopathy is needed in order to carry out these schemes. Ramamoorti (2008), on the other hand, suggested that the fraudster is adept at social engineering, the ability to systematically manipulate others, such that even if the fraudulent person lacks the skill to bypass security (such as in computer networks for example), s/he can manipulate those who have those skills and compromise them and their access.

Techniques by which the fraudulent individual will neutralise inhibition to behave in this way depend on the target or victim. Members of large organisations will rationalise that the company deserves to lose revenue, or that people further up the hierarchy are gaining more income for inferior work. In fraud involving personal contact, seeing the victim as complicit in their own defrauding is another form of neutralisation. A common theme here that an honest person cannot be conned because the lure into the scam is not attractive, in the same way as a fish that is not hungry will not take the bait and be hooked. There seems to be an implicit agreement that it is only in violent crime that anyone is hurt. In addition, those crimes in which the victim seems to enter willingly, such as ploys for evading tax or putting money into schemes that promise seemingly impossibly high returns, are apparently the easiest to rationalise, and Blum (1972) first suggested that the fraudster attributes success to inherent greed in the victims. This in turn might signal an inherent misanthropy in those committing fraud, with an implicit view of the victim as dishonest as him/herself.

The victim type is important in considering the psychology of fraudulent offending. A large company is essentially faceless to the person embezzling from it, but the person persuading an elderly widow to invest her pension in a get rich quick scheme is acting on a very personal level. The victim, then, is not faceless in organised fraud, but the empathy normally derived from person-to-person contact is not present. However, fraud can be committed at a distance in any form, whether the victim is an organisation, such as a company or government department, or another person. A worrying development in recent years has concerned the growth in the widespread use of electronic media to attempt to defraud. Fraud has always been committed with the unwitting aid of the media, such as newspaper advertisements for schemes etc., and this means there are reduced social cues normally present in personal communication. Using email and the Internet makes access to victims much easier, and eliminates the need for social interaction and the problems and inhibitions inherent to it.

A 'blanket' email will be ignored or deleted by the majority of recipients, but some must be attracted otherwise the method would not continue to be used. How many days go by without receipt of an email claiming to be from a person who has many millions of pounds held in your name in a bank to which only you can gain access? There are several forms of email fraud, including spoofing, phishing and spamming. This does not require personal contact with a victim beyond the composition of words in an email. These schemes are termed advance fee frauds, and still gather victims worldwide. There is little social interaction and hence few social cues are given to the offender. It is this that leads to a reduction in the influence of social norms and constraints.

Types of email fraud

Spoofing – the email is written so that it appears to come from a genuine person or organisation, such as a bank or Internet sites such as eBay. Removing the actual information about the sender, software replaces it with a supposed other sender. Senders rely on the routing of the message through several servers to hide the location of the email initiator. Remailing, for example, is an attempt to avert detection by sending the email first to a server that strips off the initiating address and replaces it with another.

Spamming – sending out a message to a large number of recipients, usually routed through an unsuspecting company's mail server. The emailer uses the server as a relay point and then disappears. This is theft of services, and potentially a denial of services as well, if the volume of emails sent through the server causes it to crash.

Stealing – the unauthorised use of someone else's password and email account via shoulder-surfing (watching over someone's shoulder as they enter a password and identity details), or 'sniffing' a network (watching all the network traffic and intercepting user IDs and passwords).

Bogus freemail accounts – setting up accounts in services such as Hotmail where names and addresses are not checked. The email company cannot keep account of who opened the false account and they can be quickly discarded. Someone wishing to email illicit material, such as pornography, would use such accounts.

A type of fraud that is facilitated by electronic media but which feels very personal to the victims is identity fraud or identity theft. According to Saunders and Zucker (2010), perpetrators assume the identity of others in order to steal money or obtain loans or goods, and it can be very difficult to detect until the theft has been committed. Using electronic media means the perpetrator remains anonymous and does not even need to resemble the victim in order to impersonate them. The tracking of such criminals is carried out by forensic computing and accountancy experts. The only way to combat this is to build increasingly more impenetrable security measures, which may end up with the genuine person being locked out of their own assets.

The majority of research into fraud concentrates on the culprit, particularly when the fraud concerns millions or billions of whatever currency is lost. This runs the risk of behaving almost like the con-artist rationalising away the existence of the victim. The impact of fraud is wide, victims are not faceless, and the outcome for them may be primary effects of the crimes, such as financial hardships resulting in relationship breakdown, psychological trauma and physical health issues, and secondary impacts, such as damage to reputation and celebrity and changes in behaviour. Button et al. (2012a) carried out a survey of 800 victims of fraud and demonstrated that the primary and secondary effects of fraud are very real. The rationalising myth of a victimless crime is invalid. Perhaps the route to rehabilitation for white-collar criminals is one of restorative justice (Van Ness & Strong, 2010), in which they are made to face their victims and acknowledge the damage they have done.

SUMMARY

White-collar crime, now a term superseded by specific terminology, is inherently non-violent but is carried out in monetary terms. Psychologically speaking, those carrying out fraud, embezzlement and other types of economic crime do not think of themselves as criminal, but there may be an element of psychopathy at the root of all white-collar criminals.

Discussion point: How can we measure the impact and range of fraudulent behaviour?

White-collar crime is inherently non-violent. This does not mean that there is no impact on the victim. As Button et al. (2012a) found, there are severe impacts for the victim that go well beyond any financial loss. Being conned is at the very least embarrassing, and can cause many other psychological outcomes. How may psychologists go about assessing the impact and recommending ways in which this is alleviated and the offenders are made to face their actions?

Button, M., Lewis, C. & Tapley, J. (2012a) Not a victimless crime: the impact of fraud on individual victims and their families. *Security Journal* [advance online publication], 23 April.

Button, M., Tapley, J. & Lewis, C. (2012b) The 'fraud justice network' and the infra-structure of support for individual fraud victims in England and Wales. *Criminology and Criminal Justice* [advance online publication], 6 July.

Wallang, P. & Taylor, R. (2012) Psychiatric and psychological aspects of fraud offending. *Advances in Psychiatric Treatment* 18(May): 183–192.

Section 4

Psychology in Detection and Investigation

Psychology has some major contributions to make to the investigation of crime. Psychology in the police station looks at how psychology can be successfully applied when detecting and investigating crimes. This section relates to the practice dimension in that the psychology of crime investigation and the contribution psychology can make to criminal investigation is considered. It also relates to the knowledge dimension, as the underlying psychological theory relevant to investigation is examined, along with supporting research. Core Roles represented here are Core Role 1 (conducting applications) and Core Role 2 (research).

Chapter 12 looks at the issues surrounding profiling and crime scene analysis, applying these techniques to how a modern investigation may have tackled the infamous Jack the Ripper case.

Chapter 13 covers how psychology can help the interviewing processes when witnesses and victims are questioned by the police, and Chapter 14 applies the same question to the interrogation of suspects.

Psychology in the Investigation of Crime

12

Policing and detection

Profiling

- FBI method
  - Organised/ Disorganised classification
  - Serial killer motivation classification
  - Stages
    - Profiling input
    - Meaningful patterns
    - Crime assessment
    - Profile generation
- Statistical approaches
  - Behavioural evidence
  - Statistical analysis
- Performing profiling
  - Psychological knowledge
  - Collection and interpretation of evidence
  - Examination of bodies
  - Time since death
  - Psychological autopsy
  - Behavioural analysis of crime scenes and witnesses

Case study

- Jack the Ripper
  - Whitechapel prostitutes
  - Range of suspects
  - Crime scene analysis and linkage
  - Geographical clustering
  - Behavioural evidence – mutilation, communication

Efficacy of profiling

- Criminal personality
- Empirical support
- Ethics and professionalism

Someone is prowling through the streets of London, killing women. The murders happen at night and all the victims earned their living as sex workers. All except one have been found in the street, sometimes quite close to where other people are walking home or in pubs drinking. All the women's bodies have been horribly mutilated peri-mortem, internal organs have been neatly removed, but other mutilations have been carried out in what appears to be a frenzied manner. The last victim, found in her lodgings, was subjected to a particularly bloody attack. The police surgeon reports that the skin on her abdomen and thighs has been removed and the abdominal cavity emptied of organs. Her breasts have been removed and the arms and face had been hacked by a knife. Her throat has been cut, deeply, and her heart was missing. Being indoors had evidently given him a longer time to conduct his work than with the other women.

The police desperately need to stop this killer, but the investigative tools at their disposal are limited. How might psychology aid the processes of crime investigation and apprehension of this perpetrator?

KEY THEMES

- Criminal profiling
- FBI method of profiling
- UK Profiling: the Statistical Approach
- Collection and interpretation of physical evidence
- Medical autopsy
- Psychological autopsy

POLICING AND DETECTION

The control of crime and responsibility for protection by the state dates back as far as 1066 in England (Rawlings, 2003) when the victorious Norman rulers found themselves with a recalcitrant indigenous population to control. It is, after all, the period in which the legend of Robin Hood is set. Policing in medieval times meant either bringing a criminal caught red-handed to the presence of a Justice, or setting up a 'hue and cry', by which bystanders were summoned to help and all able-bodied men were expected to assist in finding whoever had committed the crime (Sharpe, 1996). Policing, then, is a societal necessity for the prevention and deterrence of crime and for preliminary investigation.

However, there is a distinction between policing and detection. Policing is the practice of protecting the populace and preventing crime. Detection is the systematic investigation of crimes and has a much shorter history. The formation of the first squad of detectives was in 1749, when Henry Fielding created the Bow Street Runners in London (Beattie, 2006).

More than a century later, we see psychological knowledge being used in the field of the law, usually to protect the mentally incompetent accused of crime, but sometimes in the detection and prosecution of crime.

According to Osterburg and Ward (2000), there are various approaches to criminal investigation. The first is that the investigator has certain personal characteristics that lend something to the process of investigation. The idea that a detective should appreciate the workings of the criminal mind and recognise his/her habits and habitat is not a new one, but it is understood that this should be coupled with a sense of moral justice and an ability to use logic. An alternative or complementary approach is one of process; in other words, the tasks and actions of the investigator, when outlined, clarify the purpose and process of investigation. All of these components can also be applied to the use of psychology in investigatory processes.

Psychology can be integrated into procedures of criminal investigation; hence forensic psychologists can play a number of roles. On the reporting of a crime, a forensic psychologist may be asked to act as a criminal profiler. Profiling is a task beloved by the media. It seems to have properties of dramatic or magical spectacle, but in reality is simple logic and a sound knowledge of how to apply statistical and scientific techniques (Turvey, 2008). Perhaps one of the most famous criminal detectives in fiction to employ such logic was Sherlock Holmes. Carson (2009) describes Holmes as being able to define a person down to the minutest detail with only the smallest piece of evidence on which to base his assertions. Witness the description of the absent-minded Dr Mortimer solely from the examination of the cane left on an earlier visit to Baker Street (*The Hound of the Baskervilles*). His associate, and the narrator of the stories, Dr Watson, appears unable to fathom how Holmes arrives at his deductions. However, when Holmes reveals his techniques, Watson declares them to be nothing more than simple tricks. Profiling techniques are anything but tricks. Criminal profiling involves using understanding of human behaviour, motivation and pathology so that a picture of the psychological characteristics of a perpetrator can be built (Ebiske, 2008). This can also sometimes involve crime scene analysis, the examination of elements of the crime in order to deduce the execution of the crime and the operation and methods of the perpetrator. This requires knowledge, not just of the action of offenders, but of the crime scene evidence-gathering processes and procedures.

CRIMINAL PROFILING

In order to provide a description of a person carrying out a set of crimes, a profiler needs to be able to understand and use some sort of classification system. Classification systems fall into two types: typologies and taxonomies (Bailey, 1994). A typology is a conceptual form of separating items on a set of predetermined dimensions. The dimensions are not necessarily built from empirical observations. However, in taxonomies the classification is based on measurable characteristics and they are more likely to be found in biological sciences. A profile is an analysis of the extent to which something exhibits various characteristics, and is closer to a typological classification than a taxonomic one. Hence, offender or criminal profiling is usually defined as the process of predicting the characteristics of an offender based on information gathered by police officers and scientific officers from a crime scene. More recently, however, this definition has been broadened to include other types of methods by which psychologists can provide advice to the police during investigations. Thus the description of how psychological data is used in investigation is a broader one than simply providing a profile of the perpetrators. It now encompasses crime scene analysis, the interpretation of geographical data, victimology and crime linkage.

Various terms for profiling:

Offender profiling

Criminal profiling

Psychological (criminal) profiling

FBI – criminal personality profiling

Applied or clinical criminology

Crime scene reconstruction

Sociopsychological profiling

Behavioural investigative analysis

According to Petherick and Turvey (2008), there are two approaches to dealing with the data that emerges from a criminal investigation. Idiographic or individual case study leads to in-depth knowledge about the characteristics of a particular case, and can be useful if an understanding of the unique characteristics of a crime or crime series is needed. A profile created from such a knowledge base means that those using it can relate it to singular cases. This is often found in crime fiction and seems to be a favourite of the depiction of a profiler. It is pretty much how Agatha Christie's Miss Marple operates. She compares the details of the case in question to an example from her own experience and the solution is derived from the ensuing unfolding of that compared case. This is a very concrete way of operating. Outside the fictional arena it involves a comparison to a real-world case. In contrast, a nomothetic process of deduction is that which uses an average. It is not specifically related to any one case example, and is therefore akin to theory generation rather than real-life examples.

Due to this variety, the use of psychology in investigation now has many different forms, depending on the model or method by which the psychologist operates. There are several such methods available.

The FBI method of profiling

The Federal Bureau of Investigation was the first agency to systematically develop a form of profiling in order to detect and classify the personality and behavioural characteristics of an individual based on analysis of the crime or crimes committed (Ressler et al., 1988). In addition to the USA, the method is used in several countries around the world.

The FBI method has several stages. Assimilation is the gathering of information from the crime scene, victims, witnesses, etc. This may use photographs, post-mortem reports, victim profiles, police reports and witness statements. Classification is the integration of the data into a framework, which can allow the perpetrator to be identified as 'organised' or 'disorganised'.

Organised offenders have social skills, are able to plan, can gain/maintain control over the victim, and leave little forensic evidence. If the crime is murder, sexual acts will occur before the death of the victim.

The disorganised offender is seen as impulsive, possesses little social skill, the crimes are opportunistic, and crime scenes suggest a lack of planning or attempts to avoid detection. Murderers may engage in sexual acts after the death of the victim, due to sexual dysfunction or lack of sexual knowledge (Canter et al., 2004).

The next stage is identification, which is an attempt to construct the behavioural sequence of the crime, the steps the offender went through in order to commit the crimes, and any behaviour that was not necessary to the offence. Finally, a profile is generated, which may contain detailed information regarding the offender's demographic characteristics, family characteristics, education, personality, in addition to any other information the profiler can determine. A great deal of the FBI method concentrates on the classification stage.

The organised/disorganised classification

The classification used by the FBI is much more applicable to murder and rape than other types of crime. The organised offender is assumed to have some form of cunning, which may or may not manifest itself as the ability to plan, which is often reflected in the crime scene. There is also a need for control, to the extent of a fixation with the condition of a crime scene and its aftermath. In terms of a killing, Hickey (2001) states that the organised offender will signal this through the way the murder is approached, the condition of the body and its clothes, the way the body is disposed, etc. An organised offender is antisocial, but presents the façade of normality, maintaining friendships, etc. S/he is more likely to be forensically aware, that is s/he will understand the concept of exchange of material, possibly even the idea of identification through fingerprints or DNA, and s/he will be adaptive, mobile and creative. S/he will have a preferred type of victim; this will be more evident for a murderer or a rapist. When considering a serial murderer, the bodies may be concealed or disposed of in such a way as to shock or frighten the community, such as dismemberment or sexually displaying a body. This offender may be aware of police procedures and even be obsessed by them. In the FBI study of incarcerated serial killers, those that were seen as organised were able to overcome emotions at the time of killing to remain calm and select victims that conformed to a fantasy. Indeed, the selection may form part of the fantasy. This last is not supported by research, simply anecdotal evidence, such as Ted Bundy selecting women with long dark hair, who were similar in appearance to a former fiancée. Organised killers also improve techniques between each murder.

There are several problems with this typology, including contradictory positions of the killer remaining calm, but at the same time feeling quite deep negative emotions. This makes the motivation very unclear, as anger or frustration as negative feelings would suggest that the murder is driven by emotion. The emotionally driven behaviour might suggest a psychodynamic drive underlies the killing, with an Oedipal conflict explaining a hatred of women or father figures. However, this kind of drive is only seen in certain killers, driven by revenge or hatred.

The Freudian explanation is much more apparent in disorganised offenders. Sexual murder and accompanying acts, such as necrophilia, suggest that this offender kills for sexual

	Organised	Disorganised
Murder scene	Planned Victim — targeted stranger Control including restraints, and conversation/ speech Aggression before death Body hidden or moved from crime scene Weapon and evidence absent	Spontaneous Victim — known by offender Little control Sexual acts before death Body not hidden, or left at crime scene. Evidence present
Murderer	More-than-average IQ Skilled occupation Controlled mood Living with partner Mobile — for example, car Socially competent Sexually competent High birth order status Father's work stable Inconsistent discipline as child Use of alcohol during crime Follows crime on news Limited change in behaviour after crime	Less-than-average IQ Unskilled Uncontrolled Living alone Lives near crime Socially incompetent Sexually incompetent Low birth order status Unstable Harsh discipline as child Alcohol not used during crime Does not follow crime on news Major behaviour change after crime

Figure 12.1   FBI Organised/Disorganised typology of murderers and murder scenes

gratification (Federal Bureau of Investigation, 1985). This killer is not sociable and does not plan his crimes, mainly because he cannot maintain the social interaction. The FBI argues that these offenders are motivated by uncontrolled sexual drives, reflected in impulsive behaviour and an inability to adapt to unexpected events. This would be seen in a situation where the killer is murdering a woman and her husband arrives home. The husband may then be killed simply because the killer has no way of reacting to such a situation.

The disorganised murder is essentially driven by sex, but Fox and Levin (1994) suggest that this sexual element is more to do with the power and control seen in rape, and hence indicates a need to dominate.

A disorganised offender is also not forensically aware, leaves lots of evidence at the scene, such as fingerprints, body fluids (semen from a male offender, blood or sweat), and demonstrates little planning. The killing may seem more frenzied and occurs early in the whole set of actions. The victim may be depersonalised by mutilation and sexual humiliation (such as inserting objects into sexual orifices, described as repressed necrophilia).

The characteristics of the organised/disorganised typology are pressented in Figure 12.1.

Criticism of the classification

The classification is not as dichotomous as it appears at first glance. There is a significant overlap of behaviours from one to the other, such as emotionally driven states in the organised typology and an ability to revise the crime scene in the disorganised typology. It is difficult to reconcile a disorganised emotionally driven killer with one that remains unseen long enough to perform necrophilia, cannibalism, post-mortem mutilation, etc.

There is also a problem with determining the psychology of such a classification. Why, for example, do serial killers not find their desires assuaged by one killing? Why do they carry on? The typology also does not allow for an understanding of victim selection or a desire for a specific type of location; it simply says that they exhibit such.

In order to address such criticisms, the FBI enhanced the application of the classification in terms of motivations.

Visionary motivations

Visionary serial killers suffer from psychotic breaks with reality, sometimes believing they are another person or are compelled to murder by entities such as the Devil or God. David Berkowitz, aka 'Son of Sam', was a visionary killer because he thought he received his orders to kill from a demon residing in his neighbour's dog.

Mission-oriented motivations

These killers think they are cleaning up the world, as they have a mission to get rid of certain types of people. This can range from prostitutes to homosexuals to those of a particular religion.

Hedonistic motivations

Hedonism means pleasure seeking, and hedonistic killers kill as a means of gaining thrills and pleasure; people are therefore expendable. There are several subtypes: there are lust killers for whom sex is the primary motive; there are thrill killers, who seek to inflict pain or fear and receive a thrill from hunting and capture, and possibly torture; and there are comfort or profit killers, who kill to maintain a comfortable lifestyle.

Power/control motivations

Power killers kill to gain control over victims. This is the killer who is mostly likely to have been abused as a child, leaving him or her feeling powerless. They may rape their victims, but the power over the victims is not necessarily sexual, as in the hedonistic killer.

Profiling originally appeared to be more appropriate for certain types of offence than others (Stevens, 1997). Currently, the most common crimes for which it is used are murder and the more serious sexual offences, especially where it appears that there is a series of connected crimes. The FBI believes that property crimes and robberies are not particularly suitable for profiling, as such offences are unlikely to reveal many clues about an offender's underlying personality. The FBI also stresses that the profiles need to have a clear set of guidelines about inferring behavioural evidence from crime scenes. The profile generation therefore has several stages to navigate:

Stages of FBI profile generation

1. Collation of information is the first stage and is referred to as profiling inputs. This will include a full description of the offence that has taken place and of the crime scene. An account of the victim may be included too. A report on forensic evidence and any interpretation where possible, including (where appropriate) autopsy, blood and fluid analysis, and description of wounds, estimated time and cause of death, and type of weapon. This will be studied in order to extract any behavioural elements that can be identified.
2. Once the information is collated it will be organised into any meaningful patterns. The objective of this stage is to build decision process models; in other words, to form a structure on which to build the profile. So, the type and style of the crime is identified. For example, in a murder case, the crime(s) would be classified by whether it was a single offence or they were a series of offences (serial murder) or multiple offences (mass or spree killings), and there is a further classification dependent on the relationship of the killer to the victims: family, known or stranger. The second item to be identified in the decision tree is the level of victim risk (low risk means those people who present easier targets to the killer), offender risk (how much risk was involved in committing the offence), escalation (whether the offender is moving or is likely to move from, for example, voyeuristic acts to sexual assault), time factors (time of day, how long the commission of the crime took, etc.), location (where first contact with the victim took place,

where the crime was actually committed, etc.). All of these pieces of information allow the building of a picture of the crime in terms of the decisions the offender took to reach the crime itself and afterwards, such as disposing of a body.

3. The third stage is the assessment of the crime in terms of the sequences of events and the behaviour of the victims and the offender, as well as these can be determined. This provides specifics based on the decision model from stage 2. At this point, the organised/disorganised classification is made from the strategies and sequences the offender has used. Other elements are also used, such as the motivation of the offender and the crime scene dynamics. The motivations are often difficult to determine; it is much easier with an organised offender as s/he premeditates and plans and can often carry out a plan that is logical. The disorganised offender can be motivated by delusions resulting from mental illness, or from the patterns of behaviour driven by drugs and alcohol. Crime scene dynamics, on the other hand, are the elements common to all crimes scenes, such as location and, in violent crimes or murder, the cause of wounds or death, method of wounding, etc. These are examined in the light of similar cases and the body of knowledge that investigations have accrued.

4. The fourth stage is the generation of the profile. This means identifying the type of person the offender is and their behavioural organisation within the crime itself. For the FBI, this also means identifying strategies for investigation and interrogation. The profile will include the offender's demographics, physical characteristics, habits, beliefs and values, pre- and post-offence behaviour. At this stage, the profiler can validate the profile generated by ensuring that it fits with the reconstruction of the crime, the evidence and so on.

5. During the investigation stage, the profile is used to its best advantage by the investigative agency and a second point of validation is made if a suspect is apprehended and charged (stage 6).

The FBI method has been criticised for a lack of rigour and scientific method. One major point to be raised is that validation/evaluation of the profile is somewhat circular. The FBI uses their process to investigate the most serious crimes, such as serial murder or rape or kidnapping. In order to profile serial murderers, for example, there needs to be a process by which crimes can be linked, and subsequently linked to a single offender (or a single group). The FBI process does this by determining and classifying the characteristics of the actions carried out at the crime scene (Woodworth & Porter, 2001). For this to be successful, the procedure needs to be reliable and empirically testable. In other words, the system needs to have validity.

The FBI process of classification (the organised/disorganised dichotomy) has become an 'industry standard' due to a certain level of reliability, but it lacks theoretical and empirical foundations and assumptions (Canter, 2004). The classification system is derived from a single, interview-based study with 36 incarcerated serial killers in the USA. While this might have been a pivotal piece of work, it seems precarious to base a whole investigatory process upon it. Canter further criticises the system in that it does not meet the criteria of a typology. He proposes that a more analytical or statistical approach is needed (Canter, 2004).

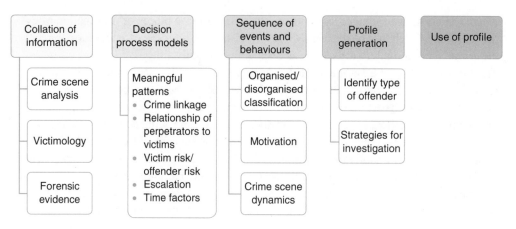

Figure 12.2   FBI profiling process

UK profiling: the statistical approach

Canter's first case, in which he used his preferred, more statistical methods, was that of John Duffy and David Mulcahy, the 'Railway Killers'. During 1982–85 large numbers of women had been raped near railway stations. The press dubbed the offender the 'Railway Rapist' until December 1985, when Alison Day was strangled after being raped. At that point, the nickname naturally changed to the Railway Killer. Police asked David Canter to examine the evidence using his approach, which suggests that the interaction between a criminal and the environment in which the crime took place means clues are left. This is not the same type of evidence that forensic scientists gather, such as hair, physical traces, bodily fluids or fingerprints, but is concerned with the behaviour of the offender, their treatment of the victims and anything they say, etc. Also, in serial offences, such as murder, rape or stalking, larger patterns of behaviour can be deduced, and subsequently overall impressions can be generated.

For example, in the Railway Killer case, Canter noticed that there were significant periods of time when the offender was operating during normal working hours. This meant that he was able to be missing from work or normal activities without being noticed or attracting suspicion. In addition, the person responsible for the attacks must have had a good knowledge of the area around railways in North London. The attacks were planned, so the perpetrator was fairly well educated, and the sexual acts performed suggested that he was sexually experienced. It was also possible that there was more than one rapist involved, given the ways the women were subdued and attacked. All this information, when generated into a profile, meant that John Duffy, a previously known suspect, was moved up the list. Canter (2004) insists that this is all profiling can really do. Psychological science simply allows profilers to add details to the forensic evidence already in place. When Duffy was arrested, following a woman in a secluded area, he was charged with all the rapes and murders, but did not say anything about an accomplice until after his conviction. In 1997, he named David Mulcahy, and it subsequently emerged that Mulcahy was the main perpetrator, the one who had decided to move from rape to murder for a greater thrill (Bennetto, 2000).

The UK method of profiling, pioneered by Canter, brings profiling into the arena of systematic methodologies with complex statistical methods of analysis. This is the distinction between what might be referred to as the UK and the USA methods. The use of empirical and statistical techniques in the UK system emphasises psychological crime scene evidence and the input of this information into databases allows an analysis of the coexistence of patterns across similar offences. For example, stranger rape has many elements in common, such as surprise and a high probability of violence, etc. But in addition to the commonalities, there are other elements that may be specific to one set of rapes, such as apologising or torture (Howitt, 2002). If several rapes in relatively close proximity to each other occur and the rapist typically says something specific, such as apologising or uttering a particular type of threat, this allows the linkage of those offences to one particular offender. If details have been entered into a database, it is possible to statistically analyse the likelihood of these being committed by different offenders. Additionally, if the rapist also commits other offences during the attack, such as theft, it is likely that he is already known to the police for this other type of offence and therefore this can be added into the profile in order to refine it and identify possible suspects. Of paramount importance in the Duffy case was the recognition that he was very familiar with the area in which the crimes took place. Such data form the fundamental elements of geographical profiling, one of the statistical techniques that aid the generation of criminal profiles. Algorithms (procedures or instructions to follow to reach a certain point) are used that analyse the movements of serial offenders in an attempt to identify probable locations in which they operate (i.e. their home, the home of a friend, workplace, etc.).

Canter's success with the Duffy case, and subsequent effective contributions, do suggest that profiling can be a productive aid in the detection of crime. However, the caveat mentioned in Chapter 1 about the Rachel Nickell case must be borne in mind. Profiling aids investigation and detective work, coupled with thorough forensic science, but it cannot replace any of these. Empirical evaluation of the practice of profiling is still under way, and recent studies are still questioning the applicability the underlying hypotheses of behavioural profiling (Trojan & Salfati, 2011). Such validity measurement is complicated by the difficulty of establishing any criteria by which to measure success. Even if arrests and convictions follow from profiling, it is difficult to say with any certainty what contribution the profile may have made in addition to conventional police investigation. Further difficulty comes from the perception of senior officers of the efficacy of the profiling techniques. Although a very small proportion of senior officers have expressed an opinion of profiling that suggests it has contributed to the success of police work (Alison et al., 2004), it is much more likely that such officers prefer to attribute success to standard police practice. A further examination of all of these elements is still needed.

HOW IS PROFILING CARRIED OUT?

Profiling requires a thorough knowledge of psychological theory, particularly that related to personality and personality types, statistical analysis of psychological data and the ability to interpret it correctly, and an understanding of the ways in which people reason. It also needs keen observational powers and the ability to think laterally. A profile is generated by collating all of the evidence available, which will include interpretation of physical evidence and any DNA comparisons, autopsy reports, if appropriate, and any behavioural evidence from the crime scene.

Collection and interpretation of physical evidence

The most basic principle of scientific criminal detection is that material is always left at the scene of a crime by a perpetrator or other personnel entering the crime scene. This can include hair, fibres, soil, fingerprints, footprints or shoeprints, bodily fluids and documents. All of these pieces of potential evidence must be gathered in a systematic way. It is also now known that it is likely that a perpetrator has unknowingly taken similar things away from a crime scene. This is called Locard's Exchange Principle, after Edmond Locard (1877–1966), whose work on the application of scientific methods and logic to criminal investigation and identification is now seen as the cornerstone of forensic science.

   Police officers and scientific officers – often called scenes of crime officers (SOCO) or crime scene investigators (CSI) – will protect and preserve the immediate crime scene and some of the area around it, together with any potential suspects' homes or vehicles. This is to ensure that the collection and documentation of evidence is carried out methodically and with minimal contamination. In this way, the chain of custody can also be maintained; this is evidence about evidence, ensuring that it has not been tampered with and can be shown to be genuine. According to Giannelli (1996), any alteration of an article can reduce or negate its probative value, as it is no longer in the same condition as at the time of the crime. The only people who should deal with evidence are the officers who collect it, the scientists who analyse it, or, in the case of a body or serious injury, the medical examiner who carries out the forensic medical or post-mortem examination. In addition, other experts may need to be consulted and to examine the evidence, such as forensic anthropologists or forensic odontologists. The psychologist rarely steps into these particular arenas because the direct examination of physical evidence is not within that purview. However, many early advocates of psychological profiling, such as Robert Ressler, suggest that there are psychological aspects of the Exchange Principle that are also important in the examination of a crime scene, and this can then lead to a profile (Turvey, 2008). The study of the commission of a crime from which these pieces of evidence have been recovered can aid the analyst or can be given an alternative account by a psychological examination.

Examination of a homicide victim

Sudden and/or unexpected death is usually examined by medical personnel – medical examiners or forensic pathologists – who are qualified to certify the cause and manner of death. The elements of determination of a death as unnatural or natural, by the deceased's own hands or another's, requires careful examination of a large number of factors concerning the mechanism of death and immediate and proximate causes. As such, the examiner employs specialised techniques to answer specific questions relating to sudden unexpected death and that distinguish such a death from one of natural causes. This information may be presented in court so the examiner also needs to be proficient in translating scientific and medical information to a lay jury.

If it is determined that a murder has taken place, all relevant examinations of the crime scene will be carried out. The placement of the body may be of importance to both the physical and psychological interpretation of a crime scene. Therefore the body will not be removed until a medical examiner releases it, and after any crime scene scientists have gathered pertinent evidence. At the scene, the medical examiner may be able to give an estimate of the time since death by determining the internal temperature of the body, although a more accurate estimation will be given during the autopsy procedure at the laboratory/morgue. The temperature of the body, the temperature at the crime scene, the weight of the victim and all other appropriate variables are then applied to a formula designed to predict the time since death. According to Payne-James et al. (2011), core body temperature drops at 1.5°C each hour from the time of death, so the difference between the temperature when the body is discovered and the usual living temperature provides a rough estimate of time since death, taking into account other variables. Other ways of estimating time since death include stiffening of the body (rigor mortis), pressure of fluid in the eyes and pooling of blood in the body.

In addition to gathering physical information from the victim, crime scene officers will attempt to record any fingerprints, collect items such as hairs and fibres, and document any blood spatter evidence. An accurate picture of the crime scene will be needed so photographs will be taken to document the position of the body and other aspects of the scene. An important element at the scene or at the laboratory/morgue is the identity of the victim. Sometimes this is difficult to establish without the aid of other experts, such as forensic odontologists, forensic anthropologists, etc.

Once the body is removed to the morgue, it will be examined by a forensic pathologist. A forensic medical autopsy is an external and usually an internal examination of the body to determine cause of death. It also provides a more accurate estimate of the time since death.

Estimating time since death

There are several elements by which time since death can be determined. The level of decomposition in the body is one of the major ways in which this is measured. For example, immediately after death muscles relax, but then there is a gradual onset of rigidity. This is not the same rigidity seen when muscles contract under conscious effort. This hardening is called rigor mortis and is caused by the conversion of glycogen into lactic acid. This decreases the pH of the body (the more acidic the body is, the lower is the pH) and causes a chemical reaction in the muscles. As there is a chemical reaction taking place, it is affected by the temperature of the air around the body, accelerating in hotter air and slowing down in cold air. Highly acidic conditions will also accelerate the process. For these reasons, and also because the perception of rigidity is subjective, rigor mortis is not regarded as a highly effective way to determine time since death (Swift, 2006). Rigor dissipates from the body anywhere between 12 and 36 hours after onset (Prahlow, 2010).

A second form of mortis is livor mortis, which is the settling of blood in the lower parts of the body due to gravitational pressure after the heart has stopped pumping. The pooling of blood causes the skin in the lower parts of the body to take on a darker colouring, but this is affected by contact with the floor or other objects and clothing. The body can be examined to see if it has been moved some time after death or if clothing has been removed.

The third form of change is algor mortis, which refers to the cooling of the body, mentioned above. Body temperature is a range, and is affected by exercise, illness, decomposition, infection and ambient temperature. The body cools by radiation (transfer of heat to the air), convection (transfer through moving air currents) and conduction (transfer by contact with another object). Consideration of the scene and other factors need to be taken into account when interpreting cooling rate.

There are several other changes to the body that can assist with determining time since death. There are changes to the eyes in terms of colour and shape, for example. There are also chemical changes in the body that can be measured most accurately by the fluid in the eye.

After the body is received at the mortuary, it is photographed and the clothing is examined. Any material on the external surfaces of the body is collected, together with hair and blood samples, and any material from under the nails. If a sexual assault is suspected, the anogenital areas of the body are also photographed and swabbed for analysis at the forensic laboratory. The body is then undressed and examined for wounds, etc., then cleaned and weighed. A record of the general description of the body, concerning ethnicity, sex, age, hair colour and length, eye colour and distinguishing features, is made. In some jurisdictions, the autopsy may stop at this point if the cause of death can be determined from the external examination only. However, it is common practice in other places to carry out an internal examination too. The chest is opened in order to gain access to the internal organs (and the body may be eviscerated). It is then examined, and other samples may be taken. It is usual that the stomach contents will be examined too, as the time of the last meal and the extent to which it is digested can be enlightening in determining what the victim was doing before death. The next area to be examined and opened is the head, allowing the brain cavity to be inspected for signs of infection or trauma. As with crime scene evidence collection and examination, the forensic autopsy is a carefully conducted process, with meticulous record keeping being an essential component.

A medical autopsy will often determine the cause of death. For example, in simplistic terms, water in the lungs will indicate death by drowning, whereas petechial haemorrhages in the face and upper body can indicate death by asphyxiation. However, it is not always possible to determine the manner of death, or whether the death was due to murderous intent, accident or suicide. Such a question may sometimes be answered by a psychological autopsy.

Psychological autopsy

If the results of the medical autopsy are inconclusive, a psychological autopsy may be called for. This is essentially an examination of the mental state of the deceased in the time immediately prior to death. There are a number of reasons why it might be appropriate to undertake a psychological autopsy, although the most common is to assist in determining the nature or manner (rather than cause) of death. The term 'psychological autopsy' was first used by E.S. Shneidman (1981) to describe a posthumous evaluation, via thorough retrospective investigation, to determine the deceased person's intentions, in terms of his or her death, in circumstances where the mode of death was ambiguous in nature. Therefore, this will include several themes of investigation.

Cause relates to how the person died. While this may be ambiguous, it is often the clearest item to determine. Mode is the set of circumstances leading to the death, classified in terms of natural causes, accidental, suicide or homicide. Shneidman (1981) suggests that in between 5% and 20% of deaths examined by a medical examiner the mode is unclear. This might then lead to the investigation of motives to determine whether the death was suicide: if there is little motivation to kill oneself, then the verdict of suicide may be inappropriate. The person conducting the psycholegal autopsy needs to establish any reasons and/or events that prompted the individual to act. However, it may not be possible to gain this type of insight directly. Sometimes it must be inferred from other evidence (Biffl, 1996). In addition to motive, intent is an important consideration because, without intent, the death may be accidental or due to misadventure. Determining intent is often done by examining the level of lethality or risk-taking in the behaviour that led to death.

There are several ways to conduct a psychological autopsy. However, a review of records – the medical reports, any mental health reports and the personal documents of the deceased – is required. Interviews with survivors, family members and friends can give a clear time line, and also some insight into the mental state of the deceased. The difficulty with the process is actually one of its strengths – its flexibility in use – which means there are no guidelines on how to carry out the procedure in any standardised way, and hence no training can be given (LaFon & Dvoskin, 2007). It is difficult to support such an intuitive process, even including the objective data described above, as a means of providing irrefutable evidence, but such a criticism can be levelled at the use of psychology in all aspects of the legal and investigative process, of course.

The psychological autopsy is essentially a data collection tool, the most common source being interview data obtained from the family and friends of the deceased person, together with medical records. There is some evidence to support its validity (e.g. Brent et al., 1993). However, Knoll (2009) attempted to set out clear guidelines and suggested that it should include:

- biographical information (age, marital status, occupation)
- personal information (relationships, lifestyle, alcohol/drug use, sources of stress)
- secondary information (family history, police records, diaries)
- alcohol and drug history, history of dealing with stress, medical history, family medical history, recent stressors in the victim's life, military history, employment history, educational history, sexual history, dietary history
- interpersonal relationships, writings by the deceased, books and music owned by the deceased, websites visited, phone calls made, recent conversations with friends, acquaintances, relatives, co-workers and teachers, interests and hobbies shared with others, old and current enemies
- reactions by any of the above parties to the victim's death, especially as to the degree of lethality, as well as the usual questions about early warning signs and who might have intended harm
- assessment of intention about the role of the decadent in their own demise, including any sub-intentional, covert or unconscious role; this is obtained by analysing the pattern of how the victim went about accomplishing their goals or life plans
- fantasies, dreams, thoughts, premonitions, fears or phobias of the victim, socio-emotional mood swings, mental status examination, concentration and judgement abilities, IQ
- timeline of events leading up to the day of the deceased's death.

Collating evidence for a profile

The above describes the types of evidence that can be gathered from a crime scene, and how that is done. The evidence from the victim is obviously an important element of that. With a living victim, such as someone who has experienced a sexual assault or robbery, then the evidence to be gathered is slightly different. A victim in this case is an important witness to what went on, but s/he must be treated with sensitivity. There may also be physical/biological evidence that can be collected from living victims.

Once all the information is collated, a profiler may be requested to examine it with a view to building the profile required. At this point, however, there are still two types of evidence to be considered and these are essentially psychological in nature. First, there is the testimony of any witnesses/living victims and the psychological or behavioural elements of the crime scene. While detectives and crime scene officers have hopefully compiled a comprehensive dossier of evidence, these may not have been considered from a psychological perspective. A psychologist can aid the interviewing process and also identify issues within the crime scene that may not have been considered.

Psychological elements of crime scenes and witnesses

Examination of a crime scene reveals several pieces of behaviour that an offender or offenders have carried out. The first is all the actions necessary to carry out the crime, such as breaking into a house, subduing a victim, etc. This is called the *modus operandi*, or method of operation, and is often shortened to MO. Crimes can be classified in terms of MO (the first systematic record of an MO was made by Scotland Yard during the 1890s) so that a pattern of criminal habits can be maintained to track offenders and crimes. The Scotland Yard classification of MO had ten elements to be recorded, such as means of entry, transport, etc. Douglas et al. (2006) describe the components of the MO as behaviour that will ensure the success of a crime's commission, allow the perpetrator to escape from the scene and evade detection. This is learned behaviour. The form of the MO will also evolve as offenders can learn from experience; it is therefore dynamic. An unfortunate effect of the success of profiling, or at least its publicity, is that offenders can also learn to exhibit false change in their MO, such as changing geographical areas or types of victim, in order to confuse detectives and profilers. Hence, *modus operandi* is not necessarily the only psychological element that should be noted. There are, however, two other items to be inferred from the scene.

The signature is a combination of behaviours that is not needed to successfully execute the crime but is something that the offender must do – they may even be the reason that the crime is carried out. In general, signature is a combination of behaviours. Douglas et al. (2006) describe it as the behaviour an offender needs to do to fulfil some emotional need above and beyond that needed to accomplish the crime. It often seems strange that this behaviour occurs because it may mean the perpetrator spends longer at the crime than is necessary. They are more indicative of the needs and patterns of the offenders and include behaviours such as wound patterns, verbalisations, particular sex acts, ways of controlling or subduing the victims(s), the taking of souvenirs, or ways of destroying evidence. Hence the signature is seen as a compulsion to express part of the offender's personality. It will never change in its essential expression but it may escalate. For example, if the signature is a form of body mutilation, this may increase or become more complex from victim to victim (Keppel, 2005).

A final part of the psychology of the crime scene is ritual behaviour. There is disagreement over whether this is viewed as a sub-signature behaviour or a behaviour in its own right. Ritual behaviour is fundamentally unusual behaviour and may be based on the psycho-sexual or emotional needs of the offender. Douglas et al. (2006) state that while the ritual may evolve, its themes are consistent throughout a series of offences. However, there may be additional elements that are designed to taunt, such as leaving notes or signs, writing on walls or signs in or on the body that may change.

Presenting a profile

The above are all elements that require a psychological interpretation because they may be indicative of psychopathology and are not the fundamental elements required to commit a crime, but they are required in the offender's mind. Therefore to produce a profile, these elements and their interpretation are vital in order to ascertain the cognitive processes underlying the offender's motives and behaviour.

Hence, we now have a description of all the things needed to compile a profile, i.e. the crime scene description, geographical data, witness statements, forensic scientific results and, in the case of suspicious death, the autopsy report and any information about the victim, up to the detail of a psychological autopsy. In addition to these inputs, the profiler would also need to determine the MO, signature and rituals from the crime scene information, including hypotheses about demographic and physical characteristics, behavioural habits and personality dynamics of the perpetrator.

The use of Canter's profiling techniques in the Railway Killer case was extremely successful, but there are instances in which it has been less useful. The real test of profiling is whether it can lead to a solution either in studies where the perpetrator is known but those attempting to profile are blind to this, or in so-called 'cold cases' that have never been solved. There is an argument in the scientific and legal community on whether the first paradigm has been adequately followed in order to demonstrate the validity and efficacy of profiling. Kocsis (2006) states that it has been carried out, but not in all forms of profiling; that the so-called statistical forms have not been fully validated even while claiming to have the only valid format to be followed. He claims that the so-called statistical forms have not been fully validated, even though proponents of this format claim it is valid, the only one that can be used with confidence.

The second way to examine the use of profiling is to look at cases that have not been solved. This exposes the format of profiling to scrutiny without complicating or distracting the full investigatory process. Let us return to the first paragraph of this chapter and see how profiling can aid the investigation of these horrific cases.

Profiling serial murders

Prostitutes are favourite victims of serial murderers; the sex worker is extremely vulnerable for several reasons. First, his or her work is often carried out in the dark, alone with the client, who is often a stranger. Additionally, several killers have described the wish to kill prostitutes because of what they do. For example, Peter Sutcliffe (the 'Yorkshire Ripper') claimed that he had heard God telling him to rid the world of prostitutes (Salfati et al., 2008). The murders of prostitutes may often be accompanied by sexual acts, and it is the emergence of new technology and forensic testing that has aided police investigations of such crimes. However, the police investigating the crimes described at the beginning of this chapter did not have such technology and science available. The murderer of Mary Nichols, Annie Chapman, Elizabeth Stride, Catherine Eddowes and Mary Kelly did not need to fear

DNA or physical traces on the bodies or the crime scenes, as these murders took place many years before the use of scientific evidence was commonplace. The 'Jack the Ripper' murders took place in 1888 and the perpetrator's identity will remain a mystery. However, we can examine the evidence that is available and determine how a profiler might have used it.

The murders took place in Whitechapel, an area in the East End of London. This was a severely deprived area, and many women needed to supplement their income selling sex. As a result, the area was frequented by men seeking the services of prostitutes and a stranger would not look out of place. So any theoretical supposition about Jack's socio-economic class is simply that, theory. The suspects that the contemporary police and history have given us range from a prince of the realm to a Polish immigrant barber, from an Oxford don and well-known author to an American quack doctor. The only thing all of the accused have in common is that they are white and male, although the man in charge of the case, Inspector Abberline, did posit the theory that Jack should, in fact, be called Jill.

The population of the East End of London was predominantly white in the 1880s; all the victims were white. Statistically, serial murderers kill within their own race, so there is a high probability that Jack was white. The women were under-nourished but had reputations for drinking heavily. They supported this habit, and the need for food and lodging, with prostitution. As such, they were at high risk of becoming victims to violence. They were accessible, and it is even highly likely that they approached the killer themselves. All the victims except the last known victim were killed outdoors, in the early hours of weekend mornings, very quickly and with post-mortem mutilation. All were killed within a short distance of each other, although the first victim was slightly apart from the others. It is possible that the first victim was in the area in which the killer felt comfortable or safe. Once the victim was found and the police investigation started, he may have moved his operation to a secondary area, seen on the map in Figure 12.3 as a close triangle of sites.

Figure 12.3   Whitechapel and the Ripper victims (1894 map courtesy of Ordnance Survey)

Contemporary and modern analyses of the Ripper's victims agree that the five victims found within the triangle are definitely his murders (these are referred to as the Canonical cases), but some suggest that there were other deaths in the area that may be attributed to him (or her). Keppel et al. (2005) note that 11 women were killed in this area during this period, but only five can be definitively identified as being the victims of the same killer in question. The linkage is due to distinct, personal signature characteristics, including domination and control of the victim, unusual body position, sexual degradation, mutilation, organ harvesting, etc.

The MO of this killer is the way in which the victim was chosen, approached, attacked and disposed of. Each of these is very similar in each of the five murders identified above, but some behaviour changed and was elaborated upon from one victim to the next. The postmortem mutilation of the women's bodies appears to be some form of acting out a sexual fantasy of penetration, known as piquerism, a paraphilia in which sexual arousal or satisfaction is derived from stabbing, either oneself or another (Peak, 1996). According to Keppel et al. (2005), this is very rare. This ritual behaviour became highly elaborate in the last victim, the only one who was killed inside, perhaps because he had more time to act out whatever fantasies this may have been.

The Ripper murders are what is generally described in the literature as lust murders (Purcell & Arrigo, 2006). This is because the killer attacks the sexual organs or genital areas of the body. Overwhelmingly, lust murderers are male (Chan & Heide, 2009), so it is highly probable that the Ripper was male. Above, it was established that he was most likely to be white, as few such crimes are inter-racial. They also include a high level of psychopathological elements, a violent psychopathology that has its typical onset in the mid to late 20s. The murderer was also able to engage with the victims and evade detection, so it is unlikely that he was a young age. He was also able to blend into the environment and not look out of the ordinary, but at the same time let his victims know that he was a potential client of their prostitution.

It is highly likely that he had fantasies of domination, cruelty and mutilation of women. He probably worked in an occupation that did not bring him into a lot of contact with many people, but which followed a normal work pattern (Monday to Friday) as the murders happened at weekends. Given the confidence with which he killed and then mutilated the bodies, it is also likely that he had some experience of anatomy, but this could be as a butcher or as a mortician. It is unlikely that he lived with someone, such as a wife, who would have noticed his movements late at night or him coming home covered in blood. He may have had a venereal disease if he had frequented prostitutes in the past. After each murder he would have needed to access somewhere where he could clean himself of the blood and possibly change his clothing.

An interesting feature of this murderer is that he allegedly wrote letters to the press, although there is some question as to the true identity of the writer. It was these letters that gave rise to the name 'Jack the Ripper'. Many hoax letters were received during the period of the murders. Experts believe some of these to be genuine, in particular one containing a piece of a human kidney. Such communication is rare, according to Guillen (2002). The genuineness can be verified by the inclusion of details that can only be known to the killer and the police, and they also often include information that is relevant to the motive for the crimes, albeit unconsciously. Some letters are a plea for help. The so-called 'Lipstick Killer', in Chicago in 1946, wrote 'For heaven's sake, catch me before I kill more; I cannot control myself' on the wall of one of his victims (Kennedy et al., 1947). Some move the investigation to different levels. For example, in the case of the Zodiac Killer in San Francisco in the 1960s, police did not initially link the murders as they were in different jurisdictions. The killer made calls to the press and police, and sent indecipherable coded letters, all of which led police to link the murders and decide it was indeed a serial killer who was responsible for all of them (Graysmith, 1986). Unfortunately, the communications are rarely enough to help apprehended a murderer. Of the hundreds of letters sent to the newspapers offices and the police during the Jack the Ripper investigation, three are believed to be genuine. They either mention elements of the crimes that were not made public at the time and, indeed, predict the double murder of 30 September, or were accompanied by the grisly package of half a human kidney, thought to be removed from Catherine Eddowes. The letter ridiculed the police efforts to apprehend the murderer.

Sadly, the Ripper was never caught, and it is obviously difficult to tell whether a modern profile could have added anything to the investigation. London police in 1888 did not have at their behest all the forensic science we are accustomed to seeing; this includes the input of forensic psychology.

THE EFFICACY OF PROFILING

Profiling faces challenges from both the scientific community and from the criminal justice system in which it finds itself operating. These challenges rest upon the questions that psychology is also wrestling with, namely whether personality is consistent between situations and across time, and whether perceptions of behaviour by others accurately reflect personality and characteristics. In profiling, the first question means that the knowledge base of personality theory, and the research upon which it sits, is questioned when a profile is presented, in that those using it need to know whether the idiographic representation is accurate and reliable. Secondly, the profile is also questioned in terms of the nomothetic application of personality theory to the interpretation of the crime scene elements such as the signature.

Trait-based theories of personality assume that personality remains consistent across situations and time. Hence, if criminal profiling relies on the assumption that the 'criminal personality' is consistent, then offenders will exhibit similar behaviour across all of their offences independently of any situational differences in each offence site and type. A further assumption is that these behavioural traits are extended into everyday lives outside the offending arena. Unfortunately, this is as flawed as the theory underlying these assumptions. It is now recognised in personality theory that situational factors should be taken into account when assessing personality, but this has not extended to any profiling knowledge base. (Situational factors contribute as much to the prediction of behaviour as personality dispositions.) This is likely to be equally true when predicting criminal behaviour. The importance of situational factors is apparent when one considers research in the profiling domain. For example, offenders rarely display high levels of behavioural consistency across the crimes they commit, and do not necessarily display any more consistency in other parts of their lives than the rest of us. However, there may be a case for showing consistency across different types of crimes. For example, rapists who break into their victims' homes are more likely to have prior offences of breaking and entering (Santtila et al., 2005).

A further question is whether the actions of the profilers are any better than those designated as non-profilers. Comparing the performance of professional profilers with that of non-profilers in mock profiling scenarios is a typical experiment to evaluate the accuracy of profiles. Participants review details of a case and make inferences about the offender. These inferences are categorised on the basis of offender cognitions (such as remorse), the physical evidence presented and crime scene behaviour. These are then checked against the genuine attributes of the case. Meta-analyses of the literature in which these studies are published showed that the profilers were found to be more accurate than non-police personnel on overall measure of profile accuracy and on examination of the physical evidence, but their predictive accuracy was no better than the non-profilers in examining the cognitive processes of offence behaviour (see Snook et al., 2007). However, if police officers are removed from the profiler group and placed in the non-profiler group, the results become much clearer (Kocsis et al., 2008). In this set of studies, the results suggested that the profilers were better (but the differences were not statistically significant) across all predictor categories, and particularly so in terms of the overall profile and its predictions. This might therefore suggest that it is the putting together all of the elements of a profile that make a profiler's success, but that police officers with a good grasp of criminology can produce profiles as successfully as those calling themselves profilers. Indeed, Snook, Gendreau et al. (2008) suggest that any belief in profiling is misguided as it has no theoretical grounding or empirical support at all. They go on to say that the faith exhibited is merely a result of a repeated message of success, the label of expertise and the emphasis on successful cases. The human mind wishes to make sense from ambiguity, and the portrayal of criminal profiling is one of ambiguous messages and *post hoc* interpretation.

To answer these challenges we need to return to the two forms of profiling detailed above. These are not the only forms of profiling but they are the two most influential. The FBI model is presented as one-dimensional in nature; it is a simple classification into organised and disorganised. This is an out-dated oversimplification, of course. The model has moved on and now attempts to apply other forms of personality classification. Even so, this does appear to have low predictive ability, as personality appears to be consistent over time but not over situations (Bartol & Bartol, 1999). A situational approach therefore needs to take into account other items beyond the offender, including that of the victim and criminological insights such as risk factors. Such sociological and criminological inputs may not be welcomed by psychologists in the forensic field, but they may be useful to consider. Risk factors include the issues that change over time and situation, such as a person's attitudes and values, and those which remain the same, such as gender or other biological characteristics. Each of these has a unique contribution to the likelihood of becoming a criminal (Farrington et al., 2010), and progressing through the life course as one (Gavin & Hockey, 2010). As such, profiling already includes these elements: the consideration of the MO is an element that, while it may evolve, holds its core elements as a persistent set of behaviours.

The final major question to be addressed is not whether profiling is an efficient aid to investigation but, rather, is it an ethical one? As always with psychologists, whether in research or practice (or more likely, both), this is an underlying issue for every part of his/her professional life, and profiling is no exception. Perhaps profiling is also the area in which psychologists or other practitioners of profiling are under the most scrutiny. The Rachel Nickell case brings this sharply into focus. An innocent man, no matter what his fantasies may have been, was wrongly accused of the murder and the real killer was allowed to go free. The use of the profiler's input in this case was wrong, and the protest of the psychologist involved – that it should not be used to target an individual – was lost in the pursuit of what appeared to be justice for the young mother.

It must always be clear that a profile is not developed in order to target an individual but to eliminate possible suspects, suggest areas of investigation and forms of interrogation, and formulate strategies for legal cases. However, there is no formal training for profiling. Therefore, practitioners must operate under their own model and within their own professional boundaries. Profiling is not a designated profession and does not have any specialised training programmes leading to it. Hence there is no minimum standard of competency as in other area of forensic psychology. There is also no sanction that can be brought against any lack of professionalism of a profiler. Furthermore, there is no agreed methodology for producing a profile and disagreement about processes that need to be followed. It is therefore difficult to subject it to open, scientific analysis.

Another issue is that there are ethical considerations in the use of any aspect of personality theory and its application in, for example, educational or occupational as well as forensic settings. Professional bodies in psychology find themselves in a difficult situation with respect to profiling; there is no professional edict on the practice and ethics of profiling, so if a profiler appears to be behaving unethically and incompetently, there is no sanction that can be exercised. Professional bodies are now calling for peer review, education and training, and common professional standards for practitioners of evidence-based criminal profiling.

SUMMARY

The use of psychology in the investigation of crimes is not as clear-cut as in other areas of forensic application. Profiling is probably the best known but least understood of all such applications. It is beset with problems and challenges, not least because there is no agreement about how to carry it out and there are claims that it has no scientific grounding. The various methods have been evaluated in this chapter. The next chapter will examine what happens when the investigation of a crime has moved forward and evidence from witnesses and interviews with suspects need psychological input.

Discussion point: Can you profile a stalker?

'Stalking' is a term used to describe unwanted or obsessive attention by an individual or group towards an individual. This is similar to harassment and intimidation, and includes following the person, monitoring them or sending unwanted gifts or other items. It can escalate to more serious behaviours, such as kidnap or murder. One form of stalking that also contains a pathological explanation is erotomania, a delusional belief that another person is in love with the affected person. The object of the delusion is usually high status, often famous. This may be the result of psychoses. However, erotomania and psychosis does not explain all the behaviours classed as stalking, and there have been attempts to examine the phenomenon in order to classify and profile stalkers. Using the references below as a starting point, examine whether there is any support for the potential profiling of stalkers.

Miller, L. (2010) Stalking: patterns, motives and intervention strategies. *Aggression and Violent Behaviour*, 17(6): 495–506.
Wood, R. & Wood, N. (2002) Stalking the stalker. *FBI Law Enforcement Bulletin*, 71(12): 1–10.

13

Psychology in the Police Station 1: Victims and Witnesses

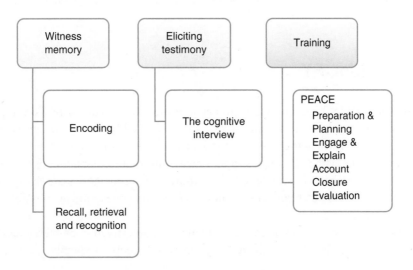

Witness memory

Eliciting testimony

Training

Encoding

The cognitive interview

PEACE
  Preparation & Planning
  Engage & Explain
  Account
  Closure
  Evaluation

Recall, retrieval and recognition

Being the victim of or witness to a crime can be very traumatic. In addition to the incident itself, there is a need to tell the authorities involved as much as can be remembered about the events surrounding what happened, as this will aid the police and forensic teams in carrying out their investigation. Due to stress and simply poor use of memory, this can be difficult and sometimes it all goes horribly wrong.

KEY THEMES

- Eyewitness memory
- Identity parade/line-up simultaneous/sequential presentation
- Cognitive interview
- Enhanced cognitive interview
- PEACE model
- Episodic memory

After a crime has been committed, the witnesses to it need to recount as much as they can remember in order to aid the investigation. Witnesses include any living victim(s) and anyone else who either saw or heard the events unfold. Hence eyewitness (and earwitness) memory is an episodic memory for the event. It is heavily relied upon in both the investigation of a crime and within the court. However, as cognitive psychology tells us, the accuracy of eyewitness memory is often negatively affected by many factors that impact upon the encoding and retrieval of the witnessed event. Several cases throughout history have demonstrated that these memories are volatile, and a growing body of research supports this position. There are issues with encoding during the event and after the event and at the point of retrieval, both immediately after the event and at a later time (such as giving testimony in court).

WITNESS MEMORY

Memory is a fickle thing, and we learn early in life that we cannot rely on it at all times. Sitting in an exam room, how many students have wished for better memories? How about watching a film in which there is an actor whose face you think you recognise but you cannot remember his name? It keeps slipping away until your companion asks 'isn't that the bloke who used to be in EastEnders?' If we know that our memories are faulty, why are we so ready to rely on another person's memory to send someone to prison, possibly for the rest of his or her life?

In 1973 Elizabeth Loftus started the first empirical investigation of eyewitness testimony. The first set of studies looked at the ways in which people remembered a car accident.

She showed people pictures of an accident and then altered the wording of the questions she asked about it. For example, if she described the two cars as smashing into each other, the estimates of the damage were much higher than when she said they had hit each other (Loftus & Palmer, 1974). Loftus and her team then investigated what effect leading and misleading questions had (Loftus, 1975). This led to the development of the misinformation effect paradigm, which demonstrated that not only were memories for the event itself faulty, but that they could actually be altered due to exposure to incorrect information. This was the first real experimental work that showed how malleable memory is. It showed that eyewitnesses can be open to suggestion in even unintentional ways. What's more, the experiments have been reproduced many times.

Encoding events

The work of Loftus and her associates demonstrates that there are several problems with the memory for events, starting with the accurate encoding of elements during a crime. The first is concerned with remembering faces, which is a major element in using eyewitnesses to identify perpetrators. Megreya and Burton (2008) performed three experiments that showed that, even under non-stressful conditions, people struggle to correctly identify unfamiliar faces, whether presented with a live person (video) or in photographs. They conclude that this is one of the components of encoding difficulty in crime scenes, and that it contributes a large proportion of the inaccuracy of testimony.

The area of the brain involved in encoding and recognising faces is called the fusiform face area. It appears to function in a unique way in comparison to other visual recognition areas. Faces are therefore a highly specific set of memory stimuli (Kanwisher & Yovel, 2006). Wells and Hasel (2007) took this knowledge a step further and suggested that the holistic representation of faces in memory may hinder the recall of faces in certain investigative processes such as composite face matching, which gives cues at the feature level. Other issues are also important in the encoding and retrieval of case, such as the 'other-race effect' (see the discussion point at the end of the chapter).

In addition to the established difficulty with face recognition, other elements of the crime incident affect adequate encoding. Trauma during the event may result in the information being repressed from conscious processing. This may also trigger dissociation, in which the person involved psychologically and emotionally removes themselves from the event, a form of coping mechanism. In the more severe cases, such trauma can result in post-traumatic stress disorder (PTSD) or psychogenic amnesia. PTSD can affect explicit memory – the conscious

Fusiform face area (FFA) – the area of the brain that appears to be involved in processing visual information about faces. There is some debate about this, although there is evidence from patients with prosopagnosia (a neurological impairment of the ability to recognise faces) that shows that the FFA behaves differently in people without the impairment.

recall of experiences and information – making it difficult for people to recall specific events, including those associated with the trauma that caused the issue. According to Amir et al. (2010), implicit memory, the more unconsciously, deeply encoded memory, remains unaffected in PTSD. Similarly, psychogenic, or dissociative, amnesia can affect explicit memory for events, particularly after witnessing a very violent crime. However, as Bourget and Whitehurst (2007) report, this effect is treated with some scepticism, as most cases arise from the perpetrator claiming to have no memory for the crime, and hence building a defence of diminished responsibility (see Chapter 16).

In a less dramatic way, memory can still be affected by stress or mood, and events are best controlled when the recall context is similar to the point of encoding. This, of course, will not be appropriate for crimes, but it is the hypothesis on which the idea of crime reconstruction is based (Houck et al., 2012).

Other encoding questions centre around the attention paid to some aspects of the crime event, such as a weapon. Presence of a weapon, such as a firearm, knife, etc., would make those witnessing the crime focus upon it due to fear, making the weapon the most salient aspect, and the most memorable (Hope & Wright, 2007). The problem arises in that the witness is less likely to be able to remember the other aspects of the crime as the weapon focus has narrowed attention and taken up encoding resources due to the highly aroused state that a weapon causes (Pickel, 2009). Conversely, concentrating on too many aspects at once can negatively impact on memory too, as cues interfere with each other.

Recall, retrieval and recognition

Once the crime has been committed and the witness is trying to recall the events, several factors can contribute to information being inaccurately recalled. Memory distortions mean that the witness alters the account of the events, not consciously, but because the misinformation is becoming confused with the actual recall. People report what they think they have witnessed, but this can be a false memory. In 1974 and since, Loftus' experiments in recall show very clearly what deliberately giving participants misinformation can do to the retrieved memories, although Echterhoff et al. (2005) demonstrated that this post-event misinformation can be mediated by the credibility of the source. Those taking witness statements are trained to provide warnings about misinformation.

In addition to misinformation, some mistaken identifications are due to unconscious transference. This means an inability to distinguish between the perpetrators and other people encountered at the scene. This is due to the implicit processing that has taken place, making other people appear familiar as the general features of faces are encoded. Hence, it is more likely that misidentification will happen when there is another person present with similar features to those of the perpetrator. The witness misattributes the sense of familiarity to a bystander. Identity parades and 'mugshot' presentations are being updated to take this into account.

A police line-up is an opportunity for the witness to view a series of faces that may or may not include a person suspected of the crime under investigation. Ideally, a witness will be able to pick out a guilty person from the line-up, but occasionally a completely innocent person is identified. There are detailed guidelines for the police who use the line-up method with witnesses, ensuring they reduce the pressure the witness may feel, and also that they inform the witness that the suspect may not be in the line-up, to prevent forcing identification when the witness is unsure. Police officers should also take steps to prevent the witness being given any information about who is in the line-up, so often a police officer who is not involved in the investigation will accompany the witness through the line-up procedure. In addition, the witness may be presented with the faces of the individuals in the line-up in different ways. Presenting one at a time, for example, allows the witness to compare the photo to memory independently of all the others. This is quite challenging as it means the witness is making an absolute judgement about each face. A simultaneous line-up, on the other hand, requires relative judgements and leads to more correct identifications, although sequential presentation results in fewer incorrect identifications (Steblay et al., 2003). As a result, the issue of interference and misattribution of familiarity is less likely to happen when each face is scrutinised independently and matched to recall.

A second form of interference is retroactive, in which new information is encoded that then obstructs retrieval of old information. The problem arises in witness testimony when investigators' bias leads them to inadvertently suggest something to the witness that then interferes with their accurate recall. Additionally, if there are several witnesses, they may contaminate each other's testimony. Gabbert et al. (2003) showed that the conformity effect, in which people's discussion of events leads them to add items to their testimony, affects accuracy negatively. In their experiment, people were encouraged to discuss a video of any event in which only one person saw particular things. All went on to report items that they could not have seen and had only heard about from other witnesses. Those who did not discuss the videos did not show as much inaccuracy in their later recall. Gabbert et al. (2003) suggest that this is a social influence due to conformity, and that it is not mediated by age-related memory deficits in any way. This demonstrates that the confidence with which a witness makes identifications or recalls events is very important, because Lachman and Andreoletti (2006) showed that confidence in ability to recall strengthens the accuracy of the memory.

ELICITING TESTIMONY

As discussed above, one important way of getting information from a witness is in the police line-up and other face recognition exercises. However, the identification of suspects will usually take place after the witness has described the events that took place. The ways in which police conduct their interviews can have a major impact on both the accuracy and quality of the information the witness can give. While police officers are naturally anxious to get as much information from the witness as possible, they need to be aware that pushing the witness can result in confabulation – the presentation of untrue information which the person believes is their correct and accurate recall. Pezdek et al. (2007) carried out a series of experiments in which the participants, as witnesses, were forced to make a response to an unanswerable question. In comparison to the unforced condition, people confabulated material, leading the researchers to conclude that pressing for information may not be the best practice. In addition, issues of suggestibility need to be taken into account, as police interview techniques may include suggestive and leading questions.

Geiselman et al. (1985) examined the ways in which police could enhance the memory of witnesses in interviews. They compared the then standard police interview, hypnosis and a 'cognitive interview' based on retrieval mnemonics, and concluded that both the cognitive and hypnotic techniques were superior to the standard procedure. However, as it is not practical to train police officers in the techniques of hypnosis, the cognitive interview technique has been adopted as the most effective method of police interview.

The cognitive interview

The cognitive interview is a technique by which eyewitnesses or victims report their memories of the events of the crime through four retrievals. It helps minimise the misinterpretation and uncertainty that can result from standard police interviews. It also overcomes the issue of confabulation that can result from being pressured to answer or being asked the same question several times (Chan et al., 2011). Suggestive and/or repeated questioning can lead to distortions in memory and can even increase suggestibility. If officers offer misleading information to a witness, this can receive more attention than previously encoded material and witnesses change testimony to include the erroneous elements. Chan et al. (2011) go further and suggest that the repetition of questions and of erroneous information can alter the witness's own view of what happened. Using open-ended questioning instead can overcome these problems and allow the witness to move along the events at their own pace and without manipulation.

So what does the cognitive interview consist of? The witness is taken through four stages of retrieval:

1. *Mental reinstatement*: The first thing an interviewee will be asked to do is to mentally revisit the event. Forming a mental picture re-accesses the environment, and they may be asked to remember things that are seemingly trivial, such as the placement of furniture or the temperature of the room. They will also be asked to think about how they were feeling at the time, to revisit their mental state. This allows all the features of the event to aid in recall.

2. *In-depth reporting*: The interviewee is encouraged to report every detail, no matter how peripheral it may seem to the main incident. Geiselman et al. (1985) identified this as being important because initial reporting may only include what the interviewee thinks is important. Even though they are unaware of the value of any of it, in-depth reporting might provide recall cues to other information.

3. *Narrative reordering*: The recounting of an event from start to finish is the creation of a narrative. If the witness is then prompted to recount it from different points in the unfolding of events, or to think of it from end to start, this may provide a new perspective, leading to new information. Recounting backwards, for example, means later elements provide cues to earlier ones rather than the other way around.

4. *Reporting from different perspectives*: Asking the witness to think about how things would be viewed from another person's point of view can give them insight into their own thinking.

After these stages have been completed, supplementary techniques can be used in order to elicit specific items from the narrative. These are questions to the interviewee that may allow some further detail to be recalled, such as asking if the perpetrator reminded them of somebody, or whether s/he used any unusual words or speech patterns.

Cognitive interview/Enhanced cognitive interview – a technique for eliciting information from witnesses that minimises misinterpretation and distortion. The enhanced version includes more social settings.

These processes have all been found to be useful in interviews, but research and practice has also led to suggestions about enhancing the cognitive interview.

The enhanced cognitive interview

The enhanced version of the cognitive interview contains the same four retrieval rules as the original, but adds more social aspects to the setting and procedure that appear to improve communication. These include minimising distractions, allowing for pauses between questions and their responses, and being sensitive to the level of language used to suit the witness (see below). This allows for an environment in which the interviewee can be comfortable and can increase the context reinstatement.

The enhanced cognitive interview (ECI) therefore differs from the cognitive interview (CI) as the control is handed over to the interviewee, who is encouraged to strengthen the contextual reinstatement by the use of focused memory techniques. This means the production of fundamental imagery that can be probed, such as clothing and objects at the scene, which might provide additional cues. Research demonstrates that the ECI is significantly better than other methods at eliciting accurate recall, but also shows a slightly increased chance of eliciting inaccurate recall, but less confabulation (Memon, 2006). Shorter versions of the ECI, which are less time-consuming and just as helpful to investigators, have also been developed. These contain fewer instructions for change order and change perspective since these have been shown to be less effective cognitive strategies. If time is tight, then the shorted version of the ECI may be better.

TRAINING – USING THE COGNITIVE INTERVIEW

Training for police officers now follows the PEACE model – Preparation and Planning, Engage and Explain, Account, Closure, Evaluation.

- Preparation and Planning: Interviewers are encouraged to plot events on a timeline (for information), to understand what is known and established about the interviewee, to plan the aims and objectives of the interview, to identify what points and facts need to be verified, to identify any practical issues (access to the witness, whether the witness is vulnerable, etc.) and to write up the plan.
- Engage and Explain: Interviewers are encouraged to engage in a conversation (and not just fire off questions), to manage the first impressions, to explain the purpose of the interview clearly, and to manage the expectations.
- Account, Clarification, Challenge: Interviewers allow the witness to relate the narrative uninterrupted (with prompts only), make high use of open questions and summaries, ask the interviewee to expand and clarify the account, use question loops, open questions, probe questions, and keep summarising and repeating until all is clear. If the interviewee is deceptive, this is the point at which it starts to emerge. Challenging the account exposes inconsistencies and lies, and using the interviewee's own words backs up evidence or exposes more inconsistencies. Asking the interviewee to explain the account and the evidence means they are sure in their own mind that they have given the full account.
- Closure: Closing down the interview properly reinforces rapport. Interviewers should ask the interviewee to contact officers again if needed.
- Evaluation: Interviewers establish whether the process has revealed everything needed, or if there were lies and inconsistencies not followed up by the officers.

Within the PEACE framework, the CI is taught to police officers using a tiered building-block approach (tiers 1–5). The tier of training represents experience and expertise, with tier 5 being the most skilled. All officers are required to complete tier 1 training (Milne & Powell, 2007). Research about the effectiveness of PEACE is limited, but currently it is supported as the best method available for training.

PEACE model – a model of training for police officers in how to interview witnesses.

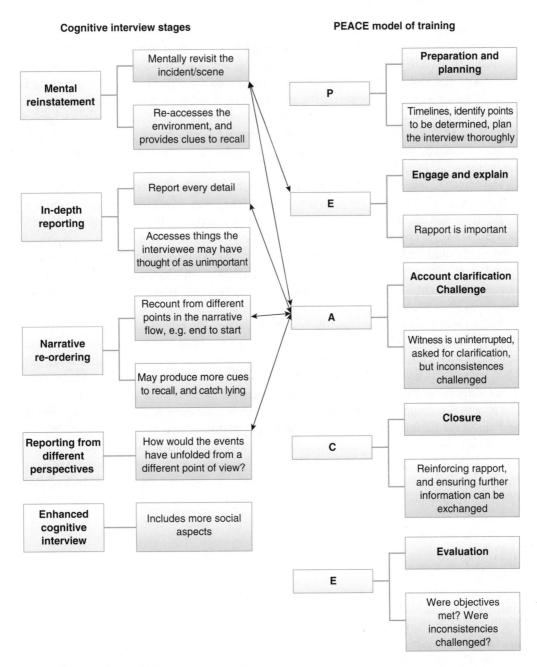

Figure 13.1   The cognitive interview and training to use it

Limitation of CI/ECI

The cognitive interview and its developments have received some criticism, suggesting limitations in its effectiveness. Police officers find the technique time-consuming and difficult to conduct as it requires a great deal of concentration on the officers' part. The technique is also not useful with uncooperative witnesses. Lack of cooperation means rapport is difficult to establish and the communicative relationships cannot be made. Other research suggests that the CI/ECI is not effective in enhancing memory for recognising suspects in situations such as a line-up. In fact, it appears that the CI can be obstructive in correctly identifying faces (Finger & Pezdek, 1999).

The cognitive interview has been modified for use with children but it has been shown that it is not generally effective for younger children. They may have more difficulty adhering to the more advanced components of the cognitive interview. This difficulty in comprehending the more cognitive aspects of the interview, and hence being unable to comply, is particularly difficult for change perspective instructions (Memon et al., 2010). Children can, however, provide coherent answers to concrete questions, such as those about clothing and sequences of events. Variants of the CI are therefore available for use with children, and they have been shown to be very effective (Verkampt & Ginet, 2010).

At the other end of the age spectrum, it might be expected that older adults would have more difficulty in remembering details. In fact, the CI has been shown to a very useful strategy with older witnesses. In a review of the literature, Memon et al. (2010) discovered that older witnesses produce much more reliable and accurate information with the CI technique, particularly in the environment context restatement part.

There is one group of vulnerable people who are not necessarily aided by the use of CI, and this is adults and children with intellectual disabilities, such as significantly impaired cognitive functioning or acquired brain damage. In addition to being vulnerable to victimisation, as witnesses, people with intellectual disability may be susceptible to suggestibility and confabulation. As a result, interviewing needs to avoid leading questions and not rely on open-ended questioning.

SUMMARY

The trauma of being a witness to a crime can lead to some significant errors of memory. Such errors might lead to the misidentification of suspects or the inaccurate recall of events. Applying psychology to these issues has resulted in training for police interviewers in the use of various interview techniques designed to enhance memory and elicit accurate information. The next chapter will consider how psychology can be used in interrogation of suspects rather than in the interviewing of witnesses.

Discussion point: Why are people misidentified?

Facial recognition is a major element of eyewitness testimony. Why, then, do so many witnesses misidentify people when they have seen them quite clearly or fail to identify them altogether? One element is clearly familiarity with types of face. Evans et al. (2009) showed that there is a general effect of own-race versus cross-race identification, and that cognitive interview elements, such as contextual reinstatement, only enhanced own-race recognition. Shriver et al. (2008) suggest that the impact of the other-race effect is very important. They carried out experiments that demonstrated superior recognition for same-race faces and this effect was mediated by perceived social class. Critically evaluate this research and examine how you might carry out research examining whether this is changing as there is more interchange and communication between races in society.

Evans, J., Marcon, J. & Meissner, C. (2009) Cross-racial lineup identification: assessing the potential benefits of context reinstatement. *Psychology, Crime & Law*, 15(1), January: 19–28.

Shriver, E., Young, S., Hugenberg, K., Bernstein, M. & Lanter, J. (2008) Class, race, and the face: social context modulates the cross-race effect in face recognition. *Personality and Social Psychology Bulletin*, 34(2): 260–274.

14

Psychology in the Police Station 2: Investigative Interviews and the Psychology of False Confession

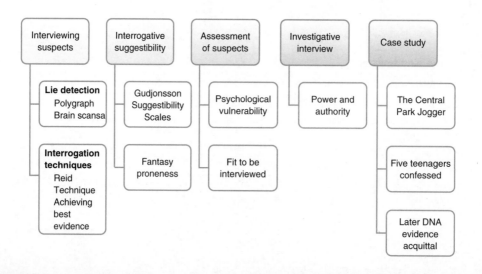

Interviewing suspects	Interrogative suggestibility	Assessment of suspects	Investigative interview	Case study
Lie detection Polygraph Brain scansa	Gudjonsson Suggestibility Scales	Psychological vulnerability	Power and authority	The Central Park Jogger
Interrogation techniques Reid Technique Achieving best evidence	Fantasy proneness	Fit to be interviewed		Five teenagers confessed
				Later DNA evidence acquittal

In 1989, Trisha Meili was a 28-year-old investment banker in New York. She had degrees from Wellesley College and Yale University, and a promising career at a prestigious Wall Street bank. She kept fit by jogging in Central Park. On 24 June, while she was running after dark, as usual, she was brutally assaulted and raped, and left for dead. Her injuries were horrific: she had been elaborately bound, dragged almost 300 yards and beaten. Her skull had been fractured to such an extent that her eye was out of its socket and, when found, she had suffered severe blood loss and was hypothermic. She could only be identified by an unusual ring she was wearing that her colleagues recognised. When taken to hospital, physicians thought she would die or be in a permanent coma, but she recovered, albeit with no memory of the attack. This case caused a huge outrage, and Meili became known around the world as the Central Park Jogger. The assault itself was horrific; the New York Governor called it 'the ultimate shriek of alarm'. Meili made an extraordinary recovery and identified herself as the victim in 2003. However, what happened in the police station over the days and months following the attack caused a good deal of outrage too.

The police arrested a group of teenagers who were taking part in an activity known as 'wilding', running in packs, attacking people in their path. Undoubtedly, these young men were not behaving well that night. Not only did they confess to the attack on Meili, but they also implicated each other, and in 1990 were convicted of physical assault and rape. In 2002, DNA evidence showed that another man, a convicted serial rapist and later killer, was the real perpetrator. He confessed and insisted that he was alone that night in 1989. The five young men had their convictions vacated (made legally void), although they had spent some years in jail, thus becoming one of the best known cases of false confession in global legal history. It was difficult to believe that anyone could confess to a crime they did not commit, but the Central Park Jogger case, while possibly the best known, is not the only example of this strange phenomenon.

KEY THEMES

- Investigative interviews
- Confabulation
- False confession/false memory
- Interrogative suggestibility
- Fantasy proneness/fantasy prone personality
- Lie detection
- Interrogative techniques
- Reid Technique
- Assessment of suspects
- Fit to be interviewed

Psychological knowledge has been applied to events inside the police station. As Gudjonsson (2003) suggests, the interrogation of suspects is an area fraught with difficulty, and, if something goes wrong, it can lead to problems such as false confessions and unsafe convictions. None of these is a new idea. As early as 1908, Hugo Munsterburg, in his treatise *On the Witness Stand: Essays on Psychology and Crime*, was reporting on the confession of a young man to murder whom Munsterburg was convinced was innocent. He was publicly derided for this belief because it does seem fantastical that someone could be condemned to death on the strength of a confession when he or she was innocent. Cognitive psychology also tells us how unreliable human memory can be, so knowledge of psychology or recourse to psychological assistance can be helpful in interviewing witnesses and identifying suspects.

INTERVIEWING SUSPECTS

Interviewing someone in connection to a crime – a suspect – requires a good deal of skill on the part of the police officer. Interrogation techniques are largely informed by psychological knowledge and the belief that the suspect is going to lie. There are several processes, therefore, to take into account: the detection of lies, the persuasion to tell the truth and the logic of events and behaviour.

Lie detection

Police officers need to be able to identify lies in testimony, especially those given by people who are suspected of crimes. There are several ways of doing this, including mechanical/electronic means and use of interview techniques.

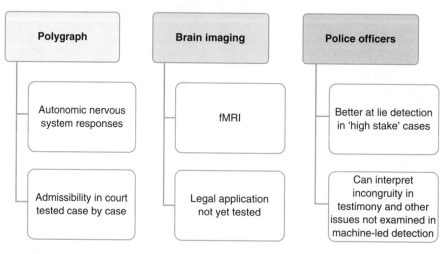

Figure 14.1   **Lie detection**

When the term 'lie detection' is used, many people think of the lie detector machine, also called the polygraph. It was invented in 1921 by John Larson and is routinely used by many law enforcement agencies to interrogate suspects, and even by some organisations to screen job applicants. Essentially, the polygraph measures several psychophysiological responses, such as respiration, heart rate and galvanic skin resistance, and records changes in these as the subject responds to questions asked by the operator. Theoretically, as the autonomic nervous system is not under conscious control, any fluctuation in these aspects is taken to be linked to psychophysiological stress in response to questions in which the responder is lying. The validity of the polygraph is widely questioned, with many asserting that the changes in heart rate, etc., are open to many different interpretations, no matter how reliably these are observed to happen. It is regarded in much of the scientific community as simply an unstructured interrogation technique with little real-life validity, at best giving support to an opinion that someone is lying. Iacono (2001) stated that it does not meet the standards of a scientifically credible process and that it can be 'beaten' by augmenting responses to control questions. While it is not strictly inadmissible in court, the production of polygraph evidence has been challenged extensively in many jurisdictions. The use of the polygraph during an investigative process rather than a judicial one is less rigorously tested and can be an aid to police officers in determining the route of questioning of suspects.

New technology has been considered in the area of lie detection. The ability of brain imaging techniques to accurately depict activity in the central nervous system has led to the potential for a lie detection method superior to the psychophysiological measurement in the polygraph.

Brain scans and lying

There are several ways in which the brain can be 'mapped' using imaging technology. One of these, magnetic resonance imaging (MRI), is captured by a device with powerful magnets within it. The area to be imaged (here, the head) is placed inside the machine and then bombarded by the magnetic fields and radio frequency fields produced by the machine. Essentially, what happens is that hydrogen atoms in the body's cells all line up on the axis of the field. When released from this lining up, they give off a miniscule amount of energy, and it is this that is measured in order to provide the very clear images seen in MRI scans. When the MRI is used to image the brain, successive measurements are taken that show changes in the blood flowing through specific areas, indicating activity, and in this case the scans are called functional magnetic resonance images, or fMRI.

In order to map changes in the fMRI to specific events, changes in the ratio of oxygenated and deoxygenated blood in brain regions are interpreted as indicative of higher or lower relative brain activity in those regions. The idea is that in order to detect lying, the suspect is asked the same sorts of question that would be asked in a polygraph test while within an MRI machine, and the activity in their brain is monitored. First, there might be some practical difficulties with this, not least that the MRI is one of the noisiest pieces of medical equipment anyone will ever encounter, and a not inconsiderable number of patients have experienced claustrophobic episodes while in it, although there have been developments to make people with claustrophobia more comfortable (Spouse & Gedroyc, 2000). The second is that lawyers might be reluctant to allow such exposure, citing safety concerns, or at least use those concerns to prevent their clients from being required to go through this. The third objection might be on the grounds that everyone has the right to silence and that this technology is being used to self-incriminate when the suspect/defendant is exercising the right to silence (Boire, 2005). Langleben (2008: 4–5) deals with this objection quite neatly:

> This line of criticism fails to make the important distinction between mind-reading and lie-detection applications of fMRI. Deception is not a thought but a voluntary act. … Thus, while unauthorized access to one's thoughts and opinions (i.e. mind-reading …) may be obtained using fMRI tools developed to study addiction and schizophrenia … lie detection demands that there is a lie, i.e. a conscious and voluntary response to a query.

The difficulty with this is, of course, that those not trained in the sciences involved in fMRI and its interpretation will tend to think of it as an exact measure and that testimony based on it will determine guilt or innocence because the technique will definitely tell us if someone is lying or not. In the same ways as DNA is seen to be an unofficial gold standard of biological evidence (see Chapter 15), will the fMRI lie detector become the same for psychological evidence? Spence (2008) pointed out that replication of findings in legal and mock legal scenarios has yet to be done, and in 2012 Langleben and Moriarty concluded the same has yet to be finished.

When considering the skills of human interrogators, however, there are only a few studies in which police officers have attempted to demonstrate their ability to detect whether someone is lying. Franzten and Can (2012) suggest that, although experiments show that people are generally bad at lie detection, police officers are significantly better at it, specifically in what might be regarded as high-stake situations, such as when interviewing someone suspected of murder or another violent crime. Ironically, they found that property crime detectives are significantly more confident in their ability to detect lies than those investigating violent crimes. Johnson and Morgan (2013) conducted a review of studies in which police officers' abilities in lie detection were examined. In this, they describe how the officers' own viewpoints and biases were important in what led them to determine who was lying, and that training to overcome the negative effects of stereotypes were supportive in the aim to be more accurate. It is tempting to police officers, they contend, to assume that the stereotypes they can build up about the typical perpetrators of particular types of crime are similar to the offender profile that experienced behavioural analysts will produce, and that it is legitimate to seek to apprehend or question individuals who fit that stereotype. This can be unconscious stereotyping, done without the police officer even being aware that it has been done, even those who have received training to avoid doing it. It is difficult, according to Williams (2007), not to allow stereotypes, particularly unconsciously held ones, to colour one's perception if a scruffily dressed person is lurking in a residential area when no one else is evident. Williams' study involved the behaviour of European police officers operating closed-circuit TV cameras remotely, and showed that they targeted such individuals excessively, to the detriment of focusing on others.

Johnson and Morgan (2013) also discovered that studies reveal ways in which police officers are able to successfully spot lying, including such abilities as interpretation of incongruity in evidence and testimony (such as failure to explain the presence of trace evidence), and interpretation of non-verbal cues (such as non-fluidity of speech or inappropriate emotional expressions). Such skills can be of value in the interrogation phase of an investigation.

Interrogation techniques

Interrogation is a word that appears to have a great deal of negative connotation, seeming to describe an aggressive approach to questioning suspects (Kassin et al., 2010). In the latter half of the twentieth century, it became apparent that physically coercive forms of questioning were unacceptable, from both a human rights perspective, and due to the risk of false confessions. Under scrutiny from the media and the courts after several high-profile cases of unsafe convictions, police interrogation tactics were deemed to be instrumental in producing false confessions. For example, during the 1970s, there were several pub bombings in Birmingham, UK, in which 21 people died. Birmingham police obtained confessions from six Irishmen who were resident in the city, and the Birmingham Six, as they became known, were all sentenced to life imprisonment. However, they all later claimed to have confessed because they had been beaten, and they retracted the confessions. Due to increased public pressure after cases such as this, in 1984 the Police and Criminal Evidence (PACE) Act came into being. This sets out rules about the way in which suspects are arrested, detained and interviewed, providing safeguards for suspects and police officers alike, in that all interviews are now recorded, ensuring non-coercive techniques of interview are used. This means that police officers need to be trained in appropriate interrogation techniques.

In training police officers and others involved in interrogation, one of the most influential techniques in both the USA and the UK was the 'Reid Technique', which was developed by John E. Reid in 1947 in Chicago. Reid had established a private polygraph firm and amalgamated the experiences of operatives in using these techniques. The technique is a three-stage process of crime solution, comprising factual analysis, a neutral interview of suspects (termed a 'behaviour analysis interview') and an accusatory interview of suspects. Gathering as much information as possible in the first stage means that the interrogator is operating from a position of power. The Reid process of interviewing comprises nine steps:

1. Direct positive confrontation, allowing the suspect to know that the investigation suggests s/he is responsible for the crime.
2. Theme development. The investigator offers possible reasons for the criminal behaviour, reinforcing the justifications the suspect may already have and allowing him/her to think

about confessing. Someone who is innocent will reject any form of justification, but a guilty suspect will also deny at this stage.

3. Addressing statements made during step 2 in response to themes. The investigator reinforces the themes and does not address the denial. Part of this procedure is simply maintaining a flow of words during theme development.
4. Addressing statements, but monitoring for signs of deception.
5. Focusing the suspect's attention to the theme(s).
6. Responding to the suspect's passive mood. The investigator condenses theme concepts to one or two central elements and moves into the next step of the process, which is designed to elicit the initial admission of guilt.
7. Presenting alternative explanations for the crime, usually one negative and one positive, but both would be admission of guilt.
8. Developing an oral confession.
9. Converting the oral confession to a document.

The Reid Technique has been a successful method for interrogations, evidenced by 50 years' usage in the USA and recommendations to police officers in the UK and Canada. It is clearly a more acceptable form of dealing with suspects than physical intimidation or aggression, and is designed to produce an atmosphere in which suspects can answer questions without coercion. It also conforms to the more recent legislative practices in terms of interviewing by police officers. However, although it advocates non-coercive methods of interviewing suspects, it has been heavily criticised by psychologists and courts in both the UK and USA. The Reid procedure is to be followed when the police have a denying suspect whom they regard as guilty. Unfortunately, the advice on how to decide whether someone is guilty is at odds with published research on how to detect and interpret behavioural clues to lying. Training people to use the technique in this way does not improve lie detection performance. Therefore, while the Reid Technique militates against coercive practices in the interrogation room, it does not necessarily lead to better investigative processes. Neither does it prevent false confessions from those detainees who are the most vulnerable.

Guidelines on both interrogations in general and vulnerable people in particular are included in documentation from agencies such as the UK Ministry of Justice (MoJ). The most recent UK guidelines are outlined in *Achieving Best Evidence in Criminal Proceedings* (Ministry of Justice, 2011) (ABE), which is a generic guide to preparing to interview witnesses and suspects, and on how to make decisions about whether holding an interview is appropriate or not.

In the UK, after the PACE implementation, interrogation was deemed to be much more open and transparent and avoided the types of case which it was introduced to prevent. However, a critical report in 1992 highlighted issues of concern, such as poor interviewing techniques and assumptions of guilt (Milne & Bull, 1999). This led to the standardised framework for ethical interviewing known as PEACE (see Chapter 13), which may be suitable for some suspects (see below).

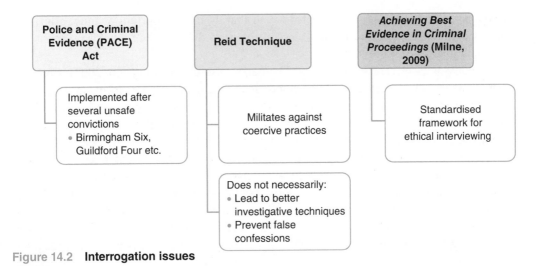

Figure 14.2   **Interrogation issues**

INTERROGATIVE SUGGESTIBILITY

When Gudjonsson and Sigurdsson (1994) interviewed 229 prison inmates, 29% reported that they had made false confessions. While, sceptically, we can assume that some of those were false protestations, it does beg the question about the testimony given in police custody. Kassin et al. (2012) found that, of the US convictions that were overturned due to new DNA evidence, more than 25% involved a confession that was clearly false. As these authors point out, this does not include cases where there is no reliable new evidence, such as a modern DNA test result, that could exonerate those who later claim to have given a false confession. Such data can also be found in other countries. For example, in studies in seven European countries, Gudjonsson et al. (2009) found that 14% of juveniles claimed to have confessed to a crime they did not commit. It is clear, then, that false confessions are a problem, and that some people are more prone to making them due to interrogative suggestibility.

Gudjonsson et al. (2008) found that there were individual differences in vulnerabilities to making false confessions. Measuring compliance in social situations, he found that those scoring high are eager to please and to avoid confrontation, particularly with those in authority. These findings led to the development of the Gudjonsson Suggestibility Scale (GSS), and later refinements, which can determine individuals whose memory reports can be altered by misleading questions and negative feedback (Gudjonsson, 1984). These are the people who can be persuaded to confess when they are not guilty, simply by being led to believe that they actually did do something when they did not. High GSS scores are also linked to poor memories, high levels of anxiety, low self-esteem and a lack of assertiveness.

Gudjonsson and Petursson (1991) also found that a large proportion of those who later retract confessions made to the police score high on the GSS, but those who resist and maintain innocence score low.

Gudjonsson also reports a link to psychological disorder (Gudjonsson, 2003). Common symptoms include distorted perceptions and memories, impaired judgement, anxiety, mood disturbance and impulse control problems. There may even be a form of serial false confessor, as Redlich (2010) found that prison inmates with a mental illness report that 22% of confessions are false. This is considerably higher than in those without illnesses.

Research demonstrates that there are several factors that contribute to interrogative suggestibility leading to false confession. In addition to the social compliance issues and mental health problems already cited, Gudjonsson (2006: 68) defines such vulnerabilities as 'psychological characteristics or mental state which render a witness prone, in certain circumstances, to providing information which is inaccurate, unreliable or misleading'. The model of interrogative suggestibility that grew out of this research shows that interrogation depends on uncertainty, interpersonal trust and expectations of success experienced by the suspect, and the ways in which they cope within these variables.

Interrogative pressure – the influences exerted upon suspects during interviews – is anything that interferes with the accuracy of the suspect's approach to reporting the events under question. For example, negative feedback can be used to some extent in interviews to allow an interviewee to know that their answers are not satisfactory. If the interviewer suggests the suspect is lying, this is negative feedback, but it will have a different effect on different types of interviewee. If the interviewee accepts the negative feedback as accurate, then uncertainty is increased and the interviewer is relied on to address the imbalance in self-esteem that is experienced. Hence, the element of uncertainty is one way in which a vulnerable suspect could be led to a state in which s/he will comply with the interviewer's directions.

A further factor in vulnerability is age, with younger interviewees/suspects being more likely to be compliant to interviewer suggestions and hence to a false confession. Gudjonsson (2003) found higher suggestibility in children younger than 12 years, but with adolescents between 12 and 18 years there was no higher GSS scores, but they were more susceptible to negative feedback. Older people (over 65 years) are more likely to experience memory impairment compared to younger people, but recent research (e.g. McMurtie et al., 2012) suggests that they are no more vulnerable to shifts in response to repeated questions in interviews than are younger adults.

There are, it would seem, problems with a certain proportion of reports made during police questioning, with some people being more vulnerable to interrogative suggestibility and hence making a false confession. However, in addition to these internal conditions, there are also external factors to take into account. The first is the interview situation itself, regarding duress and coercion, which legislation such as PACE, and in particular code C, has sought to minimise.

Miranda warning – the name given to the police caution in the USA:

they have the right to remain silent;

anything the suspect says can be used against them;

they have the right to have an attorney present before and during the questioning; and

they have the right, if they cannot afford an attorney, to have an attorney appointed at public expense to represent them before and during the questioning.

This is a rule to ensure that police officers protect an individual in custody and subject to direct questioning from a violation of the Fifth Amendment right against compelled self-incrimination. It is called a Miranda warning after the case of Miranda vs. Arizona, in which the Supreme Court ruled that eliciting statements from a suspect without informing him of these rights violated both the Fifth and Sixth Amendments (right to legal advice). In 1963 Ernesto Miranda had been held on suspicion of kidnap and rape. In court, his written confession led to his conviction and sentencing to 20–30 years in prison, but his appeal was that he had not been informed of his rights and this meant that his confession was no longer admissible. He was re-tried without the written confession being given in evidence and was convicted in 1966.

PACE code C (Home Office, 2012), refers to the procedures to be followed when someone is arrested and detained, and then interviewed in police custody. The normal procedures include being cautioned before any questions are asked. This means that the person is informed that anything they say will be recorded and may be given in evidence, and that they have the right to remain silent. In the USA, this is known as the Miranda warning (see text box). In addition, code C sets out additional rights of which the detainee must be informed, namely to have someone informed of their arrest, to be able to consult a solicitor privately, and to inspect the codes of practice. They should be given a written notice informing them of these rights, what the arrangements are for obtaining legal advice, a copy of the custody record and of the caution. If the detainee is a foreign national, they should also be told about their right to communicate with the High Commission, Embassy or Consulate, whichever is appropriate (for further details see www.homeoffice.gov.uk/publications/police/operational-policing/). The caution is a requirement to inform the person being questioned of their legal rights, and is of importance if that person is later charged with an offence. Their understanding is therefore crucial to any process of questioning. In Scotland, there is no standard wording of the police caution, although officers are trained to make statements which contain all the elements of the caution used in England and elsewhere. This no-standard wording further increases the importance of ensuring that the person being questioned has an adequate understanding of their rights (Cooke & Philip, 1998), and in particular the right to silence.

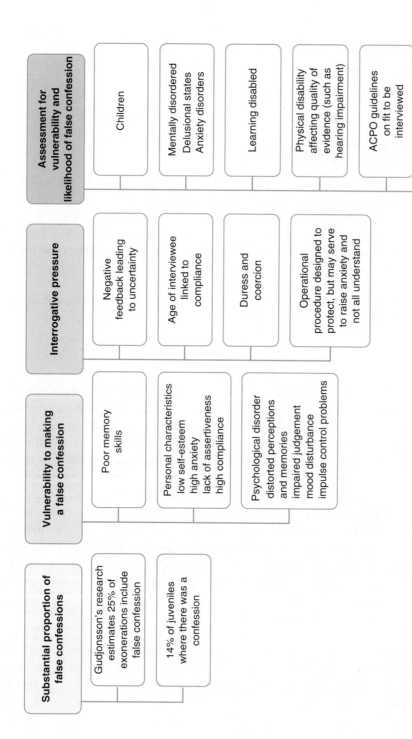

Substantial proportion of false confessions

- Gudjonsson's research estimates 25% of exonerations include false confession
- 14% of juveniles where there was a confession

Vulnerability to making a false confession

- Poor memory skills
- Personal characteristics
  low self-esteem
  high anxiety
  lack of assertiveness
  high compliance
- Psychological disorder
  distorted perceptions and memories
  impaired judgement
  mood disturbance
  impulse control problems

Interrogative pressure

- Negative feedback leading to uncertainty
- Age of interviewee linked to compliance
- Duress and coercion
- Operational procedure designed to protect, but may serve to raise anxiety and not all understand

Assessment for vulnerability and likelihood of false confession

- Children
- Mentally disordered
  Delusional states
  Anxiety disorders
- Learning disabled
- Physical disability affecting quality of evidence (such as hearing impairment)
- ACPO guidelines on fit to be interviewed
- Risk assessment

Figure 14.3 **Interrogative suggestibility**

All of these operational procedures are designed to protect the person who has been arrested, but also have the effect of ensuring that s/he understands the gravity of the situation in which s/he finds him or herself. It can also be intimidating and hinder understanding of what is happening. Cooke and Philip (1998) demonstrated that the Scottish variant of cautioning often means that suspects are presented with a caution that is more complex in terminology than the standard one used elsewhere. They developed the Scottish Comprehension of Caution instrument, and, using this, discovered that there was a very low level of comprehension of a caution statement in a sample of 100 young offenders, with only 11% showing full understanding even though 89% had claimed to understand what was said to them (Cooke & Philip, 1998). While this was linked to cognitive function, it was not linked to any other variables they examined, i.e. demography and criminal justice backgrounds. Hughes et al. (2012) then took this further. Using the same instrument, they demonstrated that comprehension of the police caution is variable across the general population. In this research, adults with low or high educational attainment were separated into three groups which were either given a verbal or written representation of the standard police caution, or were given both. Despite 95% of their research sample declaring that they fully understood the caution, only 40% fully understood it when given both verbal and written versions, and 5% understood it when presented verbally only (Hughes et al., 2011/12).

If comprehension of the situation of being arrested and questioned is low, this begs the question as to the status of information gained in police interviews, not just specifically with vulnerable people, but in general, and of admissibility of any such information in court. This also means that it is imperative that understanding be raised, and that vulnerability must be addressed early on in the process, and those seen as vulnerable should be assessed.

ASSESSMENT OF SUSPECTS

Roberts and Herrington (2011) suggest that psychological vulnerability – the cognitive challenges facing people with a mental illness or intellectual disability – is of paramount importance in police interviews, as it impacts on the integrity of the evidence to be gained. Figures given by the Mental Health Foundation (2013) suggest that a quarter of all adults will experience some form of mental disorder at some point, although the majority of these experiences do not last longer than 18 months. It is therefore also likely that a figure approaching this must be represented in those questioned by the police either as witnesses or suspects. As such, it is necessary to assess both witnesses and suspects in police custody as to their psychological vulnerability (Milne et al., 2009). However, there is no standard definition of psychological vulnerability that can be used to guide police officers in the identification of people who may need assessment, or, indeed, for the mental health professional faced with making such an assessment. Gudjonsson (2006) suggests that it is a range of psychological states that make individuals prone to providing unreliable information. The Ministry of

Justice guidelines (Milne et al., 2009) state that those who are vulnerable require special measures to assist them in giving their evidence, either in the police station or in court. Those who are defined as vulnerable are, according to the Ministry of Justice, children (under 18 years) and/or those who have a mental disorder, a learning disability that affects their intelligence or social functioning, or a physical disability that may affect the quality (completeness, coherence or accuracy) of their evidence.

Psychological vulnerabilities can affect memory in the same ways as witness memory can be affected. When this is coupled to a wish to hide something from the police, the accuracy of any answers a suspect may provide is going to be impaired. Additionally, a suspect may have linguistic impairment, such as a limited vocabulary, or use language in a disorganised fashion due to a psychotic illness. Delusional states can also make a suspect or a witness problematic in behaviour and communication. Anxiety disorders, on the other hand, may lead to overwhelming stress levels and make it difficult for the interviewee to be coherent or to concentrate on what is being asked. All such conditions can also affect memory, making it impossible to give a coherent account of behaviour during the time frame of the crime/incident they are being questioned about. Dealing with these issues in the police interview is a very difficult matter. The Association of Chief Police Officers (ACPO) in England and Wales, for example, currently has guidelines for dealing with the individual who may display psychological vulnerability. This guidance (ACPO, 2012) stresses the importance of gathering as much information as possible about the arrested person so that a decision can be made as to whether a medical assessment for fitness to be interviewed is required. Police officers are not trained psychologists or mental health practitioners, of course, and as such cannot be expected to always recognise whether a suspect has a psychological vulnerability. In clinical settings, assessment would be based on multiple information sources, which would not necessarily be available to police officers. However, the ACPO guidance does recommend what do to if a problem of this nature is suspected, such as with suspects who exhibit unusual speech or behaviour (ACPO, 2012).

The final issue is whether someone with a psychological vulnerability fully understands their legal rights, that is, their right to have legal representation or to refuse to answer. The problem comes when the issue is less discernible, or the individual is masking their own vulnerability due to the stigma attached to it. In the UK, there are screening instruments that can be used, such as form 57M (Metropolitan Police). Essentially, form 57M is a comprehensive risk assessment, covering assessment of illness or injury in detained persons before they are questioned. Other forms and guidance are under development across other police forces. Some police authorities use an assessment of the likelihood of suicide or self-harm when someone is taken into the custody suite, providing a warning for officers who are going to question this person. Custody officers should always complete a 'Detained Person's Medical Form' when an issue is suspected or identified, together with noting any medication required (National Centre for Policing Excellence, 2006). This means there are clear instructions to and from the custody staff about the possible vulnerability of the detained person. The form should indicate whether the person requires medication and whether s/he has been seen by an appropriate healthcare professional (and how soon this happened after being detained). It can also record whether any information has been obtained from national records about this person, such as whether they have a record on the Violent and Sex Offender Register or on the police national computer.

There are a range of screening tools that are available to the police in addition to the procedures mentioned above. They need to be specific enough to pick up symptoms of a particular condition, but not so broad as to miss borderline cases of vulnerability. As most instruments are designed with professional psychological use in mind, it is difficult to verify whether any are useful enough in a police interview situation. Accordingly, more interviewees are being assessed by mental health professionals for their 'fitness to be interviewed', even though this phrase does not appear in guidelines such as those for PACE. There are therefore no criteria by which to establish whether someone should or should not be assessed, or what the outcome of that assessment means for the interviewer's next step.

The risk to the police officer is that, at the very least, unreliable information may be gained when a suspect is psychologically vulnerable, and may extend up to and include false confessions. Compromising the information here has implications for anyone moving through the judicial system, as unreliable first interviews are problematic for evidence in court and for any sentencing that may occur. The PEACE model (Savage & Milne, 2007) used with witnesses (see Chapter 13) may be applicable to interviews with vulnerable suspects. However, it may not be appropriate across the whole range of suspects.

THE INVESTIGATIVE INTERVIEW

The interview of a suspect is important to the investigative process. Research provides guidance to operational procedures about best practice, such as using open-ended questioning, active listening, avoiding unnecessary repetition of questions, allowing the interviewee to answer fully, not interrupting, and so on. For example, Walsh and Bull (2010) examined 142 suspect interviews focusing on the ways in which interviewers did or did not build rapport. They noted that it was those officers who maintained rapport throughout the interview who acquired the best quality of evidence and information. However, Snook et al. (2012) contend that police officers find it difficult to implement best practice for various reasons, including a lack of training, supervision and feedback. They examined 80 police suspect interviews between 1999 and 2008, and found that almost 40% of the questions used were closed, with less than 1% being a fully open question. Other types of question used were probing, leading, forced choice and multiple questions, and questions asking for clarification. They concluded that guidelines to enhance the quality of evidence provided are often not followed, particularly with respect to facilitating extraction of information. Police officers tended to dominate the talking time and ask short-answer questions, instead of letting the interviewee talk.

Problems that arise in interviewing witnesses are also present in suspect interviews, and sometimes training in best practice does not translate to the field (Bull & Soukara, 2010). Snook et al. (2012) conclude that officers use open-ended questioning very infrequently and that this is because officers may have a bias towards believing that a suspect will not provide testimony on their own accord and that there is a need to 'pry' it out of them with specific questions. Kassin et al. (2003) showed how preconceived views of guilt lead to confirmation-seeking questions. This is not supported by research, as Vanderhallen et al. (2011) found that suspects who are treated ethically and humanely are more likely to voluntarily give reliable and accurate information, and this can lead to reliable confessions. They conclude that empathy, respect and interview clarity are highly correlated with reliable interrogation evidence: open-ended questions (including free narratives) produced nine times more than closed, yes–no questions and unsolicited information is more likely to be generated from open questions which avoid narrowing the scope of their investigation.

In addition, Walsh and Bull (2010) contend that rapport and communication, as recommended in the witness interview model, is very important in interrogation interviews too. However, they also report that maintenance of this throughout an interview is very difficult. The purpose of an interview with a suspect is to gain reliable and truthful information. A good deal of the research has concentrated on how to avoid the false confession and hence the vulnerability of suspects to this issue. However, there is also a need for psychology to be applied in the pursuit of reliable information and a true confession. Walsh and Bull (2011) looked at the way in which false denials are overcome by examining 85 interviews with suspects. They concluded that this was more likely when using interview tactics recommended by the PEACE model, and that it was particularly effective to use the model when physical evidence was lacking. They found that it was the attitude of the interviewer that was the most effective determinant of the potential for a confession that was not inherently affected by the elements that lead to false confession. The attitudes here were the behavioural aspects of how the interviewer handled the interviewee and their responses, and were more indicative of a set of tactics in questioning. The conclusions were that there were 11 attitudes (such as preparedness, calmness and being an active listener), coupled with up to 22 questioning tactics (e.g. regular summarising, gentle prods and emphasising contradictions) that led to a successful outcome, that is a confession that was not likely to be a false confession due to coercion and other tactics, and that could therefore lead to a safe conviction (Walsh & Bull, 2011).

The interviewer must therefore be well trained in all the appropriate forms of questioning and understand his/her own personally held beliefs and what effect they may have on the interviewee and how to overcome this. The interviewer must also understand how to appear to be at a disadvantage in order to allow his/her interviewee to feel comfortable enough to talk. Haworth (2006) examined the way in which power and control were negotiated between interviewer and suspect. The background to her research indicates that police interviews have a built-in asymmetry, and that there is an implicit negotiation demonstrating the status of each participant, in that the police officer(s) usually have all the power in the interview setting but that this is not always the best tactic to use. She described interviews in which this power relationship was apparently, from the suspect's point of view, in the opposite direction to the usual scenario, as she had analysed the tapes of a set of police interviews with Dr Harold Shipman.

Shipman was convicted in 2000 of the murder of 15 of his patients, but it is estimated that he murdered more than 200 people during 27 years of his practice as a GP. This only came to police attention because he had forged a signature on a patient's will, disinheriting her lawyer daughter and benefiting himself, and because a taxi driver finally realised that too many of his customers were dying and contacted police (Baker & Hurwitz, 2009). Haworth's analysis of the interviews the police undertook with Shipman showed the asymmetry she had already identified, but that the power and control appeared to reside with Shipman (Haworth, 2006). As a GP, Shipman had a high level of status within the community and society in general. In an interview scenario, the suspect/interviewee has control only in that they can choose what to reveal, and it is the interviewer's task to assert power over that control. In Shipman's case, the control was considerably harder to assert than in other interviews due to his status, so the interviewer allowed Shipman to behave as if the power was all in his hands. This established a particular kind of rapport and allowed Shipman so much leeway that he relaxed and revealed points that, while they did not lead to a confession, allowed the police case against him to strengthen.

Therefore, while the interview appears to be atypical, it demonstrates the points of good interviewing procedure in that the interviewer was prepared (he had all the information he needed in terms of evidence and likely behaviour, together with the intention to let the interview proceed as if Shipman was in control throughout), he used active listening skills (when contradictions appeared in Shipman's testimony, the police officer allowed Shipman to complete the point he was making), he was flexible (he allowed Shipman to deviate from the questions being asked and introduce a new topic, emphasising his medical expertise), and so on. This also demonstrates that the experience gained by police officers in interviewing is of paramount importance, as an inexperienced officer may not have been able to respond to the situation in the same way. While a confession in Shipman's case would not have been a false one (and he never confessed at all, but maintained his innocence until his death), gaining a confession in circumstances that were not ideal, such as appearing to be coercive, would have been disastrous for this (and any) case. A false confession is therefore not only detrimental to finding the real perpetrator of a crime, but it also damages the reputation of the police and their credibility as investigators.

The Central Park Jogger

Trisha Meili recovered from her ordeal and is now a motivational speaker. The defendants in the original case are suing the city of New York for an as yet undisclosed sum. The confessions they made are reported to be false, but there are many within the police and the US courts who still believe that the five were somehow culpable. The man identified as her rapist,

Matias Reyes, cannot be examined under oath as the statute of limitations for the crime has expired (i.e. legally there has been too much time between the commission of the crime and confession for him to be tried for it). Although it is highly probable, on the basis of the DNA evidence, that Reyes committed the rape, whether he did this unassisted and was the only one who beat Meili is still unclear. As yet, the case for damages has not been settled.

SUMMARY

As Kassin (2012) suggests, a confession will always have more weight as testimony than other evidence, particularly so if any other evidence is weak. The Central Park Jogger case demonstrates this very clearly. The five juveniles were convicted on the basis of their confessions, which could not be shown to be false until other, more compelling evidence was found. It is perhaps only conflicting confessional testimony or DNA evidence that will lead anyone to question the veracity of a confession, even if it is later withdrawn. False confessions appear to be the result of many elements, including the suspect's vulnerability and the expertise of those questioning him or her. Gudjonsson's research into the concept of interrogative suggestibility and Kassin's into false confessions are invaluable places to start when attempting to ensure that questioning suspects leads to justice, and not wrongful convictions.

Discussion point: Why do we believe false confessions?

Many cases of false confession, when exposed, make the headlines around the world. Has this attention lowered the likelihood of those viewing confessions to believe them? Kassin et al. (2005) examined how accurate people were when deciding if confessions were false or not. Even when told that half of the videos they were viewing contained false confessions, the general population (represented by students) were more accurate than police officers. If media attention had changed the public's and/or police officers' understanding that false confessions can be gained, then this result should be altered today. How would you go about designing a study that would examine that hypothesis?

Kassin, S., Meissner, C. & Norwick, R. (2005) 'I'd know a false confession if I saw one': a comparative study of college students and police investigators. *Law and Human Behavior*, **29**(2): 211–227.
Loftus, E. (1997) Creating false memories. *Scientific American*, **277**: 70–75.

Section 5

Psychology in the Court Room

The court room can be an intimidating place to find yourself, even for witnesses who are not being accused of a crime. Even the expert witness can find it somewhat difficult. This section examines what happens in the the court room and what witnesses need to be prepared for. These chapters therefore relate to the practice dimension of the competences of forensic psychology training. The issues of testimony and evidence are addressed as well as the knowledge dimension in terms of the underlying psychological theory and research in the study of the court room. The Core Roles represented here are Core Role 1 (conducting applications) and Core Role 2 (research).

Chapter 15 examines the atmosphere of the court, how this is handled, and exactly what is testimony from witnesses, victims and expert witnesses. The court requires evidence for lawyers to interpret that evidence. What exactly is evidence and how are standards of evidence determined?

Chapter 16 considers several cases of homicide committed by people who were deemed to be not responsible for their own actions, or at least who claimed to be not responsible. This allows an examination of the mind of the defendant and how the criminal justice system deals with those whose mind is atypical.

Chapter 17 looks at the other people in the court room upon whom so much depends – the jury. What is it like to be a juror, and what is expected of them? Is trial by jury the fairest way to determine guilt or innocence? How can we possibly know? Psychological research tells us some things but is heavily criticised for its lack of ecological validity. So how is this problem overcome?

Psychology in Court 1

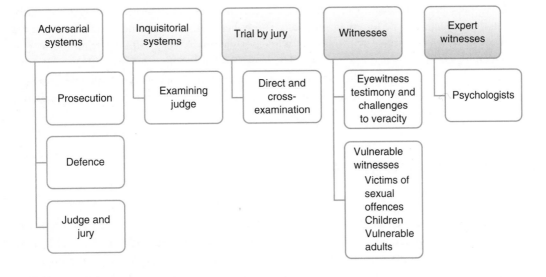

- Adversarial systems
  - Prosecution
  - Defence
  - Judge and jury
- Inquisitorial systems
  - Examining judge
- Trial by jury
  - Direct and cross-examination
- Witnesses
  - Eyewitness testimony and challenges to veracity
  - Vulnerable witnesses
    Victims of sexual offences
    Children
    Vulnerable adults
- Expert witnesses
  - Psychologists

It might seem like we are familiar with the inside of court rooms, given the popularity of dramas that allow us to look inside them. From *Perry Mason* and *Boston Legal* in the USA to *Kavanagh QC* and *Judge John Deed* in the UK, it would appear that we know exactly what happens in the court, how people behave and what would happen if we need to appear there. In fact, not surprisingly, the reality is as far from the drama as everything else we have encountered in the forensic field. Finding yourself in a court room is bound to cause anxiety, unless, presumably, you are a lawyer or judge and are there for professional purposes. The psychology of being a witness ranges from issues about eyewitness memory to the credibility of expert witnesses.

KEY THEMES

- Adversarial systems
- Inquisitorial systems
- Direct examination/examination-in-chief
- Cross-examination
- Trial by jury
- Eyewitness
- Earwitness
- Expert witness
- Eyewitness memory
- Vulnerable witness

If you have been a witness to, or victim of, a crime, the whole process of recalling and describing the incident can be traumatic in itself. The police station can be quite daunting, but the ways in which the police will question witnesses/victims is very different from the way in which they will be treated in court. The UK and USA have what is termed 'adversarial court systems', in which there are two sets of lawyers attempting to put a case about a defendant to a jury. Other countries operate different court systems, such as the 'inquisitorial court system', in which the court is part of the investigation process.

ADVERSARIAL SYSTEMS

British and American court systems are called adversarial, as there are two advocates attempting to represent their party's position before an impartial judge or jury. The judge or jury then attempts to make a finding of fact based on the evidence of the positions given to them. This system is adopted in the majority of common law countries around the world, with exception in those countries for the more minor offences. The adversarial system means that there is a prosecution case, usually presented by the state, and a defence, working on behalf of the accused. The report of the cases heard by an adversarial system is usually referred to as *State vs. Defendant*, for example, in the UK *Regina* (queen) *vs. Harold Shipman* (the case in 1999 of Dr Harold Shipman, who murdered several of his patients, see Chapter 2) or *Virginia vs. Atkins* in the USA (see Chapter 16). The prosecution case is usually heard first, as the burden of proof is on the accuser, not the accused. Hence, someone is presumed innocent until proven guilty by the court. The judge is an impartial hearer of evidence, who ensures that the rules of court and evidence are not transgressed. The rules of evidence in a particular case are therefore decided by the judge in response to requests by each set of advocates to present or to object to the presentation of evidence.

> Adversarial court system – the prosecutor is the legal representative of the state (country or other jurisdiction) making a case against the person being accused. The accused has the right to representation by a legal team who will present a defence to the prosecution.

INQUISITORIAL SYSTEMS

In contrast to the adversarial system, an inquisitorial court involves some officers actively in the investigation process of a case. They are found most commonly in countries that use a civil legal system. This means that the court is the system within which the question of criminal procedures is determined and how enquiries are conducted, and not the question of which crimes can be prosecuted and the sentences for them. An example of an inquisitorial system is that used in France. Here, the examining judge (juge d'instruction) conducts the investigation into serious crimes. S/he may question witnesses and suspects, although this is usually done by the law enforcement officers assigned to the case.

It is sometimes claimed that one of the types of court system is more or less fair than the other. No statistics or research exists in which the two systems have been directly compared, so it is difficult to judge which is better, if either. However, the adversarial system allows for processes such as plea bargaining, in which a defendant accepts a lesser charge in exchange for other testimony, and the inquisitorial system allows for an examining judge to decide if there is a case to be answered. The accused can then be sent for adversarial trial by jury, which is also presided over by a different judge. So, in effect, the two systems are very similar. A trial heard by an impartial judge and a jury is still the most likely process by which a defendant's guilt or innocence is examined.

TRIAL BY JURY

During an adversarial trial in front of a jury, the prosecution case will be heard first. The lawyers for the state will outline the case and present evidence that suggests that the crime was committed by the person accused of it. It is likely that witnesses – the people who saw or heard what happened – and possibly the victim will give testimony about the crime. The witnesses for the prosecution may be subject to direct examination (in the USA) or examination-in-chief (in the UK) by the prosecution lawyers, and then cross-examined by the defence lawyers(s), which means the answers given in direct examination can be reinterpreted. This can then be followed by redirection from the prosecution. After the prosecution case is heard, the roles are reversed, and the defence lawyers can call witnesses, to which they ask direct questions and the answers they give can be cross-examined by the prosecution lawyers.

> Trial by jury – a legal proceeding in which a jury either makes a decision or makes findings of fact, which are then applied by a judge. It is distinguished from a bench trial, in which a judge or panel of judges make all decisions. The right to be tried by a jury has been part of documented English law since 1215 and the signing of the Magna Carta, the charter which guaranteed all free men (sic) the right to due process.

> Due process – the legal requirement that the state must respect all of the legal rights that are owed to a person.

Cross-examination serves two main functions: to elicit evidence favourable to the cross-examining lawyer's case and to weaken the opposing side's case by discrediting unfavourable evidence and/or the person who provided it (Hampton & Wild, 2000). This means that it can not only present a different interrogation of the evidence and testimony produced, but it can also undermine the testimony and the credibility of the witness. A cross-examining lawyer may seek to challenge a witness's credibility by questioning the witness's ability to have seen what s/he claims to have seen (e.g. questioning the eyesight of an older witness, or disputing the witness's memory), suggesting the witness is being dishonest, or asking questions in such a complex or ambiguous manner that the witness has difficulty understanding them. Preparing witnesses for this eventuality is quite demanding as most people are not familiar with the process of the court and of trials, or even of having their accounts of what happened challenged. Wheatcroft and Ellison (2012) suggest that familiarising witnesses with the process of cross-examination is likely to lead to higher witness accuracy once in court, thus maximising the quality of

> Direct examination or examination-in-chief – the questioning of a witness by a lawyer in order to present a case from evidence and testimony.

> Cross-examination – the questioning by the opposing legal team in order to rebut the evidence. It may involve the attempt to discredit the witness.

> Re-examination – questioning after cross-examination in which the party who offered the witness has a chance to explain or otherwise qualify any damaging or accusing testimony brought out by the opponent during cross-examination.

evidence and testimony given. Such guidance appears to allow accessibility to cognitive information that allows questions and answers to be processed more effectively and to deal with the potentially misleading tactics of a cross-examining advocate.

An interesting point to note is that the accused is not compelled to give evidence, unlike witnesses, and therefore is not always subjected to the cross-examining of the prosecution. However, the jury is allowed to make inferences on the basis that the accused is not giving evidence.

The production of evidence is also subject to rules and regulations in court. Evidence and testimony can be produced by either side and challenged by the other, with the judge deciding whether or not it will prejudice the trier of fact (the jury), and whether it is actually evidence and not hearsay.

So, the components of a trial are the two sets of lawyers, the defendant, witnesses/victims and, of special interest to the forensic psychologist, the expert witness. In the remainder of this chapter we will consider the witnesses. The defendant is considered in Chapter 16 and the jury is dealt with in Chapter 17.

THE WITNESS

Witness testimony is a critical factor in the court room as it has been established that first-hand accounts are very persuasive pieces of information. Witnesses are therefore essential to the presentation of a case and to the ability of those hearing it to conceptualise what has happened (Boccaccini, 2002). Given the weight that witness evidence is accorded in court, legal counsel often attempt to prepare witnesses before they give their testimony, because the way the witness behaves during both direct and cross-examination is a crucial aspect of his or her credibility. According to Brodsky (2009), the preparation of the witness is often haphazard but is improved by the use of psychological knowledge about the court room, particularly regarding stress and coping techniques. While any unethical 'tampering' with witness is not allowed, giving the witness an idea of what to expect in court, particularly in cross-examination, is quite common, particularly with vulnerable witnesses or victims. For the latter, this has been shown to reduce the risk of revictimisation (Horn et al., 2009). Enhancing communication and credibility, and reducing the fear of the unknown for a witness is clearly beneficial, as long as the content of testimony is not altered in any way. Witnesses who are oriented to court procedure and the practice of the adversarial system are less anxious and confused than witnesses who are without such preparation (Boccaccini, 2002), and a lawyer who is prepared on the content of the testimony and the level of anxiety a witness can feel will allow for better consistency in direct examination.

In addition to preparing the witness for the experience, examining the non-verbal behaviour and non-verbal content of the verbal testimony can alert the legal teams to any characteristics that may hinder the presentation of the testimony. For example, highly emotional witnesses have been shown to have negative effects on jurors (Wessel et al., 2012), even if the topic is a highly emotionally charged one, whereas being confident and consistent has a positive effect, even though Odinot et al. (2012) suggest that this is not always a reliable indicator of accuracy. Such variables, of course, are as true for the defendant as they are for the witness/victim.

Once on the stand, the witness is also greatly influenced by the court situation itself, and any lack of confidence about memory, or indeed any errors in recall that are quite natural, can be exaggerated by anxiety and picked up by lawyers examining the testimony being given. It has been established that a lack of knowledge about the court proceedings can lead to heightened emotional states which are then amplified when giving testimony (Konradi, 1999), but that this can be assuaged by having a supporter in the court room, such as a victim advocate (Konradi, 2010). This is particularly important in cases in which there is an allegation of rape or sexual assault. A lot of progress has been made recently in the treatment of the victim of rape or similar crimes, such as guaranteed anonymity and the right not to have past sexual history discussed in court. In the USA, this is referred to as 'rape shield laws', and includes the rights that a rape/sexual assault victim has not to be identified either before, during or after the trial, and that a person's past sexual history is irrelevant and immaterial to the case against his or her attacker. Such rulings highlight the progress that has been made to protect vulnerable witnesses in courts, such as victims of sexual offences, children and those with other types of vulnerability.

The vulnerable witness
Victims of sexual offences

The laws surrounding rape and other sexual offences have long been criticised for the ways in which the victims of such offences have been treated by the criminal justice system. In Chapter 8, secondary victimisation – the potential for further trauma to be experienced by a victim due to poor handling of the case – was discussed. This potential extends to the case being heard in court. When a person is accused of rape, the main, and sometimes only, witness to the attack is the victim. Because it is the state that brings the case, the victim is simply a witness in court and is therefore, hypothetically, only accorded the same rights as any other witness. However, it is now recognised that being the witness in such a position can be very traumatic, in addition to any of the anxiety usually felt when put in such an intimidating situation. In the UK, for example, the Sexual Offences (Amendment) Act 1976 attempted to regulate the use of sexual history evidence – the examination of a victim's past sexual behaviour, number of sexual partners, etc. – but this became undermined in legal practice (Adler, 1987).

Helena Kennedy, a leading barrister and advocate for women's rights, pointed out that the mythology of rape almost serves as a legal precedent (the ruling in a prior case that is applied in the present one). Such myths include the idea that rape is only committed by strangers, at night, with a weapon or means of force, that the victim is always injured because they will always resist, that victims, particularly women, put themselves at risk of rape by 'provocative' clothing or other behaviour, that a lack of prompt reporting means the rape was not 'real' and that everyone behaves the same way after being raped (RapeCrisis, 2012). Other beliefs that colour the ways that victims of sexual offences are viewed in terms of their sexual history reflect contemporary sexual mores. Beliefs about sexual promiscuity, for example, lead to fewer rights in a person's choice of whether or not to have sex with a specific person, and that a sexually promiscuous person is less trustworthy and therefore less credible when accusing a person of rape or similar crimes, and that men's sexual urges are irresistible, coupled with the idea women lead men on and sometimes say no when they do not mean it. Such beliefs underlie the tendency for courts to examine the sexual history of the victim (Kelly et al., 2006). The failure of the original legislation to prevent such evidence influencing the jury was addressed in section 41–43 of the Youth Justice and Criminal Evidence Act 1999, which now states that no sexual history evidence should be admitted. Questions by the defence about it are not allowed unless the judge rules that it lies within several exceptions to the rule, and those exceptions should be transparent to the court.

Research suggests that this ruling has had no impact on the ability to acquit the defendant in rape trials (Kelly et al., 2006), although the conviction rate for rape is very low and the attrition rate (the rate at which reported crimes fail to reach the courts) is high (Jehle, 2012). Therefore, protecting a victim of rape or other sexual offence when s/he is a witness is now part of the regular legal process and it has no discernible impact on the findings of the case. This still does not prevent the witness being emotionally vulnerable during the trial, but it does prevent his or her sexual behaviour, other than that within the purported attack, being discussed and influencing the jury.

Children as witnesses

It is recognised that children, particularly those who are victims of a crime, are atypical witnesses due to their age and the associated issues of memory and suggestibility, their potential for confabulation and their ability to tell right from wrong (Zajac et al., 2012). Chapter 5 discussed the age of responsibility for crimes, but here the issue of a child's ability to tell right from wrong, and falsehood from truth, is the issue that a court must determine.

Child witnesses must be questioned to ensure they understand that they need to tell the truth and that they understand what truth is. This is not easy to determine, particularly with very young children. It requires knowledge of cognitive psychology and the development of cognition in a child. There is also a need to verify that a child's memory and accuracy of recall is sufficient to withstand both direct and cross-examination, and there is the issue of credibility for the jury (Segovia & Crossman, 2012). Chapter 13 highlighted the ways in which the police treat children and how investigative interviews are modified when used with child witnesses/victims. Many adversarial court systems now have processes in place to maximise the veracity of direct evidence from children, but they will often still be subject to cross-examination.

There has been considerable concern over children's ability to cope with the process of the legal system. For example, in British courts, the barristers and judge usually wear highly ritualistic wigs and gowns; in courts where children are often questioned, such as in the Family division,[1] the ceremonial dress is not worn as it may intimidate children. However, even with all measures in place, a child may still be exposed to cross-examination. Some research has suggested that being a witness can have profound effects of a child's mental health and the future likelihood of them re-engaging with the legal system in any way. This is especially so when the child is a victim. Zajac et al. (2012) describe the ways in which various jurisdictions have attempted to minimise the trauma of a court appearance for children, such as allowing children to have support people, including in the court, and sometimes allowing special measures such as giving testimony via closed-circuit TV so that the child does not have to be in court with a lot of people, including the accused. However, this really only applies during direct examination, and cross-examination, even by CCTV, can still be problematic. Even adults used to giving evidence (see 'expert witnesses' below) can find cross-examination stressful (Brodsky, 2009), and this form of verbal exchange, in which someone accuses the witness of lying, or suggests that s/he is mistaken, is very unfamiliar to a child. In addition to problems for the child's welfare, there is also the problem that s/he may not respond appropriately. Zajac and Cannan (2009) found that 75% of children can change their testimony during cross-examination, even to the point of retracting accusations, usually after leading questions that challenged the account the child was giving.

The difficulty with trying to minimise the effect of cross-examination on children and on their testimony is that the right to cross-examine is built into the adversarial system. Cross-examination serves not to elicit evidence, but to test the evidence that has been presented in direct examination of a witness. If this right is altered in any way, the question arises as to whether the system is being fair to the accused. Many countries have now implemented cross-examination by a third party, in which the cross-examining lawyer's questions are transmitted (either verbatim or interpreted) by a person sitting with the child in order to reduce the negative effect. Krähenbühl (2011) noted that there is little accord between layers and intermediaries about the appropriate forms of communication and interpretation. The recommendation is that lawyers and judges should adhere to the interview and questioning protocols described in *Achieving Best Evidence in Criminal Proceedings* (Milne et al., 2009).

Vulnerable adults as witnesses

It is not only children who are deemed as vulnerable within the court system; some adults need to be treated with care and sensitivity too. The investigative interviewing

---

[1]Family Division, a division of the High Court in England and Wales where matters such as divorce, child custody and medical treatment are dealt with.

of vulnerable adults – those with psychological vulnerabilities, intellectual impairments, etc. – is addressed in Chapters 13 and 14. However, such vulnerabilities are also evident when people need to give evidence in court, and cross-examination seems to be as problematic for them as it is for children. Keane (2012) suggests that the techniques of cross-examination in particular can confuse vulnerable adults, reducing their ability to understand what is being asked of them. He suggests that this is due to the lack of understanding on the part of lawyers of the special needs of such witnesses, and their unwillingness to abandon the forms of cross-examination that they are trained to use, rather than any deliberate wish to exploit the vulnerability of the witness. It is now recommended that courts adopt the same provisions that they have for child witnesses for an adult witness identified as vulnerable.

The understanding, or lack of it, of development and cognitive issues with respect to witness cross-examination is only one way in which psychology is important to the court system. Another way in which psychologists may find themselves involved in court is as an expert witness.

THE EXPERT WITNESS

An expert witness is someone who, acting in their professional capacity, provides an opinion based on their expertise that assists the finder of fact (jury or judge). They may provide this opinion as expert testimony in court where it can be subject to rebuttal via cross-examination. An expert witness can be anyone with a recognised knowledge or experience of a particular field and who can therefore be relied on to give evidence that is legally sound and that is the testimony of opinion. A witness is usually giving evidence of fact, that which they have personally experienced, such as hearing a gunshot or observing a car hitting a lamppost. The court then decides whether that evidence of fact is sufficient to attribute cause, for example, whether the gunshot heard was the one fired at the victim or whether the car was being driven recklessly. To assist the court in making the link between the evidence of fact and the decision, the expert opinion could be used, for example, that the victim died of a gunshot wound made at about the time the witness heard the gunshot, or that the driver of the car had a blood alcohol level consistent with the likelihood of impaired driving behaviour.

Expert testimony is admissible whenever such evidence is required. The types of expert witness vary according to the case, but the one people will be most familiar with is in the medical field. The forensic pathologist is a medical expert who is concerned with determining cause of death by examining a corpse or parts of a corpse. S/he has completed

Pathology – the study and diagnosis of disease through the examination of organs, tissues, bodily fluids and corpses. Forensic pathology is the sub-specialty of anatomical pathology concerned with the determination of cause of death.

training in medicine and anatomical pathology, specialising in forensic pathology. In most cases the pathologist will determine the manner of death as well as the cause, but may need to be assisted in that investigation by experts in other fields, including a forensic psychologist (see Chapter 12 regarding the 'psychological autopsy'). During a medical autopsy the forensic pathologist may also gather other physical evidence for other experts to examine, such as trace material from a body, including semen or other fluids deposited, fibres, dirt and skin from under the fingernails. There may also need to be a determination of the identity of the deceased, which would also be in the purview of the forensic pathologist in some cases.

An expert in forensic medicine can also be called on to testify on a variety of other issues than cause and manner of death, including the health of detainees in police custody, deaths in custody, sexual offence examination, torture, driving under the influence of drugs or alcohol and child abuse.

Other experts who may be tasked with examining physical evidence are usually called forensic scientists, although there may also be specialities within this category, such as forensic archaeology (examination of skeletal remains), forensic odontology (the examination of teeth and bite marks), or chemists, biologists and experts in drugs and toxicology.

In addition to physical evidence, opinions regarding psychological information may be required. In this case the expert is a psychologist or psychiatrist.

The psychologist as expert witness

Psychological or psychiatric opinion is sometimes needed in order to aid a criminal investigation or a trial. The use of psychology in investigation is covered in Chapter 12. Here the opinion and testimony would refer to evidence such as fitness to plead. The determination of whether an individual is fit to attend court, is competent to assist the legal team in preparation of his or her defence, and then to be sentenced, if necessary, can require physical, psychiatric and psychological assessments. The determination may be made by a forensic psychiatrist or psychologist.

A forensic psychiatrist has completed medical training and additional courses and his/her experience that blends medicine and law. A forensic psychologist does not have training in medicine, but in psychology, law and the application of psychology to the legal process. There are therefore differences in both education and outlook between a psychiatrist and a psychologist who specialises in forensic settings. Education, service methods and therapeutic approaches therefore differ. However, they can both serve as expert witnesses in courts and in relation to medical-legal issues, and face similar issues, such as matters of competence of the defendant, and so on. However, psychologists often have more training in the development, use, application and interpretation of psychological tests than a psychiatrist, so the administration of tests may fall into the purview of a psychologist.

Tests might include the Wechsler Adult Memory Scale (WMS), the Wechsler Adult Intelligence Scale (WAIS), and the Wechsler Intelligence Scale for Children (WISC). Other tests include the neuropsychological battery, visual retention tests, and so on. This scientific approach to the investigation of brain–behaviour relations provides forensic neuropsychology its unique professional standing (Kaufmann, 2009). The testimony of mental health experts presents important evidence to be considered by the criminal courts to determine questions arising throughout the adjudication process. Most commonly, this includes determining competence to stand trial, criminal responsibility or legal insanity, and sentencing in capital and non-capital cases (Redding et al., 2001). The psychologist will then prepare a report on the findings from those assessments and may be called to give evidence to that effect in court.

The evidence provided in court by other witnesses may also be examined with reference to psychological expertise. A psychologist is the more likely expert when testimony on issues such as eyewitness memory is needed. For example, Professor Elizabeth Loftus (see Chapter 13) has an international reputation as an expert in the field of eyewitness memory, and has testified and advised courts many times about it. One of her first articles about conflicting witness memory in a murder trial (Loftus, 1974) came to the attention of lawyers and led to her being consulted about the issue. She gave one of the first expert testimonies on memory and its fallibility. She has testified in or advised on the trial of O.J. Simpson for the murder of his wife and her friend, the trials of Ted Bundy, Angelo Bueno and the Menendez brothers in the USA, and the Bosnian war trial in The Hague (Haggbloom et al., 2002). Not every psychologist who provides evidence to courts and other parts of the criminal justice system is quite as eminent of course!

SUMMARY

The court room is a strange place, in which those unfamiliar with it can be intimidated simply by the process and administration of justice. A child or a vulnerable adult is likely to find it an even more bewildering experience. In most jurisdictions, a witness is likely to encounter an adversarial system in which the defending and the prosecuting legal teams present a case. Cross-examination, as experienced in adversarial systems, can be overwhelming, as lawyers will tempt to rebut evidence produced in direct examination in any way possible, including discrediting the witnesses and/or his/her testimony. This applies to all kinds of witnesses, from eyewitnesses to expert witnesses, and the effect on vulnerable witnesses is of particular interest to psychology. The next chapter deals with a different kind of witness altogether – the person who is accused of the crime, the defendant.

Discussion point: What are the ethical considerations of giving psychological testimony in court?

Professional societies, such as the British Psychological Society and the American Psychological Association, set out codes of conduct for psychologists in many roles, including that of expert witness. How do these principles and guidelines apply if the psychologist is called to give evidence in their professional capacity?

British Psychological Society (nd) *Code of Ethics and Conduct Guidance*. Leicester: BPS/Ethics Committee of the British Psychological Society. Available at: http://www.apa.org/ethics/code/ (pdf).

Edens, J., Smith, S., Magyar, M., Mullen, K., Pitta, A. & Petrila, J. (2012) 'Hired guns,' 'charlatans,' and their 'voodoo psychobabble': case law references to various forms of perceived bias among mental health expert witnesses. *Psychological Services*, **9**(3): 259–271.

Kaufmann, P.M. (2009) Protecting raw data and psychological tests from wrongful disclosure: a primer on the law and other persuasive strategies. *Clinical Neuropsychology*, **23**: 1130–1159.

Psychology in Court 2: The Defendant's Mind

16

```
Mental state
of the
defendant
    │
    Mental
    Capacity
    Act 2005

Fit to plead
    │
    Thomas
    Nugusse

Intellectual
capacity
    │
    Daryl Atkins

Insanity and
the law
    │
    Actus reus
    and mens rea
    │
    M'Naghten
    rules

Case study
    │
    John George
    Haigh – the acid
    bath murderer
        Incompetency
        and insanity
        rejected
    │
    Sara Thornton/
    Joseph McGrail
        Domestic
        Violence,
        Crime and
        Victims
        Act 2004
        Battered
        person
        syndrome
```

In 1949 John George Haigh was living beyond his means. Gambling was a vice he could not resist. In order to obtain money, he conducted several small fraudulent ventures, but was soon caught and imprisoned. It became clear to him that if he murdered his victims, he would have no complaining witness when he stole their belongings and money. He also thought that if there was no body to be found there was no risk of prosecution for murder. Unfortunately for him, he was wrong, and when he was finally caught, he attempted a plea of insanity in order to avoid the death sentence.

Was Haigh insane? What does 'insane' actually mean? In order to answer these questions, the issue of what happens when the mentally ill or incapacitated come into contact with the criminal justice system needs to be examined.

KEY THEMES

- *Actus reus/mens rea*
- Defendant's mental state
- Fit to plead
- Intellectual capacity
- Insanity/insanity defence
- M'Naghten rules

Previous chapters have examined the ways in which psychological evidence is obtained and prepared for use in investigation and prosecution, how psychologists might be used as expert witnesses, and also how the experience of being in court can affect those caught up in the system. In addition to those forms of involvement, a psychologist may also be asked to make a judgement on the competency or mental state of an accused person. This question goes further than the issues of mental disorder and criminality discussed in earlier chapters. Here, it refers to either the mental health or intellectual capacity of a potential defendant, and the examination of this as part of the judicial process. This chapter will explore how the defendant's state of mind can become crucial evidence.

There are several ways in which the mental state of an accused person can affect whether or not s/he is charged, tried or convicted. Someone may be found not fit to plead, not guilty by reason of insanity or even escape typical punishment for crimes due to mental incapacity. Pleas of insanity or incompetence are rarely made (Zapf et al., 2009); it is difficult to demonstrate and may not have a reasonable alternative outcome to prison for the defendant. A person found not guilty due to insanity or incompetence, or found not fit to plead, may be compelled to indefinite detention in a psychiatric hospital (Reid, 2006). This might be seen as preferable and even fair, if a guilty verdict could lead to a death sentence or an indefinite time in prison, but not if there would be a finite limit to a normal prison sentence; such cases may seem at first sight to be cruel and unjust punishment.

Michael Jones

In 1975, Michael Jones was arrested for attempted shoplifting in Washington, DC, USA. Jones was examined after his arrest and found to be suffering from paranoid schizophrenia. Despite this, he was determined to be fit to plead and stand trial, but then was found not guilty by reason of insanity. He was committed to a psychiatric hospital to be held until he recovered. After several appeals and re-examinations by psychiatrists and psychologists, he was finally released in 2004, having been institutionalised for almost 30 years after an offence which carried a maximum sentence of one year.

There are several questions raised by the Michael Jones case. The first may be why he was found fit to stand trial, but the second is why he was detained, albeit in a secure hospital, decades longer than he would have been if he had simply been convicted of shoplifting (G. Morris, 2002). In the District of Columbia, where Jones was arrested and his case heard, people found not guilty by reason of insanity can be committed to a psychiatric hospital for up to 50 days and then re-examined. At the 50-day hearing, Jones was determined to be a danger to himself or others. A second hearing was held after he had been hospitalised for more than one year, which was the maximum period he could have spent in prison if he had been convicted of shoplifting. The Superior Court denied his request for a civil commitment hearing, reaffirmed the findings made at the 50-day hearing, and continued his commitment. It was further affirmed that the court had the right to confine him to a mental institution until such time as he regained his sanity or was no longer a danger to himself or society (Margulies, 1983; US Supreme Court Center, 1983).

THE MENTAL STATE OF THE DEFENDANT

There are several ways in which the defendant's mental state can lead to a trial process that is unconventional in terms of the outcome. These include whether a defendant is fit to plead and stand trial, whether the defendant is not guilty by reason of insanity, and considerations of the state of mind of a convicted defendant. The issues for psychologists or psychiatrists involved in this process concern an understanding of the relationship between the science and the law.

In the UK currently, the main statutory framework for people who are lacking in the capacity to make decisions for themselves is the Mental Capacity Act 2005, which came into force in April 2007 (www.legislation.gov.uk). The Act sets out the procedures for determining whether someone lacks capacity, and how to allow another person or a court to make decisions in that person's best interests. As might be expected, the legal position is more complex in the USA, as each state conducts its legal business with a certain amount of autonomy, but generally the exercise of judgements of insanity or incompetence follow the same guidelines as the UK, and other Western legal systems are comparable in application. The legislation is not, however, designed specifically for use in the aid of the mentally incompetent defendant, and still needs interpretation in terms of deciding fitness to plead or determining not guilty by reason of insanity (Scott-Moncrieff & Vassall-Adams, 2006).

FIT TO PLEAD

Lack of understanding is hazardous to your freedom

It might be argued that Michael Jones should never have been tried, and the mental illness he had could have made him unable to participate fully in his own defence. Defendants who do not possess sufficient competence can be excluded from criminal prosecution, although what happens to such a person then will vary. In the UK, the exemption from prosecution relies on lack of adjudicative competence, that is, the defendant is not voluntarily able to plead guilty for a crime that s/he committed. In the USA, protection for defendants who do not demonstrate adjudicative competence has been ruled by the United States Supreme Court to be guaranteed as part of due process. As Eliason and Chamberlain (2008) point out, these legal positions are clearly open to abuse, such as the faking of symptoms.

For a defendant to be ruled competent to stand trial there must be several pieces of evidence in place. These relate to understanding their position with respect to the law, and the ability to comprehend instructions and advice from legal representatives and to make decisions based on that. A defendant should also be able to testify coherently and refrain from behaviour detrimental to his/her defence during legal proceedings (Zapf et al., 2009). Tests of competence may need to be carried out at several points in the judicial process, either at arrest, before trial or after conviction. There is also the issue that may arise of change in adjudicative competence, as many things can happen on the pathway to a day in court, as in the case of Thomas Nugusse.

Arsema Dawit and Thomas Nugusse

Eritrea is an East African nation bordering the Red Sea. It has been a place of troubled conflict for some 60 years, where children, girls as well as boys, are drafted into the army at a very young age (C. Morris, 2010). Many flee to seek safe haven in countries such as England. Arsema Dawit's family was one such, establishing themselves as respected members of the Eritrean community in London. Arsema was a devout Christian and regularly attended church and sang in the choir. It appears that it was at church where she met Thomas Nugusse. Nugusse was six years older (she was then 13, he 19), an age difference that may seem unconventional or uncomfortable for many in the UK. However, this reflects Eritrean culture, in which women marry very young, become their husband's property and remain confined to the home (Woldemicael, 2007). It appears Nugusse regarded his girlfriend in this way, but Arsema was more attracted to the relative freedom of British women.

Nugusse was possessively jealous and his controlling behaviour was too much for a young woman finding her place in British society. When Arsema tried to end the relationship, he punched her in public, and this was the beginning of a series of escalating stalker-like incidents. These were reported to the police, but on 2 June 2008, Thomas Nugusse stabbed the now 15-year-old Arsema at least 30 times in her neck (Reuters, 2009a). She was discovered in a lift shaft at the block of flats where her family lived. Nugusse left her to die and phoned 999, saying he had killed 'his girlfriend' and was about to jump off a bridge. He was arrested and charged with murder, but three weeks later tried to hang himself, suffering irreversible brain damage in the process (Dodd, 2009). He was found not fit to plead and, on Wednesday 20 May 2009, a jury was ordered to find Nugusse 'guilty of the act or not'. A conventional finding of guilty or not guilty was not possible due to him being unfit to plead because of the brain damage. The jury found that he was indeed guilty of the acts and he was detained for life in a secure psychiatric hospital.

Nugusse's suicide attempt meant that his brain had been starved of oxygen for a crucial amount of time, resulting in irreparable damage. His level of impairment was such that he was unable to participate in his defence. He was assessed by tests of neurological and cognitive function, which include measurement of several modes of memory, attention and reaction time, linguistic ability, decision-making and response control. His performance was so poor that it allowed the psychological experts to testify that he was unable to function at a reasonable cognitive level (Church & Watts, 2007). Thus he was unfit to plead but was found guilty and hospitalised indefinitely.

Such incapacity can have far-reaching consequences for defendants at different stages of the judicial process, and these can be positive or negative, depending on your viewpoint.

INTELLECTUAL CAPACITY

Being retarded can save your life
Daryl Atkins

In 1996, Daryl Atkins, then 18 years old, and an accomplice called William Jones abducted Eric Nesbitt, a 21-year-old US airman, from Langley Air Force Base. According to Walker (2009), they forced Nesbitt to withdraw money from an ATM machine and then took him to an isolated field where he was killed by being shot eight times. This was a horrendous crime, poorly performed. The extortion of money was captured on the ATM camera and, during the course of the shooting, Atkins was shot in the leg. They were quickly apprehended.

The two men blamed each other for the actual murder, but it appears that Jones' argument was the more convincing. When the two men were tried, in 1998, Jones was given a life sentence as a result of a plea bargain (providing evidence of the guilt of an accomplice for a reduction in severity of sentence). Atkins was sentenced to death. Perhaps the reason that

Jones was more compelling was that Atkins is, in American legal terms, retarded. His IQ in 1998 was measured, using the Wechsler Adult Intelligence Scales (WAIS), at 59 (Everington & Olley, 2008). In a landmark ruling, prompted by Atkins' case, the Virginia Supreme Court decided that the State of Virginia would not execute people with an IQ below 70 (Mossman, 2003). This cut-off point of 70 is two standard deviations below the average (100) and 95% of the population will score within two standard deviations on either side of the average, with the remaining 5% being above or below this point. This means that the legal definition of retardation, at least in Virginia, is having an IQ score in the bottom 2.5% of the population (Everington & Olley, 2008).

All well and good. Atkins is saved from the lethal injection because he has a very low IQ. There were also some irregularities in the presentation of evidence. It is clear, however, that he did, and may still, present a danger to the public. Atkins confessed to several violent crimes prior to Nesbitt's murder, including the robbery of a pizza deliveryman and the maiming of a woman during an attempted robbery (Walker, 2009). It was agreed that he should remain incarcerated. However, Nesbitt's family wanted a little more retribution. In 2004, his IQ was tested again and appeared to have risen to 74. There are several possibilities why this might be: he may have been able to fake his original score (but why didn't he fake the second?), or, as his defence team suggested, his interaction with lawyers, abstinence from alcohol and drugs, and enjoyment of informative TV, have all raised his IQ. Rather strangely, the prosecution state his IQ as 76, 2 points higher than the defence claim. It seems rather arbitrary to argue over 2 points when simply having a score over 70 would make the case. This is due to the statistical nature of the IQ distribution, the standard deviation, and the standard error of the mean (Everington & Olley, 2008). The SEM of the IQ distribution is 5. If the SEM is taken as an indication of the range of a true score, then 76 would inarguably lie above the level of retardation, but 74 would be ambiguous. This, together with other evidence of prosecutorial misconduct in the presentation of Jones' case, meant that Atkins' death sentence was commuted to life imprisonment in June 2009.

The case has become quite notorious, with many considerations about how to apply the ruling on retardation and guilt (Bonnie, 2004). Forensic psychologists need to be aware not only of how to administer and interpret tests of intellectual ability, but of the statistical, psychometric nature of such measurements. Mental incompetence is a difficult concept to understand, but when complicated by legal systems, definitions and applications, it becomes something of a quagmire. However, intellectual incompetence may be easier to measure and present for psychologists than the issues surrounding the insanity defence.

INSANITY AND THE LAW

An insanity defence is a claim that the accused was acting under the influence of an internal derangement (disturbance) of the mind. An external derangement would be one with an external cause, such as a head wound. An internal derangement means that there is no externally observable evidence of the derangement. A defence made on the basis of an internal derangement is a complex matter because insanity is a legal term, not a medical one (Weinstein & Geiger, 2003). For a defendant to have the potential to be convicted, two elements must be shown to be true beyond doubt, *actus reus* and *mens rea*. These refer to the act itself being regarded as an illegal behaviour (*actus reus*) and the knowledge in the mind of the perpetrator that the behaviour is illegal (*mens rea*). These elements have been a fundamental component of common law since at least the seventeenth century, when Sir Edward Coke (1616) added the concept of a guilty mind to the prosecution of a crime (McSherry, 2003). Coke's addendum is *Actus non facit reum, nisi mens sit rea* – an act does not make someone guilty unless his mind is guilty (Heller, 2009). Thus, the prosecution must prove that criminal conduct was voluntary, in addition to the accused having possessed the relevant fault element, such as intention, knowledge, recklessness or negligence. *Actus reus* is interpreted as the events or actions of the act under scrutiny. However, in combination with the action, there needs to be *mens rea*, the demonstration that the accused had a mental state in keeping with committing the offence. Often this is taken to mean 'intent', in other words, the question of whether the accused was legally insane at the time the offence was committed. In order to determine this, the court needs to rely on the application of the M'Naghten rules.

The M'Naghten rules

There are standardised rules used by the court to determine whether a person who offers an insanity defence was legally insane at the time of the offence. These rules originate in a debate in the House of Lords on the outcome of the 1843 case of M'Naghten.

On 20 January 1843, Daniel M'Naghten attempted to assassinate the Prime Minister, Robert Peel, because he believed the Government, in conspiracy with the Pope, was persecuting him. Approaching Downing Street, he fired a single shot into the back of a man, thinking it was Peel, but it was Edward Drummond, the Prime Minister's secretary. Drummond died five days later. M'Naghten was tried and acquitted on the ground of insanity and committed to Bethlehem Royal Hospital (commonly known as Bedlam).

The case gave rise to questions in Parliament about the legal status of defendants who may be classed as insane, and the ensuing debate resulted in guidance for courts. The rules so formulated are now known as the M'Naghten rules.

On entering an insanity plea, the defendant is subjected to psychiatric/psychological examinations set out by the rules. If these are satisfied, the accused may be judged 'not guilty by reason of insanity'. According to Allnut et al. (2007), this is not the same as 'not guilty' as the defendant may still be subject to a sentence and a period of treatment in a secure hospital facility or similar institution. The application of the rules means that juries are told that every defendant should be regarded as sane, and to possess a degree of reason of responsibility, unless it is proved otherwise. This proof must be clear evidence that, at the time of committing the act, the accused had such a defect of reason, due to disease of the mind, that s/he did not understand the nature and quality of the act or that it was wrong.

The burden of proof that an insanity plea should be accepted is on the defence, unlike when a case for conviction is being presented, where the burden of proof is on the prosecution. In an insanity plea, the prosecution will have the opportunity to rebut any evidence and produce evidence of sanity. The first element of the rules that should be determined is the question of whether a particular condition amounts to disease of the mind legally, rather than medically, and whether the effect that the disease of the mind had was caused by external or internal factors, and was under the control of the defendant (Torry & Billick, 2010). Thus, a person with epilepsy who causes harm during an epileptic episode is deemed to have suffered from a disease of the mind with an internal cause. However, in the case of a diabetic who committed assault during a hypoglycaemic state resulting from consumption of alcohol with no food, the condition would be deemed to be caused by external factors, over which the defendant could exercise control.

The second point to be determined is the physical nature and quality of the act, and whether the defendant did not know what s/he was physically doing at the time. For example, if someone deliberately scythes another person's head off under the delusion that it will be fun for the two of them to play football with it, then this is deemed an insane delusion. The physical nature of the act is clearly wrong, and would attract an accusation of murder. Such a delusion would mean that the defendant does not understand the consequences of the act, and therefore is legally deemed insane. Again, this is a legal definition in that the defendant must be functionally unaware that the actions are legally wrong at the time of the offence to satisfy this requirement. If a defendant has killed someone, but suggested to police officers or lawyers that s/he knew they would be punished, then, even if suffering from a mental illness, they would be judged to have knowledge that the act was wrong.

As may be imagined, there are some criticisms of the application of a legal assessment of insanity. The major one is that psychological theory and practice has moved on since the nineteenth century, but the legal definition and determination of insanity has not. The second objection concerns the burden of proof of insanity, as everyone is deemed to be legally sane until proven otherwise (Hathaway, 2009).

The rules also do not make any distinction between a defendant who may represent a danger to the public or themselves and those who do not. For example, certain illnesses, if they remain untreated, can cause temporary mental aberrations. Diabetes, as mentioned above, if inadequately monitored, can cause someone to lapse into a hypoglycaemic state, which in turn means there is an inadequate supply of glucose in the brain. This leads to neuroglycopenia and subsequent impairment of function. However, such conditions can be controlled by medication or diet, and therefore the accused with such a condition would not generally be a danger.

There is also the question of how the justice system treats those convicted of crimes but who are judged insane. If a defendant's defence counsel lodges an insanity plea and the defendant is convicted for murder, then s/he can be confined indefinitely in a psychiatric hospital, whereas a conviction for murder without insanity being shown may result in a finite sentence. In contrast to the public view of insanity being a loophole in which defendants can evade due punishment (see Bloechl et al., 2007), a defendant might view a short sentence as preferable. A further difficulty is the definition of the 'disease of the mind', as in law it need not be a disease of the brain or psychiatric condition as epilepsy and diabetes have both been shown to cause an internal derangement. As such, then, the disease must be one that interferes with the process of reasoning or understanding in the defendant, and s/he must demonstrate lack of awareness of the nature of the act, not the moral or legal nature. Alternatively, the defendant may demonstrate that s/he did not know that the act was legally wrong, or that s/he acted under such a delusion that the act was not wrong.

Therefore, it can be seen that a defendant and his/her counsel, on wishing to enter an insanity defence, enter a legal, moral and medical minefield (Dalby, 2006). The most disturbing cases of murder often lead us to think that the person accused of the killing must be insane – we are unable to imagine that someone sane will do the things that the killer is reported to have done. This is particularly true of cases that include the peri-mortem or post-mortem mutilation or dismemberment of a body. However, there are some cases where even the most macabre acts demonstrate that a murderer is very sane indeed, in the most cold-blooded and amoral way.

The acid bath vampire

On 20 February 1949, Constance Lane reported her friend, Mrs Olive Durand-Deacon, missing. Mrs Durand-Deacon was a 69-year-old widow who lived in the Onslow Court Hotel, London. She had recently struck up an acquaintance with another hotel resident, John George Haigh, and he had offered to help her with a small business venture. What Constance did not know was that Haigh had lured Olive to a storeroom in Leopold Road, shot her in the back of the head, drained and drunk some of her blood (or so he claimed) and then dissolved her body in a vat of sulphuric acid. He had disposed of at least six people in this way; Mrs Durand-Deacon was simply his last victim (Thomas, 2006).

Gekoski (1998) reports that Haigh was born in Yorkshire, the son of John and Emily, who belonged to a conservative religious group called the Plymouth Brethren. Haigh was to later claim that his strict religious upbringing led to nightmares and delusions. His early adult life was littered with petty crimes, and he was in prison when his wife, Betty, gave birth and gave up the baby for adoption. Haigh moved to London and became chauffeur to William McSwann. However, Haigh wanted to set up his own business, and did so, ending up in prison again for fraudulently practising as a solicitor.

This prison term appears to be where he planned his 'perfect murder', including the disposal of the body in acid. Meeting McSwann again after his release, Haigh was introduced to McSwann's parents, Donald and Amy. William McSwann disappeared, and Haigh later confessed to killing him and dissolving his body in a 40-gallon drum of sulphuric acid. The resulting sludge was poured down a drain. He told William's parents that their son had vanished because he was trying to dodge the military draft. They became suspicious that he had not returned after the war, so Haigh murdered them too, making a lot of money from disposing of their belongings. However, it was not enough to fund his lifestyle for long, and Dr Archibald Henderson and his wife were his next victims, the first to be disposed of in his workshop in Leopold Road, Crawley. The last was Olive Durand-Deacon.

A full description of the medical evidence given at Haigh's trial can be found in the Medico-Legal (1949). Haigh was defended by Sir David Maxwell Fyfe KC, who decided to enter a plea of insanity in mitigation against the murder of Mrs Durand-Deacon. The evidence for this defence was supplied by Harley Street psychiatrist Dr Henry Yellowlees. Dr Yellowlees had examined Haigh on three occasions in jail before his trial. He concluded that Haigh had a 'paranoid constitution', deriving from his descriptions of a strict religious upbringing, his hallucinations of a bleeding Christ, and demonstrated by the cheerful callousness with which he viewed his crimes. Haigh had never denied carrying out the murders, hence Haigh knew what he had done, but Fyfe was looking to suggest that he was unaware of how wrong it was. The legal test of the M'Naghten rules was on two points: did Haigh demonstrate the legal definition of paranoia and does paranoia constitute a true application of legal insanity?

Psychiatric definitions in the 1940s suggested that conditions such as a paranoid constitution were due to biology and environment in combination. Yellowlees was using as his reference a textbook on mental disease written by Tanzi in 1909. His report on Haigh was therefore based on views of mental disorder that were already out of date. He suggested that anyone reared in the kind of environment Haigh described of his childhood would be predisposed to escape into a fantasy world. He was particularly interested in the dreams of a bloodied Christ and concluded that Haigh had fantasies based on desire for blood. This, Yellowlees said, explained the act of drinking his victim's blood, a fact never verified and only mentioned by Haigh himself (Medico-Legal, 1949).

Using Tanzi's (1909) descriptors of mental disorder, Yellowlees diagnosed Haigh as an egocentric paranoid (also referred to in the book as 'ambitious' or 'mystical' paranoid). Yellowlees went on to say that such a person feels he is omnipotent and, in a religious person, this might manifest as being guided by God, and therefore, possibly, above the law even when committing unlawful acts. Of particular interest was the supposed compulsion to kill for blood (to drink). It is thought that such compulsions are linked to a sexual deviation, such as haematophilia or hematolagnia (APA, 2002) or vampirism (Prins, 1985), but Haigh gave no indication of paraphilia of this kind and, indeed, seemed to have no interest in sex. Another point to note is that one element of Yellowlees' assessment was that Haigh was too lucid and intelligent not to know what he was doing. Haigh is also reported to have written to the doctor, describing similar personalities throughout history, including Hitler, as a comparison to his own abnormality. Something that Yellowlees did not know (it was not part of his remit) was that Haigh had known someone who worked in a psychiatric hospital and, due to his interest, had found out a great deal of information about how someone with a mental illness would behave (Gekoski, 1998). He was also a consummate confidence trickster and had passed himself off as many different types of people in the past. A mental patient would be just one more impersonation for him. In fact, viewing the proceedings with the benefit of hindsight, Yellowlees seems to have failed to find out a great deal about Haigh.

Haigh pleaded not guilty on the day of the trial, but his counsel did not suggest his competency to stand trial was in any way impaired. Thirty-three witnesses were presented by the prosecution, with only four being cross-examined. The defence then mounted a case in which Haigh's mental state was its only strategy. Fyfe was clearly attempting to show that Haigh had behaved aberrantly, that his behaviour was peculiar and atypical, and thus have it recognised as a sign of a disease of the mind. For example, Haigh had apparently been seen in good humour at a restaurant some short time after Mrs Durand-Deacon's death (Lustgarten, 1968). Fyfe also entered the confessions into evidence and various other pieces of behaviour, with the implication that Haigh's mind was genuinely disordered. Fyfe described the type of mental illness from which, he suggested, Haigh suffered and told the court that it would affect his ability to understand that what he did was legally or morally wrong. He then attempted to substantiate this by calling Dr Yellowlees to the stand.

The psychiatrist testified that he had interviewed Haigh and diagnosed him as having a mental condition consistent with delusional paranoia. However, the psychiatrist could only give evidence relating to the mental condition and not to whether this prevented him from appreciating right from wrong. On cross-examination, Yellowlees admitted that he had only spent something like two hours in consultation with Haigh and that there was no objective evidence, beyond Haigh's word, that the accused had any such condition as described. Yellowlees also acknowledged any seemingly aberrant behaviour could have been carried out to give the impression of mental illness. He also agreed, under oath, that Haigh appeared to know right from wrong, as he had attempted to cover the traces of his crimes and thought that he could not be prosecuted for murder if there was no evidence of a body (Medico-Legal, 1949). This all but sealed the case for the prosecution and the defence offered no other testimony. The outcome was that Dr Yellowlees could not prove Haigh was insane, and his testimony gave more credence to the prosecution case than it could to the defence.

All that was left now was the summing up and the judge's direction to the jury. The prosecution attested that there was only one issue to be decided. Haigh had not denied murdering Mrs Durand-Deacon, but the case rested on the question of his sanity. This had not been demonstrated to the court's satisfaction by the psychiatrist called by the defence, as his entire diagnosis rested on the unreliable statements of the accused and the questionable motivation for the aberrant behaviour (Lustgarten, 1968). Haigh had also asked his arresting officers about the possibility of release from an institution such as Broadmoor, thereby demonstrating the intent to show himself to be insane but also indicating that he knew the acts would bring him to prosecution. The defence KC spoke only of the mental illness that Yellowlees had insisted was impossible to fake. He spoke of how Haigh had been seen to drink his own urine (but, as it turned out, only once and in front of prison authorities) and that he wanted to drink blood (Hemphill & Zabow, 1983). These, he said, were evidence of a disturbed mind. Fyfe tried to convince the jury that Haigh was delusional and that this level of delusional fantasy life meant he could not distinguish right from wrong.

The judge's direction was clear. He told the jury that they could not rely on anything entered into evidence from the mouth or pen of Haigh as he was unreliable and had not testified to its veracity. Here, he seemed to be dismissing the confession, which the defence had entered into the court, but in fact the prosecution did not need this. The judge reminded the jury that they had to be sure beyond reasonable doubt of the guilt of the prisoner, but that if they decided that the evidence suggested the prisoner was guilty but insane, then they must consider whether that insanity meant he did not know right from wrong for these acts.

Fifteen minutes after leaving the court, the jury returned with a guilty verdict.

After the trial Haigh was examined by several doctors, who decided he was faking a mental illness. The Home Secretary was able to order a special medical enquiry under the Criminal Lunatics Act 1884. Executing a criminal was a serious undertaking – the state did not execute lightly and there were legislative procedures in place to ensure the sentence was carried out with due consideration. Three psychiatrists examined Haigh after sentence was passed and they all reported that he was not insane and did not suffer from a mental disease or defect that would indicate he had no moral responsibility for his actions. Haigh was examined by a total of 12 doctors, including psychiatrists, before and after his trial. He was subjected to a variety of examinations, including an EEG. The medical personnel decided that Haigh was sane and faking the aberrations. They also concluded that he was responsible for his actions. On 6 August 1949, John George Haigh was executed by hanging for the murder of Olive Durand-Deacon.

To most people the acts that Haigh committed would seem to be the result of a deranged mind, and the dreams, fantasies and delusions that Haigh tried to convince the psychiatrists he was experiencing are evidence of this derangement. The fact remains that there is no proof to corroborate Yellowlees' diagnosis of the unbalanced, paranoid state of Haigh's mind other than what Haigh himself presented in prison. In addition, all of the murders were committed for gain; pure and simple greed is a rational purpose most of us can understand, even if we would not go quite as far to feed it.

The legal situation is also clear. We do not need to understand Haigh's crime and all of the alleged attendant gruesomeness; we need to know that the legal state of insanity could not be proved. The defence must show that the defendant is insane; the prosecution does not have to prove he is not. In Haigh's case, his cheerful confession and the knowledge that he might end up in Broadmoor, together with the uncertain testimony of his expert witness, did not validate the premise that he was insane, and he paid for this with his life. His body was not subject to the indignity of dismemberment and submersion in acid, as he had done with those of his victims. He was immortalised as an exhibit in Madame Tussaud's Chamber of Horrors.

Since Haigh's trial and execution, the death penalty has been abolished in the UK. Subsequently, and probably consequently, the use of insanity as a defence has diminished, even though, according to Bloechl et al. (2007), the public thinks it is used more frequently. Where it is used, the application of the rules has become increasingly difficult, not least because of the complex yet vague definitions of 'disease of the mind'. There is some way to go before we have a complete understanding of the issues concerning fitness to plead and the relationship between insanity and diminished responsibility. Diminished responsibility is a partial defence available in England and Wales to reduce a charge of murder to manslaughter. It has been the focus of a great deal of critical attention, according to Loughnan (2005), who also argues that the use of medical evidence in presenting a defence of diminished responsibility is a major, if not the only, opportunity to consider aspects of the defendant's context. He also suggests that the technical nature of an enquiry into the defendant's 'mental responsibility' provides some certainty in evaluation of whether a defendant is responsible or not. Hence, diminished responsibility is generally used only as mitigation against prosecution for murder, but not for manslaughter.

A clear example of how this applies is in the cases of battered person syndrome (formerly known as battered woman syndrome). This term refers to the medical and psychological condition of a person who has been the victim of persistent emotional, physical or sexual abuse from another person, usually within the family, and hence is an outcome of domestic violence. The Domestic Violence, Crime and Victims Act 2004 is a set of amendments to legislation governing fitness to plead and insanity. The amendments recognise the existence of 'battered woman syndrome' (although this could apply equally to male defendants) and the possible defence of extreme provocation (Rix, 2001). In some cases, where a person has been subjected to long-term abuse inside their relationship, the killing of the abusive partner leads to a charge of premeditated murder. This is more likely in the case of a woman killing a violent husband as she needs to seek the means of homicide. A man provoked into killing his wife after prolonged abuse may be physically capable of striking a blow that will kill. A wife in similar circumstances may not have that physical capability and therefore may need to furnish herself with a weapon (Rix, 2001). Psychological evidence may be required if the defence for any subsequent charge of murder is provocation and diminished responsibility. In several notable cases in the UK, women who killed their husbands/cohabitees after (what is described as) years of violent abuse have been convicted of murder. When representation is made to the court of appeal, on the basis of provocation and a mental state consistent with battered person syndrome, the conviction is often overturned. The burden of proof is once again on the defence to show that the defendant had lost her self-control suddenly and temporarily as a result of the provocation and that a reasonable person would have reacted in the same way as the defendant. The difficulty here is not just the mismatch between the psychological evidence, much of it based on feminist theory and lobby, and the legal position, but also the inability to demonstrate the reasonable person issue (Rix, 2001: 136).

In 1989, Sara Thornton killed her abusive husband, Malcolm. He had been charged with assault, but she stabbed him to death before he appeared in court. She was convicted of murder. At the trial, the judge said she should have left the room when she was being beaten. An appeal on the basis of a long-term provocation lost. She was finally set free in 1996 after her conviction was reduced to manslaughter (Bennett, 1996).

Joseph McGrail's partner, Marion Kennedy, was an alcoholic and nagged him. So, in 1991, he killed her by repeatedly kicking her in the stomach when she was drunk. At his trial he was given a two-year suspended sentence and walked free, the judge telling him that he (McGrail) was living with a woman who would have tried the patience of a saint. Marion Kennedy never attacked her common law husband physically, yet he was determined to have been provoked into murder. In the case of Malcolm Thornton there were several recorded cases of battering his wife, there was clear evidence that she felt that she and her daughter were in danger, yet she was convicted of murder.

These cases led to the formation of the UK campaign group Justice for Women, which points out that men who kill their female partners often justify their actions by claiming that they lost control. In court, judges express sympathy for this defence, suggesting men who were nagged or cheated on by female partners were justified in killing them. However, there is little sympathy for women who kill after experiencing domestic violence. The dominant emotions in people who are battered are fear and despair, not a sudden, explosive loss of self-control. Hence the distinction between the acts appears to be an acceptance of (male) reactive aggression and a condemnation of acts which seem to be instrumental. A woman is unlikely to be in the position of killing her often physically larger and stronger husband in a physical altercation, and she must therefore leave the situation to get a weapon, and this makes the act appear premeditated. Historically, women who killed husbands in this way were seen as mentally unbalanced and were committed to an asylum, if indeed they escaped the death sentence. In the USA, it is estimated that there are over 2,000 women in prison because they have murdered an intimate partner in self-defence (Messing & Heeren, 2008).

Battered person syndrome as a defence for killing is highly controversial. It evokes many emotions, some of which are dependent on the sex of the observer. For those who do not live in fear every day it is difficult to comprehend how such feelings can lead to killing another human being. It also appears to be difficult for courts to accept that such feelings constitute diminished responsibility.

SUMMARY

To summarise, then, the weight of psychological evidence in court is to demonstrate the adjudicative competence of the accused. What should be clear from this is that the psychologist and his or her testimony is simply another piece of evidence that is used by lawyers to the means of justice. Psychologists therefore have several responsibilities with respect to the legal situations in which their evidence can be used (Rogers et al., 2008). First, to determine at what stage of the legal process the evidence is being produced, and whether or not testimony in court is required. Secondly, that the production of an assessment is within their professional expertise, and that they are familiar with the administration and interpretation of tests of competence. Thirdly, to ensure the testimony deals with only the pertinent facts and does not go beyond the stated circumstances; even though psychological scientific methods allow us to infer for evidence, the legal situation does not welcome this. Finally, that they abide by the ethical considerations of their profession and the relevant professional body at all times.

Discussion point: Can modern technology aid in determining insanity?

The psychiatrists determining Haigh's sanity had little technology to aid them. Dr Yellowlees was working from a textbook that was already out of date. Modern psychological assessment now has a battery of tests at its disposal, but what about the most modern element of our equipment – the neurological measurement and neuroimaging technology? Neuropsychology in the late twentieth century grew in stature due to the ability to accurately depict what is going on in the brain. Using equipment like EEG and MRI allows us to pinpoint areas of the brain that are actively working in response to particular stimuli, or areas that are subject to some form of disease or dysfunction. Forensic neuropsychology is the practice of providing neuropsychological advice and opinions to aid in the resolution of legal issues. The articles below discuss the use of neuropsychology in forensic settings.

Bush, S. & Lees-Haley, P. (2005) Threats to the validity of forensic neuropsychological data: ethical considerations. *Journal of Forensic Neuropsychology*, **4**(3): 45–66.
Kolla, N. & Brodie, J. (2012) Application of neuroimaging in relationship to competence to stand trial and insanity. In J. Simpson (ed.), *Neuroimaging in Forensic Psychiatry: From the Clinic to the Courtroom*. Chichester: Wiley-Blackwell.
Palermo, G. (2012) Does neuroimaging have a role in assessing criminal culpability? *Journal of Offender Therapy and Comparative Criminology*, **56**(2): 171–173 (editorial).

Psychology in Court 3: The Mind of the Jury

17

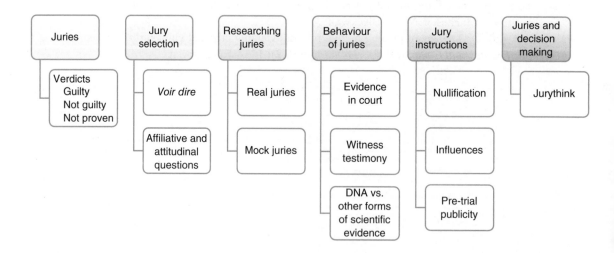

Between 2 April and 14 June 1982, the United Kingdom and Argentina engaged in a conflict concerning the sovereignty of a group of islands in the South Atlantic, generally referred to as the Falkland Islands. By the time of the Argentine surrender, 649 Argentine military personnel, 255 British military personnel and three Falkland Islanders had died. The largest single loss of Argentine lives was during the sinking of the *General Belgrano*, an Argentine light cruiser. The sinking caused a good deal of controversy. Some claimed that the ship was outside the exclusion zone (an area defined for the benefit of neutral vessels needing to pass the war zone), and others, including the former captain, stating that it was inside the exclusion zone and therefore a legitimate target. The question became public knowledge because two key documents were passed to a Labour (opposition) MP by the civil servant Clive Ponting, in direct contravention of the Official Secrets Act 1911. Ponting was subsequently prosecuted for this. His defence was that the leaking of the documents was in the public interest. At his 1984 trial, the judge clearly directed the jury to convict Ponting of a criminal offence as he had admitted the disclosure and that 'the public interest is what the government of the day says it is'. The jury acquitted him, resulting in modifications to the Official Secrets Act to remove the defence of the right to know.

Notwithstanding the interesting legal history made by Ponting's actions and his defence, the case also shows us something about the psychology of the court room. The jury's action in acquitting Ponting is an example of jury nullification, the bringing of a verdict contrary to law in which the jury considers that the defendant should not be punished. It also demonstrates the power of a concept that is at the heart of democratic legal process – trial by jury.

KEY THEMES

- Jury
- Juror
- Adversarial courts
- Inquisitorial courts
- Verdicts
- Grand jury
- Hung jury
- Affiliative questions
- Attitudinal questions
- Mock jury
- Field experiment (juries)
- Jury instructions
- Inadmissible evidence
- *CSI* effect

- DNA database (CODIS)
- Pre-trial publicity
- Groupthink
- Jurythink
- *Voir dire*
- Jury nullification

JURIES

A jury is a group of people assembled in order to determine a verdict. In legal terms, this would be on a question set to them in court or to set a penalty. The most common question set to a jury in law is the guilt or otherwise of someone accused of a crime. The verdicts rendered, therefore, are 'guilty', 'not guilty', or sometimes 'not proven', which is usually seen in Scottish courts. Jurors are usually laypeople; they are not professionals of the courts, such as lawyers or judges. In some jurisdictions, juries are also convened to determine whether or not there is enough evidence in a case to proceed to the further trial by jury.

Juries are most commonly found in the court systems which are adversarial in nature, that is, where two arguments are presented, one from the plaintiff and one from the defendant. In criminal cases, the plaintiff is usually the state, represented by the prosecuting counsel. The defendant usually has his or her own legal team too. The jury will hear the evidence presented by both sides, and will then usually take instruction from the presiding judge and retire to decide their verdict. The majority in the jury will decide the verdict; this will often need to be a unanimous decision, or simply a decision of a majority of the jurors. A jury may be unable to come to a verdict, in which a case it is referred to as a 'hung jury'. One of the alternative forms of court system is the inquisitorial system found in countries such as France (Glendon et al., 2008). Here the court is actively involved in investigating the case instead of being an impartial mediator between prosecution and defence.

In the majority of states in the USA, a grand jury, comprising 15 people, will examine a case to determine whether there is sufficient evidence to take it forward to a jury trial. Again, these people are lay

Verdict – the formal finding of fact (decision) made by a jury on matters or questions submitted to the jury by a judge. In criminal court the verdict can be:

- Guilty (followed by judgment of conviction by the judge then sentencing)
- Not guilty (the accused is acquitted and free to go, unless other findings are to be made)

In Scotland a verdict of 'not proven' can be made. The burden of proof of guilt rests with the prosecution. It is used if the judge or jury does not have enough evidence to convict but is not sufficiently convinced of the defendant's innocence to enter a 'not guilty' verdict.

persons, but the grand jury examines evidence presented to them by a prosecuting counsel. A grand jury may see this evidence without a suspect being notified of the proceedings and can be used to issue a sealed indictment against a suspect who is unaware of the whole procedure. In England, the practice of the grand jury was abandoned in 1933 and a committal procedure is used instead. Here the defendant is charged with the offence in a preliminary hearing where it is decided whether or not there is sufficient evidence for a jury to be able to make a decision.

JURY SELECTION

Of those citizens qualified for jury service, attendance is mandatory. Juries are required to be impartial and the panel is therefore composed of those who are seen to be fit to serve and who meet certain procedures and requirements. These include fluency in the language to be used and the ability to understand the procedures of the court. Jurors are selected from a pool of those who have been compelled to attend for their service and selection involves a drawing at random from the pool when the jury is needed. In England and Wales, the objection to a juror being selected for the panel can only be made if there is a very good reason, such as knowing the defendant personally. In some jurisdictions, however, the professionals involved in the case have the right to test jurors or otherwise exclude jurors who might be deemed to be less than impartial. Hence there may be some form of questioning of potential members of the panel that will take place. This process is known as '*voir dire*' and it does not happen in British courts, but it does in the USA and some other jurisdictions.

> *Voir dire* – from Old French meaning to 'speak truth', the process of questioning potential juries to determine their competence to take part in the jury or their impartiality. It can also refer to the admissibility of evidence (in the UK).

However, an examination of the process reveals a lot of information about the psychological processes within the jury. The process of *voir dire* is intended to ensure that the juror is capable of making impartial decisions, is competent to understand the legality of right and wrong, and is not biased to one side or the other. The process of selection and challenging differs depending on the country. In the USA and in some other countries, the defence and prosecution are both allowed a certain number of challenges to jurors. These are unconditional and no reason has to be given for not selecting a juror. However, in recent years, an effort must be made to make a jury as race-neutral and gender-neutral as possible. Therefore, if a minority group member is challenged by one side or the other, the challenge must be a good reason for the exclusion and not based on race or gender. In practice, the lawyers tend to attempt to exclude jurors who appear to favour the opposing side.

Questions that are designed to reveal any tendency to favour the prosecution or defence tend to be either 'affiliative' or 'attitudinal'. Affiliative questions probe the prospective juror's identification with social or cultural groups that are either traditional or liberal in outlook. Questions about demographic information, including occupation or religious and political views, are accompanied by indirect questions about television viewing habits, contributions to charities, membership of social organisations, etc. Other questions are those that are more probing in terms of a juror's views on social issues and whether s/he espouses extreme political attitudes.

Attitudinal questions are those that examine consciously held and expressed beliefs, attitudes and opinions about issues that are important to the case. This may refer to beliefs about the criminal justice system, the presumption of innocence, circumstantial evidence and other legal principles, and reveal some psychological matters of interest to cognitive and social psychologists. Further questions might focus on attitudes to race or religion, credibility of evidence, etc.

Attitudinal questions focus on bias in respect of the issues to be discussed in court. This has contributed to knowledge about bias and attitude, and the understanding that many attitudes are not consciously held. The difficulty comes when attempting to exclude a juror on the basis of attitudes that are not consciously disclosed. A further set of questions probing personal experiences has been called for but is not yet used universally.

RESEARCHING JURIES

Research aimed at understanding the psychological processes involved in being a juror can be done in two ways. Interviews with jurors after they have given a verdict and finished their service will access certain types of information, but must rely on reconstruction of memories, thoughts and decisions. It is also impossible to manipulate any variables in research involving real juries. So the alternative is to use a mock jury setting, in which participants are told to behave as if they were in a real court situation.

Research with real juries

Jury research is important not only to discover how people behave and think on a jury, but also because of what this tells us about human decision making and social groups. Studying how jurors perceive, interpret and remember evidence, and the ways in which they reach consensus with the group, provides a microcosm of the real world in terms of studying reasoning. There are two major ways in which research can be done using the participation of real juries, that is, the group of people who have listened to and deliberated upon evidence presented in a real, not simulated, court case. The first is to use archival material on verdicts, and the second is to use post-trial interviews.

Research undertaken with juries can only be undertaken once the trial and deliberations are over. The danger of trying to undertake research when a trial is in progress is that the very act of researching may alter the process by which jurors make decisions, and this would be problematic for legal due process. However, once the jurors are released from the duty, interviews, questionnaires and so on can be used. Carrying out such studies means that researchers need to gain approval of court officials and the presiding judge. In a national survey in the USA, Lewis et al. (2005) found a rate of only 15% cooperation, citing non-approval from judges as the main reason for refusal, but more locally based studies report higher rates. Concerns are based on whether the jurors or jury pool members are treated fairly and ethically, which is relatively easy to assure.

Another concern, in quantitative research at least, is that the samples drawn are representative of the population. The stated purpose of jury selection is to ensure that the pool from which it is drawn, and the makeup of those 12 members, is as representative as possible, although several things may militate that. If legal teams are allowed to veto the inclusion of some members, for example, then this may reduce representativeness, as may the fact that jurors need to be retried with the state in some way (on the electoral roll in the UK, for example).

Archival material accessed for jury research relies on analysing verdict patterns across a range of case types. The danger here is that this may not be complete material. Lee and Waters (2011) found that there may be a bias in what is recorded because there is a tendency to record cases in the same way the media does, in terms of sensationalism or large compensation awards.

Post-trial interviews and questionnaires offer a potentially more robust source of material. Using them to assess jurors' impressions of the material and the way in which they made a decision gives a first-hand account of the process. It is, of course, subject to imperfect reconstruction, and still does not necessarily access the process, of which the juror is unconscious, such as bias affecting decisions, etc.

Field experiments on jurors have occurred but are extremely rare. Heuer and Penrod (1995) investigated the use of procedural variations in trials, such as whether jurors are allowed to ask questions during the evidence giving. Their conclusions were that a more interactive jury style is advantageous to the final decision-making process, but such research is subject to many logistic problems so it is likely that simulations will remain the more likely format of jury research.

Research with mock juries

The alternative to carrying out studies with real juries is to use the so-called mock or simulated jury paradigm. One of the major concerns here is about ecological validity. A great deal of the research used student participation, which is argued to be not representative of the population as a whole, and a jury pool in particular. Here we have the representativeness question in a different form. While actual juries are deemed to be representative of a general

Mock jury – a group of people (acting as a jury panel) who will take part in research about jury trials that are not being heard in a real court situation. They are used in research, and in some educative situations, in order to create a trial-like setting for learning which does not involve the actual legal system. They may employ varying degrees of realism.

population, in simulations it is whether a finite and select pool of research participants represents what is basically another selected sample.

The first systematic examination of this question was undertaken by Bornstein (1999). He concluded that more care was needed in terms of considering methodology to be used in simulations, but that such research and attendant problems should not be viewed negatively. However, if the intention of simulations is to inform practice in the court room, attention must be paid to validity, as viewed by those outside the psychological research community. The value of simulations rests on three things: whether the members of the mock jury are truly representative of the pool from which real jurors are selected; whether the material presented in the mock jury experiment accurately reflects that which would be given in a real trial; and whether the psychological status of assessing a fictional set of material is an equivalent experience to the decision-making process in real trials. Bornstein's meta-analysis of mock jury research concludes that there was no confirmation of the effect of realism of material or of participant sample type on research results (Bornstein, 1999).

BEHAVIOUR OF JURIES

Research with juries, particularly the mock jury paradigm, has exposed a good deal about how people behave within a group like a jury. Such findings cover aspects such as the attention paid to evidence, decision-making processes, social psychology of group, and so on.

Evidence in court and the jury

In an adversarial legal system, one in which a prosecution and a defence team present and rebut evidence, lawyers need to be confident that the jury is listening and understanding what is being presented. The issue of expert witness testimony was addressed in Chapter 15; here the research considered will be that concerning the evidence presented by lawyers and the cross-examination of witnesses.

Daftary-Kapur et al. (2010) reviewed research that discovered that jurors do have difficulty understanding more complex legal constructs, even when these are summarised by a judge at the end of the trial. However, recent research has suggested ways in which this can be improved and the comprehensibility of legal concepts raised. One question that has not been fully answered by research is the effect of inadmissible evidence. This is when a piece of evidence is presented but is for some reason ruled to be irrelevant to the case or is deemed to have a dubious legal status. For example, it was usual, before legislation was enacted to prevent it, for a rape victim's previous sexual experience to be discussed in court during the trial. Until this was ruled inadmissible evidence, a jury would hear this even though it had no bearing on the matter in hand. After legislation prevented such evidence being heard in court, it was not unknown for the defence counsel to accidentally, or even intentionally, mention in court whether or not the victim was sexually experienced. A usual scenario would then be that the prosecution counsel would object and the information would be ruled inadmissible, but of course by then the jury had already heard it. Levanon (2012) states that courts are quite clear that previous sexual experience is irrelevant to the question of consent that is at the heart of rape accusation, but she goes on to say that such considerations do not take into account the bias in favour of rape victims who are sexually inexperienced. If juries are representative of the general population, then they are subject to the same biases as that population. Inadmissible evidence should be ignored if presented, but there is an effect that feeds into the bias present in the mind of each jury member.

In addition to problematic evidence, juries have difficulty, according to Levanon (2012), in assessing scientific evidence, including that from forensic scientists and psychologists. The admissibility of such evidence is subject to scrutiny, but that has also revealed that the content presented in court, and the impact it has on decision making, needs to be addressed. During a trial, a huge amount of information is given to juries, in addition to information about legal process. This means that juries are under a good deal of pressure and are working with high cognitive load. Inadmissible evidence, once heard, cannot be easily forgotten, and there may be the additional problem that it interferes with other material. Steblay et al. (2006) examined 48 studies in which juries were exposed to contested evidence and found that almost half of jurors were more likely to convict if they had heard evidence that was problematic for the defendant. This persisted even when juries were instructed to disregard it, particularly if there was no explanation as to why this evidence was to be excluded.

The impact of evidence on juries: the 'CSI effect'

The issue of inadmissible evidence brings us to the question of the impact of evidence in general, and a relatively new phenomenon, the so-called 'CSI effect'. *CSI: Crime Scene Investigation* is an America procedural drama series following the work of forensic science teams in Las Vegas, with spin-offs depicting the same premise in New York and Miami. It is one of the most popular drama series ever made (Gorman, 2010). It is also somewhat unrealistic. In each episode, the team investigates a homicide, gathering and analysing forensic evidence, questioning witnesses and apprehending suspects. In reality, CSI personnel do not undertake all tasks from gathering evidence and analysis to talking to witnesses and apprehending suspects. Also, DNA, fingerprints, etc., even if they are obtained as easily as is shown on TV, take weeks to process.

Schweitzer and Saks (2007: 358), in their analysis of the effect of *CSI* viewing on jury participants' perception of evidence, declared that the TV shows portray forensic science as 'high-tech magic'. The '*CSI* effect' refers to the impact of this TV show, and similar programmes, on the decisions made by jurors about scientific evidence, whether by creating unrealistic expectations about scientific evidence, thereby burdening the prosecution, or by creating an exaggerated faith in evidence, thereby burdening the defence. Cooley (2007) suggested that there is a concern that juries with members who watch such shows regularly will acquit if the form of evidence shown in *CSI* is not presented. This, in particular, refers to whether DNA evidence is included, even though research on potential jurors demonstrates that they do not understand what it is, and the less they understand, the more likely they are to believe that it is infallible (Goodman-Delahunty & Hewson, 2010).

DNA evidence is usually used to determine whether a person was present at a particular location. It is not used to prove they were not. If DNA is present, the matching of that biological sample to a particular person is done on the random match probability basis, that is, the frequency of occurrence of a particular genetic structure and calculations made on those frequencies of occurrence. According to Brenner (2004), these probabilities are generated by determining the proportion of each allele in the DNA profile being examined. The frequency of that allele is compared to the proportion in a standard database of DNA profiles. The next step is to estimate the frequency of genotypes and from that the overall frequency of the DNA profile that has been examined. This is then expressed as the probability of that DNA profile appearing in more than one person and is termed the 'random match probability'. This is the probability an expert would give in court when asked about the DNA sample obtained at a crime scene from bodily fluids, hairs, skin, etc. Research into how to express this to a jury focuses on the ways in which the testimony should underline the probative value of the DNA profile but not negate the value of any other evidence. This is difficult when in dramas such as *CSI* DNA evidence is extracted and analysed and then prepared for presentation in court in almost every episode, usually within ten minutes of the end credits rolling. There is good deal of emphasis on how valuable this is to the prosecution case.

Allele – the alternative form of a gene located at a specific position on a specific chromosome. The DNA codings determine inherited traits.

Genotype – the alleles that appear at a particular locus.

DNA database – a computerised record all the DNA profiles of all those convicted of a recordable offence. The first national database was set up in the UK in 1995. The largest database is that in the USA, the Combined DNA Index System (CODIS).

Kim et al. (2009) studied the *CSI* effect on a set of jurors in a field experiment. They had observed many of the simulated studies that had been carried out with student participants. Their design was to ask the potential jurors to fill out a questionnaire in which they recorded their willingness to convict a defendant of murder or physical assault based on circumstantial evidence only or eyewitness testimony only. Jurors also recorded how much they watched

CSI or similar programmes. The scenarios did not include any scientific evidence as the researchers wanted to look at the effect of watching *CSI* on evidence perception, and not scientific knowledge. They also measured expectations about receiving scientific evidence, and various demographic characteristics. They found that jurors' race, educational level and gender were all factors that needed to be taken into account when presenting evidence, but that exposure to *CSI* did not significantly impact on decision making.

> CSI effect – the possible effect that watching dramas such as *CSI* has on the way the juries view evidence.

The *CSI* effect is simply a label for the wider impact of prior knowledge on a jury's decision-making process. There are other issues that influence the ways in which juries perceive and interpret what they see and hear in court, such as the credibility of witnesses (expert or otherwise), the personal characteristics of the witness/victims and the jurors themselves (as seen in the study by Kim et al., 2009), the comprehensibility of the evidence, and the instructions to the jury.

JURY INSTRUCTIONS

Jury instructions are the set of legal rules that jurors are required to follow when they decide on the case they have heard. This includes how to go about discussing the case and what processes they should follow to decide as a group on the verdict. Instructions are given to the jury by the judge, usually in written form (the procedures) and verbally (a summary of the case and the legal points that specifically relate to it, such as ignoring inadmissible evidence). In England and Wales, the procedural elements are referred to as 'standard instructions' and are approved by the Judicial Studies Board. In the USA, they are often referred to as 'pattern instructions'. They also appear to cause quite a few problems.

Cronan (2002) found that juries who were given no such instructions understood the law better than those who did receive them, with the implication that there is a greater potential for misinterpretation and miscarriage of justice in the latter case. According to Heuer and Penrod (1994), the already complex matter of making decisions as a jury is intensified when they have the added incomprehensibility of the legal position outlined to them. The questions that arise here, then, are whether justice is being served when it is being considered by a confused jury, and how to make instructions easier to understand. If they do not understand, they have to rely on their own, possibly uninformed, opinion of what is just. Finkel (2009) termed this 'intuitive justice' – the notions that a juror brings with him or her in order to judge a defendant and to uphold

> Jury instructions – the rules given to a jury governing how they should conduct themselves with respect to what they hear in court and the decisions they make about that.

the law. Gordon (2012) examined how schemas, or the pre-existing notions held by jurors, affected how they use jury instructions. She found that even when jury instructions are given in what is termed 'plain language' the use of them is still affected by pre-existing schemas for legal concepts, even if they are inappropriate. She went on to suggest that the courts need to pay more attention to the research in cognitive psychology to develop schemas into applicable legal concepts. Any failure to do so would appear to be extremely problematic.

In 2013, Vicky Pryce, the ex-wife of a former energy minister in the British government, was being tried for perverting the course of justice. In 2003, her then husband, Chris Huhne, was caught speeding, incurring penalty points that would have led to the suspension of his driving licence. He persuaded his wife to say that she was driving, thus effectively transferring the points to her licence, which would not have been suspended as she did not have as many existing penalty points. In 2011, Pryce divorced Huhne after he revealed he had had an extramarital affair. She told police that she had been forced to say that she was driving the car when the speeding penalty was incurred. In 2012, the Director of Public Prosecutions decided that Huhne and Pryce would be charged with perverting the course of justice (Chapman, 2012). Pryce entered a plea of not guilty and announced she would be advancing the defence of marital coercion. Her trial started on 4 February 2013. On 20 February the trial collapsed and the judge ordered a re-trial after the jury was unable to reach a majority verdict (BBC News, 2013a). It was what happened then that is of interest here.

It was reported that the jury had posed ten questions during their deliberations, the nature of which prompted the judge, Mr Justice Sweeney, to declare that he had never seen such a fundamental lack of understanding in a jury in 30 years of criminal trials (BBC News, 2013b). According to the media reports, the questions were regarding the definition and extent of 'marital coercion', the nature of 'reasonable doubt', the difference between drawing inferences and speculating about evidence, whether a juror can come to a conclusion based on information not presented as evidence during the trial, whether there is an obligation to present a defence and if one was not presented what could be inferred from that, whether the defendant's state of mind can be speculated upon, whether her religious beliefs could be used as evidence of the defendant feeling compulsion to carry out her husband's wishes (even though that was not presented in court) (BBC News, 2013b). It would be easy to sneer at the jurors, as many commentators did, but while some showed a fundamental lack of understanding of plain English, others suggested that the points of law had not been explained to the jurors in ways that they could understand as applying in this case. The arrogant way the judge handled this could not have helped their anxieties over being at the centre of a high-profile case either (Stern, 2013). However, one positive outcome may be that researchers could be allowed more access to study jury reasoning processes, as two senior legal figures suggested this may help to support the jury system (Jones, 2013).

In some court systems, usually inquisitorial rather than the adversarial systems, juries are assisted in their decision-making process by judges. There is a better understanding of the legal process in such cases, but there is the danger of the jury deliberations being affected by the experiences and opinions of the judges. Hence both forms of jury input have been criticised.

Rose and Ogloff (2001) suggested that there is a low level of understanding of the law when instructions are given if they contain so much legal jargon that the jurors are unable to comprehend a large portion of it, or how it pertains to the case they are hearing. This can lead to the case of jury nullification, which was seen in the Ponting case, and other issues. For example, Kramer and Koening (1990) found that jurors knew that they had to be convinced beyond reasonable doubt of the guilt of the defendant before returning a guilty verdict, but they had no idea how to define or determine what reasonable doubt means. Even when the concept was defined, 52% of jurors who had not yet been instructed thought that reasonable doubt was based solely on evidence presented and not the interpretations to be drawn from it, but once instructed, 68% made this mistake. In addition, only 25% knew that if they had reasonable doubt they should return a not guilty verdict. This seems to be an unacceptable risk to justice and fairness.

In addition to any misunderstanding of the law, there are other things that can influence the jury's decision, such as any publicity about the trial before it is heard, perceptions of evidence and witnesses, and what is said in court by the lawyers and judge(s).

Influences on the jury

Any information about the case brought to the court by the jury members is termed pre-trial influence. This includes publicity surrounding the case. The more sensational the case the more likely it is that jurors will have been exposed to it. This can affect two things: the factual elements of the case and the emotive element, particularly regarding the prejudging of guilt. Ruva et al. (2012) analysed the content of mock jury deliberations when they had either been exposed to pre-trial publicity that was negative (anti-defendant) or had received no exposure. Those in the exposure group were more likely to discuss items of the trial scenario that supported the prosecution case compared to the defence case than the control group was. They also ignored jury instructions about not discussing the information brought in from the publicity. Ruva and LeVasseura (2012), exploring this further, found that mixing the type of publicity (anti-defendant or pro-defendant) showed a recency effect, in that the most recently read publicity was the more salient and affected the verdict more than other material seen or heard.

Such pre-trial material can affect the ways in which juries approach the material presented at the trial, but other issues during the trial are important influences too. In addition to expert testimony, material brought to the trial by witnesses is very important. Witness evidence is very powerful, as Loftus (1974) established in experiments on witness memory and testimony. In these studies, mock jurors were given three types of evidence: a witness with good eyesight, a witness with poor eyesight and no witness. When there was no witness, the mock jury convicted on only 18% of the occasions, but when a witness with good eyesight and one with poor eyesight gave evidence, there was little difference (72% and 68% respectively). So the presence of a witness is extremely important irrespective of whether that testimony is of good quality or not.

But what about the perception of an individual witness? If a witness is perceived as likeable and credible, then their testimony is more likely to be believed. These perceptions can be altered by several things, such as whether the witness is seen as attractive or whether they smile in appropriate or inappropriate places (Able &Watters, 2005), or whether the witness has a criminal record (although there are rules governing the exposure of such information). The content of the testimony is also important, beyond its legal value. Allison et al. (2012) investigated the impact of salacious material. They presented mock jurors with evidence from a witness in which the defendant was provided with an alibi. When the alibi was engaged in salacious activity (such as watching a pornographic movie together), the testimony was more likely to be rated as believable.

The confidence which a witness is perceived as having when they present their evidence is also important. Brewer and Burke (2002) examined the relationship between consistency of testimony and the confidence with which eyewitnesses presented their evidence and what impact this had on mock jurors' decisions. They found that confidence had a much stronger impact on jurors, irrespective of whether the testimony was consistent or not.

The way in which jurors construct evidence is also an important influence on their decision making. According to Conley and Conley (2009), the evidence as a whole is constructed as a narrative form of information. There is limited data on how this happens, as narrative analysis on real jurors' deliberations has been carried out only infrequently. However, the ways in which jurors remember the evidence they have seen and use those memories in the jury room is an important topic for research. The preparation of witnesses and defendants for appearance in court may be influenced by an understanding of the ways in which jurors construct their perception of those giving testimony and remember the versions of the stories that they hear.

JURIES AND DECISION MAKING

Juries, having heard the evidence and making individual perceptions of witnesses, eyewitnesses and scientific testimony, must then retire to make a decision that will lead to a verdict. The way in which this is done relies on social and cognitive psychology. Social psychology informs us about the way in which groups come to a consensus (or not) about what they have seen and heard. Cognitive psychology tells us much about the ways in which people remember what they are told and how they construct this into an internal narrative to be used for later memory.

Groupthink (Janis, 1982) is a well-established phenomenon. Individuals in groups suppress their opinions if they tend to be outside the 'norm' of the group. Early research on how the jury, a very specific type of group, might be subject to the phenomenon of groupthink suggests that there are specific actions of the group that go beyond the individual level of analysis. Lybrand et al. (nd) proposed that there is a phenomenon akin to groupthink, which they termed 'jurythink', which happens in jury deliberations. Studying real cases, they discovered that jurors who state that they are confused by the evidence will then discuss those points so they are assessed openly. However, the accuracy or level of understanding is not necessarily any greater in those who attempt to clarify than in those who declare confusion. What also happens is that the jury room becomes a place in which the entire group can discuss and interpret, and even argue about the case and the evidence in it, and the ways in which each side presented it, whether those interpretations are accurate or not. At this point, Lybrand et al. (nd) suggested, the jurors are no longer acting as independent thinkers but, as a whole, they are constructing a collective reality. This, they propose, is where jurythink supersedes individual thoughts and decisions. The similarities to groupthink lie in the ways in which positions that vary from the group consensus are suppressed, and those who hold opinions that are different from this consensus are criticised and excluded to the point at which their positions are relinquished.

However, such social processes do not mean that jurors are not actively processing information as individuals. Jurors need to make sense of a lot of information in a relatively short time and, according to Bornstein and Greene (2011), information processing models are an appropriate way to examine the ways in which they do this. Experiential or heuristic processing seem to be the ways in which jurors assimilate discrete pieces of information, assessing them in terms of probative value, with issues such as the availability and representative heuristics (Gavin, 1998) ensuring that easy-to-retrieve information and the over-attending to more salient pieces of information impacts on the decisions they make. In addition to this, the emotions of the juror, either their personal emotions or reactions to emotive evidence and testimony, also affect the decision-making processes in both the court and the jury room. Feigenson and Parks (2006) suggested that emotion and mood affects jury judgements because it influences information-processing strategies and has a tendency to incline judgements in the direction of the valence of the emotion or mood. They further suggested that there is a distinction between various affective influences that are dependent on whether emotion is provoked by a source integral or incidental to the judgement task, and whether it has a direct influence on the judgement being made.

However, simply because jurors' decision-making processes are affected by emotional content and their own affect, and they are processing heuristically, does not lead to the conclusion that this processing is inaccurate. Feigenson and Parks (2006) contend that emotion can aid the understanding, empathy and decision-making ability of the jury. Additionally, the literature on heuristics suggests that their use leads to inaccurate decisions, but this is not always the case; they may have positive effects, such as the ability to assimilate, retrieve and understand information. Vidmar and Diamond (2001) demonstrated that jurors do pay attention to testimony in a systematic and careful way. Jurors also view themselves as able to carefully evaluate evidence (Devine et al., 2007).

> Probative value – the status of evidence in terms of relevancy to the case or its ability to demonstrate something in a trial, for example, the value that forensic scientific findings have in showing the defendant was present at a particular location.

The final issue to be considered about the mind of the jury is the effect of the testimony on each person. During a trial, jurors may be exposed to some horrific details and they also view any trauma that witnesses describe. The juries in several sensational, high-profile trials have been offered counselling as it has been recognised that details within cases concerning murder and/or rape can traumatise jury members (McAree, 2004). The problem with studying trauma and stress is that there are restrictions on jurors in terms of how much they can discuss the case, and the restrictions on questioning jurors for the same reasons. Robertson et al. (2009) carried out a study on jurors in England via an online survey, complying with the prohibitions of contempt of court laws around talking to jury members. Gathering information about the trial each juror had attended, together with psychometric measurements of stress, prior trauma, trauma symptoms and response to the trial, Robertson et al. (2009) found 23% were experiencing moderate to severe stress, with 13% scoring well above the levels for severe clinical stress. This was more apparent in female jurors, and in jurors where the trials involved crimes against the person and repellant or horrific evidence. On the basis of these findings, Robertson et al. (2009) suggested ways for mitigating stress without compromising the legal restrictions about discussing what is heard in the court room.

SUMMARY

Jury service is a civic duty in many countries, and the majority of people undertake this willingly and with a good deal of thought and deliberation once they are in the court room and the jury room. There are a lot of psychological factors that impact on the juror, including social pressure and cognitive load. Research on real juries is difficult due to the need for juries to be independent and the admonition against discussing the case. Some researchers therefore use the mock jury paradigm, but this is criticised in terms of its ecological validity. However, researchers agree that the experience of being a juror is quite stressful due to the need to pay attention to what, in some cases, can be very complex, or even horrific, information.

Discussion point: What effect do the personal characteristics of jurors and the witness/defendant have on verdicts?

The demeanour and perceived credibility of witnesses is important in the unconscious processes of a juror. In addition to hearing the evidence, the jurors are also making decisions about the witnesses based on their appearance. To what extent are the characteristics of the witnesses of fact, expert witnesses and the defendant important when juries make decisions?

Alicke, M. & Zell, E. (2009) Social attractiveness and blame. *Journal of Applied Social Psychology*, **39**(9): 2089–2105.

Bergeron, C. & McKelvie, S. (2004) Effects of defendant age and severity of punishment for different crimes. *Journal of Social Psychology*, **144**(1): 75–90.

Neal, T.M., Guadagno, R.E., Eno, C.A. & Brodsky, S.L. (2012) Warmth and competence on the witness stand: implications for the credibility of male and female expert witnesses. *Journal of the American Academy of Psychiatry and the Law* [Online], **40**(4): 488–497.

Section 6

Psychology in Prison

A major employer of forensic psychologists is the prison system. This section is concerned with the psychology of prison and why we imprison criminals. It discusses what imprisonment is supposed to achieve and what the effects of imprisonment are on inmates. The chapters relate to the practice dimension in terms of the discussion of the use of psychology in prisons, but also the knowledge and research dimension as the underlying psychological theory and research is also discussed. The Core Roles are therefore Core Role 2 (research) and Core Role 1 (conducting applications).

Chapter 18 examines the question of punishment and rehabilitation, why we need to lock criminals away from society and what this is meant to achieve. Once someone is locked up, how should we treat them and how do we minimise the risk of recidivism?

A high proportion of people in prison are suffering from a mental disorder. Chapter 19 is a description of the ways in which psychology is attempting to find out why and to treat those who are in this situation.

Chapter 20 looks at the ways in which some prisoners end their life in prison, either in terms of a long-term sentence, a life sentence or a death sentence, but also looks at what happens on release from prison after many years.

Psychology in Prison

18

Punishment

- Universal social constant
- Denial of freedom

The prison psychologist

Imprisonment

- Number of imprisoned and the homogeneity of society
- Prison categories
- Effects of imprisonment
  - Solitary confinement
  - Psychological harms
  - Physical harms
  - Risk factors

Rehabilitation

- Treatment/ education
- After prison
  - Parole

Case study

- Sex offender treatment programmes
  - CBT
  - Core/ extended
  - Physical harms
  - Assessment
  - Psychological processes

On 20 August 1971, Stanford psychology professor Philip Zimbardo announced the end of an unusual experiment. The study was terminated after six days instead of the planned 14, but only after one person outside the study expressed concern about what was going on. In a simulated prison, students were acting as inmates and guards, but adaptation to their roles was beyond what was expected. 'Guards' imposed strict authority and even, it is reported, subjected 'prisoners' to psychological torture. The prisoners were passive, and accepted much of what was meted out to them, even harassing other prisoners at the instigation of guards. Some rioted. Zimbardo himself, playing the role of superintendent, was sucked into the role play and allowed the abuse to continue. The design and findings of the study have been heavily criticised and its generalisability questioned. However, some 33 years later, conditions at the Abu Ghraib American military prison in Iraq were brought to public scrutiny; the physical and psychological abuse there made many think of Zimbardo's experiment and question what prisons are for and what they do to those inside them.

KEY THEMES

- Imprisonment/incarceration
- Punishment
- Rehabilitation
- Risk factors
- Recidivism
- Reoffending

PUNISHMENT

Punishment is the imposition, by some authority, of a negative or unpleasant experience on to an individual or group in response to unacceptable behaviour. In legal terms, the unacceptable behaviour is a crime, and the negative or unpleasant experience is usually some form of deprivation of liberty or imprisonment (Duff, 2008). Why do we need to punish in return for a perceived wrong? If someone has commited a crime, what does society need to do about it? According to Walker (1991), punishment is a universal social constant. It is found in every society and has the same basic form: punishment is intentional and carried out by someone perceived as having the authority to do so, and it results from a voluntary action or omission infringing a law or custom, and there is a clearly expressed justification of the punishment and its severity.

Imprisoning those who are deemed to have committed a crime serves several functions: justice, deterrence, safety and reform. Denial of freedom punishes in order to make those imprisoned pay a moral debt to victims and society, as well as ensuring that they do not commit any more crimes. In addition to such a penalty, a good prison system should educate inmates so that they do not commit crimes again, or treat any illnesses that have caused people to commit crime. In the latter endeavour, the prison psychologist has a major contribution to make.

THE PRISON PSYCHOLOGIST

In the UK, a large proportion of people who are qualified as practising forensic psychologists work within the prison service and its research and development unit. Within the prison setting, psychologists are responsible for the development and delivery of the rehabilitation programmes, but may also support prison staff in their own training. They can also assist with the issues of mental disorder (see Chapter 19) and other psychological services to inmates, including evaluation for services and/or release and to provide recommendation to prison authorities about the management of inmates.

IMPRISONMENT

According to the world prison population list (Walmsley, 2010), almost 10 million people are in prison around the world. However, the rate of imprisonment varies across the globe, with the USA holding 2.29 million of them, although 59% of countries hold fewer than 150 per 100,000. The UK rate is around the 150 mark, depending on the specific jurisdiction. Figure 18.1 shows the imprisonment rate across the world as number of prisoners per 100,000.

The reason for this variation between nations is thought to be linked to the homogeneity of a society. Communities that are more homogeneous are less likely to experience crime

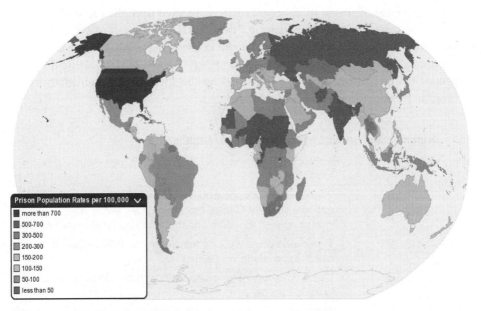

Figure 18 1   **National imprisonment rate across the world (number of prisoners per 100,000 population)**

and are therefore less likely to need prisons (Neopolitan, 2001). Whether the reasons for heterogeneity of a society lead to higher crime rates is unclear, particularly as rates in the UK, arguably one of the most heterogeneous societies in Europe, are relatively low.

In England and Wales, the prison service categorises prisoners on the basis of the level of security their imprisonment entails. Male prisoners are sent to one of four categories of prison. Category A prisoners are those whose escape would present the most danger to the public or national security. Therefore Category A prisoners are those convicted of murder, attempted murder, manslaughter, wounding with intent, rape, indecent assault, robbery or conspiracy to rob (with firearms), firearms offences, importing or supplying class A controlled drugs, possessing or supplying explosives, offences connected with terrorism and offences under the Official Secrets Act 1989. Category B prisoners are those who do not require maximum security, but whose escape needs to be made very difficult, and Category C are those who cannot be trusted in open conditions but who are unlikely to try to escape. Category A–C prisons are closed prisons, whereas a Category D prison is an open prison, housing those who can be reasonably trusted not to try to escape. Some Category D prisoners may be released on temporary licence to work in the community or to go on home leave once they have served at least a quarter of their sentence. Table 18.1 lists these categories.

Female adult offenders are also classified into four categories. Restricted status is similar to Category A, Closed conditions is similar to Category B, Semi-open conditions is similar to Category C, and Open conditions is the same as for men (see Table 18.2).

Juveniles and young offenders (under the age of 21) are also housed in four different types of unit: secure training centres, secure children's homes, juvenile prisons or youth offender institutions, and young offender institutions (see Table 18.3).

Those convicted of sexual offences are often segregated from the rest of the prison population for their own protection, under the Prison Services Rule 45 or 49 in juveniles units (www.justice.gov.uk, 2011). They may even be housed in specialist secure units if they are at exceptional risk from other inmates, such as HMP Usk and HMP Wakefield.

In the USA, prison facilities are classified by the level of governmental organisation involved in running the prison (see Table 18.4).

Table 18.1   Prison categories in England and Wales, adult males

Prison type	Category	Description
Closed	A	Those whose escape would be highly dangerous to the public or national security. Crimes include murder, some sexual offences, violent crimes, terrorism and threats to national security
Closed	B	Those who do not require maximum security, but for whom escape needs to be made very difficult
Closed	C	Those who cannot be trusted in open conditions but who are unlikely to try to escape
Open	D	Those who can be reasonably trusted not to try to escape, and are given the privilege of an open prison. Potential release on temporary licence

Table 18.2   Prisoner categories in the UK, adult females

Category	Description
Restricted status	As for adult male prisoners
Closed conditions	Any prisoner (female, young person or young adult male) convicted or on remand whose escape would present a serious risk to the public and who is required to be held in designated secure accommodation
Semi-open conditions	Those who cannot be trusted in open conditions but who are unlikely to try to escape
Open conditions	Prisoners who present a low risk; can reasonably be trusted in open conditions and for whom open conditions are appropriate

Table 18.3   Prisoner categories in England and Wales, young offender and juveniles

Category	Description
Secure training centres	Privately run, education-focused centres for offenders up to the age of 17
Secure children's homes	Any prisoner (female, young person or young adult male) convicted or on remand whose escape would present a serious risk to the public and who is required to be held in designated secure accommodation
Youth offender institutions	15–18 year olds
Young offender institutions	18–21 year olds

There is a further distinct category of prisoner, but this is outside the Prison Service's classifications. A political prisoner is a person who has been detained or imprisoned because s/he has opposed or criticised the government of his/her own country, or because s/he has participated in political activity which is not necessarily illegal. This definition can become blurred, especially when activist groups campaign for the release of a particular prisoner or group. For example, Irish nationalist activists in Northern Ireland, protesting against what they termed 'British occupation', were imprisoned in facilities such as the Maze prison in Belfast. They, and support groups in the community, identified themselves as political prisoners, even though they had been convicted of crimes such as causing explosions and conspiracy to commit murder (O'Hearn, 2009).

Leaving aside political prisoners, most people are imprisoned after conviction for a crime, usually of the most severe type. Prison is therefore punishment for a crime, but is also intended to prevent those imprisoned from committing more crimes, and to act as a deterrent against committing crimes in the future. When linked to the idea of rehabilitation, prison removes criminals from society, thereby protecting people from crime and preventing further crimes from being perpetrated, and provides the opportunity to educate criminals away from the acts of committing crime. These are worthy intentions but in practice prison may fall short of some of them.

According to Coyle (2005), prison is primarily intended as a punishment to those who have committed crimes, to protect the public from crime and criminals, to act as a deterrent to potential criminals, to reform those who have committed crime and to reduce re-offending. Coyle further pointed out that in the UK this costs around £35,000 per year, per prisoner. However, rates of re-offending are high, despite imprisonment. The Social Exclusion Unit (2002) reported that 60% of those released from prison re-offend and return within two years. Dye (2010) suggested that prison also has many unintended effects, such as increased substance abuse, physical and mental health problems and higher suicide rates. Even if the goals of punishment and public safety are achieved by locking criminals away from society, the psychological effects of imprisonment are not necessarily conducive to the educative purposes avowed by the justice system. Zimbardo's experiment, even allowing for the unusual circumstances and question of generalisability, clearly demonstrates that prison has an effect on all of those within it that is not necessarily positive.

The effect of imprisonment

Imprisonment is based on the separation of those convicted of crime from the rest of society. It depends upon the isolation of those within the walls from both the world at large and, to a certain extent, from each other. Solitary confinement is used within prison to separate some inmates from everyone else; it can be used either as a further safety measure or for further punishment. However, some research suggests that this is counter-productive.

Table 18.4 **Prison categories in the USA**

Category	Security level	Description
Federal prison Run by the federal (national) government	Minimum	Work or program oriented with low staff to inmate ratio
	Low	Higher staff to inmate ratio, but strong work and program components
	Medium	Higher staff to inmate ratio, work and treatment program focussed, high internal controls
	High	United Sates Penitentiaries: high security perimeters, high staff to inmate ratio, close control of inmate movement
State prison Run by individual state governments	Similar categories to above	

Grassian (1983) described symptoms such as delusions, claustrophobia, depression, panic attacks and various other psychopathological issues within those subjected to solitary confinement as a result of social isolation and sensory restriction. Such symptoms are suffered by those in prison in general, not just those in solitary confinement, and are indicative of a mental illness commonly known as prison neurosis (but also termed chronophobia, or the fear of (doing) time).

In addition to the psychological harm imprisonment can inflict, there are real physical dangers to inmates. In a review of literature concerning violence in prisons, Schenk and Fremouw (2012) reported that 15.6% of guards and 21% of inmates have been the victim of physical assault by another prisoner. They also identified those at high risk of committing violence inside prison: young men convicted of violent crime with low educational attainment and a history of mental instability or illness. Sexual assault is also a real risk within prison settings. Gonsalves et al. (2012) reported that 21% of male inmates in the USA have experienced at least one incidence of sexual assault or rape while incarcerated. The risk factors here include victim stature (with smaller men being easier to intimidate and overpower), low position in prison hierarchies, age and ethnicity, with 75% of perpetrators reported as being African-American.

While there is little research on sexual coercion in female prison populations, recent research has also suggested that the risk factors in male inmates may also apply to women in prison, albeit in much smaller numbers. Issues such as these are considered of paramount importance within both practice and research literature, giving rise to initiatives such as the Prison Rape Elimination Act (PREA) of 2003 in the USA.

This would therefore suggest that the issue of mental illness is of paramount importance to the prison system, both as a direct result of imprisonment and as a further risk factor for all within the system.

Risk factors for mental illness in prison

Some of those sentenced to imprisonment already have mental illnesses and may spend their period of imprisonment in a secure hospital (see Chapter 19 for more details). However, there are risk factors associated with prison life which may lead to mental health problems. Some prisoners experience incarceration as a major source of stress due to loss of contact with family and life outside, lack of personal choice and privacy. There are several factors that mean this stress may have more of an impact on some individuals than others. For example, Bartol and Bartol (1994) reported that younger inmates are more resistant to the ways in which prisons are structured and run, and this makes them more likely to be victimised. In addition, curtailment of movements, wearing of uniforms, restriction of privileges and other aspects of prison makes some inmates feel dehumanised, as described by Zimbardo (2011). This includes the effect and extent of isolation from both the outside population and that of the prison. If this is not to become a medical or psychiatric problem, the needs of prisoners must be met in terms of safety, access to food and activities to relieve boredom, and access to rehabilitative programmes.

REHABILITATION

If prison has the objective of being rehabilitation in addition to punishment and public safety, then the programmes prisoners join must be effective and reliable, and based on sound psychological and educational practices. The Prison Service in the UK have made a large investment in programmes based on the cognitive–behavioural model, such as Reasoning and Rehabilitation (R&R) (Porporino & Fabiano, 2000) and Enhanced Thinking Skills (ETS) (Clark, 2000). Both programmes cover problem-solving skills, perspective taking and social skills, creative thinking, moral reasoning, management of emotions, and critical reasoning.

Evaluations are difficult. The main measure of the effectiveness of such programmes is levels of recidivism. Studies such as Beech et al. (2012) suggested that recidivism is significantly different between control (no treatment) and programme groups and between in-prison and community-based programmes. Furthermore, critics suggest that the evaluative studies themselves are biased, as they only consider those who voluntarily opt in to the programme. Grady et al. (2012) addressed this by considering the impact of volunteerism by comparing a sample who volunteered and one that did not, with a non-treatment control group. They found that there were no significant differences in recidivism between the two treatment groups, but there was a difference in some aspects, including the risk for future offending, measured by STATIC-99.[1] Nevertheless, other criticisms include a lack of attention to aspects such as opportunities and motivation of the individual and some suggest that interventions focused on change and development would be more fruitful.

Other issues focus on the implementation of these programmes without full evaluation, as this took place after the programmes had been in place for some time and included a wide variety of offenders and offences (Merrington & Stanley, 2000). In order to address such criticisms, the implementation of the programmes across the UK has been done within a framework of accreditation. This aims to minimise threats to integrity as it puts in place a thorough monitoring and evaluation programme (Home Office, 2000). The accreditation process relates to both design of the programmes and quality assurance. To meet these criteria a programme must be assessed by an independent Joint Accreditation panel made up from representatives of the prison and probation services and independent experts. One such programme is the Sex Offender Treatment Programme (SOTP).

Sex Offender Treatment Programme

During the 1990s, a major concern about recidivism in sex offenders led to the implementation of accredited programmes as part of a UK national prison strategy for assessment and treatment. These are now delivered in the various high-security hospitals and

---

[1]STATIC-99 is a 10-item psychometric instrument for measuring the risk of recidivism. It is specifically designed for use with adult male sex offenders (Hanson & Thornton, 2000).

specialist sex offender units, although some are designed to be delivered in the community. There is a Core Programme with several enhanced or supplementary programmes. Treatment can be for the needs of all forms of sex offenders, including child sex abusers and rapists. The programme can be delivered to individuals, but group programmes are the norm. The programme follows a CBT model in the same way as other prison treatment programmes do. This means the learner is encouraged to recognise patterns of distorted thinking that allow and rationalise illegal acts, together with understanding the impact that such behaviour has on victims. It also aims to identify the triggers to that behaviour and in this way addresses the prevention of such behaviour.

The Core SOTP combines several target areas that are fundamental to sexual offending behaviour. It does this through developing strategies to deal with deviant arousal, recognition and modification of distorted thinking, promotion of victim empathy, reduction of denial and minimisation, and relapse prevention. The primary aim is to increase offenders' motivation to avoid re-offending and to develop the self-management skills necessary to achieve this. The average treatment of the Core Programme is 180 hours (Beech & Mann, 2002), typically, in two-hour sessions, several times a week.

The Extended SOTP

Sometimes offenders have treatment needs that go beyond the Core Programme, in which case they can be referred for further stages. An Extended Programme is designed to identify and challenge patterns of dysfunctional thinking, improve the management of emotions, improve relationship and intimacy skills, address deviant fantasy and sexual arousal and the links of these issues to sexual offending. There are further programmes, for example, the Enhanced Thinking Skills (ETS) Programme, which is designed to combat antisocial behaviour that results from an inability to demonstrate prosocial behaviour due to a lack of cognitive skills. Such deficiencies are not related to intelligence or educational attainment but with styles of thinking and attitudes that lead to antisocial behaviour. The programme targets impulse control problems, deficits in perspective taking and empathy, and critical reasoning. Alternatively, the Healthy Sexual Functioning Programme is run as an individual programme for offenders who need additional work to help them deal with deviant sexual fantasy and arousal, by teaching strategies to manage them appropriately via behavioural modification.

Assessment and treatment of criminogenic needs

The approach to treatment of sexual offenders in UK prisons is based on assessment of the level of problems in four identified risk domains (Thornton, 2000). These domains are:

deviant sexual interest
pro-offending attitudes
social competence problems
self-management difficulties

The Structured Assessment of Risk and Need (SARN) is used by the Prison Service as a standard assessment tool to assess sexual offenders' risk, need and progress in treatment.

Table 18.5   **Programmes appropriate for needs in each risk domain**

Risk domain	Prison programme
Sexual interests (resulting in deviant arousal) Sexualised violence Sexual preoccupation Other offence-related sexual interest	Healthy Sexual Functioning Programme (in development) Core 2000 Sex Offender Treatment Programme (SOTP) One-to-one work
Distorted attitudes Adversarial sexual attitudes Sexual entitlement Rape-supportive beliefs View of women as deceitful	Core 2000 (SOTP) Extended SOTP
Socio-affective functioning Grievance thinking Lack of emotionally intimate relationships with adults	Core 2000 SOTP Extended SOTP Enhanced Thinking Skills Programme
Self-management Lifestyle impulsiveness Poor cognitive problem-solving Poor emotional control	ETS Programme Extended SOTP

Depending on the assessment outcomes, offenders can be channelled into various programmes of treatment (see Table 18.5).

Beech et al. (1998) undertook the first assessment of Sex Offender Treatment Programmes using 12 treatment groups in six prisons, comprising 82 child sex offenders. This evaluation was expanded into the STEP (Sex Offender Treatment Evaluation Project). Assessing the offenders pre- and post-treatment, with a variety of psychometric tests, they gathered data about denial of deviant sexual interests and offending behaviours, pro-offending attitudes, predisposing personality factors, and relapse prevention skills. They conclude that the programmes helped offenders achieved positive changes, with 67% of the samples showing an effect of treatment. There was an effect of length of treatment, the longer programmes achieving more success that could be maintained with support. A further study (Beech et al., 2001) examined the reconviction data for 53 treated child sex offenders six years after release. Only 10% of men who had been originally identified as benefiting from treatment re-offended within that period and 23% of men who were classified as 'not having responded to treatment' re-offended.

The CBT programmes are not the only form of treatment, however, as one of the key domains – deviant sexual interest – has been treated with anti-libidinal hormonal treatments in conjunction with the psychological intervention. Unfortunately, these treatments have side-effects and are only used with strict guidance from medical specialists. Selective serotonergic reuptake inhibitors (SSRIs), such a fluoxetine (Prozac), are often used instead, particularly when deviant sexual interests are closely allied to anxiety and depressive disorders.

With such a range of therapeutic interventions available, the key to success is often in terms of efficient diagnosis and selection for treatment.

Assessing suitability for treatment

All treatment is voluntary and there are several categories of prisoner to whom the treatment can be offered. Those who should *definitely* be considered for the Core Sex Offender Treatment Programme are those with:

- a conviction for a sexual offence unrelated to consensual sex, or
- a previous conviction for a sexual offence where the prisoner falls into medium- or high-risk groups (measured by Risk Matrix 2000) (Thornton et al., 2003), or
- a homicide conviction where there is a clear sexual element to the homicide.

There are others who may be suitable but who need further assessment and definition of problem behaviours. For example:

- those sentenced to life imprisonment for offences in which there is a suspected sexual element (e.g. clothing disarranged or removed) but where this is strongly denied
- prisoners who request treatment and admit to sexual offending but who do not have convictions
- sexually offensive behaviour that has occurred in custody and would be construed as an offence if it happened in another context (e.g. indecent exposure to prison staff)

Suitability assessment can still lead to exclusion from the programmes, even if the above criteria are met. After consultation with psychology staff, exclusion is considered if the prisoner has:

- a high score on either the PCL-R or PPI-R, as this indicates a lack of certain capacities necessary for change to be assisted by a cognitive-behavioural programme.
- medium scores, although this does not mean automatic exclusion. Additional criteria would be recent evidence of dishonesty, poor responsibility, manipulation, impulsivity, callous behaviour or lack of goal-setting/achievement.
- an IQ less than 80 (measured via the WAIS screen). There is an Adapted SOTP available if needed.
- a current mental illness that is acute and damaging to the ability to relate to others or concentrate on treatment-type work. If the illness is stabilised on medication, the prisoner may still be suitable for SOTP.

Exclusion may not be irredeemable as there are certain criteria by which prisoners can be deemed to be not ready for treatment but there is the potential for them to benefit from treatment at some point in the future. These might include total denial of the offence, refusal of treatment, the prisoner does not speak English, has a physical disability (but the institution needs to make adjustments), poor literacy (as the Core and Extended Programmes rely on written homework, although literacy programmes are available), or the prisoner is suicidal or self-harming.

As screening for entry to the programme is very thorough, a lot of data is generated. Similarly, the evaluation of the programmes in the UK has exposed a good deal about the offenders who navigate through it, in addition to any issues around recidivism and offending. What is becoming clearer through this research is what the psychological processes are behind sexual offending behaviour.

Psychological processes in sexual offending in men

Since its first implementation in 1991, the set of Sex Offender Treatment Programmes in prison has been evaluated on a regular basis. The main measure of success is clearly re-offending rates, but the evaluation of the SOTPs has also led to some understanding of the thought processes involved in violent sexual offending, and whether these can be successfully addressed by the offenders themselves. These processes relate to the characteristics of the course participants, the motivation for offending, and implicit theories that offenders hold about the world, which can in turn lead to motivations for offending behaviour. The following findings are summaries of the research by the Sex Offender Treatment Evaluation Project (STEP).

Characteristics of course participants

The course is offered to anyone who meets the criteria (see above) and participation is voluntary, although there may be incentives offered for successful completion. The course participants therefore include those who have offended against adults and those against children, and some have killed. Within the samples studied, murderers have slightly higher IQs than rapists/molesters, but all are within the normal range, as this is one of the criteria for inclusion. The majority of participants are low to medium risk for reconviction as measured on the risk assessment measures (Thornton et al., 2003). In the samples studied, the murderers tended to be slightly younger than rapists at the time of their index offence (the offence for which they were considered for inclusion). The rapists in the sample were more likely to have a history of violence than the murderers, but both groups had high levels of previous contact with psychiatric services, both as children and adults. Similarly, a large proportion reported experience of physical and/or sexual abuse in childhood, including a third of the groups who had been sexually abused by women, including the biological mother. The programmes discussed here are only for male offenders; the question of treatment of female offenders is a complex one (see below).

Motivations for sexual offending

Grievance-motivated offenders have little insight into their own issues and are suspicious and resentful of others. They display avoidant, negativistic, self-defeating and dependent personality styles. Offending behaviour exhibits impulsivity and vengefulness, and attendance in the programme needs to address rape justification and grievance thinking. Even after treatment, they continue to blame others for their actions, but the level of rape-supportive beliefs and grievance towards women can decrease significantly and victim empathy can improve. However, they still have problems with emotional regulation.

Sexually motivated offenders plan and fantasise about sexual offences, selecting victims in terms of accessibility, and include violence only where necessary, for example, to avoid detection. As such, they tend not to be impulsive, hostile or aggressive and are motivated to address their problems. These issues include stereotypical gender views and male entitlement to sex. This can be addressed, however, and treatment can lead to them taking more responsibility for their offending and improving victim empathy, attitudes about rape and emotional regulation, although it does not seem to target their stereotypical views about women and attitudes about the acceptance of violence against women.

Sadistically motivated offenders are found within the sexual murderer groups. They show a fascination with sexual violence and are sexually aroused by thoughts such as death or torture. They plan, and the sexual offending is accompanied not only with murder, but with sadistic behaviour and post-mortem sexual interference or mutilation. Strangely, they do not hold offence-supportive attitudes, but they do show callousness, shallow affect and anger. Treatment leads to them taking responsibility for their offending and lower levels of hostility and anger.

Implicit theories in sexual murderers

In addition to the statistical analysis of groups above, the STEP researchers have also carried out in-depth qualitative interviews with several sexual murderers. Several implicit theories held by sexual offenders (i.e. their personal constructions about the world) were revealed. These include:

'Dangerous world' – where the individual concerned felt that he had been treated unjustly and abusively, resulting in feelings of anger and resentment which were taken out against his victim

'Male sex drive is uncontrollable' – where offenders reported that their urges were so compelling and compulsive that they led to rape and murder

'Entitlement' – where offenders reported an entitlement to sex

'Women as sexual objects' – where women were seen as little more than sexual objects

'Women as unknowable' – where women were viewed as being deliberately deceptive.

These are also found in the literature about rapists. The STEP research found that these theories were held in combination by the participants in such a way as to identify separate grouping of thought processes. Those who held both the 'dangerous world' and 'incontrollable male sex drive' theories were motivated by fantasies about killing and raping, whereas those who held the 'dangerous world' theory only were more likely to be motivated by grievance and resentment towards women.

None of these findings is particularly surprising. It is clear that no one rapes a woman or kills her in a sexually motivated manner without harbouring some atypical attitudes towards women. What it does show is that implantation of a programme of prison treatment is not the end of this matter. The evaluation not only measures the effectiveness of a programme, but can also add to our understanding of the psychology of offending. The programme is delivered by prison psychologists or other suitably trained personnel.

Other prison treatment programmes

In addition to the Sex Offender Treatment Programmes, there are several other treatment programmes available in prison. They may include drug rehabilitation programmes, in which the physical and psychological needs of those recovering from substance addiction are assessed and dealt with. These are also based on the CBT model and appear to be effective in lowering drug use and related crime in prisoners, parolees and probationers in the USA (Bahr et al., 2012). In the UK, research such as that by Clarke et al. (2004) and Neale et al. (2005) sought to determine if the needs of prisoners in the UK were different from those in North America, which is where most data has been derived, and whether these differences were also evident in comparing drugs users in and outside prison, and male and female addicts. These studies appear to be the earliest research that was done to address these questions and they reveal some interesting results.

Neale et al. (2005) found that there were inconsistencies when comparing North American and UK services because drug-focused criminal justice interventions were less readily available at that time. There was also a tendency, within the UK service provision, to perceive the drug-using population in and outside prison as homogeneous, when this was not the case, even though drug users are more likely to be arrested and given custodial sentences than other members of the community. Neale et al. (2005) also advised that female and male drug-user participants within prison may not benefit from the same types of intervention because those for male prisoners contain elements targeted at behavioural issues such as anger management, which may not be appropriate for female inmates.

Prisoners who are not sexual offenders or in need of drug rehabilitation can still be offered rehabilitative treatment programmes, including those targeted at cognitive deficits related to offending behaviour. These programmes are based on the link between a lack of cognitive skills, which are unrelated to intellectual ability but to styles of thinking and attitudes, and antisocial behaviour, due to an offender's ability to achieve goals in prosocial ways. These programmes also incorporate cognitive-behavioural elements, focusing on thinking skills or patterns. Examples of such programmes are Reasoning and Rehabilitation (R&R), which targets, among other things, self-control, interpersonal skills, critical reasoning and cognitive style, and Enhanced Thinking Skills (ETS), which is formally adapted for the UK offender population, due to the emphasis on group working, an important aspect for programmes to run in the UK. The effectiveness of these programmes in the UK has been evaluated (see, for example, Friendship et al., 2003). They have been found to produce significant reductions in the reconviction rate of those who had participated compared to those who had not.

Clarke et al. (2004) also attempted to access prisoner views of the programmes. They reported that prisoners sometimes felt coerced to participate in the programmes, despite their voluntary nature. This affected both the motivation of the prisoners and the group dynamics. Some prisoners were told that participation was a condition of them being considered for parole, when in fact graduation from the course is seen as an added point in the favour of a parole applicant, not a condition of being considered. There was also a lack of linkage between the skills which could be developed through the courses and desistance from offending.

There is a general consensus in the evaluative and research literature that the treatment programmes have a good deal of value in terms of reducing reconviction and recidivism. However, there are a few studies that attempt to access what prisoners think of treatment. All the programmes aim to shift the process of thinking in some way, whether to understand that anger is not an appropriate response to social interactions, or that sexual needs can be expressed in a way other than violence. This shift in thinking is then focused on ways to desist from reoffending and learning that prosocial actions to achieve goals are much more rewarding.

AT THE END OF A SENTENCE

According to data compiled by the European Commission (2007), the percentage of prisoners classed as long-term varies across nations, with some countries having rates as low as 20% (such as India) and others being around 40% (as in England and Wales). Of course this means that a high proportion of people are sentenced to relatively short periods in prison, and will be released. The majority of long-term prisoners will also be released at some point. Prisoners on fixed term (also called determinate) sentences are normally released half way through this term, and if the term was 12 months or more they will be released on parole.

Parole

Parole is a term to describe a conditional release from prison, once a prisoner has served some of the term of sentence. The conditions may include doing unpaid work, completing a training course or getting treatment for addictions and will include having regular meetings with an offender manager. This person monitors whether or not the prisoner on release is meeting the conditions of that parole.

While there is a set of services set up around prisoners being released from prison, what is also clear is that some prisoners experience problems when returning to the outside world, particularly after serving several years. Problems such as homelessness are a major social problem. Released prisoners make up a significant proportion of those without appropriate accommodation and there is a clear link between this and reconviction rates (Williams et al., 2012). In addition, a study in New York (Lim et al., 2012) established that the risk of mortality in relapsed prisoners was twice that of the general population. The risk was strongly correlated with the length of time in prison, and there was a high level of association

> Parole – conditional release from prison to complete a sentence in the community.
>
> Probation – alternative sentencing outside prison.

between this and homelessness. The issues are all seemingly exacerbated by problems such as drug use and mental disorder. The latter is addressed in Chapter 19.

SUMMARY

Putting people in prison when they have committed a crime is regarded as both punishment for the individual and protection of society from crime. It is also seen as a deterrent against committing future crimes. Across the world, imprisonment is seen as an effective solution to most forms of crime. However, nations and cultures differ in terms of how much they use imprisonment and how effective that process is. Evaluations of treatment within prison show that it can be an effective solution for some offenders.

Discussion point: How effective is the SOTP for female sex offenders?

The programme discussed in this chapter is only for male offenders. Female sex offenders, while a minority proportion of the female prison population, do represent a risk to both children and adults. The SOTP for men includes assessments such as attitudes to women and deviant sexual fantasy. What assessments and treatment approaches might be useful in female offenders?

Bunting, L. (2007) Dealing with a problem that doesn't exist? Professional responses to female perpetrated child sexual abuse. *Child Abuse Review*, **16**: 252–267.

Ford, H. (2009) Female sex offenders: issues and considerations in working with this population. In A. Beech, L. Craig & K. Browne (eds), *Assessment and Treatment of Sex Offenders: A Handbook*. London: John Wiley & Sons.

19

Imprisonment and Mental Disorder

Mental health in prison
- Large numbers of mentally disordered inmates
- Causal issues
  - High levels of psychiatric morbidity in prisons globally
  - 70% of prison inmates have mental health issues
  - Gender difference
  - Mental health is seen as the most important factor contributing to disruptive behaviour in prison

Research in mental health in prison
- Higher incidence of violent altercations
  - Damage to the cell, health and hygiene violations, intentional self-injury

Secure hospitals
- Detained under the Mental Health Act 2007
- Treatment without consent
- Studying violent crime and mental disorder

Serious mental illness and serious crime
- Increasing criminalisation

Suicide in mentally ill prisoners
- High rates in prison, higher among the mentally ill in prison
- Risk factors – self-harm
- Gateway theory
- Third variable theory

Managing mental health in prison
- Solitary confinement
- Continuity problem

Case study
- Richard Dadd
  - Celebrated artist
  - Murdered his father
  - Extradited from France
  - Bethlem Hospital
  - Broadmoor
  - Paintings of supernatural beings

Richard Dadd is one of the most celebrated Victorian artists, and his paintings of fairies and other supernatural subjects are arguably among the best ever created. One, *The Fairy Feller's Master Stroke*, even inspired a song by Queen, the British rock band. He was a founding member of a group of artists called 'The Clique', who opposed the ideals of the Royal Academy. Dadd was also commissioned to accompany Sir Thomas Phillips on his Grand Tour in order to document and illustrate their journeys across Europe and the Middle East.

While the early part of this tour appears to have been a great success, and Dadd produced many beautiful pictures, Sir Thomas later became concerned about Dadd's health and sent him home in 1843. His concern was well founded; Dadd was criminally insane. When he reached home, he murdered his father in the belief that the Egyptian god Osiris wanted him to do so (Tromans, 2011). Dadd fled to France, attempting another murder on the way, but was arrested and put into a succession of French asylums. He was finally returned to England (he was the first person to be legally extradited from France), where he was placed in Bethlem Hospital in London. After 20 years, he was among the first male prisoners to be sent to the newly opened Broadmoor Hospital for the Criminally Insane. He continued to paint, and some of his most famous works of art were produced while he was under the care of the psychiatric authorities, including *Fairy Feller* (Stevens, 2011).

KEY THEMES

- Social exclusion in prisoners
- Comorbidity
- Secure hospitals
- Suicidal ideation
- Self-harm

According to Durcan (2008), there is a large proportion of the prison population that has need of support for their mental health and the majority of prisoners experience high levels of psychological distress. This conclusion was based on a study carried out in five standard prisons, not secure hospitals, in the West Midlands of the UK. The units included one housing young offenders, one for women inmates, one Category B and two Category C (see Chapter 18 for descriptions of these categories). One of the Category C prisons included a facility for vulnerable prisoners. Durcan interviewed prisoners and staff at all the units. Interviews with inmates included questions on their offending, their life before prison, their use of mental health services, both inside and outside prison, and the problems they experienced, again inside and outside prison. The report of this study concluded that there is a great deal of inconsistency of the experience of mental health issues and services across all of the prisons represented. Durcan suggested that prison itself may contribute to the damage to mental health observed, but also acknowledged that mental illness may contribute to criminality and subsequent imprisonment. Durcan (2008) observed how screening for mental health problems was often inadequate and prisoners rarely had access to medical services that could meet their mental health needs.

By 2012, however, the picture was becoming brighter, with the HM Chief Inspector of Prisons for England and Wales' Annual Report 2011–12 stating that physical and mental health care in prison had generally improved, despite the need for those services to expand. The remaining question for researchers, in addition to the provision of services for those in prison, is why are there so many prisoners in need of mental health screening and support?

MENTAL HEALTH IN PRISON

Fazel and Seewald (2012) reported on the global issue of mental health in prisoners. Their review covered 24 countries, and they found that high levels of psychiatric morbidity are regularly reported across the countries involved. According to the Mental Health Foundation, a UK charity concerned with research, policy and service improvement in mental health, one in four adults experience mental illness at some point in their lives. However, according to the Social Exclusion Unit (2004) at that time, more than 70% of the prison population suffered from some form of mental health disorder. This suggests that either being imprisoned leads to mental health problems or that there is a higher likelihood of being imprisoned if you have a mental health disorder. In addition, the same report indicated that male prisoners were 14 times more likely to have two or more disorders comorbidly than men in the general population, and this rises to being 35 times more likely in female prisoners. Within prisoners, experience of abuse, deprivation, homelessness, unemployment and substance misuse is also high in comparison with the general population (Fazel & Danesh, 2002), and this is often coupled to low educational attainment, numeracy and literacy problems and below-average IQ (HMIP, 2000). As such, psychological difficulties, including psychotic illnesses and personality disorders, are prevalent in the prison population. The question this gives rise to is why this might be the case, and what is done about addressing the needs of those in prison with psychological difficulties.

According to Rich et al. (2011), much of the increase in incarceration can be attributed to the refusal to treat mental illness as a medical problem that can lead to criminal activity. First, this means that those who are mentally ill and who commit crimes are not dealt with as being ill, but as being criminal. Secondly, the mentally ill are being deinstitutionalised, and because they cannot be treated appropriately in society, the burden of care for those who are mentally ill and who have committed crimes has shifted to the prisons.

This poses a large problem for the Prison Service, which is constructed on the premise that it houses the criminal, not the mentally ill. Friedman et al. (2008) reported that prison staff view mental disorders as being the most important factor contributing to disruptive behaviour in inmates. As prison occupancy figures rise, and more patients with mental disorders are treated in the community and not inside hospital, the issue is becoming an urgent one, notwithstanding the improvement in provision of services. Adams and Ferrandino (2008) reported that the prison population experience the more serious forms of mental illness in high numbers, including depression, bipolar disorder and schizophrenia, alongside substance abuse issues and personality disorders, including antisocial personality disorder. If prison inmates are experiencing the same mental health problems as the general population, but in increased and increasing numbers, it would certainly suggest that a mental disorder is more likely to lead to some form of criminal behaviour either as a direct or indirect result of the mental illness. Psychological research and practice issues are therefore concerned with the effects of mental illness on those in prison, including violence and self-injury, together with the reasons for high levels of mental illness among prison inmates.

RESEARCH IN MENTAL ILLNESS IN PRISONS

Research has established that there is a close relationship between mental disorder and violence within prisons. Seminal studies by Adams (1983, 1986) found that people who had been previously diagnosed with mental illness, but who were incarcerated, were more likely to be involved in violent altercations both outside and inside prison. Issues discovered within prison include damage to the cell, health and hygiene violations, and intentional self-injury. This was later supported by Friedman et al. (2008), who found that issues such as paranoia increased the risk of violent behaviour, but that this was not always linked to psychiatric diagnosis *per se*. Even if there was a high correlation between violence and mental disorder, there would remain the problem that exists in all such studies that such an observed relationship could be spurious.

Although there is an evidenced view that mental illness and violence do share such risk factors, including gender, socio-economic status, stressful life events and prior abuse (Silver & Teasdale, 2005), this is by no means a straightforward relationship. It would necessarily not include several issues of importance and cannot make any statements about a causal relationship. Therefore extrapolating this to the link between mental illness and criminal behaviour and subsequent incarceration would be just as spurious. Even more specifically, the possibility that mental disorder provides motivation for violence and criminal behaviour is just as difficult to establish. The frustration–aggression hypothesis suggests a form of reactive aggression (Berkowitz, 1988) in which negative affect leads to aggression, but is mediated by inhibitory factors, such as cognitive interpretation of stimuli that led to the affect. If cognition is disordered in some way, then interpretation is skewed, resulting in behaviour which is socially inappropriate. Depression should therefore predict aggression, as the inherent chronic negative affect should lead to a higher likelihood of reactive aggression.

On the other hand, for instrumentally determined aggression, violence is acted upon when the costs are weighed lower than the potential outcome, such as gaining rewards, fighting offensive behaviour directed against the self, or defending already achieved goods, etc. If decision-making processes are flawed, then again, inappropriate aggression might ensue. Mental illness can lead to disordered thinking and result in aggression and violence, particularly in situations where, for example, paranoia can lead a person to assume normal behaviour in others is directed aggressively towards them. Hence violence becomes a seemingly rational choice in inappropriate circumstances.

None of these perspectives sheds much light on the two major questions about mental disorder in prisons, namely is mental illness a high-risk factor that can lead to imprisonment, and does imprisonment lead to higher levels of mental disorder. There are, of course, further questions, such as if mental disorder is a risk factor for crimes that lead to imprisonment, why is the disorder not being recognised at an earlier stage and the individual diverted into mental health services intervention. If it is recognised, then the question becomes one of how to ensure the recognition is sufficient and timely enough to enable those convicted of crime to be treated appropriately, rather than simply imprisoned?

Mental disorder and crime is in itself a major issue. If people with psychological difficulties are committing crimes, then there is a serious question to be raised about the mental state of those being brought to the attention of the police and the court. Chapter 16 addresses the questions concerning insanity as a legal. What remains to be examined is whether those who are deemed to have committed crime due to their mental illness are treated accordingly in the criminal justice system, and throughout imprisonment. Those who have been convicted of a crime, or are deemed guilty but insane, or not guilty due to insanity may be incarcerated in a secure psychiatric hospital – one of the forms of mental health provision within the criminal justice system.

SECURE HOSPITALS

Individuals can be detained under mental health legislation such as the Mental Health Act 2007 in the UK. This means they can be committed to psychiatric hospital or forced to undergo treatment against their wishes, if it is deemed that doing so will protect either the individual or society. Someone detained in such a way and who has either been found guilty of serious crimes or declared unfit to plead for such crimes will be housed in a high security psychiatric hospital. Many of these units have been converted from institutions previously known as criminal lunatic asylums, but there has been a very clear change in attitude and terminology.

Within England and Wales, there are three high security psychiatric hospitals: Broadmoor, Rampton and Ashworth. Broadmoor now houses only male patients, although the first patients admitted to it were women (Stevens, 2011). The hospitals have high walls and very visible security features as well as siren systems at nearby schools and other facilities. It is therefore easy to think of them as prisons. However, the emphasis is very much on therapy and treatment rather than incarceration and punishment. Current practice places governance of secure hospitals within the remit of the National Health Service and the Department of Health. In addition to therapy, there is a set of research projects currently being performed within some of the institutions, such as new diagnostic and therapeutic practices for those patients who are the most dangerous in terms of risk to others.

In addition to the high security hospital units, there are also low to medium security hospitals, which house people on remand for, or convicted of, offences but who are also detained under mental health legislation but who represent a lower risk than those within high security units. For example, Pulsford et al. (2012) reported on a study about nurses' responses to aggressive behaviour in patients. They suggest that the attitudes of nurses and other care staff who may need to respond to violence will influence the management strategies used. They also investigated the attitudes of patients within the units, as agreement between the two sets of people involved is likely to lead to more acceptance of the strategies they adopt. Their findings reveal the ideas that people hold about the causes of aggression and the ways to control it, including medication, seclusion and restraint, and also suggests ways in which cooperation can be included in management strategies.

The problems of aggressive behaviour within secure hospitals are not the only issues to be researched. Within these units there is a very high proportion of people who have committed homicide, whether or not they have been charged with murder. By studying those who have committed homicide, it is possible that the reasons for lethal behaviour by the mentally ill can be determined and future risk averted. In addition, accepting responsibility for what they have done and its consequences is a vital part of both the patient's recovery and the intent of the Prison Service's aim of rehabilitation and justice. Attitudes towards this redemptive position provide knowledge about whether these processes are taking place.

Ferrito et al. (2012) attempted to address these issues by conducting in-depth interviews with seven men who had killed but who were serving their sentences within high security hospitals. The analysis revealed several themes of need within the group of patient participants which were indicative of the progress of recovery and therapy in people who have committed the most violent of crimes and the ways in which they move towards understanding their actions and the consequences of them. For example, the majority of men recalled instances of abuse in childhood that illustrated extremely difficult relationships with their abusive mothers. This led to difficulties with later relationships, whether implicitly or explicitly understood by the patient to have had that effect. Loss of control over emotions, possibly linked to early trauma of this nature, then led to loss of control over reality for several of the men, resulting in the devastating event(s) which led to lethal violence. In coming to terms with what they did, the progress of the therapy the men were undergoing can be evaluated. Ferrito et al. (2012) did not consider whether developing understanding of their actions would lead to further trauma for the men, something which may be a source of future research.

Many people in secure hospitals have been transferred there from prison or have been referred by the courts at some point during prosecution. They may also be sent to a secure hospital if it is decided they represent a high risk to either themselves or other people.

However they have reached this position, the needs of patients are diverse and complex. To work in such units requires a high level of commitment to treating people with several and complex mental health problems and to be comfortable within an environment of high security. Teams tend to be multidisciplinary, including nurses, medical doctors and psychiatrists, as well as psychologists.

SERIOUS MENTAL ILLNESS AND SERIOUS CRIME

Some people who have been convicted of a serious crime but who have not been assessed for psychological illnesses will find themselves in prison. Lurigio (2011) reported a 40-year observation that people with serious mental illnesses are becoming increasingly criminalised. In other words, they are being processed through criminal justice systems when it would be more appropriate to divert them to mental health professionals. According to Fazel & Seewald (2012), high proportions of prisoners worldwide have some form of mental illness, in comparison to national trends for non-imprisoned people. This means that people with such illnesses are over-represented in prison.

Lurigio points out that this is not necessarily a direct result of the closing of psychiatric hospitals, such as seen in the UK and the USA, as those with serious mental health issues were not always transferred from hospital to community care. However, removal from psychiatric hospital did sometimes mean that there was a lack of support, and many needed to commit crime in order to replace support that was not forthcoming in the community. The link between mental illness and crime is not straightforward, however, and the removal from hospital into prison is hardly a direct route, whether intended or not.

Whatever the reason, for people with mental illness committing crime and then ending up in prison, what is clear is that this is happening. According to a report written for the Sainsbury Centre for Mental Health (Khanom et al., 2009), there are 16 times as many people in prison with some form of psychosis than there are in the general population. In terms of depression and anxiety, the figures are no less problematic, with more than three times the population rate, and more than four times for drug or alcohol dependency. This is perceived as leading to a higher likelihood of various problems occurring, including suicide, attempted suicide or self-harm among prisoners, and violence against other prisoners or staff.

SUICIDE IN MENTALLY ILL PRISONERS

The suicide rate in prison is high in comparison with the general population. These figures are higher among female prisoners and for those with already identified mental health problems, although there is a downward trend of those with drug dependency problems in committing or attempting suicide (Humber et al., 2011). It is clear that one way of addressing such issues is to identify suicidal ideation at an early stage of imprisonment, if the individual has not been assessed before. One study (Godet-Mardirossian et al., 2011) demonstrated a close link between childhood adversity, personality characteristics and suicidal thoughts, assessed by both assessment inventories and clinical interviews. They stressed the importance of early screening too.

Self-harm, which can include attempted suicide that has been incorrectly classified, includes episodes of cutting, insertion of various types of object, swallowing non-food and non-medication items, and hanging. Appelbaum et al. (2011) carried out a study in 39 US prison systems examining the prevalence and extent of self-injurious behaviour among inmates. Although they report that such behaviour is carried out by less than 2% of the prison population, based on answers to a 30-item questionnaire, these incidents occur weekly or more frequently in a large number of facilities, so there appears to be something anomalous in these figures. Either a very small proportion of people are self-harming on a regular basis (although 2% of the US prison population is around 44,000 inmates, according to Walmsley [2010], which begs the question of why they are not being transferred to hospital, or there are more people self-harming than reported. This is an important question, as self-injurious behaviour is a risk factor for suicide (Hamza et al., 2012); it often precedes successful suicide attempts.

Theories of the links include the possibility of self-injurious behaviour acting as a gateway to suicidal behaviour: self-injury that does not, and could not, result in suicide is one end of the spectrum and successful suicide is on the other (Brausch & Gutierrez, 2010). As self-injury onset is usually seen in a younger population than the average age for suicide or attempted suicide, the gateway theory is a compelling explanation for the link between the two. However, this is limited by the ability to carry out clear longitudinal and causal research in a group of highly vulnerable, often young, people. Many also view self-injury as a form of practice behaviour, although Snow (2002) clearly distinguished two groups within those who self-injure in prison: those not expressing any suicidal ideation are more likely to have been precipitated into their behaviour by negative thoughts, and the suicidal group are motivated by concrete factors such as court appearances or drug withdrawal.

An alternative explanation is termed the 'third variable theory'. The suggestion that there is a causal or at least precipitative link between self-injury and suicide appears to be unclear, and some suggest that there is another explanation, or at least a mediating factor present in the pathway from injury to fatal harm. This third variable is the presence of diagnosable psychiatric disorders or psychological distress. Nock (2010) reported that similar rates of psychiatric disorder occur in those hospitalised for intentional self-injury and those committing suicide (approximately 85–90%). If this is the case, then the hypothesis that self-injury in prisoners, when linked to mental illness, will lead to suicide attempts bears examination.

Screening and identification of prisoners with mental health problems or the capacity for self-harm is therefore of paramount importance, given, as Epperson et al. (2011) pointed out, they are over-represented in the criminal justice system. However, another point to consider is how people are treated within prison, whether or not they have an identifiable mental illness. Metzner and Fellner (2010), in a study of US prisons, reported that difficult or dangerous prisoners are often managed by using solitary confinement. Many such inmates will have mental illness, and solitary confinement is seen to exacerbate the symptoms. This situation cannot be helpful for either the prison or the staff, and will place a load upon the prison system in general since the risk of re-offending in prisoners with mental illness is much higher than in those without (Baillargeon et al., 2010).

MANAGING MENTAL HEALTH IN PRISON

Managing mental health problems in prisons is, of course, challenging both for staff and inmates, but at least it does provide an opportunity for prisoners to engage with mental health services, perhaps for the first time. However, the challenges within prison also extend to issues after release. Ensuring continuity of care for released prisoners is difficult; according to Lennox et al. (2012), release from prison for the mentally ill prisoner presents a range of negative outcomes, including increased mortality and suicide.

In their longitudinal study of released prisoners in the South of England, Lennox et al. (2012) examined continuing contact with mental health services by those identified with a serious mental illness. They found that less than 10% of the sample prisoners assessed as having enduring and serious mental health issues were in contact with community mental health teams a year after release. This represents a worrying trend that suggests that it is difficult for inmates to sustain the good work being done in prisons once they are in a community setting, possibly because of all the other issues with which released prisoners need to contend. This may be even more evident in prisoners who are released after long terms in prison. The next chapter will consider this in prisoners who may or may not have mental illnesses, and also what effect never being released may have on those inside prisons. Not all prisoners have the skills or interests that facilitate coping with incarceration.

Richard Dadd spent many years in the Bethlem Hospital, first, and then, after 20 years, in Broadmoor. In addition to the imaginative paintings of fairies and landscapes, he also drew images depicting his inner turmoil. Each work of art was intricate and delicately drawn, even those depicting his personal demons. It is hard to reconcile such beautiful artistic creations with the reports of a man who was violent and often binged until he vomited. And yet, when left alone, he was tranquil, building excellent relationships with the medical doctors who were responsible for his care. Therapy in Victorian asylums did not extend much beyond exercise and fresh air. The doctors did not have the range of therapeutic tools available today. Dadd appears to have been content and wonderfully creative. It is difficult not to speculate what might have happened if drugs and psychotherapy had been available. He died in Broadmoor's medical wing in 1886, aged 68 (Stevens, 2011).

SUMMARY

Mental disorder is a risk factor for offending. Some individuals with serious mental illnesses, who also offend, will have access to screening and treatment at some point in their progress through the criminal justice system. People who commit crimes must be dealt with appropriately, nevertheless, those with mental health problems need to be dealt with in different ways from those without. If the latter adjust well to prison, then it is clear that the risk of developing illness is low for them, and it appears that recidivism is also prevented in some prisoners. However, there are those with serious problems who do not receive screening and diversion to hospital for some reason, and they invariably end up in prison. It is also clear that for some prisoners the development of serious mental health problems can be linked to their incarceration. Whatever point at which this is identified, access to mental health services is of paramount importance in the prison system in order to prevent self-harm, suicide, violent behaviour, drug dependency and potential recidivism.

Discussion point: Does prison cause mental illness or does mental illness cause people to be placed in prison?

This question is one of the most difficult to answer, as the correlational relationship between mental health and prison is highly complex. The statistical analysis of the numbers entering prison, and the proportion of those arriving with mental health problems, does not necessarily show that the psychiatric issue led to crime. Nor does it mean that prison will lead to higher levels of mental illness. But, of course, it does not prove the obverse either. Could research and analysis shed any light on these questions, and if it did, what policy decisions could be recommended?

Brandt, A. (2012) Treatment of persons with mental illness in the criminal justice system: a literature review. *Journal of Offender Rehabilitation*, **51**(8): 541–558.

Harner, H. M., & Riley, S. (2013). The impact of incarceration on women's mental health: responses from women in a maximum-security prison. *Qualitative Health Research*, **23**(1): 26–42.

Long-term and Life Imprisonment

20

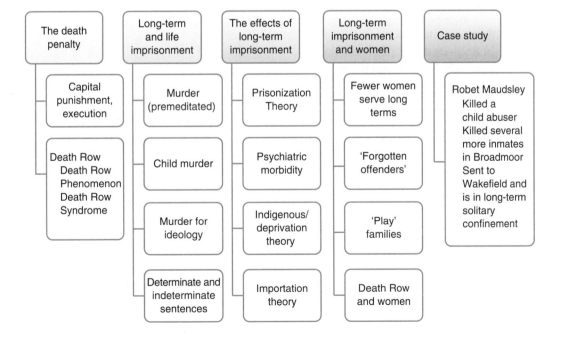

The death penalty	Long-term and life imprisonment	The effects of long-term imprisonment	Long-term imprisonment and women	Case study
Capital punishment, execution	Murder (premeditated)	Prisonization Theory	Fewer women serve long terms	Robet Maudsley Killed a child abuser Killed several more inmates in Broadmoor Sent to Wakefield and is in long-term solitary confinement
Death Row Death Row Phenomenon Death Row Syndrome	Child murder	Psychiatric morbidity	'Forgotten offenders'	
	Murder for ideology	Indigenous/ deprivation theory	'Play' families	
	Determinate and indeterminate sentences	Importation theory	Death Row and women	

Robert Maudsley has a genius-level IQ and enjoys classical music, poetry and art. He would like to study for a degree in music theory. People who know him describe him as gentle, kind and highly intelligent, good company with a great sense of humour. He is also officially classified as Britain's most dangerous prisoner, presenting such a high risk that he is in virtual isolation in Wakefield Prison. Maudsley lives in a cell with a perspex wall, which will be very familiar to anyone who has watched '*Silence of the Lambs*', but this was built years before the film aired. He will remain in his solitary cell, with no contact with other inmates, for the rest of his life. He is one of fewer than 100 people in the UK who are placed under a whole-life tariff, meaning he will never be released from prison.

KEY THEMES

- Life imprisonment/life sentence
- Whole-life tariff/ whole-life order
- Parole
- Minimum tariff
- Death sentence/Capital punishment
- Death Row
- Death Row Phenomenon
- Death Row Syndrome
- Prisonization theory
- Solitary confinement
- Indigenous model of imprisonment
- Imported model of imprisonment
- 'Play' families

The most serious of crimes are punished with the most severe of sentences. Historically, in many Western societies, and today across the world, some of these punishments can mean a death penalty, life imprisonment or an indeterminate sentence. The death penalty has a long, and some would say ignominious, past and remains the subject of much controversy.

THE DEATH PENALTY

Also called capital punishment, death sentence or execution, the death penalty has not been used in the UK since 1963 but is retained in several US states and some other places in the world (see Figure 20.1).

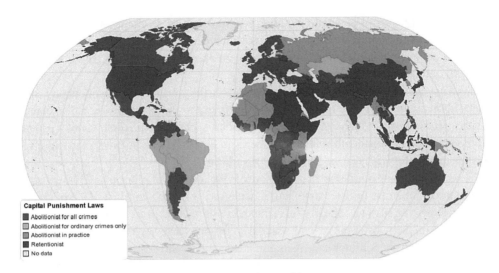

Figure 20.1   The use of the death penalty around the world

There are several different forms of execution used, including hanging, electrocution, firing squad, lethal injection, gas chamber and, less commonly, strangulation, decapitation (by axe, sword or guillotine), crushing, impalement, crucifixion, burning, boiling, disembowelment and stoning. Historically, even more bizarre methods have been employed, such as sawing, scaphism (eaten alive by insects) and, notably in seventeenth-century Prague, defenestration, or throwing a person from a high window (Howe, 1983).

In modern USA, a prisoner sentenced to death is often housed in what is referred to as 'Death Row', a part of the prison separate from other prisoners, or even a specific prison, and close to the place where the execution will take place. The prisoner may be kept in solitary confinement, with little or no contact with other prisoners or visitors except for legal team members. Capital prisoners can spend a long time on Death Row, as there are complex and time-consuming legal procedures after a death sentence is passed and before a prisoner is executed. US Department of Justice figures (Snell, 2011) indicate that the average time to wait is 15 years. This had led some opponents of capital punishment to suggest that the mental cruelty imposed by living under threat of death in this manner leads many inmates to become mentally ill and suicidal (Harrison & Tamony, 2010), an unintentional, if somewhat ironic, effect. The effect of this so-called 'Death Row Phenomenon' (being held in solitary confinement and/or waiting for a death sentence to be enacted) leads to what some call the Death Row Syndrome. Although not officially recognised in either the DSM or the ICD (Smith, 2008), this syndrome is defined as the psychological ill-effects of being held in Death Row. While many psychiatric and psychological experts in prison psychology accept that this is a real set of psychological harms, the denial of its status as a recognised illness means it is not a clinical or legal condition which can be treated or used as an extenuating circumstance for legal defence teams to base an appeal on, although some of the specific clinical outcomes can be (Yanofski, 2011).

As a psychological condition, and an unusual legal status, having prisoners on Death Row does allow an examination of the mental adjustment to the harshest form of incarceration. Although solitary confinement is used in some cases where the prisoner is not a capital case, this, in addition to the death sentence, appears to be the issue that causes the more specific, unique psychological issue of Death Row Syndrome.

Solitary confinement means that a prisoner is locked in a cell for up to 23 hours a day, and the period of exercise is also carried out in isolation. It is used within a range of disciplinary punishments, but also to control prisoners and to protect them from other inmates, or other inmates from them, as in the case of Maudsley. In some cases, whole prisons are built on the premise of solitary confinement of its inmates, such as the so-called Supermax prisons of the USA (Rhodes, 2004). It is well established that such isolation can cause many psychological issues, ranging from a catatonic state to high levels of violence, suicidal thoughts or even suicide attempts. Some effects are comparable with symptoms of psychoses, including paranoia, visual and auditory hallucinations, self-mutilation, suicidal thoughts, depression and loss of a sense of reality (Harrison & Tamony, 2010). Such effects are very damaging, and solitary confinement is, in some places, used as a heightened-level torture, commonly seen in survivors of brainwashing (Haney & Zimbardo, 2009).

A number of countries have prohibited the use of solitary confinement with mentally ill offenders. This is, of course, a circular position, as it may be the solitary confinement itself has led to the conditions in which the prisoner has become mentally ill (see Chapter 19). It is estimated that 45% of those living within high security units are mentally disordered, but that this rises to around 65% in Death Row units. Whether this is the result of being confined is not known, but the added anxieties of waiting to be executed, and the stress that rounds of appeals incurs, leads to the position in which Death Row Syndrome is recognised in many prisons, even if it is not officially recognised in the psychological community.

The time taken from sentence to execution does vary. In the USA, the only country with capital punishment that publishes statistics, the longest time between sentencing and execution was that of Michael Selsor, who was sentenced to death in Oklahoma in 1976 and executed in 2012 – some 36 years on Death Row (dailymailonline.com, 2012). Selsor had already had his death sentence commuted to life imprisonment when Oklahoma's mandatory death penalty statute was invalidated by the US Supreme Court. His lawyers then instigated an appeal against conviction, and he was granted a retrial, at which he was resentenced to death.

This lengthy period before execution is due to the full legal process of appeals that a capital sentence produces, sometimes against the wishes of the prisoner. In so-called 'death row volunteering', someone sentenced to death requests that appeals are abandoned and advocates for his or her own execution. According to Rountree (2012), 11% of such prisoners volunteer and, as Schildkraut (2012) notes, this does call into question their competency to decide their own fate. Opponents of the death sentence point out that this delay constitutes 'a cruel and unusual punishment', due to the lengthy periods of time, prolonging the sentence, and the psychological effects of waiting for execution, thereby enacting two punishments for one crime. Additionally, if it causes illness, particularly psychological issues linked to confinement and high levels of anxiety, then it can indeed be seen as a cruel and unusual punishment. As such, the Death Row Phenomenon and its syndrome do allow a comparison of the issue of a death sentence and long-term imprisonment. Solitary confinement and other ways of managing long-term imprisonment do seem, in themselves, to be problematic, and are exacerbated by a death sentence and anxiety about approaching execution, but they should also be addressed in terms of how long-term imprisonment is experienced.

LONG-TERM AND LIFE IMPRISONMENT

Life imprisonment is a sentence that can be given for crimes such as murder, severe child abuse, rape, high treason, severe or violent cases of drug dealing or human trafficking, or aggravated cases of burglary or robbery resulting in death or grievous bodily harm.

In the UK, life imprisonment is only applicable to those aged 21 or over. Young offenders (18–21 year olds) are sentenced to custody for life. Minors, aged under 18, are sentenced to detention during Her Majesty's pleasure for murder, or detention for life for other crimes where life imprisonment is the sentence for adults. However, people under age 21 may not be sentenced to a whole-life order, and so must become eligible for parole. There are two other kinds of life sentence in which the defendant may be imprisoned or detained for public protection, when the crimes committed would not attract a life sentence but that s/he is deemed to pose a danger to the public and will be incarcerated until it can be decided they no longer do so. The implication is that the convict will spend the rest of their natural life in prison, but in reality a large number of people will be eligible to request parole at some point in their sentences. There are fewer than 100 people in the UK who are subject to a whole-life order or tariff.

In UK law, a whole-life order or whole-life tariff can be applied to someone convicted of very serious offences. In 1983, the UK Home Secretary received the right to impose a whole-life order, meaning that the prisoner will remain in prison for the rest of his or her life. The power was removed from the Home Secretary in 2011, and there have been subsequent changes to the law that remove the right of politicians to set minimum sentences. Now judges are expected to recommend minimum sentences to be served before consideration for early release (or parole). To date, only two women, Myra Hindley and Rosemary West, have received such a tariff.

Crimes that could attract a whole-life tariff are:

a. Murder of two or more persons, where each murder involves:

    i. a substantial degree of premeditation or planning and/or
    ii. the abduction of the victim and/or
    iii. sexual or sadistic conduct.

b. Child murder involving the abduction of the child or sexual or sadistic motivation.
c. Murder for the purpose of advancing a political, religious or ideological cause.
d. Murder by an offender previously convicted of murder.

Other offences are if the court considers that the seriousness of the offence (or the combination of the offence and one or more offences associated with it) is exceptionally high.

Generally, offenders are sentenced to determinate sentences, which mean that the person must be released at the end of that term. The alternative to this is an indeterminate sentence. Prisoners given an indeterminate sentence – Imprisonment for Public Protection (IPP), as it is known in the UK – do not have the automatic right to be released, and they must serve a minimum period of imprisonment. This period is announced by the trial judge in open court and is known commonly as the 'tariff' period. It can be whole-life, as described above, or for any other specific number of years. Release on expiry of the tariff period is also not automatic, and will only occur if the Parole Board is satisfied that the risk of harm the prisoner poses to the public is acceptable.

In many jurisdictions, including in the UK, courts must impose a life sentence on any individual convicted of murder. In some states in the USA, there was, until recently, a mandatory death sentence for murder (see the case of Michael Selsor above), but this mandatory sentencing has been overturned by the US Supreme Court. Life imprisonment is the maximum, but not mandatory, sentence that can be imposed for a number of other types of offence, such as manslaughter and arson, particularly where there was endangerment to life. An offender who has committed murder and is aged between 10 and 18 at the time of the offence (see Chapter 5), is detained at Her Majesty's pleasure, and if s/he is between 18 and 21 at the time of the offence, then s/he will be placed in custody for life.

Discretionary life sentences, in cases where there is no case for a mandatory life sentence but the crime is severe, can be imprisonment for life, detention for life (for 10–18 year olds), and custody for life (for 18–21 year olds). An automatic life sentence was used before 2005, but has been replaced by the indeterminate sentence for IPP.

Release from life or indeterminate sentences can take place after the minimum tariff imposed by the court, but only if the Parole Board is satisfied that the prisoner is no longer a danger to the public, or the risk is acceptable. A prisoner will be released on licence and supervised by the Probation Service, officers of which will ensure that the parolee meets certain conditions specific to that individual. This licence remains in place for the rest of the person's natural life, and s/he can be recalled at any time if those conditions are not met.

Although a whole-life order applies only in mandatory lifer cases, it is open to a trial judge in non-murder cases to decline to set a minimum period of imprisonment, which has the same effect. In either case, the prisoner can appeal.

THE EFFECTS OF LONG-TERM IMPRISONMENT

Death Row and its attendant problems are a special case, as the majority of those convicted of murder and crimes of similar severity around the world are sentenced to long-term or life imprisonment. In 2009, those serving life sentences, as a proportion of all prisoners, was 9.5% in the USA and 19.3% in England and Wales (Griffin & O'Donnel, 2009). This represents a large number of people convicted of crimes who will be spending a significant portion of their lives inside prison. This raises two questions: What happens to those living a long time in prison? And how do people who have served long sentences adapt to life outside prison? A 'life sentence' does not always mean the prisoner will end his or her life inside. In the absence of whole-life orders, there is provision for the prisoner to request parole, at some point, and to spend the rest of his or her natural life outside prison. There are therefore several things to consider about long-term imprisonment: the reason why the sentence may be given, discussed above; the effect of being in prison with or without the possibility of release; and adapting to life outside prison after spending long periods incarcerated.

The potential for those convicted of serious crimes is to spend the rest of their lives in prison. The release or otherwise of a prisoner after long-term incarceration throws into relief the issue of long-term imprisonment and its effect on the individual.

Traditionally, studies of the effect of life or long-term imprisonment have concentrated on Prisonization Theory (Thomas & Petersen, 1977), which focuses on the negative effects of socialisation within prisons, and the process of acceptance of incarceration and the role of being a prisoner. This largely ignored the psychological effects, until studies in the 1990s started to consider longitudinal designs, covering behaviour and the cognitive and emotional experience associated with long-term confinement. These later studies addressed the issues of prisonization, the adoption of the prison culture by inmates, as being dependent on both prisoners' own personal traits and the prison environment, rather than simply on the latter. A large number of such studies note high rates of mental illness, in comparison to those outside prison and as an increasing phenomenon within prison. However, alongside this, some psychiatric studies, performed with the intent of examining mental disorder in long-term imprisonment, showed some contradictory findings. For example, Dettbarn (2012) showed, via an analysis of psychiatric reports before and after long-term sentences, that the rate of morbidity in psychological disorder had decreased, as had hostility, emotional instability and depression. This was a notable result, as only 42.5% of her sample had undergone any form of psychotherapy. However, these positive findings can be contrasted with the fact that the sample members were still demonstrating a higher number of mental disorders in comparison to the non-prison population, and this psychological improvement was not accompanied by any increasing physical health or changes in intelligence test performance. This contrasts with studies that relate higher levels of psychological disorders to longer periods spent in prison, such as Dudeck et al. (2011), who report that 14% of European inmates are experiencing such high levels of trauma in prison as to develop clear symptoms of PTSD as a result. Additionally, 50% of their sample were in need of psychological treatment because of their experience of prison, with one-third of all those examined having attempted suicide. Such contrasts depend on the perspective, it seems, as a focus on morbidity does suggest that the effect of prison is not only compounding already present psychological difficulties, but that the experience of prison can increase the risk of developing psychological and medical problems.

Research is clearly now turning from the prisonization focus to examining the behavioural, emotional and psychological reactions to imprisonment, and this is more readily achieved when examining long-term prisoners due to the potential for longitudinal studies and the likelihood of problems being more detectable. Behavioural components include the extent to which prisoners engage in activities and programmes (rehabilitative and educative), socialise and interact (whether they have visitors, etc.). Emotional components are accessed via direct questioning about their feelings and thoughts about imprisonment, and psychological components are accessed via assessment. In this way, research can therefore address the effects of factors inherent to the prison and its environment and influence, and those brought to the environment by the prisoners.

There are several theoretical models of long-term imprisonment. The indigenous approach, also termed the deprivation model, suggests that the conditions experienced by the individual in prison are the primary influences on responses to imprisonment. Once deprived of liberty, and access to family, friends and sexual partner, a prisoner experiences loss of control and deprivation of previously enjoyed goods and services. Zamble (1992), in his study of long-term inmates, found that the most keenly felt deprivations were more emotional than physical, except for missing sex. This study followed prisoners over seven years and was one of the first to attempt to address emotional states and cognitions over a period of time. Prisonization theory concentrates on the negative aspects of the socialisation to the prison environment, but general psychological functioning had not been considered in the detail that Zamble employed. This, together with some methodological flaws, such as biased samples suffering attrition, means that previous studies had not been sensitive to the prisoners' individual adaptation to prion life. Zamble's study was among the first to include a wide range of measures over an extended period of time, and concluded that there is no generalised pattern of emotional damage that prisonization theory would suggest. The sample here had increased levels of work activity over the period of the study and, although the amount of socialisation had declined, the number of friends had not. The qualitative responses to interview questions about this suggested that the decreased time spent in socialising was more to do with conflict avoidance than lack of opportunity for positive social contact.

In addition to factual reporting of behaviours, this research also explored needs, concluding that support, emotional connection, safety, freedom and privacy were the most missed. Hence it is the very things that prison deprives the imprisoned of that are major explanatory factors in adaptation to imprisonment. This supports the indigenous model in that it is the prison environment that affects the prisoner's adaptation, and this can be tested via examination of the behavioural and emotional adjustments prisoners make in terms of the type of prison and length of sentence. The type and strength of behavioural adaptations change in relation to length of time in prison; shorter sentences equate to limited adaptational behaviour, but longer term prisoners engage more with the activities of the prison. The latter also maintain contact with family and friends, and appear to experience a reduction in feelings of hopelessness. Misbehaviour is also reduced.

An alternative approach to viewing the inherent or indigenous properties of imprisonment as an explanation for adaptation to imprisonment is to regard it as reflecting the inherent properties of the prisoner and his or her previous lifestyle. These properties are therefore imported, and this theoretical position is termed the importation model. If this model correctly represents the effect of prison, it would mean that there is an association between how the prisoner adapts to prison life and their personal characteristics. Wright (1991) found that there was a significant effect regarding level of education on adaptation, with lower educational attainment linked to fewer physical problems and more rule violations. On the other hand, previous unemployment status was linked to higher levels of physical problems and distress, and risk of violent episodes, than those who had been employed. Finn (1995) found clear relationships between prior economic deprivation and disruptive behaviour in prison. The effects of all of these variables were independent of race, age or prior imprisonment. As Zamble (1992) points out, these factors may work in combination, and most studies have examined each in isolation.

It is also likely that the two models are not mutually exclusive, but it is difficult to examine them in combination. Dhami et al. (2007) attempted to examine the ways in which long-term prisoners in the USA adapted to life inside, and whether this was due to indigenous or imported factors. They studied 712 federal prisoners whose sentences ranged from two years to more than five. Prisoners completed a survey, answering questions on life in the prison (taking part in regime activities, prison treatment programmes, contact with others inside and outside the prison, thoughts of missing things such as friends and sex, emotions, and misconduct), their offence and sentence, and time served, and life outside prison. They found that, taking into account length of sentences and the type of prison they were examining, there were direct effects of length of time spent in prison on participation in activities, prisoner thoughts and emotions, and misbehaviour. There was also a direct effect of their quality of life before prison on participation, misconduct and emotions, although this did not directly affect thoughts. There were interactions with quality of previous life and time in prison on contact with the outside world through visitors, etc. Dhami et al. (2007) made some complex statistical analyses of their findings to draw out this information, exposing positive effects of prison life that had not been observed, dependent on the quality of life prisoners had before entering prison and the more time they spent inside. Those prisoners whose life before prison was of low quality participated more in prison activities, which, as the researchers point out, may mean they have higher motivation to attain skills in order to improve themselves, or that they were alleviating boredom. They also distinguished between prisoners who use time and those who fill time, and their findings here were consistent with their conclusion about motivations. However, these positive findings are tempered with the negative effects that prison life exposed, including the higher likelihood of disciplinary actions against prisoners whose life before prison was of poor quality, and more feelings of hopelessness with longer time spent, and to be spent, in prison.

None of these alone is surprising, but it makes it clear that there is no simple model to be constructed about life in prison. The effects of being in prison are complex and far-reaching, but may not be the whole story. An alternative approach to examining adjustment, which looks simply at the assessable aspects of a prisoner's behaviour, coupled with some emotional and cognitive issues, is to use a more direct approach to access a prisoner's coping strategies. The adaptation approach examines observable facts of prison life and the prisoner's situation, and a coping strategy approach examines the prisoner's own adjustment and well-being while in prison. In a wide-ranging review, Picken (2012) examined research attempting to approach prison life in this way. This contrasts with earlier research that suggests that prison, particularly long-term imprisonment, always has a negative impact on psychological and physical well-being, with later studies suggesting that this is not the whole picture. The research that Picken noted reflects a mixed set of findings regarding the adjustment and well-being of inmates. Here, it is suggested, it is the coping styles of the prisoner and the level of therapeutic community within the specific prison that determine the ability of prisoners to cope with life inside, and that this is reflected in their adjustment and behaviour. Therefore, the indigenous aspects of the prison environment interact with the assorted imported issues that the prisoner brings with him or her. The review concludes that a therapeutic environment is much more conducive to allowing prisoners to cope with their imprisonment and to reduce infractions and aggressive behaviour that appear to be endemic to life inside.

One aspect that is noted in the research quite clearly is that the majority of studies on prison life have concentrated on male offenders. There is little research on female prisoners and, indeed, research that considers whether the findings are even applicable to female prisoners.

LONG-TERM IMPRISONMENT AND WOMEN

Studies of the effects of long-term imprisonment have centred squarely upon male prisoners. There are fewer women in prison in general, and the percentage of long-term prisoners who are female is very small. For example, according to the UK Ministry of Justice (2012), women represent less than 5% of the overall prison population, 59% of whom serve sentences less than six months. In addition, in figures provided by the Ministry of Justice (2010), women are subject to more punishments than are male prisoners, and are more likely to commits acts of self-harm, but are less likely to commit suicide. They are also serving shorter sentences on average, but this appears to reflect differences in the types of crime for which women are convicted. Men are more likely to be perpetrators of violent crimes such as assault, sexual assault and murder, all of which attract longer custodial sentences than non-violent crimes. However, although crime rates appear to be falling in relative terms, one crime that is on the increase is violent crime perpetrated by women and girls. Whether or not this is an artefact of changes in reporting and arresting behaviour, and consequent changes in the way the criminal justice system perceives and deals with women, as Schwartz et al. (2009) suggest, this does mean that the proportion of the women sentenced to custody is rising, due to the rising number convicted of violent crime. The number of those who are sentenced to long-term imprisonment is growing. According to the UK Ministry of Justice statistics, the number of women being sentenced to prison grew by 27% between 2000 and 2010 (Ministry of Justice, 2010). As with men, the women with longer-term sentences tend to have been convicted of more violent crimes. In 2008–09 the proportion of women arrested for violent crimes was 33%; for men in the same year it was 30%. So although there are much smaller numbers of women arrested and convicted overall, the distribution of crime type is comparable. This does not mean of course that their experience is comparable.

Mackenzie et al. (1989) carried out one of the first examinations of women serving long-term prison sentences. In their study, they called women inmates in general 'forgotten offenders', and suggested that this is a very appropriate term for the long-term female incarcerated. They pointed out that simply allowing the smaller number of female inmates to be regarded as the same as men was doing them a disservice, as the problems they face are often completely different. For example, female prisoners often have children, and the emotion a mother feels when separated from her children may be unlike that of fathers. We just do not know. The problems experienced by the children of incarcerated parents, whether mother or father, are well documented. For example, Arditti (2012) examined in detail the effect that maternal and paternal incarceration has on the family, but even here Arditti does not separate out the issue that the incarcerated parent might experience into respective parental gender. Very little research accesses the effect on the incarcerated parent of separation from children. Some, such as Secret (2012), examined the parenting capacity of imprisoned fathers and how they valued and perceived their fatherhood, concluding that, with non-violent offenders, the amount of contact was an important determining factor in their willingness and ability to engage and re-engage with the fathering role. Going broader, Dyer et al. (2012) reviewed the research that examines fathers and the theoretical positions that attempt to explain how men manage their family relationship when in prison and on release. However, there are no such studies on mothers. Any issues are likely to be comparable to those for men, but not necessarily similar, because, as Collica (2010) notes, women are perceived to experience the separation from families more harshly than men.

Imprisoned women in general also exhibit differences in adjustment the longer they have been in prison and the longer they will be in prison. Newly entered inmates, irrespective of length of sentence to be served, have not yet developed the coping strategies of women spending longer periods inside, as would be expected. This finding was partially supported by Thompson and Loper (2005), but they found that long-term female inmates exhibited higher levels of conflict and institutional misconduct, rather than changes in emotional adjustment, but that this differed significantly from the pattern in long-term male inmates.

Mackenzie et al. (1989) noted that a major difference in male and female prisoners was their participation in what is termed 'play' families, a social grouping which may or may not involve sexual relationships. These families can be a supportive social network that ameliorates the pains of imprisonment, such as separation from family, and engenders prosocial behaviour (Collica, 2010). However, Mackenzie et al. (1989) noted that long-term prisoners tend not to engage with these, or have left the engagement behind in an earlier phase of their sentence. They concluded that these social groupings are a social support strategy that women inside for longer terms no longer need after an initial period of adjustment. They also found that women serving longer sentences were more likely to experience environmental strain linked to being away from families, etc. (Mackenzie et al., 1989). However, anxiety and ability to cope with the situation did not seem different for long-term prisoners. Later studies support this finding. Thompson and Loper (2005) found that the longer the term women served, the higher the likelihood of reporting higher feelings of conflict and committing institutional offences. However, there was no relationship between length of sentence and emotional adjustment, but they conclude that there are still identifiable needs for different interventions in long- and short-term female prisoners.

A criticism of studies such as these is that often there is only one aspect considered, with other contributing factors being ignored, which may explain why there are contradictory findings – it is an artefact of focusing on only one factor without considering the interaction with others. Van Tongeren and Klebe (2009) attempted to take a multidimensional approach to studying women in prison, particularly in terms of adjustment over time. Their findings indicate that it was women whose adjustment was to the prison culture rather than institutional structure that were in fact the more likely to exhibit persistence in criminal thinking and an inability to obtain psychological and physical support systems and engage in rehabilitative processes. They suggested that an enhancement of prisonization theory is a suitable framework in which to view the adjustment of long-term female prisoners, in that it is those inmates who exhibited higher levels of the factors described there, such as acceptance of prison culture and rejection of institutional services, who adjust badly.

An examination of women in prison long term would not be complete without looking at those who are destined to end their lives there. Some women sentenced to life, or even medium terms, will die in prison, but there are some who face a death sentence. In the USA in 2010, there were 3,158 inmates on Death Row, 58 of whom were women (Snell, 2011). In 2011, 43 US prisoners were executed, none of them women. The last woman to be executed in the USA was Teresa Lewis in September 2010. She was the only female inmate of Virginia's Death Row at that time, and there was a great deal of controversy about her sentence and execution. She was convicted of using sex and money to arrange the death of her husband and stepson in order to benefit from an insurance policy. The two men who carried out the murders were given life sentences. Lewis was also of very low IQ (72) and her case bears obvious and ironic comparison to that of Daryl Atkins (see Chapter 16).

In 2010, fewer than 2% of the prisoners waiting for execution were women (Schmall, 2012). It would be easy to overlook such a small number, but the cases of these women do attract attention, usually in highlighted comparison to male capital offenders, such as the contrast between Lewis and Atkins. Even though a much smaller number of women are given capital offences, there are still female inmates on Death Row awaiting execution, and who have been there for some years (in the same way as male inmates are). However, we know nothing about their propensity for Death Row Syndrome, as there has been no such research involving these women. In fact, there is little research on any aspect of women on Death Row beyond a quantitative examination of the factors that put them there and a delineation on demographics, such as that compiled by Streib (2010). The psychology of women under sentence of death is unknown. Perhaps they are the epitome of the 'forgotten offenders' that Mackenzie et al. (1989) described.

SUMMARY

Capital sentences are still used around the world, although many are then commuted to life imprisonment. The pains of being sentenced to death are often exacerbated by the stress due to the length of time between sentence and execution, such that many claim there is a Death Row Phenomenon, leading to a set of psychological issues terms the Death Row Syndrome.

Long-term imprisonment is used as a viable alternative to the death sentence in many parts of the world, and is therefore handed down to those who have committed the most violent and serious of crimes, including murder. Initial research showed that, despite the belief that imprisonment means deterioration in physical and mental health, and that long-term imprisonment should be related to higher levels of difficulties, in fact it does not, and prisoners adjust to long-term imprisonment quite well. This may not be the case for those prisoners who are sentenced to long terms, including life, who enter prison with the most serious problems, but even the seriousness of those issues cannot be mitigation for crimes.

Robert Maudsley claims to have experienced physical and sexual abuse in his childhood, the major problems starting when he was taken from foster care and returned to his parents at 9 years old. It was an impoverished and violent family in which there were eventually 12 children. He claims the abuse he received there resulted in him running away and developing a serious drug addiction in his teens, which he supported by life as a rent boy. In 1974, one of his clients boasted about abusing young children, so Maudsley garrotted him. He was sentenced to life imprisonment and sent to Broadmoor Hospital for the criminally insane. While there, in 1977, Maudsley and another inmate tortured a convicted child sex offender to death. The dead man was found with a spoon in his open skull, with part of his brain missing, assumed eaten. Maudsley was then sent to Wakefield Prison for the manslaughter of this prisoner. In 1978 Maudsley killed a further two inmates on one day. He killed convicted sex offender Stanley Darwood in his cell, hiding the body under the bed, and then hunted down Bill Roberts. He hacked at his head, before smashing it into a wall. Maudsley is deemed too dangerous to be housed with the rest of the prison inmates and has been in solitary confinement since 1983, where he will stay for the rest of his life, despite the progress psychiatrists report at Broadmoor and other prisons in which he has been housed. He regularly makes the 'most depraved' or 'most disturbing' lists on the internet. His is one of the saddest cases of life behind bars, if you are inclined to feel sympathy for someone who has killed several people. He does, however, demonstrate some of the things this book has discussed. A poor start to life and other exceptional circumstances can lead to explosions of murderous rage. Maudsley shows us that the psychology of crime is as fascinating as it has ever been, and that we should not stop trying to discover what goes on in the minds of criminals.

Discussion point: Is life imprisonment simply a death sentence by another name?

High numbers of prison inmates die in jail, while prisoners sentenced to death often spend many years waiting for their execution. Some calling for prison reform suggest that a long prison sentence is simply a different way of ensuring, albeit unintentionally, those offenders die in prison. However, due to the issue known as Death Row Phenomenon, and its pathological companion, Death Row Syndrome, there may be measurable differences in capital and long-term prisoners that justify the distinction. How might this issue be investigated?

Harrison, K. & Tamony, A. (2010) Death Row Phenomenon, Death Row Syndrome and their effect on capital cases in the US. *Internet Journal of Criminology*: 1–16

Ross, J. (2012) Why a jail or prison sentence is increasingly like a death sentence. *Contemporary Justice Review: Issues in Criminal, Social, and Restorative Justice*, **15**(3): 309–321.

Schlosser, J. (2008) Issues in interviewing inmates: navigating the methodological landmines of prison research. *Qualitative Inquiry*, **14**(December): 1500–1525.

Glossary

These terms are defined in respect of their relation to forensic psychology, and may have other meanings in other settings.

Acquisitive crime: Theft and robbery; crimes in which items or goods are stolen from another person or an organisation.

Actus reus: The committing of an act that has guilt attached to it. *See also Mens rea*

Adversarial courts/systems: Courts in which two advocates represent two parties' position (such as defendant and prosecutor) before an impartial judge or jury. *See also* Inquisitorial system

Affiliative questions: Questions probing the identification with particular social issues. In jury selection, they may be used to determine if a potential juror is likely to be sympathetic to a defendant or not.

Age of criminal responsibility: The age at which a child is deemed to understand the difference between right and wrong, and is therefore old enough to take responsibility for the crime s/he has committed.

Antisocial personality disorder: A mental health condition in which a person has a long-term pattern of manipulating, exploiting, or violating the rights of others.

Arson: The act of illegally setting a fire.

Assessment of suspects: The determination of whether someone is fit to be interviewed.

Attachment failure: The lack of close emotional relationships, particularly in childhood, leading to emotional difficulties.

Attitudinal questions: Questions probing consciously held and expressed attitudes. In jury selection, they may be used to determine a potential juror's attitudes to issues to be discussed in a case.

Biological differences: The theoretical position that any observed difference between genders, races, ages, etc., are the result of biological factors such as genetics, body chemistry, etc.

Biosocial theories of crime: A theoretical position that stresses the interdependence of genetic and environmental factors and which can be applied to the study of crime and anti-social behaviour.

Bribery/corrupting public officials: Giving money, gifts or favours that alter the behaviour of the recipient, particularly to influence the actions of public officials.

Burglary: Illegal entry to a property in order to steal items inside.

Capital punishment: *See* Death sentence

Child sex abuse/molestation: The use of a child, by an adult or older child, for sexual stimulation.

Cognitive interview: A method of questioning victims or witnesses of a crime about what they remember, using cognitive retrieval strategies in order to minimise misinterpretation, faulty recall and confabulation.

Collection and interpretation of physical evidence: The gathering of material left at a crime scene, its analysis, and understanding its relation to the crime.

Comorbidity: The presence of one or more disorders in addition to the primary disorder and/or the effect of their existence alongside each other.

Confabulation : Memory disturbance or faulty memory characterised by the person recalling believing that the memory is accurate.

Corporate psychopath: Someone exhibiting the traits identified in psychopathy but who has used those traits to engender success in business.

Criminal profiling: Also called offender profiling or forensic profiling, a behavioural and investigative technique whereby the characteristics of an offender are determined in order to aid the process of investigation of crime.

Cross-examination: The interrogation of someone giving testimony in court by an opposing legal team. *See also* Direct examination

CSI effect: The suggested effect on the perceptions and attitudes of people, more specifically jurors, of watching TV programmes or films in which the collection, analysis and presentation of evidence from crime scenes is portrayed as part of the drama. This is as yet established, but it is thought to be negative in that the absence of such evidence is likely to lead jurors to discount the importance of other evidence.

Death Row: A reference to the prison or area in a prison where those who are sentenced to death are accommodated.

Death Row Phenomenon: The emotional stress felt due to waiting for a death sentence to be carried out.

Death Row Syndrome: The collection of psychological symptoms that sometimes develop in those waiting to be executed, particularly over long periods of time.

Death sentence/Capital punishment: The legal process of putting to death a person who has been convicted of a crime. The carrying out of the sentence is termed execution.

Defendant's mental state: The psychological status of a person who is suspected of a crime. *See also Mens rea*

Delinquency prevention: An intervention designed to prevent or avert antisocial behaviour in juveniles.

Direct examination/examination-in-chief: Questioning of a witness by the party who called him or her in a trial.

DNA: Deoxyribonucleic acid – an informational molecule encoding the genetic instructions used in the development and functioning of all known living organisms. The assumption that this encoding is unique to each individual is the basis for suspect identification in crimes where bodily fluid has been collected at the scene.

DNA database (CODIS): Storage of DNA material or profiles that can be used in the analysis of genetic diseases, genetic fingerprinting or genetic genealogy.

Doli incapax: The capacity for understanding the difference between right and wrong and hence that one has done something wrong. *See also Mens rea*

Earwitness: A witness whose testimony concerns something they have heard. *See also* Eyewitness

Embezzlement: A form of financial fraud in which assets are dishonestly withheld or diverted by someone to whom they have been entrusted.

Enhanced cognitive interview: The enhanced form of the cognitive interview. The enhancements include better social aspects.

Episodic memory: Memory for events (times, places, associated emotions and other contextual knowledge) that have been directly experienced and that can be explicitly stated.

Evolutionary models of crime: A theoretical position that suggests behaviour is a result of adaptations that are then passed to the next generation. In the study of crime, it has been applied to explanations of violent and/or sexual crimes.

Expert witness: Someone who, by virtue of education, training, skill or experience, is deemed to have expertise and specialised knowledge in a particular subject beyond that of the average person, sufficient that their testimony about evidence or fact in that area can be legally relied on.

Eyewitness: A witness whose testimony concerns something that has been seen.

Eyewitness memory: The memory of a witness for the events seen (or heard). Also the subject of study which has determined that this memory may be faulty.

False confession/false memory: An admission of guilt in which the confessor is not responsible for the crime. This can be induced through coercion or by the mental disorder or incompetency of the accused, and often involves a false memory, in which the memory of the confessor is affected such that s/he believes they committed the crime.

Fantasy proneness/fantasy prone personality: The tendency for some individuals to fantasise a large part of the time and to report that they fully experience what they fantasise.

FBI method of profiling: A profiling process that includes refining the types of crime or offender into an organised–disorganised continuum and using other classification schemes developed on the premise that behaviour reflects personality.

Feminist models of crime: A perspective in which crime is considered from a female point of view, with particular reference to patriarchy, female oppression and the physical, political and economic dominance of men.

Field experiment (juries): A study in which real-life juries are studied without interference with their duties.

Fit to be interviewed: The determination of whether someone in police custody is in a fit state to be questioned. This is a particular issue when the person is likely to be a vulnerable witness.

Fit to plead: The capacity of a defendant in criminal proceedings to comprehend the course of those proceedings and assist with his or her own defence. In the USA this may be termed 'competence to stand'.

Fraud: Intentional deception for personal gain or to damage another individual.

Fraud Diamond: A model of the constituent psychological and physical components of fraudulent behaviour based on the fraud triangle, but adding capability/skills.

Fraud Triangle: A conceptual model of the components of fraudulent behaviour containing the relationship between pressure/incentive, opportunity and rationalisation.

Functional analytical model: A model of firesetting that takes into account the variables which allow the maintenance and reinforcement of the behaviour.

Genocide: The deliberate targeting of an ethnic, religious or racial group with the intent of eradication.

Grand jury: A group of people convened in order to determine if a case has sufficient evidence or cause to be presented to a trial by jury. Most used in the USA, where a grand jury can be 15 people compared to the more usual 12 in a trial.

Groupthink: A phenomenon in which the decision of a group is seen not to depend on individuals' prior beliefs and attitudes.

Hung jury: A position in which a jury cannot return a verdict as there is no overall consensus.

Identity parade/line-up; simultaneous/sequential presentation: The presentation to a witness/victim of a series of people looking similar in appearance, which may or may not include a suspect. There are several ways of presenting the line-up, either as a simultaneous group or singly one after the other.

Imported model of imprisonment: A view of imprisonment in which the characteristics that the prisoner brings (imports) with him or her are what determines the effect of imprisonment.

Imprisonment/incarceration: The act of locking up someone convicted of a crime away from the rest of society.

Impulse control disorder: A class of psychiatric disorders characterised by a failure to resist a temptation, urge or impulse that may harm oneself or others.

Inadmissible evidence: Evidence that cannot be used in court because it falls into a category deemed 'unreliable'. Thus a court should not consider it as part of a deciding a case, e.g. testimony based on hearsay.

Indigenous model of imprisonment: A view of imprisonment in which the inherent properties of prison are what determines the effect of imprisonment.

Inquisitorial courts/systems: A legal system in which the officers of the court are actively involved in the investigation of the facts of the case, rather than being an impartial decider of fact.

Insanity/insanity defence: The legal status of being unable to take responsibility for one's (criminal) actions due to mental disturbance. As a defence, the application of the M'Naghten rules applies.

Insider trading: The trading in a company's stock or assets and having non-public information about that company.

Intellectual capacity: The capacity to understand that one's actions are wrong and/or criminal. *See also Doli incapax*

Interrogative suggestibility: The susceptibility to persuasion during interviews or interrogation.

Interrogative techniques: The process of questioning suspects in order to gain a confession or more information about the crime, and the procedures followed during questioning. *See also* Investigative interview

Investigative interview: The questioning of suspects, victims or witnesses during the process of investigating a crime, and the procedures and training followed in order to both ascertain as much information as possible and protect the rights and needs of those being questioned.

Juror: A person sitting in a jury.

Jury: A sworn body of people convened to consider the facts of a case and to deliver an impartial verdict or finding of fact.

Jury instructions: The set of legal rules that jurors should followed when considering a case. These determine how they should decide the guilt or otherwise of the defendant(s).

Jury nullification: The situation where a jury acquits a defendant even though the evidence shows they are guilty, especially in cases where the jury decides the person does not merit punishment for what they have done.

Jurythink: A position similar to groupthink in which the apparent consensus of a verdict does not reflect the individual positions of each juror.

Juvenile delinquency: The participation of young people, usually minors, in illegal and/or antisocial behaviour. A juvenile delinquent is such a young person.

Juvenile detention: The incarceration of young people who have been convicted of crimes but are deemed too young to be held in adult prisons. A juvenile detention center [*sic*] is a secure residential facility for young people in the USA; in the UK, these are known as young offender institutions.

Kleptomania: The inability to refrain from taking things which do not belong. It is classified as an impulse control disorder.

Libor scandal: Fraudulent actions involving the London Interbank Offered Rate (Libor) and the investigation of this. Banks had been falsely inflating and deflating their rates in order to profit from the trade and/or to appear more creditworthy than they were.

Lie detection: The questioning techniques used by police officers and others to determine whether someone is lying. This may involve intelligent questions or the technology developed to assist. *See also* Lie detector

Lie detector: Another name for a polygraph machine which measures various psychophysiological reactions to questions posed by the operator.

Life imprisonment/life sentence: A sentence of imprisonment for a serious crime which compels the incarceration of the convicted person for the rest of his or her life, or until given parole.

M'Naghten rules: Rules by which a person's insanity can be tested when it is offered as a defence. A person is insane if, at the time of the criminal act, s/he was labouring under such a defect of reason, arising from a disease of the mind, that s/he did not know the nature and quality of the act that s/he was committing or, if s/he did know it, s/he did not know that what s/he was doing was wrong.

Madoff scandal: A Ponzi scheme perpetrated by Bernard Madoff in which billions of dollars had been fraudulently taken from investors.

Manslaughter: Killing without intent to kill.

Mass murder: The killing of several victims in one place at one time by the same person.

Medical autopsy: The post-mortem examination of a corpse or part of a corpse.

Mens rea: The state of having a guilty mind, the intent to commit a crime. *See also Doli incapax*

Mental disorder: A psychological sickness that may or may not lead someone to be more likely to commit crime.

Minimum tariff: The minimum number of years attached to a long-term sentence.

Mock jury: A form of research protocol in which participants are asked to behave as if they were on a jury, allowing studies on jury behaviour without interfering with a real jury's actions.

Money laundering: The process of concealing the source of money obtained by illicit means.

Murder: Illegal killing.

Paedophilia: The sexual attraction to children under the legal age of consent. It is often used to refer to attraction to all children, but attraction to babies/infants is more properly referred to as infantophilia, and to adolescents as hebephilia/ephebephilia. It is often confused with child sexual abuse, but the two are not necessarily synonymous.

Parole: Early release from a prison sentence.

PEACE model: A model of training police officers in investigative interviewing that minimises false confessions. It comprises stages termed Preparation and Planning; Engage and Explain; Account; Clarify and Challenge, Closure; Evaluation.

'Play' families: Social groupings in prison, especially female prison, which may or may not involve sexual relationships.

Ponzi scheme: A fraudulent investment operation that pays returns to its investors from their own money or the money paid by subsequent investors, rather than as the result of legitimate investment.

Pre-trial publicity: The media interest in a case before any trial takes place, which may or may not have adverse effects on the impartiality of jurors.

Prisonization theory: The process of being socialised into the culture and social life of the prison community to the extent that adjusting to the outside society becomes difficult.

Psychodynamic theories of crime: Freudian theory was never directly applied to crime, but later theorists did so, emphasising the importance of childhood experiences and parent–child relationships as an influence on offending.

Psychological autopsy: The examination of the mental state of a deceased person to aid in the determination of manner of death.

Psychometrics: The field of study concerned with the theory and technique of psychological measurement. Alternatively, it may refer to the tests used in psychological measurement themselves.

Psychopathology and crime: *See* Mental disorder

Psychopathy: A personality disorder or type characterised by shallow affect, cold-heartedness, egocentricity, superficial charm, manipulativeness, irresponsibility, impulsivity, criminality, antisocial behaviour, a lack of remorse, and a parasitic lifestyle, but which may or may not be linked to crime. Closely associated with antisocial personality disorder, but not necessarily synonymous with it. Alternative words may include *sociopathy*, but this is thought to be more environmentally influenced.

Punishment: The authoritative imposition of something negative or unpleasant in response to behaviour deemed unacceptable.

Rape: Sexual assault involving sexual intercourse/penile penetration, which is initiated by one or more persons against another without that person's consent.

Recidivism: The act of repeating undesirable behaviour after experiencing negative consequences. Also used to refer to the percentage of former prisoners who are rearrested.

Rehabilitation: Training and/or treatment intended to prevent further offending in individuals undertaking the course.

Reid techniques: A method of questioning suspects and assessing their credibility.

Reoffending: Committing further criminal acts after original convictions.

Risk factors: The likelihood of committing crime or factors that predict crime.

Robbery/armed robbery: Taking or attempting to take something of value by force or threat of force or by putting the victim in fear. This may involve the use of weapons, in which case it is referred to as armed robbery.

Secure hospitals: Hospitals housing those who have committed criminal acts but are deemed to be not responsible by reason of insanity.

Self-harm: The tendency or act of harming oneself.

Serial murder: Murders of several victims (usually three or more) by the same person but separated in time.

Sex offender: A person who has committed an act of sexual assault, sexual abuse, incest, rape, etc.

Sexual legislation: Legislation designed to ensure equality between the sexes in terms of employment, healthcare, education, etc.

Sexual(ised) violence: Violence using sex as a weapon or linked to sexual behaviour.

Shoplifting: The theft of goods from a retail outlet while it is open for business.

Single murder: Murder of only one victim.

Social exclusion in prisoners: The potential for prisoners to be excluded from the benefits of social interaction, such as education, healthcare, employment prospects, etc.

Social learning theory and crime: A theoretical position that suggests that people engage in crime due to an association with others who commit crime, whom they imitate, and this behaviour is reinforced.

Sociopathy: See Psychopathy

Solitary confinement: A special form of imprisonment where the prisoner is excluded from human social contact, with the exception of prison officers. It may be a form of punishment, coercion or protection.

Spree murder: The killing of several victims within one period of time, but at different locations, by the same person(s).

Stealing: The taking of items/money that do(es) not belong to the person taking them/it.

Suicide: The intentional taking of one's own life.

Suicidal ideation: The medical term for thoughts about or an unusual preoccupation with suicide.

Suicide by terrorism: The death of a terrorist while committing a terrorist act. Also known as suicide bombing.

Theft: The taking of items/money that do(es) not belong to the person taking them/it.

Trial by jury: A legal proceeding in which a jury either makes a decision or makes findings of fact which are then applied by a judge.

Typology: The classification of crimes or criminals from investigative and legal perspectives, e.g. the typology of rapes or rapists.

UK Profiling: The Statistical Approach: An approach to criminal profiling in which the classification of crime scenes is empirically based, using statistical procedures to identify how likely features of crime scenes are to exist and coexist with another feature.

Verdicts: The formal finding of fact by a jury. This can be 'guilty', 'not guilty' or 'not proven' (Scotland).

Voir dire: Refers to a variety of procedures connected with jury trials, including the oath taken to tell the truth, the examination of the admissibility of evidence (UK) or the examination of potential jurors before selection (USA).

Vulnerable witness: A witness for whom giving evidence, or being questioned by the police, is particularly difficult. Such people may include children, victims of sexual offences and those with communication or learning difficulties. Special measures may be used to facilitate them in giving evidence, such as by video link, or with an appropriate adult accompanying them.

Whole-life tariff/whole-life order: A mechanism in which the early release of a prisoner cannot apply and no minimum tariff is set.

References

Aamodt, M. (2008) Reducing misconceptions and false beliefs in police and criminal psychology. *Criminal Justice and Behavior*, **35**, 10 October: 1231–1240.

Abel, M.H. & Watters, H. (2005) Attributions of guilt and punishment as functions of physical attractiveness and smiling. *Journal of Social Psychology*, **145**(6): 687–702.

ABFP (American Board of Forensic Psychology) (2010) http://www.abfp.com/brochure.asp

Abrahamsen, D. (1985) *Confessions of Son of Sam*. New York: Columbia University Press.

Abrahamson, D. (1960) *The Psychology of Crime*. New York: John Wiley.

Absher, J.R., Vogt, B.A., Clark, D.G., Flowers, D.L., Gorman, D.G., Keyes, J.W. et al. (2000) Hypersexuality and hemiballism due to subthalamic infarction. *Neuropsychiatry, Neuropsychology and Behavioral Neurology*, **13**: 220–229.

Adams, K. (1983) Former mental patients in a prison and parole system: a study of socially disruptive behavior. *Criminal Justice and Behavior*, **10**(3): 358–384.

Adams, K. (1986) The disciplinary experiences of mentally disordered inmates. *Criminal Justice and Behavior*, **13**(3); 297–316.

Adams, K. & Ferrandino, J. (2008) Managing mentally ill inmates in prisons. *Criminal Justice and Behavior*, **35**(8): 913–927.

Adler, Z. (1987) *Rape on Trial*. London: Routledge and Kegan Paul.

Aggrawal, A. (2005) Mass murder. In J. Payne-James, R. Byard, T. Corey & C. Henderson (eds), *Encyclopedia of Forensic and Legal Medicine* (Vol. 3). London: Elsevier Academic Press, pp. 216–223.

Agnew, R. (1992) Foundation for a general strain theory. *Criminology*, **30**(1): 47–87.

Agnew, R. (2009) Revitalizing Merton: general strain theory. In F.T. Cullen, F. Adler, C.L. Johnson & A.J. Meyer (eds), *Advances in Criminological Theory: The Origins of American Criminology* (Vol. 16). New Brunswick, NJ: Transaction.

Aichhorn, A. (1925) *Verwahrloste Jugend* (*Wayward Youth*). Vienna: Internationaler Psychoanalytischer Verlag.

Alexander, L., Ferzan, K. & Morse, S. (2009) *Crime and Culpability: A Theory of Criminal Law*. Cambridge: Cambridge University Press.

Alison, L., West, W. & Goodwill, A. (2004) The academic and the practitioner: pragmatists' views of offender profiling. *Psychology, Public Policy, and Law*, **10**(1/2): 71–101.

Allen, E., Bonell, C., Strange, V., Copas, A., Stephenson, J., Johnson, A. M., & Oakley, A. (2007) Does the UK government's teenage pregnancy strategy deal with the correct risk factors? Findings from a secondary analysis of data from a randomised trial of sex education and their implications for poliey. *Journal of Epidemiology and Community Health*, **61**(1): 20–27.

Allison, M., Mathews, K. & Michael, S. (2012) Believability: the impact of salacious alibi activities. *Social Behavior and Personality: An International Journal*, **40**(4): 605–612.

Allnutt, S., Samuels, A. & O'Driscoll, C. (2007) The insanity defence: from wild beasts to M'Naghten. *Australasian Psychiatry*, **15**: 292–298.

Almond, L., Canter, D. & Gabrielle Salfati, C. (2006) Youths who sexually harm: a multivariate model of characteristics. *Journal of Sexual Aggression*, **12**(2): 97–114.

American Psychiatric Association (1994) *Diagnostic and Statistical Manual of Mental Disorders IV–TR*. Arlington, VA: APA.

American Psychiatric Association (2013) *Diagnostic and Statistical Manual of Mental Disorders V*. Arlington, VA: APA. Available at: www.dsm5.org/Pages/Default.aspx (retrieved 12.1.13).

Amir, N., Leiner, A.S. & Bomyea, J. (2010) Implicit memory and posttraumatic stress symptoms. *Cognitive Therapy and Research*, **34**(1): 49–58.

Anderson J. (2010) Comprehending the distinctively sexual nature of the conduct. In H. Gavin, and J. Bent, (eds), *Sex, Drugs & Rock'n'Roll: Psychological, Legal and Cultural Examinations of Sex and Sexuality*. Critical Issues Series. Oxford: Inter-Disciplinary Press Ltd.

Appelbaum, R. & Chambliss, W. (1997) *Sociology* (2nd edn). New York: Longman.

Appelbaum, K., Savageau, J., Trestman, R., Metzner, J. & Baillargeon, J. (2011) A national survey of self-injurious behavior in American prisons. *Psychiatric Services*, **62**(3), 285-290.

Arditti, J. (2012) *Parental Incarceration and the Family: Psychological and Social Effects of Imprisonment on Children, Parents, and Caregivers*. New York: New York University Press.

Arnaldo, C.A. (ed.) (2001) *Child Abuse on the Internet: Breaking the Silence*. Oxford, UK, New York: Berghahn Books/UNESCO.

Association of Certified Fraud Examiners (ACFE) (2008) *Report to the Nations: Key Findings and Highlights*. Austin, TX: ACFE. Available at: www.acfe.com/rttn-highlights.aspx (retrieved 1.1.12).

Association of Certified Fraud Examiners (2012) *Report to the Nations on Occupational Fraud and Abuse* http://www.acfe.com/rttn.aspx (retrieved 1.7.13).

Association of Chief Police Officers (2012) *Guidance on the safer detention and handling of persons in police custody* (2nd edn). www.gov.uk/government/uploads/.../saferdetention–guidance.pdf (retrived 1.3.13).

Babiak, P. & Hare, R. (2007) *Snakes in Suits: When Psychopaths Go to Work*. New York: HarperCollins.

Babiak, P., Neumann, C.S. & Hare, R.D. (2010) Corporate psychopathy: talking the walk. *Behavioral Sciences and the Law*, **28**(2): 174–193.

Bahr, S., Masters, A. & Taylor, B. (2012) What works in substance abuse treatment programs for offenders? *The Prison Journal*, **92**(June): 155–174.

Bailey, K. (1994) *Typologies and Taxonomies: An Introduction to Classification Techniques* (Quantitative Applications in the Social Sciences Series). London: Sage.

Baillargeon, J., Penn, J., Knight, K., Harzke, A., Baillargeon, G. & Becker, E. (2010) Risk of reincarceration among prisoners with co-occurring severe mental illness and substance use disorders. *Administration and Policy Mental Health*, **37**(4): 367–374.

Baker, R. & Hurwitz, B. (2009) Intentionally harmful violations and patient safety: the example of Harold Shipman. *Journal of Royal Society of Medicine*, **102**(6): 223–227.

Bancroft, J.H. (2009) *Human Sexuality and its Problems*. London: Elsevier Health Sciences.

Bandura, A. (1973) *Aggression: A Social Learning Analysis*. Englewood Cliffs, NJ: Prentice-Hall.

Bandura, A. (1977) *Social Learning Theory*. Englewood Cliffs, NJ: Prentice-Hall.

Bandura, A., Ross, D. & Ross, S.A. (1963) Imitation of film-mediated aggressive models. *Journal of Abnormal and Social Psychology*, **63**: 3–11.

Barker, E., Séguin, J., White, H., Bate, M., Lacourse, E., Carbonneau, R. & Tremblay, R. (2007) Developmental trajectories of male physical violence and theft: relations to neurocognitive performance. *Archives of General Psychiatry*, **64**: 592–599.

Bartol, C.R. & Bartol, A.M. (1994) *Psychology and Law*. Pacific Grove, CA: Brooks/Cole Publishing Company.

Bartol, C.R. & Bartol, A.M. (1999) History of forensic psychology. In A.K. Hess & I.B. Weiner (eds), *Handbook of Forensic Psychology*. New York: John Wiley.

BBC News (2007) Sex attacker given four-year term, BBC News, 19.12.2007. news.bbc.co.uk/1/hi/england/london/7153044.stm (retrieved 1.3.13).

BBC News (2013a) Vicky Pryce jury discharged in Huhne speeding points case. *BBC News.* Available at: www.bbc.co.uk/news/uk-21516473 (retrieved 20.2.13).

BBC News (2013b) Ten questions posed by Vicky Pryce jury. *BBC News.* Available at: www.bbc.co.uk/news/uk-21521460 (retrieved 20.2.13).

Beattie, J. (2006) Early detection: the Bow Street Runners in late eighteenth-century London. In C. Emsley & H. Shpayer-Makov (eds), *Police Detectives in History, 1750–1980.* Aldershot: Ashgate.

Becker, H.S. (1974) Labelling theory reconsidered 1. *Deviance and Social Control*, **3**: 41.

Beech, A., Erikson, M., Friendship, C. & Ditchfield, J. (2001) *Findings 144. A Six-year Follow-up of Men Going Through Probation-based Sex Offender Treatment Programme.* London: Home Office.

Beech, A., Fisher, D. & Beckett, R. (1998) *Step 3: an evaluation of the prison sex offender treatment programme. A report for the Home Office by the STEP team.* London: Home Office.

Beech, A.R., Kalmus, E., Tipper, S.P., Baudouin, J., Flak, V. & Humphreys, G.W. (2008) Children induce an enhanced attentional blink in child molesters. *Psychological Assessment*, **20**(4): 397–402.

Beech, A.R., Mandeville-Norden, R. & Goodwill, A. (2012) Comparing recidivism rates of treatment responders/non-responders in a sample of 413 child molesters who had completed community-based sex offender treatment in the United Kingdom. *International Journal of Offender Therapy and Comparative Criminology*, **56**(1): 29–49.

Beech, A.R. & Mann, R. (2002) Recent developments in the assessment and treatment of sexual offenders. In J. McGuire (ed.), *Offender Rehabilitation and Treatment: Effective programmes and policies to reduce re-offending.* London: John Wiley, pp. 259–288.

Benmelech, E. & Berrebi, C. (2007) Human capital and the productivity of suicide bombers. *Journal of Economic Perspectives*, **21**(3): 224–225.

Bennet, W. (1996) Sara Thornton is cleared of murder Killer walks free but verdict fails to resolve legal issues over domestic violence. www.indepdendent.co.uk, 31 May 1996 (retrieved 1.1.13).

Bennetto, J. (2000) Killers cruised streets on hunting expeditions. *The Independent*, 4.10.2000. www.independent.co.uk/news/uk/home-news/killers-cruised-streets-on-hunting-expeditions-634394.html (retrieved 20.6.11).

Berkowitz, L. (1988) Frustrations, appraisals, and aversively stimulated aggression. *Aggressive Behavior*, **14**(1): 3–11.

Berkowitz, L. (1989) Frustration–aggression hypothesis: examination and reformulation. *Psychological Bulletin*, **106**(1): 59.

Berkowitz, L. (1993) *Aggression: Its Causes, Consequences and Control.* New York: McGraw-Hill.

Biffl, E. (1996) Psychological autopsies: do they belong in the courtroom? *American Journal of Criminal Law*, **1**: 123–146.

Bishop, D., Jacobs, P., Lachlan, K., Wellesley, D., Barnicoat, A., Boyd, P., Fryer, A., Middlemiss, P., Smithson, S., Metcalfe, K., Shears, D., Leggett, V., Nation, K. & Scerif, G. (2011) Autism, language and communication in children with sex chromosome trisomies. *Archive of Disease in Childhood*, **96**: 954–959.

Bladon, E., Vizard, E., French, L. & Tranah, T. (2005) A descriptive study of a UK sample of children showing sexually harmful behaviours. *Journal of Forensic Psychiatry & Psychology*, **16**(1): 109–126.

Blair, R. (2003) Neurobiological basis of psychopathy. *British Journal of Psychiatry*, **182**: 5–7.

Blair, R.J.R., Jones, L., Clark, E. & Smith, M. (1997) The psychopathic individual: a lack of responsiveness to distress cues? *Psychophysiology*, **34**: 192–198.

Blanchard, R., Lykins, A., Wherrett, D., Kuban, M., Cantor, J., Blak, T., Dickey, R. & Klassen, P. (2008) Pedophilia, hebephilia, and the DSM–V. *Archives of Sexual Behavior*, **38**(3): 335–350. [Original Paper]

Bloechl, A., Vitacco, M., Neumann, C. & Erickson, S. (2007) An empirical investigation of insanity defense attitudes: exploring factors related to bias. *International Journal of Law and Psychiatry*, **30**(2), March–April: 153–161.

Bloom, M. (2005) *Dying to Kill: The Allure of Suicide Terrorism*. New York: Columbia University Press.

Bloom, M. (2007) Dying to kill: motivations for suicide terrorism. In A. Pedahzur (ed.), *Root Causes of Suicide Terrorism: The Globalization of Martyrdom*. New York: Routledge.

Bloom, M. (2011) *Bombshell: The Many Faces of Women Terrorists*. Toronto: Penguin.

Blum, R.H. (1972) *Deceivers and Deceived: Observations on Confidence Men and their Victims, Informants and their Quarry, Political and Industrial Spies and Ordinary Citizens*. Springfield, IL: Charles C. Thomas.

Boccaccini, M.T. (2002) What do we really know about witness preparation? *Sociology of Fraud: Integrating the Behavioral Sciences and the Law*, **20**: 161–189.

Boer, D.P., Eher, R., Craig, L.A., Miner, M.H. & Pfäfflin, F. (eds) (2011) *International Perspectives on the Assessment and Treatment of Sexual Offenders: Theory, Practice, and Research*. Chichester: John Wiley & Sons.

Boire, R.G. (2005) Searching the brain: the Fourth Amendment implications of brain-based deception detection devices. *American Journal of Bioethics*, **5**(2): 62–63.

Bonnie, R. (2004) Retardation and capital sentencing: implementing Atkins v. Virginia. *Journal of the American Academy of Psychiatry Law*, **32**: 304–308.

Bornstein, B.H. (1999) The ecological validity of jury simulations. *Law and Human Behavior*, **23**(1): 75–91.

Bornstein, B. & Greene, E. (2011) Jury decision making: implications for and from psychology. *Current Directions in Psychological Science*, **20**(1) February: 63–67.

Borsboom, D., Mellenbergh, G. & van Heerden, J. (2004) The concept of validity. *Psychological Review*, **111**(4): 1061–1071.

Borum, R. (2004) *Psychology of Terrorism*. Tampa, FL: University of South Florida Press.

Bouchard Jr., T., Lykken, D., McGue, M., Segal, N. & Tellegen, A. (1990) Sources of human psychological differences: the Minnesota study of twins reared apart. *Science*, **50**: 223–250.

Bourget, D. & Whitehurst, L. (2007) Amnesia and crime *Journal of the American Academy of Psychiatry Law*, **35**:469–480.

Brausch, M. & Gutierrez, P.M. (2010) Differences in non-suicidal self-injury and suicide attempts in adolescents. *Journal of Youth and Adolescence*, **39**: 233–242.

Brenner, C. (2004) Forensic mathematics of DNA matching. *DNA Profile Probability*. Available at: http://dna-view.com/profile.htm (retrieved 12.2.13).

Brent, D., Perper, J., Moritz, G., Allman, C., Roth, C., Schweers, J. & Balach, C. (1993) The validity of diagnoses obtained through the psychological autopsy procedure in adolescent suicide victims: use of family history. *Acta Psychiatrica Scandinavica*, **87**(February): 118–122.

Brewer, N. & Burke, A. (2002) Effects of testimonial inconsistencies and eyewitness confidence on mock-juror judgments. *Law and Human Behavior*, **26**(3): 353–364.

Brezina, T., Tekin, E. & Topalli, V. (2009) "Might not be a tomorrow": a multimethods approach to anticipated early death and youth crime. *Criminology*, **47**(4), 1091–1129.

Briere, J. & Runtz, M. (1989) University males' sexual interest in children: predicting potential indices of 'pedophilia' in a nonforensic sample. *Child Abuse & Neglect*, **13**(1): 65–75.

Briken, P., Hill, A., Habermann, N., Kafka, M. & Berner, W. (2010) Paraphilia-related disorders and personality disorders in sexual homicide perpetrators. *Sexual Offender Treatment*, **5**(1) [online journal].

British Psychological Society (BPS) (2013) Qualification in Forensic Psychology. http://www.bps.org.uk/careers–education–training/society–qualifications/forensicpsychology/qualification–forensic–psychol

Brodsky, S.L. (2009) *Principles and Practice of Trial Consultation*. New York: Guilford Press.

Broidy, L. & Agnew, R. (1997) Gender and crime: a general strain theory perspective. *Journal of Research in Crime and Delinquency*, **34**: 275–306.

Brown, J. & Campbell, E. (eds) (2010) *Cambridge Handbook of Forensic Psychology*. Cambridge, UK, and New York: Cambridge University Press.

Brownmiller, S. (1975) *Against Our Will: Men, Women and Rape*. Auckland, New Zealand: Pearson Education and New York: Simon & Schuster.

Brunner, H.G., Nelen, M., Breakefield, X.O., Ropers, H.H. & Van Oost, B.A. (1993). Abnormal behavior associated with a point mutation in the structural gene for monoamine oxidase A. *Science*, **262**(5133): 578–580.

Buikema, R. & Smelik, A. (eds) (1995) *Women's Studies and Culture: A Feminist Introduction*. London: Zed Books.

Bull, R. & Soukara, S. (2010) Four studies of what really happens in police interviews. In D. Lassiter, C. Meissner (eds), *Police Interrogations and False Confessions: Current Research, Practice, and Policy Recommendations*. Washington, DC: American Psychology Association, pp. 81–95.

Burgess, R.L. & Akers, R.L. (1966) A differential association–reinforcement theory of criminal behavior. *Social Problems*, **14**(2): 128–147.

Buss, D.M., & Duntley, J.D. (2006) The evolution of aggression. In M. Schaller, J. Simpson & D. Kenrick (eds), *Evolution and Social Psychology*. New York: Psychology Press, pp. 263–286.

Buss, D.M. & Schmitt, D.P. (1993) Sexual strategies theory: an evolutionary perspective on human mating. *Psychological Review*, **100**(2): 204.

Button, M., Lewis, C. & Tapley, J. (2012a) Not a victimless crime: the impact of fraud on individual victims and their families. *Security Journal*, doi 10.1057/sj.2012.11, 23 April.

Button, M., Tapley, J. & Lewis, C. (2012b) The 'fraud justice network' and the infra-structure of support for individual fraud victims in England and Wales. *Criminology and Criminal Justice*, **13**(1): 37–61.

Cameron, M.O. (1964) *The Booster and the Snitch: Department Store Shoplifting* New York: Free Press of Glencoe, pp. 160–162.

Campbell, A. (1992) *Girls in the Gang*. London: Blackwell.

Campbell, A. & Muncer, C. (2009) Can 'risky' impulsivity explain sex differences in aggression? *Personality and Individual Differences*, **47**(5), October: 402–406.

Campbell, R. & Raja, S. (1999) Secondary victimization of rape victims: insights from mental health professionals who treat survivors of violence. *Violence and Victims*, **14**(3): 261–275.

Canter, D. (2004) Offender profiling and investigative psychology. *Journal of Investigative Psychology and Offender Profiling*, **1**: 1–15.

Canter, D. (2006) The Samson syndrome: is there a kamikaze psychology? *Twenty-First Century Society*, **1**(2): 107–127.

Canter, D., Alison, L.J., Alison, E. & Wentink, N. (2004) The organized/disorganized typology of serial murder: myth or model? *Public Policy, and Law*, **10**(3): 293–320.

Canter, D.V. & Almond, L. (2007) *A Strategy for Arson*. Centre of Investigative Psychology, University of Liverpool.

Canter, D. & Fritzon, K. (1998) Differentiating arsonists: a model of firesetting actions and characteristics. *Legal and Criminological Psychology*, **3**: 73–96.

Canter, D. & Youngs, D. (2003) Beyond 'offender profiling': the need for an investigative psychology. In D. Carson & R. Bull (eds), *Handbook of Psychology in Legal Contexts*. Chichester, UK: Wiley.

Canter, D.V., Bennell, C., Alison, L.J. & Reddy, S. (2003) Differentiating sex offences: a behaviorally based thematic classification of stranger rapes. *Behavioral Sciences & the Law*, **21**(2): 157–174.

Caputi, J. (1989) The sexual politics of murder. *Gender & Society*, **3**(4): 437–456.

Carlsmith, K., Wilson, T. & Gilbert, D. (2008) Interpersonal relations and group processes: the paradoxical consequences of revenge. *Journal of Personality and Social Psychology*, **95**(6): 1316–1324.

Carson, D. (2009) The abduction of Sherlock Holmes. *International Journal of Police Science & Management*, **11**(2): 193–202.

Carver, K., Joyner, K. & Udry, J.R. (2003) National estimates of adolescent romantic relationships. In P. Florsheim (ed.), *Adolescent Romantic Relations and Sexual Behavior: Theory, Research, and Practical Implications*. Mahwah, NJ: Lawrence Erlbaum Associates.

Casey, P. (2001) Multiple personality disorder. *International Journal of Psychiatry in Clinical Practice*, **7**(1): 7–11.

Casoni, D. & Brunet, L. (2002) The psychodynamics of terrorism. *Canadian Journal of Psychoanalysis*, **10**(1): 5–24.

Cavanagh Johnson, T. & Friend, C. (1995) Context of child sexual abuse evaluations. In T. Ney (ed.), *True and False Allegations of Child Sexual Abuse*: *Assessment & Case Management*. New York: Brunner Mazel, pp. 49–68.

Cécile, M. & Born, M. (2009) Intervention in juvenile delinquency: danger of iatrogenic effects? *Children and Youth Services Review*, **31**(12): 1217–1221.

Celbis, O., Ozcan, M. & Özdemir, B. (2006) Paternal and sibling incest: a case report. *Journal of Clinical Forensic Medicine*, **13**(1): 37–40.

Chabrol, H., Van Leeuwen, N., Rodgers, R. & Séjourné, N. (2009) Contributions of psychopathic, narcissistic, Machiavellian, and sadistic personality traits to juvenile delinquency. *Personality and Individual Differences*, **47**: 734–739.

Chan, H.C.O. & Heide, K.M. (2009) Sexual homicide: a synthesis of the literature. *Trauma, Violence, & Abuse*, **10**(1): 31–54.

Chan, J.C. & LaPaglia, J.A. (2011) The dark side of testing memory: Repeated retrieval can enhance eyewitness suggestibility. *Journal of Experimental Psychology: Applied*, **17**(4): 418.

Chandra, A., Martino, S.C., Collins, R.L., Elliott, M.N., Berry, S.H., Kanouse, D.E. & Miu, A. (2008) Does watching sex on television predict teen pregnancy? Findings from a national longitudinal survey of youth. *Pediatrics*, **122**(5): 1047–1054.

Charters, S., Horn, R. & Vahidy, S. (2009) *Best practice recommendations for the protection and support of witnesses*. Project Report. Special Court of Sierra Leone.

Chapman, J. (2012) Huhne pays for his infidelity: minister's career in ruins as feud with ex-wife lands them both in court over speeding points. *Daily Mail*, 4 February.

Charlton, D., Fraser-Mackenzie, P. & Dror, I. (2010) Emotional experiences and motivating factors associated with fingerprint analysis. *Journal of Forensic Sciences*, **55**(2): 385–398.

Church, M. & Watts, S. (2007) Assessment of mental capacity: a flow chart guide. *The Psychiatrist*, **31**: 304–307.

CICAS (2012) Criminal Injuries Compensation Authority, www.justice.gov.uk/victims-and-witnesses/cica (retrieved 1.12.12).

Clark, D. (2000) *Theory Manual for Enhanced Thinking Skills*. Prepared for the Joint Prison Probation Service Accreditation Panel.

Clarke, A., Simmonds, R. & Wydall, S. (2004) *Delivering Cognitive Skills Programmes in Prison: A Qualitative Study*. London: Home Office Research, Development and Statistics Directorate.

Clarke, C. & Milne, R. (2001) *National Evaluation of the PEACE Investigative Interviewing Course*. Research Award Scheme, Report No. PRSA 149. London: Home Office.

Clarke, R.V. & Felson, M. (eds) (1993) *Routine Activity and Rational Choice: Advances in Criminological Theory* (Vol. 5). New Brunswick, NJ: Transaction.

Cleckley, H.M. (1976) *The Mask of Sanity*. St. Louis, MO: Mosby. (Originally published 1941.)

Clement, P. & Hess, A. (1990) *History of Juvenile Delinquency: A Collection of Essays on Crime Committed by Young Offenders in History*. Amsterdam: Scientia Verlag.

Coccaro, E.F.; Kavoussi, R.J. & Hauger, R.L (1989) Physiological responses to d-fenfluramine and ipsapirone challenge correlate with indices of aggression in males with personality disorder. *International Clinical Psychopharmacology*, **10**(3): 177–179.

Cohen, P. & Shim, M. (2007) Hyperpituitarism, tall stature, and overgrowth syndromes. In R. Kliegman, R. Behrman, H. Jenson & B. Stanton (eds), *Nelson Textbook of Pediatrics* (18th edn). Philadelphia, PA: Saunders.

Cohen, S. (1973) Some sociological problems in the study of adolescent violence. *Proceedings of the Royal Society of Medicine*, **66**(11): 1131.

Coid, J., Yang, M., Ullrich, S., Roberts, A. & Hare, R.D. (2009) Prevalence and correlates of psychopathic traits in the household population of Great Britain. *International Journal of Law and Psychiatry*, **32**(2): 65–73.

Coke, E. (1616) *Acts of the Privy Council*. In S. Shepard (ed.) (2003) *Selected Writings and Speeches of Edward Coke* (Vol. 3). Indianopolis, IN: Liberty Fund.

Collica, K. (2010) Surviving incarceration: two prison-based peer programs build communities of support for female offenders. *Deviant Behavior*, **31**(4): 314–347.

Conley, R. & Conley, J. (2009) Stories from the jury room: how jurors use narrative to process evidence. In A. Sarat (ed.), *Studies in Law, Politics, and Society* (Vol. 49). Bingley, UK: Emerald Publications, pp. 25–56.

Cooke, D. & Philip, L. (1998) Comprehending the Scottish caution: do offenders understand their right to remain silent? *Legal and Criminological Psychology*, **3**(1): 13–27.

Cooley, C.M. (2007) CSI effect: its impact and potential concerns, *New England Law Review*, **41**: 471–502.

Cornish, D.B. & Clarke, R.V. (2003) Opportunities, precipitators and criminal decisions: a reply to Wortley's critique of situational crime prevention. *Crime Prevention Studies*, **16**: 41–96.

Coyle, A. (2005) *Understanding Prisons*. Maidenhead: McGraw–Hill International.

Cressey, D.R. (1953) *Other People's Money: A Study in the Social Psychology of Embezzlement*. Glencoe, IL: Free Press.

Cronan, J.P. (2002) Is any of this making sense? Reflecting on guilty pleas to aid criminal juror comprehension. *American Criminal Law Review*, **39**: 1187.

Cullen, R. (1993) *The Killer Department*. New York: Ivy Books.

Daeid, N. (2005) *Fire Investigation*. Boca Raton, FL: CRC Press.

Daftary-Kapur, T., Dumas, R. & Penrod, S.D. (2010) Jury decision-making biases and methods to counter them. *Legal and Criminological Psychology*, **15**(1): 133–154.

Dahmer, L. (1994) *A Father's Story: One Man's Anguish at Confronting the Evil in His Son*. New York: HarperCollins.

Daily Mail (2010) Prison guard's casual glance at CCTV screen stopped the 'Crossbow Cannibal' from killing himself. *Daily Mail* [online], June 2010 www.dailymail.co.uk (retrieved 12.6.10).

Daily Mail (2012) Death row killer executed by lethal injection after final meal of Kentucky Fried Chicken. *Daily Mail* [online], 2 May, www.dailymail.co.uk (retrieved 22.11.12).

Dalby, J.T. (2006) The case of Daniel McNaughton: let's get the story straight. *American Journal of Forensic Psychiatry*, **27**: 17–32.

Dallam, S.J. (2001) Science or propaganda? An examination of Rind, Tromovitch and Bauserman. *Journal of Child Sexual Abuse*, **9**(3/4): 109–134.

Daly, M. & Wilson, M.I. (1994) Some differential attributes of lethal assaults on small children by stepfathers versus genetic fathers. *Ethology and Sociobiology*, **15**(4): 207–217.

Damio, W. (1974) *Urge to Kill*. Edinburgh: Pinnacle Books.

Danto, B.L. (1982) *Alternative Approaches to the Violent Criminal: The Human Side of Homicide*. New York: Columbia University Press.

Darcangelo, S. (2007) Fetishism, theory and pathology. In R. Laws & W. O'Donahue (eds), *Sexual Deviance: Theory, Assessment, and Treatment*. New York: Guilford Press.

Day, L., Maltby, J., Giles, D. & Wingrove, V. (2000) Psychological predictors of self-reported shoplifting. *Psychology, Crime & Law*, **6**(1): 71–79.

de Boer, S. & Koolhaas, J. (2005) 5–HT1A and 5–HT1B receptor agonists and aggression: a pharmacological challenge of the serotonin deficiency hypothesis. *European Journal of Pharmacology*, **526**(1–3): 125–139.

de Viggiani, N. (2007) Unhealthy prisons: exploring structural determinants of prison health. *Sociology of Health & Illness*, **29**(1): 115–135.

Dean, G. (2007) Criminal profiling in a terrorism context. In R.N. Kocsis (ed.), *Criminal Profiling: International Theory, Research, and Practice*. New York: Humana Press.

Dearing, R., Stuewig, J. & Tangney, J. (2005) On the importance of distinguishing shame from guilt: Relations to problematic alcohol and drug use. *Addictive Behaviors*, **30**(7): 1392–1404.

Decker, S. (2004) *Understanding Gangs and Gang Processes*. Greenbelt, MD: ACA.

Dees, M., Vernooij-Dassen, M., Dekkers, W. & van Weel, C. (2010) Unbearable suffering of patients with a request for euthanasia or physician-assisted suicide: an integrative review. *Psycho-oncology*, **19**(4), April: 339–352.

DeMause, L. (2002) The childhood origins of terrorism. *Caietele Echinox*, **3** (2002): 132–137.

Dennis, M.J. (1999). The ILO convention on the worst forms of child labor. *American Journal of International Law*, **93**(4): 943–948.

DesForges, A. (1999) *Leave None to Tell the Story: Genocide in Rwanda*. New York: Human Rights Watch.

Dettbarn, E. (2012) Effects of long-term incarceration: a statistical comparison of two expert assessments of two experts at the beginning and the end of incarceration. *International Journal of Law and Psychiatry*, **35**(3): 236–239.

Devine, D.J., Buddenbaum, J., Houp, S., Stolle, D.P. & Studebaker, N. (2007) Deliberation quality: a preliminary examination in criminal juries. *Journal of Empirical Legal Studies*, **4**(2): 273–303.

Devinsky, J., Sacks, O. & Devinsky, O. (2010) Kluver–Bucy syndrome, hypersexuality, and the law. *Neurocase*, **16**(2), April: 140–145. (Epublished 18 November 2009).

DeWall, C.N., Bushman, B.J., Giancola, P.R. & Webster, G.D. (2010) The big, the bad, and the boozed-up: Weight moderates the effect of alcohol on aggression. *Journal of Experimental Social Psychology*, **46**(4): 619–623.

Dhami, M.K., Ayton, P. & Loewenstein, G. (2007) Adaptation to imprisonment: Indigenous or imported? *Criminal Justice and Behavior*, **34**(8): 1085–1100.

Dhawan, S. & Marshall, W. (1996) Sexual abuse histories of sexual offenders. *Sex Abuse*, **8**(January): 7–15.

Dimas, C., Reiss, D. & Neiderhiser, J. (2008) Triangular relationships in adolescence predict adult psychopathology: an empirical validation of the Oedipus Complex? *Journal of the American Psychoanalytical Association*, **56**: 1342–1348.

Dodd, V. (2009) Mother blames police failure for girl's murder. *The Guardian*, 20 May.

Dodge, K., Coie, J.D. & Lynam, D. (2006) Aggression and antisocial behavior in youth. In W. Damon, R. Lerner & N. Eisenberg (eds), *Handbook of Child Psychology*. New York: Wiley, pp. 719–788.

Dodge, M. (2006) Juvenile police informants: friendship, persuasion, and pretense. *Youth Violence and Juvenile Justice*, **4**(3): 234–246.

Douglas, J., Burgess, A.W., Burgess, A.G. & Ressler, R. (2006) *Crime Classification Manual: A Standard System for Investigating and Classifying Violent Crimes* (2nd edn). New York: John Wiley & Sons.

Doyle, S. (2010) The notion of consent to sexual activity for persons with mental disabilities. In H. Gavin & J. Bent (eds), *Sex, Drugs and Rock & Roll: Psychological, Legal and Cultural Examinations of Sex and Sexuality*. Oxford: Inter-Disciplinary Press.

Dracker, C.B. (1996) *Counseling Survivors of Childhood Sexual Abuse*. London: Sage.

Drew, J. & Drew, M. (2010) *Ponzimonium: Madoff and the Red Flags of Fraud*. Finance Discussion Papers No. 2010–07 (Series Editor A. Akimov). Brisbane: Griffith Business School.

Dudeck, M., Drenkhahn, K., Spitzer, C., Barnow, D., Kuwer, P., Freyberger, H. & Dünkel, F. (2011) Traumatization and mental distress in long-term prisoners in Europe. *Punishment & Society*, **13**(October): 403–423.

Duff, A. (2008) Legal punishment. In E. Zalta (ed.), *Stanford Encyclopedia of Philosophy*. Stanford, CA: Metaphysic Research Laboratory, Stanford University.

Dumais, A., Lesage, A., Lalovic, A., Séguin, M., Tousignant, M., Chawky, N. & Turecki, G. (2005) Is violent method of suicide a behavioral marker of lifetime aggression? *American Journal of Psychiatry*, **162**: 1375–1378.

Duntley, J.D. & Shackleford, T.K. (2008) Darwinian foundations of crime and law. *Aggression and Violent Behavior*, **13**: 373–382.

Durcan, G. (2008) *From the Inside: Experiences of Prison Mental Health Care*. London: Sainsbury Centre for Mental Health.

Dutton, D. (2007) *The Psychology of Genocide, Massacres, and Extreme Violence: Why 'Normal' People Come to Commit Atrocities*. Westport, CT: Praeger Security International.

Dye, M.H. (2010) Deprivation, importation, and prison suicide: combined effects of institutional conditions and inmate composition. *Journal of Criminal Justice*, **38**(4): 796–806.

Dyer, J., Pleck, J.H. & McBride, B.A. (2012) Imprisoned fathers and their family relationships: a 40-year review from a multi-theory view. *Journal of Family Theory & Review*, **4**(1): 20–47.

Eadie, T. & Morley, R. (2003) Crime, justice and punishment. In J. Baldock et al. (eds), *Social Policy* (3rd edn). Oxford: Oxford University Press.

Ebbesen, E.B. & Konecni, V.J. (1997) Eyewitness memory research: probative vs. prejudicial value. *Expert Evidence*, **5**(1&2): 2–28.

Ebiske, N. (2008) *Offender Profiling in the Courtroom: The Use and Abuse of Expert Witness Testimony*. Westport, CT: Greenwood.

Echterhoff, G., Hirst, W. & Hussy, W. (2005) How eyewitnesses resist misinformation: social post warnings and the monitoring of memory characteristics. *Memory & Cognition*, **33**(5): 770–782.

Egan, V. & Taylor, D. (2010) Shoplifting, unethical consumer behaviour, and personality. *Personality and Individual Differences*, **48**(2010): 878–883.

Egeland, B., Bosquet, M. & Chung, A.L. (2002) Continuities and discontinuities in the intergenerational transmission of child maltreatment: implications for breaking the cycle of abuse. In K. Browne, H. Hanks, P. Stratton & C. Hamilton (eds), *Early Prediction and Prevention of Child Abuse: A Handbook*. Chichester: John Wiley, pp. 217–232.

Eggen, D. & Wilson, S. (2005) Suicide bombs: potent tools of terrorists. *Washington Post*, 17 July, www.washingtonpost.com (retrieved 1.11.12).

Egger, S. (1984) Working definition of serial murder and the reduction of linkage blindness. *Journal of Police Science and Administration*, **12**(3): 348–357.

Egger, S. (2002) *The Killers among Us: An Examination of Serial Murder and Its Investigation* (2nd edn). Englewood Cliffs, NJ: Prentice-Hall.

Egger, S.A. & Doney, R.H. (1990) *Serial Murder: An Elusive Phenomenon*. New York: Praeger.

Eifler, S. (2007) Evaluating the validity of self-reported deviant behavior using vignette analyses. *Quality & Quantity*, **41**(2): 303–318.

Eisenberg, N., Hofer, C. & Vaughn, J. (2007) Effortful control and its socioemotional consequences. In J. Gross (ed.) *Handbook of Emotion Regulation*. New York: Guilford Press, pp. 287–306.

Eliason, S. (2009) Murder-suicide: a review of the recent literature. *Journal of the American Academy of Psychiatry and the Law Online*, **37**(3): 371–376.

Eliason, S. & Chamberlain, J. (2008) Competence to stand trial. *Journal of the American Academy of Psychiatry Law*, **36**(2): 255–257.

Ellis, L. (1989) *Theories of Rape: Inquiries into the Causes of Sexual Aggression*. New York: Hemisphere.

Ellman, S.J. (2003) Racial profiling and terrorism. *New York Law School Law Review*, **46**: 688.

Epperson, M., Wolff, N., Morgan, R., Fisher, W., Frueh, B.C. & Huening, J. (2011) *The Next Generation of Behavioral Health and Criminal Justice Interventions: Improving Outcomes by Improving Interventions*.

New Brunswick, NJ: Rutgers University, Center for Behavioral Health Services and Criminal Justice Research.

Erikson, E.H. (1994) *Identity: Youth and Crisis (No. 7)*. New York: WW Norton.

European Commission (2007) *Long-term Imprisonment and Human Rights: Findings of an International Study*. Brussels: Directorate General Justice, Freedom and Security.

Everington, C. & Olley, G. (2008) Implications of Atkins v. Virginia: issues in defining and diagnosing mental retardation. *Journal of Forensic Psychology Practice*, **8**(1): 1–23.

Ewing, C.P. (1997) *Fatal Families: The Dynamics of Intrafamilial Homicide*. Thousand Oaks, CA: Sage.

Eysenck, H. & Gudjonsson, G. (1989) *The Causes and Cures of Criminality*. New York: Plenum Press.

Fagbaibi, S.O., Yahya, Y.I. & Longe, O.B. (2012) On the uses of data mining techniques for crime profiling. *Computing, Information Systems & Development Informatics Journal*, **3**(3): 61–68.

Farrer, T. & Hedges, D. (2011) Prevalence of traumatic brain injury in incarcerated groups compared to the general population: a meta-analysis. *Progress in Neuro-Psychopharmacology and Biological Psychiatry*, **35**(2): 390–394.

Farrington, D. (1996) Development of offending and antisocial behaviour from childhood: key findings from the Cambridge Study in Delinquent Development. *Journal of Child Psychology*, **360**(6): 929–964.

Farrington, D. (2002) Developmental criminology and risk-focused prevention. In M. Maguire et al. (eds), *The Oxford Handbook of Criminology* (3rd edn). Oxford: Oxford University Press.

Farrington, D.P. (2005) Childhood origins of antisocial behavior. *Clinical Psychology & Psychotherapy*, **12**(3): 177–190.

Farrington, D., Coid, J. & Murray, J. (2009) Family factors in the intergenerational transmission of offending. *Criminal Behaviour and Mental Health* (special issue: *Intergenerational Transmission*), **19**(2): 109–124.

Farrington, D., Jolliffe, D., Hawkins, D., Catalano, R., Hill, K. & Kosterman, R. (2010) Why are boys more likely to be referred to juvenile court? Gender differences in official and self-reported delinquency. *Victims & Offenders*, **5**(1): 25–44.

Farrington, D. & Welsh, B.C. (2006) A half century of randomized experiments on crime and justice. *Crime and Justice*, **34**(1): 55–132.

Fazel, S. & Danesh, J. (2002) Serious mental disorder in 23,000 prisoners: a systematic review of 62 surveys. *Lancet*, **359**: 545–550.

Fazel, S. & Seewald, K. (2012) Severe mental illness in 33,588 prisoners worldwide: systematic review and meta-regression analysis. *British Journal of Psychiatry*, **200**(5): 364–373.

Fazel, S., Xenitidis, K. & Powell, J. (2008) The prevalence of intellectual disabilities among 12,000 prisoners: a systematic review. *International Journal of Law and Psychiatry*, **31**(4), August–September: 369–373.

Federal Bureau of Investigation (1985) The men who murdered. *FBI Law Enforcement Bulletin*, **54**(8): 2–31.

Federal Bureau of Investigation (1989) *White-collar Crime: A Report to the Public*. Washington, DC: US Dept. of Justice, Federal Bureau of Investigation.

Federal Bureau of Investigation (2006) *Serial Murder: Multidisciplinary Perspectives for Investigators*. Washington, DC: FBI.

Feigenson, N. & Parks, J. (2006) Emotions and attributions of legal responsibility and blame: a research review. *Law and Human Behaviour*, **30**(2): 143–161.

Ferrito, M., Vetere, A., Adshead, G. & Moore, E. (2012) Life after homicide: accounts of recovery and redemption of offender patients in a high security hospital – a qualitative study. *Journal of Forensic Psychiatry & Psychology*, **23**(3): 327–344.

Financial Times (2012) Barclays fined a record £290m. http://www.ft.com/cms/s/0/2a4479f8–c030–11e1–9867–00144feabdc0.html#axzz2ZJhJPEo1 (retrieved 1.7.13).

Finger, K. & Pezdek, K. (1999) The effect of cognitive interview on face identification accuracy: release from verbal overshadowing. *Journal of Applied Psychology*, **84**(3): 340.

Finkel, N.J. (2009) *Commonsense Justice: Jurors' Notions of the Law*. Boston, MA: Harvard University Press.

Finn, M.A. (1995) Disciplinary incidents in prison: effects of race, economic status, urban residence, prior imprisonment. *Journal of Offender Rehabilitation*, **22**(1–2): 143–156.

Fisher, R.P. (1995) Interviewing victims and witnesses of crime. *Psychology, Public Policy and Law*, **1**(4): 732–764.

Fisher, R.P. & Geiselman, R.E. (1992) *Memory-enhancing Techniques for Investigative Interviewing: The Cognitive Interview*. Springfield, IL: Charles C. Thomas.

Flombaum, J.I. & Santos, L.R. (2005) Rhesus monkeys attribute perceptions to others. *Current Biology*, **15**(5): 447–452.

Fox, J.A. & Levin, J. (1994) *Overkill: Mass Murder and Serial Killing Exposed*. New York: Plenum Press.

Franklin Report (1951) *Report of a Committee to Review Punishments in Prisons, Borstal Institutions, Approved Schools and Remand Homes, Parts III and IV: Approved Schools and Remand Homes*. Cmnd 8429. London: HMSO.

Frantzen, D. & Can, S.H. (2012) Police confidence in lie detection: an assessment of crime types, Miranda and interview techniques. *Journal of Criminal Psychology*, **2**(1): 26–37.

Frazier, P.A., Mortensen, H. & Steward, J. (2005) Coping strategies as mediators of the relations among perceived control and distress in sexual assault survivors. *Journal of Counseling Psychology*, **52**(3): 267.

Freedman, S., Marks, M. & Dalgleish, T. (1996) Cognitive–behavioural treatment of shoplifting in a depressed female. *Medicine, Science, and the Law*, **36**(2): 157–162.

French Jr, J. & Raven, B. (1960) The bases of social power. In D. Cartwright & A. Zander (eds), *Group Dynamics*. New York: Harper & Row.

Freud, S. (1930) *Civilisation and Its Discontents*. London: Hogarth.

Freud, S. (1961) *The Ego and the Id*. Standard Edition of the Complete Psychological Works of Sigmund Freud. London: Hogarth Press.

Frick, P.J., O'Brien, B.S., Wootton, J.M. & McBurnett, K. (1994) Psychopathy and conduct problems in children. *Journal of Abnormal Psychology*, **103**(4): 700.

Friedmann, P.D., Melnick, G., Jiang, L. & Hamilton, Z. (2008) Violent and disruptive behavior among drug-involved prisoners: relationship with psychiatric symptoms. *Behavioral Sciences & the Law*, **26**(4): 389–401.

Friedrich, W., Fisher, J., Broughton, B., Houston, M. & Shafran, C. (1998) Normative sexual behavior in children: a contemporary sample. *Pediatrics*, **101**(4), April: 101–109.

Friedrichs, D.O. (2007) White-collar crime in a postmodern, globalized world. In *International Handbook of White-collar and Corporate Crime*. New York: Springer, pp. 163–184.

Friendship, C., Blud, L., Erikson, M., Travers, R. & Thornton, D. (2003) Cognitive-behavioural treatment for imprisoned offenders: an evaluation of HM Prison Service's cognitive skills programmes. *Legal and Criminological Psychology*, **8**: 103–114.

Fritzon, K., Lewis, H. & Doley, R. (2011) Looking at the characteristics of adult arsonists from a narrative perspective. *Psychiatry, Psychology and Law*, **18**(3): 424–438.

Gabbert, F., Memon, A. & Allan, K. (2003) Memory conformity: can eyewitnesses influence each other's memories for an event? *Applied Cognitive Psychology*, **17**(5): 533–543.

Gannon, T.A. & Rose, M.R. (2008) Female child sexual offenders: towards integrating theory and practice. *Aggression and Violent Behavior*, **13**(6): 442–461.

Gannon, T.A., Rose, M.R. & Ward, T. (2008) A descriptive model of the offense process for female sexual offenders. *Sexual Abuse: A Journal of Research and Treatment*, **20**: 352–374.

Garcia-Retamero, R. & Dhami, M.K. (2009) Take-the-best in expert–novice decision strategies for residential burglary. *Psychonomic Bulletin & Review*, **16**(1): 163–169.

Gavin, H. (1998) *The Essence of Cognitive Psychology*. London: Prentice Hall.

Gavin, H. (2005) The social construction of the child sex offender explored by narrative. *The Qualitative Report*, **10**(3): 395–413.

Gavin, H. (2010) 'Mummy wouldn't do that': the perception and construction of the female child sex abuser. In M. Barrett and T. Porter (eds), *Grotesque Femininities: Evil, Women and the Feminine*. Global Interdisciplinary Research Studies Series. Oxford: The Inter-Disciplinary Press.

Gavin, H. (2011) Sticks and stones may break my bones: an examination of the effects of emotional abuse. *Journal of Aggression, Maltreatment and Trauma*, **20**(5): 503–529.

Gavin, H. (2013) Evil or insane? The female serial killer and her doubly deviant femininity. *Fifth Global Conference on Evil, Women and the Feminine*, Prague, May 2013.

Gavin, H. & Bent, J. (2010) Sexual deviancy and the sex police: an examination of the religious, cultural and psycholegal antecedents of perceived perversion. In H. Gavin & J. Bent (eds), *Sex, Drugs and Rock & Roll: Psychological, Legal and Cultural Examinations of Sex and Sexuality*. Global Interdisciplinary Research Studies Series. Oxford: The Inter-Disciplinary Press.

Gavin, H. & Hockey, D. (2010) Criminal careers and cognitive scripts: an investigation into criminal versatility. *The Qualitative Report*, **15**(2): 389–410.

Geiselman, R.E., Fisher, R.P., MacKinnon, D.P. & Holland, H.L. (1985) Eyewitness memory enhancement in the police interview: cognitive retrieval mnemonics versus hypnosis. *Journal of Applied Psychology*, **70**(2): 401.

Gekoski, A. (1998) *Murder by Numbers: British Serial Sex Killers since 1950*. London: Andre Deutsch.

Geller, R. (2008) Firesetting. In R.N. Kocsis (ed.), *Serial Murder and the Psychology of Violent Crimes*. New York: Humana Press.

Giancola, P.R., Levinson, C.A., Corman, M.D., Godlaski, A.J., Morris, D.H., Phillips, J.P. & Holt, J.C. (2009) Men and women, alcohol and aggression. *Experimental and Clinical Psychopharmacology*, **17**(3): 154.

Giannangelo, S. (1996) *The Psychopathology of Serial Murder: A Theory of Violence*. Westport, CT: Praeger.

Giannelli, P. (1996) Forensic science: chain of custody. *Criminal Law Bulletin*, **32**(5): 447–465.

Gibson, I. (1978) *The English Vice: Beating, Sex and Shame in Victorian England and After*. London: Duckworth.

Giorgi, A. (1970) *Psychology as a Human Science: A Phenomenologically Based Approach*. Oxford and New York: Harper & Row.

Glasser, M., Kolvin, I., Campbell, D., Glasser, A., Leitch, I. & Farrelly, S. (2001) Cycle of child sexual abuse: links between being a victim and becoming a perpetrator. *British Journal of Psychiatry*, **179**(6): 482–494.

Glendon, M.A., Carozza, P.G. & Picker, C.B. (2008) *Comparative Legal Traditions*. Eagan, MN: Thomson-West, p. 101.

Godet-Mardirossian, H., Jehel, L. & Falissard, B. (2011) Suicidality in male prisoners: influence of childhood adversity mediated by dimensions of personality. *Journal of Forensic Sciences*, **56**(4): 942–949.

Goldenberg, N. (2007) What's God got to do with it? A call for problematizing basic terms in the feminist analysis of religion. *Feminist Theology*, **15**(3): 275–288.

Goldman, M. (1989) The politics of crime. *Criminal Justice Ethics*, **8**(1): 14–23.

Goldner, E.M., Geller, J., Birmingham, C.L. & Remick, R.A. (2000) Comparison of shoplifting behaviours in patients with eating disorders, psychiatric control subjects, and undergraduate control subjects. *Canadian Journal of Psychiatry*, **45**(5): 471–475.

Goldstein, A. & Epstein, S. (2008) Personality testing in employment: useful business tool or civil rights violation? *The Labor Lawyer*, **24**(2): 243–252.

Gonsalves, V.M., Walsh, K. & Scalora, M.J. (2012) Staff perceptions of risk for prison rape perpetration and victimization. *The Prison Journal*, **92**(2): 253–273.

Goodman-Delahunty, J. & Hewson, L. (2010) Enhancing fairness in DNA jury trials. *Australian Institute of Criminology*.

Goodwill, A., Stephens, S., Oziel1, S., Yapp, J. & Bowes, N. (2012) Multidimensional latent classification of 'street robbery' offences. *Journal of Investigative Psychology and Offender Profiling*, **9**: 93–109.

Goodwin, R. (1996) States are beginning to recognize that abused children who kill their parents should be afforded the right to assert a claim of self-defense. *Southwestern University Law Review*, **25**: 429–460.

Gordon, G. (2008) A cloned dog, a Mormon in mink-lined handcuffs and a tantalising mystery. *Daily Mail*, 7 August, www.dailymail.co.uk (retrieved 20.1.10).

Gordon, S. (2012) Through the eyes of jurors: the use of schemas in the application of 'plain language' jury instructions. *Hastings Law Journal*, **64**: 643–678.

Gorman, B. (2010) TV Ratings Thursday: TV by the Numbers. http://tvbythenumbers.com (retrieved 1.1.13).

Gottfredson, M. & Hirschi, T. (1986) The true value of lambda would appear to be zero: an essay on career criminals, criminal careers, selective incapacitation, cohort studies, and related topics. *Criminology*, **24**(2): 213–234.

Grady, M.D., Edwards, D., Pettus-Davis, C. & Abramson, J. (2012) Does volunteering for sex offender treatment matter? Using propensity score analysis to understand the effects of volunteerism and treatment on recidivism. *Sexual Abuse: A Journal of Research and Treatment* [online], 24 September.

Graham, J. & Bowling, B. (1995) *Young People and Crime Great Britain: Home Office Research and Statistics*. Home Office Research Study 145. London: HMSO.

Graham, S. (2008) Mother and slaughter: a comparative analysis of the female terrorist in the LRA and FARC. In J. Pretorius (ed.), *African Politics: Beyond the Third Wave of Democratisation*. Cape Town: Juta and Co.

Grant, J. (2011) Hedge fund withdrawals at highs since 2009. *Advanced Trading*, www.AdvancedTrading.com/infrastructure/hedge-fund (retrieved 1.11.12).

Grant, J.E., Kim, S.W. & Odlaug, B.L. (2009) A double-blind, placebo-controlled study of the opiate antagonist naltrexone in the treatment of kleptomania. *Biological Psychiatry*, **65**(7): 600–606.

Grant, J.E., Odlaug, B.L. & Wozniak, J.R. (2007) Neuropsychological functioning in kleptomania. *Behaviour Research and Therapy*, **45**(7): 1663–1670.

Grassian, S. (1983) Psychopathological effects of solitary confinement. *American Journal of Psychiatry*, **140**(11): 1450–1454.

Gray, J. (1970) The psychophysiological basis of introversion–extraversion. *Behaviour Research and Therapy*, **8**(3), August: 249–266.

Graysmith, R. (1986) *Zodiac: The Shocking True Story of the Nation's Most Bizarre Mass Murderer*. New York: Berkley Books.

Green, R. (2002) Is pedophilia a mental disorder? *Archives of Sexual Behavior*, **31**(6): 467–471.

Gregory, N. (2007) Offender profiling: a review of the literature. *British Journal of Forensic Practice*, **7**(3): 29–34.

Gresswell, D.M. & Hollin, C.R. (1994) Multiple murder: a review. *British Journal of Criminology*, **34**: 1–14.

Griffin, D. & O'Donnell, I. (2012) The life sentence and parole. *British Journal of Criminology*, **52**(3): 611–629.

Grossman, L.S. & Wasyliw, O.E. (1988) A psychometric study of stereotypes: assessment of malingering in a criminal forensic group. *Journal of Personality Assessment*, **52**(3): 549–563.

Grotevant, H. (1997) Coming to terms with adoption: the construction of identity from adolescence into adulthood. *Adoption Quarterly*, **1**(1): 3–27.

Groth, A. (1979) *Men Who Rape: The Psychology of the Offender*. New York: Plenum.

Groth, A.N., Hobson, W.F., & Gary, T.S. (1982) The child molester: Clinical observations. *Journal of Social Work & Human Sexuality*, **1**(1–2): 129–144.

Grubb, A. & Harrower, J. (2008) Attribution of blame in cases of rape: an analysis of participant gender, type of rape and perceived similarity to the victim. *Aggression and Violent Behavior*, **13**(5): 396–405.

Grubin, D. (2008) Medical models and interventions in sexual deviance. In R. Laws and W. O'Donohue (eds) *Sexual Deviance: Theory, Assessment, and Treatment*. New York: Guilford Press, pp. 594–610.

Guardian (2000) Did bad parenting really turn these boys into killers? *The Guardian*, www.guardian.com/uk/2000/nov/01/bulger.familyandrelationships (retrieved 1.5.11).

Guardian (2010a) Arizona execution goes ahead after stay lifted. *The Guardian*, 27 October, www.guardian.co.uk/world/2010/oct/27/arizona-execution-stay-lifted. 27.10.10 (retrieved 28.10.10).

Guardian (2010b) Stephen Griffiths: the self-styled demon who drew inspiration from serial killers. *The Guardian*, 12 December. www.guardian.co.uk (retrieved 21.12.10).

Guay, J.-P., Ouimet, M. & Proulx, J. (2005) On intelligence and crime: a comparison of incarcerated sex offenders and serious non-sexual violent criminals. *International Journal of Law and Psychiatry*, **28**: 405–417.

Guba, E.G. & Lincoln, Y.S. (1981) *Effective Evaluation: Improving the Usefulness of Evaluation Results through Responsive and Naturalistic Approaches*. San Francisco, CA: Jossey-Bass.

Gudjonsson, G.H. (1984) A new scale of interrogative suggestibility. *Personality and Individual Differences*, **5**(3): 303–314.

Gudjonsson, G.H. (2003) *The Psychology of Interrogations and Confessions*. Chichester: John Wiley & Sons.

Gudjonsson, G.H. (2006) The psychological vulnerabilities of witnesses and the risk of false accusations and false confessions. In A. Heaton-Armstrong, E. Shepherd, G. Gudjonsson & D. Wolchover (eds), *Witness Testimony: Psychological, investigative and evidential perspectives*. Oxford: Oxford University Press, pp. 61–75.

Gudjonsson, G.H. & Petursson, H. (1991) Custodial interrogation: why do suspects confess and how does it relate to their crime, attitude and personality? *Personality and Individual Differences*, **12**(3): 295–306.

Gudjonsson, G.H. & Sigurdsson, J.F. (1994) How frequently do false confessions occur? An empirical study among prison inmates. *Psychology, Crime and Law*, **1**(1): 21–26.

Gudjonsson, G.H. Sigurdsson, J.F. & Sigfusdottir, I.D. (2009) Interrogation and false confessions among adolescents in seven European countries. What background and psychological variables best discriminate between false confessors and non-false confessors? *Psychology, Crime & Law*, **15**(8): 711–728.

Gudjonsson, G.H., Sigurdsson, J.F., Sigfusdottir, I.D. & Asgeirsdottir, B.B. (2008) False confessions and individual differences: the importance of victimization among youth. *Personality and Individual Differences*, **45**(8): 801–805.

Guéguen, N. (2012) Risk taking and women's menstrual cycle: near ovulation, women avoid a doubtful man. *Letters on Evolutionary Behavioral Science*, **3**(1): 1–3.

Guerette, R.T., Stenius, V.M. & McGloin, J.M. (2005) Understanding offense specialization and versatility: a reapplication of the rational choice perspective. *Journal of Criminal Justice*, **33**(1): 77–87.

Guillen, T. (2002) Serial killer communiqués: helpful or hurtful? *Journal of Criminal Justice and Popular Culture*, **9**(2) (2002): 55–68.

Hagen, E. (2005) Controversies surrounding evolutionary psychology. In D. Buss (ed.), *The Evolutionary Psychology Handbook*. Chichester: John Wiley.

Haggbloom, S.J., Warnick, R., Warnick, J.E., Jones, V.K., Yarbrough, G.L., Russell, T.M., Borecky, C.M., McGahhey, R., Powell, J.L., Beavers, J. & Monte, E. (2002) The 100 most eminent psychologists of the 20th century. *Review of General Psychology*, **6**(2): 139–152.

Hall, L.J. & Player, E. (2008) Will the introduction of an emotional context affect fingerprint analysis and decision-making? *Forensic Science International*, **181**(13): 36–39.

Hampton, N.J. & Wild, J. (2000) Cross-examination. In B. Robertson (ed.), *Introduction to Advocacy*. Wellington: New Zealand Law Society, pp. 233–264.

Hamza, C., Stewart, S. & Willoughby, T. (2012) Examining the link between nonsuicidal self-injury and suicidal behavior: a review of the literature and an integrated model. *Clinical Psychology Review*, **32**: 482–495.

Haney, C. & Zimbardo, P.G. (2009) Persistent dispositionalism in interactionist clothing: fundamental attribution error in explaining prison abuse. *Personality and Social Psychology Bulletin*, **35**(6): 807–814.

Hansard (2005) Parliamentary business. *Hansard*, 7 July, www.publications.parliament.uk/pa/cm200506 mhansrd/vo050707 (retrieved 1.1.12).

Hanson, R.K. & Thornton, D. (2000) Improving risk assessment for sex offenders: a comparison of three actuarial scales. *Law and Human Behavior*, **24**: 119–136.

Hare, R. (1999b) Psychopathy as a risk factor for violence. *Psychiatric Quarterly*, **70**(3): 181–197.

Hare, R.D. (1982) Psychopathy and the personality dimensions of psychoticism, extraversion and neuroticism. *Personality and Individual Differences*, **3**(1): 35–42.

Hare, R.D. (2000) *Without Conscience: The Disturbing World of the Psychopaths Among Us.* New York: Guidford Press.

Hare, R.D. (1999a) *The Hare Psychopathy Checklist Revised PCL–R.* Multi-Health Systems Inc.

Harrendorf, S., Heiskanen, M. & Malby, S. (eds) (2010) *International Statistics on Crime and Justice.* European Institute for Crime Prevention and Control (United Nations).

Harris, G. & Rice, M. (1996) A typology of mentally disordered firesetters. *Journal of Interpersonal Violence*, **11**: 351.

Harrison, K. & Tamony, A. (2010) Death Row Phenomenon, Death Row Syndrome and their effect on capital cases in the US. *Internet Journal of Criminology*, 1–16. www.internetjournalofcriminology.com (retrieved 1.9.12).

Harrower, J. (1998) *Applying Psychology to Crime.* London: Hodder & Stoughton.

Harrower, J. (2001) *Psychology in Practice: Crime* (2nd edn). London: Hodder & Stoughton.

Hart, J. & Helms, J. (2003) Factors of parricide: allowance of the use of battered child syndrome as a defense. *Aggression and Violent Behavior*, **8**(6): 671–683.

Hathaway, M. (2009) The moral significance of the insanity defence. *Journal of Criminal Law*, **73**(4): 310–317.

Haworth, K. (2006) The dynamics of power and resistance in police interview discourse. *Discourse & Society*, **17**(6): 739–759.

Haywood, T.W., Kravitz, H.M., Wasyliw, O.E., Goldberg, J. & Cavanaugh, J.L. (1996) Cycle of abuse and psychopathology in cleric and noncleric molesters of children and adolescents. *Child Abuse & Neglect*, **20**(12): 1233–1243.

Heide, K. (1992) *Why Kids Kill Parents.* Columbus, OH: Ohio State University Press.

Heller, J. (2009) The cognitive psychology of *mens rea. Journal of Criminal Law and Criminology*, **99**(2): 317–380.

Hellman, D.S. & Blackman, N. (1966) Enuresis, firesetting and cruelty to animals: a triad predictive of adult crime. *American Journal of Psychiatry*, **262**: 1431–1435.

Hemphill, R.E. & Zabow, T. (1983) Clinical vampirism: a presentation of three cases and a re-evaluation of Haigh, the 'acid-bath murderer'. *South Africa Medical Journal*, **63**(19 February): 278–281.

Herndon, J. (2007) The image of profiling: media treatment and general impressions. In R.N. Kocsis (ed.), *Criminal Profiling: International Theory, Research, and Practice.* New York: Humana Press.

Hershkowitz, I. (2011) The effects of abuse history on sexually intrusive behavior by children: an analysis of child justice records. *Child Abuse & Neglect*, **35**(1): 40–49.

Heuer, L. & Penrod, S. (1994) Juror notetaking and question asking during trials. *Law and Human Behavior*, **18**(2): 121–150.

Heuer, L. & Penrod, S. (1995) Increasing juror participation in trials through note taking and question asking. *Judicature*, **79**: 256.

Hickey, E. (2001) *Serial Murderers and their Victims* (3rd edn). Belmont, CA: Wadsworth.

Higgins, G., Piquero, N. & Piquero, A. (2010) General strain theory, peer rejection, and delinquency/crime. *Youth & Society*, **36**(2): 123–155.

Hill, A., Habermann, N., Berner, W. & Briken, P. (2007) Psychiatric disorders in single and multiple sexual murderers. *Psychopathology*, **40**: 22–28.

Hirschi, T. & Gottfredson, M.R. (1995) Control theory and the life-course perspective. *Studies on Crime & Crime Prevention*, **4**(2): 131–142.

HMIC & HMCPSI (Her Majesty's Inspectorate of Constabulary & Her Majesty's Crown Prosecution Service Inspectorate) (2007) *Without Consent: A Report on the Joint Review of the Investigation and Prosecution of Rape Offences*. London: HMIC.

HMIP (Her Majesty's Inspectorate of Prisons) (2002) *HM Chief Inspector of Prisons for England and Wales Annual Report 2001–2*. London: HMSO.

HMIP (Her Majesty's Inspectorate of Prisons) (2012) *HM Chief Inspector of Prisons for England and Wales Annual Report 2011–12*. London: HMSO.

Hoertel, N., Dubertret, C., Schuster, J.P. & Le Strat, Y. (2012) Sex differences in shoplifting: results from a national sample. *Journal of Nervous and Mental Disease*, **200**(8): 728–733.

Hoffman, B. (2003) *The Logic of Suicide Terrorism*. RAND.

Hoffman, B. (2009) Radicalization and subversion: Al Qaeda and the 7 July 2005 bombings and the 2006 airline bombing plot. *Studies in Conflict & Terrorism*, **32**(12): 1100–1116.

Home Office (1992) *Memorandum of Good Practice on Video Recorded Interviews with Child Witnesses for Criminal Proceedings*. London: HMSO.

Home Office (2000) *What Works: First Report from the Joint Prison/Probation Accreditation Panel, 1999–2000*. London: HMSO.

Home Office (2009) *British Crime Survey Reports* London: Home Office, www.homeoffice.gov.uk/rds/bcs-methodological.html (retrieved 10.2.12).

Home Office (2012) *Policy Paper: PACE Code C requirements for the detention, treatment and questioning of suspects not related to terrorism in police custody*. https://www.gov.uk/government/publications/pace–code–c–2012 (retrieved 1.3.13).

Hope, L. & Wright, D. (2007) Beyond unusual? Examining the role of attention in the weapon focus effect. *Applied Cognitive Psychology*, **21**(7): 951–961.

Horgan, J. (2005) The social and psychological characteristics of terrorism and terrorists. In T. Bjørgo (ed.), *Root Causes of Terrorism: Myths, Reality, and Ways Forward*. London: Routledge.

Horgan, J. (2008) From profiles to pathways and roots to routes: perspectives from psychology on radicalization into terrorism. *Annals of the American Academy of Political and Social Science*, **618**(1): 80–94.

Horgan, J. (2009) *Walking Away from Terrorism: Accounts of Disengagement from Radical and Extremist Movements*. London: Routledge.

Horley, J. & Bowlby, D. (2011) Theory, research, and intervention with arsonists. *Aggression and Violent Behavior*, **16**(3): 241–249.

Houck, M.M., Crispino, F. & McAdam, T. (2012) *The Science of Crime Scenes*. Oxford: Academic Press.

Howe, S. (1983) *Defenestration of Prague*. New York: Kulchur Foundation.

Howitt, D. (2002) *Forensic and Criminal Psychology*. Englewood Cliffs, NJ: Prentice-Hall.

Howitt, D. & Cumberbatch, G. (1990) *Pornography: Impacts and Influences*. London: Home Office Research and Planning Unit.

Hughes, M., Bain, S.A., Gilchrist, E. & Boyle, J. (2012) Does providing a written version of the police caution improve comprehension in the general population? *Psychology, Crime & Law*, **19**(7): 1–16.

Humber, N., Piper, M., Appleby, L. & Shaw, J. (2011) Characteristics of and trends in subgroups of prisoner suicides in England and Wales. *Psychological Medicine*, **41**(11): 2275.

Husain, S. (ed.) (2006) *Voices of Resistance: Muslim Women on War, Faith, and Sexuality*. Emeryville, CA: Seal Press.

Hussain, Y. & Bagguley, P. (2013) Funny looks: British Pakistanis' experiences after 7 July 2005. *Ethnic and Racial Studies*, **36**(1): 28–46.

Iacono, W. (2001) Forensic 'lie detection': procedures without scientific basis. *Journal of Forensic Psychology Practice*, **1**(1): 75–86.

International Maritime Organisation (2013) Piracy and armed robbery against ships. http://www.imo.org/OurWork/Security/PiracyArmedRobbery/Pages/Default.aspx (retrieved 1.7.13).

Janis, I.L. (1982) *Groupthink: Psychological Studies of Policy Decisions and Fiascos*. New York: Houghton Mifflin.

Jehle, J.M. (2012) Attrition and conviction rates of sexual offences in Europe: definitions and criminal justice responses. *European Journal on Criminal Policy and Research*, **18**(1): 1–17.

Johnson, R.R. & Morgan, M.A. (2013) Suspicion formation among police officers: an international literature review. *Criminal Justice Studies*, **26**(1): 99–114.

Johnson, T.C. (1988) Child perpetrators – children who molest other children: preliminary findings. *Child Abuse & Neglect*, **12**(2): 219–229.

Johnston, V.S., Hagel, R., Franklin, M., Fink, B. & Grammer, K. (2001) Male facial attractiveness: evidence for hormone-mediated adaptive design. *Evolution and Human Behavior*, **22**(4): 251–267.

Jones, O.D. (2006) Behavioral genetics and crime, in context. *Law and Contemporary Problems*, **69**(1/2): 81–100.

Joyal, C., Black, D. & Dassylva, B. (2007) The neuropsychology and neurology of sexual deviance: a review and pilot study. *Sexual Abuse: A Journal of Research and Treatment*, **19**(2): 155–173.

Kanwisher, N. & Yovel, G. (2006) The fusiform face area: a cortical region specialized for the perception of faces. *Philosophical Transactions of the Royal Society B: Biological Sciences*, **361**(1476): 2109–2128.

Kassin, S.M. (2012) Why confessions trump innocence. *American Psychologist*, **67**(6): 431.

Kassin, S.M., Drizin, S.A., Grisso, T., Gudjonsson, G.H., Leo, R.A. & Redlich, A.D. (2010) Police-induced confessions. *Law and Human Behavior*, **34**(1): 3–38.

Kassin, S.M., Goldstein, C.C. & Savitsky, K. (2003) Behavioral confirmation in the interrogation room: On the dangers of presuming guilt. *Law and Human Behavior*, **27**(2): 187–203.

Kaufmann, P.M. (2009) Protecting raw data and psychological tests from wrongful disclosure: a primer on the law and other persuasive strategies. *Clinical Neuropsychology*, **23**: 1130–1159.

Keane, A. (2012) Cross-examination of vulnerable witnesses: towards a blueprint for re-professionalisation. *International Journal of Evidence & Proof*, **16**(2): 175–198.

Kellogg, N. (2009) Clinical report: the evaluation of sexual behaviors in children. *Pediatrics*, **124**(3), September.

Kelly, L., Temkin, J. & Griffiths, S. (2006) *Section 41: An Evaluation of New Legislation Limiting Sexual History Evidence in Rape Trials*. Home Office Online Report 20/06. London: Home Office.

Kempe, C.H., Silverman, F.N., Steele, B.F., Droegemueller, W. & Silver, H.K. (1962). The battered-child syndrome. In C.H. Kempe (ed.) (2013) *A Fifty-Year Legacy to the Field of Child Abuse & Neglect*. Springer Netherlands, pp. 23–38.

Kendell, R.E. (2002) The distinction between personality disorder and mental illness. *British Journal of Psychiatry*, **180**(2): 110–115.

Kennedy, D. (1994) *On a Killing Day*. New York: SPI Books.

Kennedy, F., Hoffman, H. & Haines, W. (1947) A study of William Heirens. *American Journal of Psychiatry*, **104**: 113–121.

Kennedy, H. (1993) *Eve was Framed: Women and Criminal Justice*. London: Vintage.

Keppel, R. (2005) Serial offenders: linking cases by *modus operandi* and signature. In S. James & J. Nordby (eds), *Forensic Science* (2nd edn). Boca Raton, FL: CRC Press.

Keppel, R.D. & Birnes, W.J. (1997) *Signature Killers: Interpreting the Calling Cards of the Serial Murderer*. New York: Pocket Books, pp. 108–113.

Keppel, R., Birnes, W.J. & Rule, A. (2004) *The Riverman: Ted Bundy and I Hunt for the Green River Killer.* New York: Pocket.

Keppel, R.D., Weis, J.G., Brown, K.M. & Welch, K. (2005) The Jack the Ripper murders: a *modus operandi* and signature analysis of the 1888–1891 Whitechapel murders. *Journal of Investigative Psychology and Offender Profiling*, **2**: 1–21.

Kester, L. & Gottlieb, D. (2012) *Dear Dawn: Aileen Wuornos in Her Own Words, 1991–2002.* Berkeley, CA: Soft Skull Press.

Kfir, N. (2002) Understanding suicidal terror through humanistic and existential psychology. *Psychology of Terrorism*, **1**: 143–157.

Khanom, H., Samele, C. & Rutherford, M. (2009) *A Missed Opportunity?* London: Sainsbury Centre for Mental Health.

Kiehl, K., Smith, A., Hare, R., Mendrek, A., Forster, B., Brink, J. & Liddle, P. (2001) Limbic abnormalities in affective processing by criminal psychopaths as revealed by functional magnetic resonance imaging. *Biological Psychiatry*, **50**(9): 677–684.

Kim, Y., Barak, G. & Shelton, D. (2009) Examining the 'CSI-effect' in the cases of circumstantial evidence and eyewitness testimony: multivariate and path analyses. *Journal of Criminal Justice*, **37**(5): 452–460.

Kimmel, M. (2007) *The Sexual Self: The Construction of Sexual Scripts.* Nashville, TN: Vanderbilt University Press.

Klemke, L.W. (1992) *The Sociology of Shoplifting: Boosters and Snitches Today.* Westport, CT: Praeger.

Knoll IV, J.L. (2009) The psychological autopsy, part II: toward a standardized protocol. *Journal of Psychiatric Practice*, **15**(1): 52–59.

Knoll, J.L. (2010a) The 'pseudocommando' mass murderer: Part I, the psychology of revenge and obliteration. *Journal of the American Academy of Psychiatry and the Law Online*, **38**(1): 87–94.

Knoll, J.L. (2010b) The 'pseudocommando' mass murderer: Part II, the language of revenge. *Journal of the American Academy of Psychiatry and the Law Online*, **38**(2): 263–272.

Kocsis, R.N. (2004) Psychological profiling of serial arson offenses an assessment of skills and accuracy. *Criminal Justice and Behavior*, **31**(3): 341–361.

Kocsis, R. (2006) Canter's investigative psychology validities and abilities in criminal profiling: the dilemma for David. *International Journal of Offender Therapy & Comparative Criminology*, **50**: 458–477.

Kocsis, R., Midldedorp, J. & Karpon, A. (2008) Taking stock of accuracy in criminal profiling: the theoretical quandary for investigative psychology. *Journal of Forensic Psychology Practice*, **8**(3): 244–261.

Koenraadt, F. (2010) Patterns of arson, In M. Herzog-Evans (ed.), *Transnational Criminology Manual.* Nijmegen: Wolf Legal Publishers, volume 2, chapter 5, pp. 91–100.

Kolko, D.J. & Kazdin, A.E. (1994) Children's descriptions of their firesetting incidents: characteristics and relationship to recidivism. *Journal of the American Academy of Child & Adolescent Psychiatry*, **33**(1): 114–122.

Konradi, A. (1999) 'I don't have to be afraid of you': rape survivors' emotion management in court. *Symbolic Interaction*, **22**: 45–77.

Konradi, A. (2010) Creating victim-centered criminal justice practices for rape prosecution. *Research in Social Problems and Public Policy*, **17**: 43–76.

Kosson, D.S., Lorenz, A.R. & Newman, J.P. (2006) Effects of comorbid psychopathy on criminal offending and emotion processing in male offenders with antisocial personality disorder. *Journal of Abnormal Psychology*, **115**(4): 798.

Krahé, B., Scheinberger-Olwig, R. & Bieneck, S. (2003) Men's reports of nonconsensual sexual interactions with women: prevalence and impact. *Archives of Sexual Behavior*, **32**(2), April: 165–175.

Krähenbühl, S. (2011) Effective and appropriate communication with children in legal proceedings according to lawyers and intermediaries. *Child Abuse Review*, **20**(6): 407–420.

Krambia-Kapardis, M. (2001*) Enhancing the Auditor's Fraud Detection Ability*. New York: Peter Lang.

Kramer, G. & Koening, D. (1990) Do jurors understand criminal jury instructions? Analyzing the results of the Michigan juror comprehension project. *University of Michigan Journal of Law Reform*, **23**: 401–437.

Krasnovsky, T. & Lane, R.C. (1998) Shoplifting: a review of the literature. *Aggression and Violent Behavior*, **3**(3): 219–235.

Krouse, W.J. (2004) *The Multi-state Anti-terrorism Information Exchange (MATRIX) Pilot Project*. Washington, DC: Library of Congress, Congressional Research Service.

Kruglanski, A.W. & Fishman, S. (2006) The psychology of terrorism: 'syndrome' versus 'tool' perspectives. *Terrorism and Political Violence*, **18**(2): 193–215.

LaBrode, R. (2007) Etiology of the psychopathic serial killer: an analysis of antisocial personality disorder, psychopathy, and serial killer personality and crime scene characteristics. *Brief Treatment and Crisis Intervention*, **7**(2):151–160.

Lachman, M.E. & Andreoletti, C. (2006) Strategy use mediates the relationship between control beliefs and memory performance for middle-aged and older adults. *Journals of Gerontology Series B: Psychological Sciences and Social Sciences*, **61**(2): 88–94.

LaFon, D. & Dvoskin, J. (2007) *Psychological Autopsies: Science and Practice*. New York: Taylor & Francis.

Lalumière, M.L., Harris, G.T. & Rice, M.E. (2001) Psychopathy and developmental instability. *Evolution and Human Behavior*, **22**: 75–92.

Lambert, S. & O'Halloran, E. (2008) Deductive thematic analysis of a female paedophilia website. *Psychiatry, Psychology and Law*, **15**(2): 284–300.

Lamontagne, Y., Boyer, R., Hétu, C. & Lacerte-Lamontagne, C. (2000) Anxiety, significant losses, depression and irrational beliefs in first-offence shoplifters. *Canadian Journal of Psychiatry*, **45**(1): 63–6.

Lane, J.D., Wellman, H.M., Olson, S.L., LaBounty, J. & Kerr, D.C. (2010) Theory of mind and emotion understanding predict moral development in early childhood. *British Journal of Developmental Psychology*, **28**(4): 871–889.

Langleben, D.D. (2008) Detection of deception with fMRI: are we there yet? *Legal and Criminological Psychology*, **13**(1): 1–9.

Langleben, D. & Moriarty, J. (2012) Using brain imaging for lie detection: where science, law, and policy collide. *Psychology, Public Policy, and Law*, 17 September (no pagination specified).

Langton, L. & Piquero, N. (2007) Can general strain theory explain white-collar crime? A preliminary investigation of the relationship between strain and select white-collar offenses. *Journal of Criminal Justice*, **35**(1), January–February: 1–15.

Lanning, K. (2001) *Child Molesters: A Behavioral Analysis for Law-Enforcement Officers Investigating the Sexual Exploitation of Children by Acquaintance Molesters* (4th edn). New York: National Center for Missing & Exploited Children.

Lassieur, A. (2000). *Serial Killers*. New York: Lucent Books.

Lawson, C. (2002) *Understanding the Borderline Mother: Helping Her Children Transcend the Intense, Unpredictable, and Volatile Relationship*. New York: Jason Aronson.

Lee, C. & Waters, N. (2011) *A Verdict on the Reporters: The Representativeness and Accuracy of Commercially Published Jury Verdict Reports*. Paper presented at the Conference on Empirical Legal Studies, Nov. 2011.

Leeners, B., Richter-Appelt, H., Imthurn, B. & Rath, W. (2006) The influence of childhood sexual abuse on pregnancy, delivery, and the early postpartum period in adult women. *Journal of Psychosomatic Research*, **61**(2): 139–151.

Lennox, C., Senior, J., King, C., Hassana, L., Clayton, R., Thornicroft, G. & Shaw, J. (2012) The management of released prisoners with severe and enduring mental illness. *Journal of Forensic Psychiatry & Psychology*, **23**(1): 67–75.

Lenz, T. & MagShamhráin, R. (2012) Inventing diseases: kleptomania, agoraphobia and resistance to modernity. *Society*, **49**(3): 279–283.

Leppard, D. (2007) Met to charge Robert Napper for Rachel Nickell murder. *The Sunday Times*, 18 November.

Leschied, A., Cummings, A., Van Brunschot, M., Cunningham, A. & Saunders, A. (2000) *Female Adolescent Aggression: A Review of the Literature and the Correlates of Aggression* (User Report No. 2000–04). Ottawa: Solicitor General Canada.

Lester, D., Yang, B. & Lindsay, M. (2004) Suicide bombers: are psychological profiles possible? *Studies in Conflict & Terrorism*, **4**(2): 283– 295.

Levanon, L. (2012) Sexual history evidence in cases of sexual assault: a critical reevaluation. *University of Toronto Law Journal*, **62**(4): 609–651.

Levin, R. & van Berlo, W. (2004) Sexual arousal and orgasm in subjects who experience forced or non-consensual sexual stimulation: a review. *Journal of Clinical Forensic Medicine*, **11**(2): 82–88.

Lewis, C., Mitchell, D. & Rugeley, C. (2005) Courting public opinion: utilizing jury pools in experimental research. Poster presented at the Political Methodology Conference, Tallahassee, FL.

Lewis, J.L., Simcox, A.M. & Berry, D.T. (2002) Screening for feigned psychiatric symptoms in a forensic sample by using the MMPI-2 and the Structured Inventory of Malingered Symptomatology. *Psychological Assessment*, **14**(2): 170.

Lewis, N.D.C. & Yarnell, H. (1951) *Pathological Firesetting: Pyromania (No. 82). Nervous and Mental Disease Monographs*. New York: Coolidge Foundation.

Lifton, R. (2000) *Destroying the World to Save It: Aum Shinrikyo and the New Global Terrorism*. New York: Holt.

Lilienfeld, S.O. & Andrews, B.P. (1996) Development and preliminary validation of a self-report measure of psychopathic personality traits in the noncriminal population. *Journal of Personality Assessment*, **66**(3): 488–524.

Lilienfield, S.O. & Widows, M.R. (2005) *Psychological Assessment Inventory Revised (PPI–R)*. Lutz, FL: Psychological Assessment Resources.

Lim, S., Seligson, A., Parvez, F., Luther, C., Mavinkurve, M., Binswanger, I. & Kerker, B. (2012) Risks of drug-related death, suicide, and homicide during the immediate post-release period among people released from New York City jails, 2001–2005. *American Journal of Epidemiology*, **175**(6): 519–526.

Loftus, E.F. (1974) Reconstructing memory: the incredible eyewitness. *Jurimetrics Journal*, **15**: 188.

Loftus, E.F. (1975) Leading questions and the eyewitness report. *Cognitive Psychology*, **7**(4): 560–572.

Loftus, E. (1997) Creating false memories. *Scientific American*, **277**: 70–75.

Loftus, E.F. & Palmer, J.C. (1974) Reconstruction of automobile destruction: an example of the interaction between language and memory. *Journal of Verbal Learning and Verbal Behaviour*, **13**: 585–589.

Lombroso, C. (1876) *L'uomo delinquent*. Milan: Hoepli (reprinted, Rome: Napoleone Editore, 1971). Translated as *Criminal Man*. New York: Putnam, 1911 (reprinted, Montclair, NJ: Patterson Smith, 1972).

Lopez, V. (2008) Understanding adolescent property crime using a delinquent events perspective. *Deviant Behavior*, **29**(7): 581–610.

Loughnan, A. (2005) The defence of diminished responsibility in England and Wales. Paper presented at the annual meeting of the American Society of Criminology, Royal York, Toronto, 15 November.

Luby, J.L., Reich, W. & Earls, F. (1995) Failure to detect signs of psychological distress in the preschool children of alcoholic parents. *Journal of Child & Adolescent Substance Abuse*, **4**(2): 77–89.

Lurigio, A.J. (2011) People with serious mental illness in the criminal justice system causes, consequences, and correctives. *The Prison Journal*, **91**(3 suppl): 66S–86S.

Lustgarten, E. (1968) *The Business of Murder*. New York: Scribner.

Lybrand, S., Dobson, J. & Solomon, S. (nd) *Jury Think ™ The Social Psychology of Group Deliberation*. Lynbrook, NY: Doar. http://www.doar.com/marketing/web/jurythink.pdf (retrieved 30.7.13).

Lyden, M. (2007) Assessment of sexual consent capacity. *Sexuality and Disability*, **25**(1): 3–20.

Lykken, D. (1995) *The Antisocial Personalities*. Mahwah, NJ: Lawrence Erlbaum Associates.

MacDonald, J.M. (1963). The threat to kill. *American Journal of Psychiatry*, **120**(2): 125–130.

MacKay, J. (2001) Global sex: sexuality and sexual practices around the world. *Sexual and Relationship Therapy*, **16**(1), February: 71–82.

MacKay, S. Henderson, J. Del Bove, G., Marton, P., Warling, D. & Root, C. (2006) Fire interest and antisociality as risk factors in the severity and persistence of juvenile firesetting. *Journal of the American Academy of Child and Adolescent Psychiatry*, **45**: 1077–1084.

MacKenzie, D.L., Robinson, J.W. & Campbell, C.S. (1989) Long-term incarceration of female offenders: prison adjustment and coping. *Criminal Justice and Behavior*, **16**(2): 223–238.

Malamuth, N.M. (1996) Sexually explicit media, gender differences, and evolutionary theory. *Journal of Communication*, **46**(3): 8–31.

Malby, S., Davis, P., United Nations Office on Drugs and Crime, Vienna International Ctr & Austria (2012) *Monitoring the Impact of Economic Crisis on Crime*. New York: United Nations.

Mandel, D.R. (2010) Radicalization: What does it mean? In T. Pick, A. Speckhard & B. Jacuch *Home-grown Terrorism: Understanding and addressing the root causes of radicalisation among groups with an immigrant heritage in Europe*. Amsterdam and Fairfax, VA: IOS Press, pp. 101–113.

Margulies, P. (1983) The pandemonium between the mad and the bad: procedures for the commitment and release of insanity acquittees after *Jones v. United States*. *Rutgers Law Review*, **36**: 793.

Markson, L., Woodhams, J. & Bond, J.W. (2010) Linking serial residential burglary: comparing the utility of *modus operandi* behaviours, geographical proximity, and temporal proximity. *Journal of Investigative Psychology and Offender Profiling*, **7**: 91–107.

Marshall, W.L. & Kennedy, P. (2003) Sexual sadism in sexual offenders: an elusive diagnosis. *Aggression and Violent Behaviour*, **8**(1): 1–22.

Martens, W.H. (2004) The terrorist with antisocial personality disorder. *Journal of Forensic Psychology Practice*, **4**(1): 45–56.

Martin, E., Taft, C. & Resick, P. (2007) A review of marital rape. *Aggression and Violent Behavior*, **12**(3): 329–347.

Masters, B. (1993) *Killing for Company: The Story of a Man Addicted to Murder*. New York: Random House.

Masson, H., Hackett, S., Phillips, J. & Balfe, M. (2013) Developmental markers of risk or vulnerability? Young females who sexually abuse – characteristics, backgrounds, behaviours and outcomes. *Child & Family Social Work*. In press

McAree, D. (2004) Reaching out to juries rocked by evidence. *National Law Journal*, **26**: 4.

McBride-Chang, C., Jacklin, C. & Reynolds, C. (1992) Mother-blaming, psychology and the law. *Southern California Law Review & Women's Studies*, **1**: 69–78.

McCauley, C. & Moskalenko, S. (2008) Mechanisms of political radicalization: pathways toward terrorism. *Terrorism and Political Violence*, **20**(3): 415–433.

McKee, A. (2007) 'Saying you've been at dad's porn book is part of growing up': youth, pornography and education. *Metro Magazine*, **155**: 118–122.

McLellan, J. (2010) *Erotophonophilia: Investigating Lust Murder*. New York: Cambria Press.

McLeod, R., Philpin, C., Sweeting, A., Joyce, L. & Evans, R. (2010) *Court Experience of Adults with Mental Health Conditions, Learning Disabilities and Limited Mental Capacity*. Ministry of Justice Research Series 9/10. London: Ministry of Justice.

McMurtrie, H., Baxter, J.S., Obonsawin, M.C. & Hunter, S.C. (2012) Consistent witness responses: the effects of age and negative feedback. *Personality and Individual Differences*, **53**(8): 958–962.

McSherry, B. (2003) Voluntariness, intention, and the defence of mental disorder: toward a rational approach. *Behavioral Sciences and the Law*, **21**: 581–599.

McWilliams, N. (1994) *Psychoanalytic Diagnosis: Understanding Personality Structure in the Clinical Process*. New York: Guilford Press.

Mealey, L. & Kinner, S. (1996) The perception–action model of empathy and psychopathic 'cold-heartedness'. *Behavioral and Brain Sciences*, **25**(1): 42–43.

Medico-Legal (1949) Medical evidence at the Haigh trial. *British Medical Journal*, **2**(4621), 30 July: 286–291.

Medler, M. (2011) Speculations about the effects of fire and lava flows on human evolution. *Fire Ecology*, **7**(1): 13–23.

Meeus, W., Branje, S. & Overbeek, G.J. (2004) Parents and partners in crime: a six-year longitudinal study on changes in supportive relationships and delinquency in adolescence and young adulthood. *Journal of Child Psychology and Psychiatry*, **45**: 1288–1298.

Megreya, A.M. & Burton, A.M. (2008) Matching faces to photographs: poor performance in eyewitness memory (without the memory). *Journal of Experimental Psychology: Applied*, **14**(4): 364.

Mehra, B. (2002) Bias in qualitative research: voices from an online classroom. *The Qualitative Report*, **7**(1): 1–17.

Mehta, P. & Beer, J. (2010) Neural mechanisms of the testosterone–aggression relation: the role of orbitofrontal cortex. *Journal of Cognitive Neuroscience*, **22**(10), October: 2357–2368.

Meloy, J.R. (2000) The nature and dynamics of sexual homicide: an integrative review. *Aggression and Violent Behavior*, **5**: 1–22.

Memon, A. (2006) The cognitive interview. In O. Hargie (ed.), *The Handbook of Communication Skills* (3rd edn). New York: Routledge, pp. 531–550.

Memon, A., Meissner, C.A. & Fraser, J. (2010) The cognitive interview: a meta-analytic review and study space analysis of the past 25 years. *Psychology, Public Policy, and Law*, **16**(4): 340.

Mental Health Foundation (2013) *Mental Health Statistics: UK & Worldwide*. http://www.mentalhealth.org.uk/help–information/mental–health–statistics/UKworldwide/ (retrieved 1.3.13).

Merrington, S. & Stanley, S. (2000) Doubts about the What Works initiative. *Probation Journal*, **47**(3): 272–275.

Merton, R. (1938) Social structure and anomie. *American Sociological Review*, **3**(5): 672–682.

Messing, J.T. & Heeren, J.W. (2004) Another side of multiple murder: women killers in the domestic context. *Homicide Studies*, **8**(2): 123–158.

Metropolitan Police (2012) *History of the Metropolitan Police*. London: Mayor's Office for Policing and Crime, www.met.police.uk/history/krays.htm (retrieved 1.11.12).

Metzner, J. & Fellner, J. (2010) Solitary confinement and mental illness in US prisons: a challenge for medical ethics. *Journal of the American Academy of Psychiatry Law*, **38**(1): 104–108.

Michaud, S.G. & Aynesworth, H. (2000) *Ted Bundy: Conversations with a Killer*. Irving, TX: Authorlink Press.

Milne, B. & Powell, M. (2007) Investigative interviewing. In B. Milne & M. Powell (eds), *The Cambridge Handbook of Forensic Psychology*. Cambridge: Cambridge University Press, pp. 208–214.

Milne, R. & Bull, R. (1999) *Investigative Interviewing: Psychology and Practice*. Chichester: Wiley.

Milne, R., Shaw, G. & Smith, K. (2009) *Achieving Best Evidence in Criminal Proceedings: Guidance on Interviewing Victims and Witnesses, and Using Special Measures*. London: Crown Prosecution Service.

Ministry of Justice (2012) *Statistics on Women and the Criminal Justice System*. London: Ministry of Justice.

Moghaddam, F. (2005) The staircase to terrorism: a psychological exploration. *American Psychologist*, **60**(2), February–March: 161–169.

Molnar, B.E., Buka, S.L. & Kessler, R.C. (2001) Child sexual abuse and subsequent psychopathology: results from the National Comorbidity Survey. *American Journal of Public Health*, **91**(5): 753.

Money, J. (1986) *Lovemaps: Clinical Concepts of Sexual/Erotic Health and Pathology, Paraphilia, and Gender Transposition in Childhood, Adolescence, and Maturity*. New York: Irvington.

Monroe, K. (2008) Cracking the code of genocide: the moral psychology of rescuers, bystanders, and Nazis during the Holocaust. *Political Psychology*, **29**(5): 699–736.

Moore, R.H. (1984) Shoplifting in middle America: patterns and motivational correlates. *International Journal of Offender Therapy and Comparative Criminology*, **28**(1): 53–64.

Morf, G. (1970) *Terror in Quebec: Case Studies of the FLQ*. Toronto and Vancouver: Clarke, Irwin.

Morris, C. (2010) Peacekeeping and the sexual exploitation of women and girls in post-conflict societies: a serious enigma to establishing the rule of law. *Journal of International Peacekeeping*, **14**(1–2), February: 184–212.

Morris, G. (2002) Commentary: punishing the unpunishable – the abuse of psychiatry to confine those we love to hate. *Journal of the American Academy of Psychiatry and the Law*, **30**: 556–562.

Mossman, D. (2003) Atkins v. Virginia: a psychiatric can of worms. *N.M. L. Review*, **33**: 255.

Muetzelfeldt, L., Kamboj, S.K., Rees, H., Taylor, J., Morgan, C.J.A. & Curran, H.V. (2008) Journey through the K-hole: phenomenological aspects of ketamine use. *Drug and Alcohol Dependence*, **95**(3): 219–229.

Munsterberg, H. (1908) *On the Witness Stand: Essays on Psychology and Crime*. New York: Doubleday, Page & Co.

Myers, M., Husted, D., Safarik, M. & O'Toole, M. (2006) The motivation behind serial sexual homicide: is it sex, power, and control, or anger? *Journal of Forensic Sciences*, **51**: 900–907.

Myers, W.C., Reccoppa, L., Burton, K. & McElroy, R. (1993) Malignant sex and aggression: an overview of serial sexual homicide. *Journal of the American Academy of Psychiatry and the Law Online*, **21**(4): 435–451.

National Centre for Policing Excellence (2006) *The Safer Detention & Handling of Persons in Police Custody*. London: Home Office/ACPO (Association of Chief Police Officers).

National Mental Health Association (2005) *Fact Sheet: Mental Health and Adolescent Girls in the Justice System*. Washington, DC: NMHA.

Neale, J., Robertson, M. & Saville, E. (2005) Understanding the treatment needs of drug users in prison. *Probation Journal*, **52**(3): 243–257.

Neapolitan, J.L. (2001) An examination of cross-national variation in punitiveness. *International Journal of Offender Therapy and Comparative Criminology*, **45**(6): 691–710.

Nee, C. & Meenaghan, A. (2006) Expert decision making in burglars. *British Journal of Criminology*, **46**(5): 935–949.

Nelson, R.J. & Trainor, B.C. (2007) Neural mechanisms of aggression. *Nature Reviews Neuroscience*, **8**(7): 536–546.

Nettler, G. (1982) *Lying, Cheating, Stealing* (Vol. 3). New York: Anderson Publishing Company.

Nock, M.K. (2010) Self-injury. *Annual Review of Clinical Psychology*, **6**: 339–363.

Norris, J. (1988) *Serial Killers*. New York: Doubleday.

NSPCC (2010) *Sexual Behaviour of Children: What Is Normal, Worrying or Abusive*? NSPCC Factsheet. London: NSPCC, www.nspcc.org.uk (retrieved 1.6.11).

Nydell, M.K. (2005) *Understanding Arabs: A Guide for Westerners. A Guide for Modern times.* Boston, MA: Intercultural Press.

O'Hearn, D. (2009) Repression and solidarity cultures of resistance: Irish political prisoners on protest. *American Journal of Sociology*, **115**(2), September: 491–526.

O'Neill, D. (2008) A Mormon, a beauty queen and manacles.... *South Wales Echo*, 29 January, www.walesonline.co.uk/news/columnists/2008/01/29/a-mormon-a-beauty-queen-and-manacles-91466-20404168/ (retrieved 20.4.10).

Odgers, C.L. & Moretti, M.M. (2002) Aggressive and antisocial girls: research update and challenges. *International Journal of Forensic Mental Health*, **1**: 103–119.

Odinot, G., Wolters, G. & van Giezen, A. (2012) Accuracy, confidence and consistency in repeated recall of events. *Psychology, Crime & Law*, **18**: 1–14.

Office for National Statistics (2011) *Families and Households*. London: ONS, www.statistics.gov.uk (released April 2011).

Ones, D.S., Viswesvaran, C. & Schmidt, F.L. (1993) Comprehensive meta-analysis of integrity test validities: findings and implications for personnel selection and theories of job performance. *Journal of Applied Psychology*, **78**(4): 679.

Ones, D.S., Viswesvaran, C. & Schmidt, F. L. (1995) Integrity tests: overlooked facts, resolved issues, and remaining questions. *American Psychologist*, **50**(6): 456–457.

OPSI (2003) *Sexual Offences Act 2003*. London: Office of Public Sector Information. Available at: www. opsi.gov.uk/acts/acts2003 (retrieved 21.1.10).

Ormerod, D. (2008) *Smith and Hogan Criminal Law* (12th edn). Oxford: Oxford University Press.

Osborough, N. (1975) *Borstal in Ireland: Custodial Provision for the Young Adult Offender 1906–1974*. Dublin: Institute of Public Administration.

Osterburg, J.W. & Ward, R.H. (2010) *Criminal Investigation: A Method for Reconstructing the Past*. London: Elsevier.

Otto, R.K. (2006) Competency to stand trial. *Applied Psychology in Criminal Justice*, **2**(3): 82–113.

Overton, J., Hensley, C. & Tallichet, S. (2012) Examining the relationship between childhood animal cruelty motives and recurrent adult violent crimes toward humans. *Journal of Interpersonal Violence*, **27**(5), March: 899–915.

Pakaluk, M. (2005) *Aristotle's Nicomachean Ethics: An Introduction*. Cambridge and New York: Cambridge University Press.

Palermo, G. & Ross, L. (1999) Mass murder, suicide, and moral development: can we separate the adults from the juveniles? *International Journal of Offender Therapy and Comparative Criminology*, **43**(1): 8–20.

Patkin, T. (2004) Explosive baggage: female Palestinian suicide bombers and the rhetoric of emotion. *Women and Language*, **27**(2): 79–88.

Patton, M.Q. (1980) *Qualitative Evaluation Methods*. Beverly Hills, CA: Sage.

Payne-James, J., Jones, R., Karch, S. & Manlove, J. (2011) *Simpson's Forensic Medicine* (13th edn). London: Hodder.

Peak, K. (1996) 'Things fearful to name': an overview of sex crimes and perversions. *Journal of Contemporary Criminal Justice*, **12**(2), May: 204–214.

Pearlman, D. (2002) Intersubjective dimensions of terrorism and its transcendence. In C. Stout (ed), *The Psychology of Terrorism: A Public Understanding*, Volume 1. Westport, CT: Praeger Publishers.

Pearson, J. (2010) *Notorious: The Immortal Legend of the Kray Twins*. London: Random House.

Peng, Z. & Pounder, D. (1998) Forensic medicine in China. *American Journal of Forensic Medicine and Pathology*, **19**(4), December: 368–371.

Perper, J. & Cina, S. (2010) *When Doctors Kill*. New York: Springer.

Petherick, W. & Turvey, B. (2008) Nomothetic methods of criminal profiling. In B.E. Turvey (ed.), *Criminal Profiling: An Introduction to Behavioral Evidence Analysis* (3rd edn). Burlington, MA: Elsevier Academic Press.

Pezdek, K., Sperry, K. & Owens, S.M. (2007) Interviewing witnesses: the effect of forced confabulation on event memory. *Law and Human Behavior*, **31**(5): 463.

Philbin, T. & Philbin, M. (2009) *The Killer Book of Serial Killers*. Napierville, IL: Sourcebooks Inc.

Pitchford, I. (2001) The origins of violence: is psychopathy an adaptation? *Human Nature Review*, **1**: 28–36.

Pickel, K.L. (2009) The weapon focus effect on memory for female versus male perpetrators. *Memory*, **17**(6): 664–678.

Picken, J. (2012) The coping strategies. Adjustment and well being of male inmates in the prison environment. *Internet Journal of Criminology*, 1–29.

Pitt, D. (1989) Jogger's attackers terrorized at least 9 in 2 hours. *New York Times*, 22 April.

Popper, Karl R. (1959) *The Logic of Scientific Discovery.* London: Hutchinson.

Porporino, F.J. & Fabiano, E.A. (2000) *Theory Manual for Reasoning and Rehabilitation (revised).* Ottawa, Canada: T3 Associates.

Porter, T. (2010) Woman as molester: implications for society. In M. Barrett (ed.) *GrotesqueFemininities: Evil, Women and the Feminine.* Oxford: Inter-Disciplinary Press.

Porter, T. & Gavin, H. (2010) Infanticide and neonaticide: a review of 40 years of research literature on incidence and causes. *Trauma Violence & Abuse*, **11**(July): 99–112.

Post, J. (1998) Terrorist psycho-logic: terrorist behavior as a product of psychological forces. In W. Reich (ed.), *Origins of Terrorism: Psychologies, Ideologies, Theologies, States of Mind.* Washington, DC: Woodrow Wilson Center Press.

Post, J. (2002) 'When hatred is bred in the bone': the social psychology of terrorism. *Annals of the New York Academy of Sciences* Issue: Psychiatric and Neurologic Aspects of War.

Post, J. (2007) *The Mind of the Terrorist: The Psychology of Terrorism from the IRA to Al Qaeda.* New York: Palgrave Macmillan.

Post, J.M. (1984) Notes on a psychodynamic theory of terrorist behavior. *Terrorism* **7**(2): 241–256.

Potter, J. & Wetherell, M. (1987) *Discourse and Social Psychology: Beyond Attitudes and Behaviour.* London: Sage.

Prahlow, J. (2010) *Forensic Pathology for Police, Death Invetigators, Attorneys and Forensic Scientists.* New York: Humana Press.

Prentky, R.A. & Knight, R.A. (2000, November) *Psychopathy Baserates among Subtypes of Sex Offenders.* In 19th Annual Meeting of the Association for the Treatment of Sexual Abusers. San Diego, CA.

Prins, H. (1985) Vampirism: a clinical condition. *British Journal of Psychiatry*, **146**: 666–668.

Prins, H. (1994) Adult fire-raising: law and psychology. *Psychology, Crime and Law*, **1**(4): 271–281.

Proulx, J., Ouimet, M., Boutin, S. & Lussier, P. (2001) La carrière criminelle des agresseurs sexuels [The criminal careers of sexual aggressors]. Paper presented at the International Academy of Law and Mental Health, Montreal, Canada, July.

Pulsford, D., Crumpton, A., Baker, A., Wilkins, T., Wright, K. & Duxbury, J. (2012) Aggression in a high secure hospital: staff and patient attitudes. *Journal of Psychiatric and Mental Health Nursing*, **20**(4): 296–304.

Purcell, C. & Arrigo, B. (2006) *The Psychology of Lust Murder: Paraphilia, Sexual Killing and Serial Homicide.* London: Academic Press.

Purkiss, D. (1996) *Witch in History: Early Modern and Twentieth-Century Representations.* London: Routledge.

Quinsey, V.L. (2002) Evolutionary theory and criminal behaviour. *Legal and Criminological Psychology*, **7**(1): 1–13.

Rae, J.A. (2012) Will it ever be possible to profile the terrorist? *Journal of Terrorism Research*, **3**(2).

Raine, A. (1989) Evoked potentials and psychopathy. *International Journal of Psychophysiology*, **4**: 277–287.

Raine, A. (2008) From genes to brain to antisocial behavior. *Current Directions in Psychological Science*, **17**(5), October: 323–328.

Ramamoorti, S. (2008) The psychology and sociology of fraud: Integrating the behavioural sciences component into fraud and forensic accounting curricula. *Issues in Accounting Education*, **23**(4): 521–533.

RapeCrisis (2012) *Myths and Facts.* www.rapecrisis.org.uk/mythsampfacts2.php (retrieved 1.11.12).

Rawlings, P. (2003) *Policing: A Short History.* Cullompton, UK: Willan Publishing.

Ray, J.B., Solomon, G.S., Doncaster, M.G. & Mellina, R. (1983) First offender adult shoplifters: a preliminary profile. *Journal of Clinical Psychology*, **39**(5): 769–770.

Rebellon, C. (2006) Do adolescents engage in delinquency to attract the social attention of peers? An extension and longitudinal test of the social reinforcement hypothesis. *Journal of Research in Crime and Delinquency*, **43**(4), November: 387–411.

Recupero, P. (2010) The mental status examination in the age of the internet. *Journal of the American Academy of Psychiatry Law*, **38**(1): 15–26.

Redding, R.E., Floyd, M.Y. & Hawk, G.L. (2001) What judges and lawyers think about the testimony of mental health experts: a survey of the courts and bar. *Behavioural Science Law*, **19**: 583–595.

Redlich, A.D. (2010) *False Confessions, False Guilty Pleas: Similarities and Differences. Interrogations and confessions: current research, practice, and policy*. Washington, DC: APA Books.

Reid, J.E. (1947) A revised questioning technique in lie-detection tests. *Journal of Criminal Law and Criminology* (1931–1951), **37**(6): 542–547.

Reid, W. (2006) Sanity evaluations and criminal responsibility. *Applied Psychology in Criminal Justice*, **2**(3): 114–146.

Reilly, B., Rickman, N. & Witt, R. (2012) Robbing banks: crime does pay–but not very much. *Significance*, **9**(3): 17–21.

Reiner, R. (2010) *The Politics of the Police* (4th edn). Oxford: Oxford University Press.

Reinhardt, J.M. (1962) *The Psychology of Strange Killers*. Springfield, IL: Charles C. Thomas Publisher Limited.

Ressler, R.K., Burgess, A.W. & Douglas, J. (1988) *Sexual Homicide: Patterns and Motives*. Lexington, MA: Lexington Books.

Ressler, R.K. & Schachtman, T. (1993) *Whoever Fights Monsters: My Twenty Years Tracking Serial Killers for the FBI*. New York: Macmillan/St. Martin's Press.

Reuters (2009a) Jilted student stabbed schoolgirl to death. *Reuters News Agency*, http://uk.reuters.com/article/idUKTRE54J3NL20090520 (retrieved 22.1.10).

Reuters (2009b) Madoff mysteries remain as he nears guilty plea. *Reuters News Agency*, www.reuters.com/article/2009/03/11/madoff (retrieved 1.11.12).

Rhodes, L. (2004) *Total Confinement: Madness and Reason in the Maximum Security Prison*. Berkeley, CA: University of California Press.

Rhue, J.W. & Lynn, S.J. (1987) Fantasy proneness and psychopathology. *Journal of Personality and Social Psychology*, **53**(2): 327.

Rich, J., Wakeman, S. & Dickman, S. (2011) Medicine and the epidemic of incarceration in the USA. *New England Journal of Medicine*, **364**: 2081–2083.

Riddle, E.M. (1927) Stealing as a form of aggressive behavior. *Journal of Abnormal and Social Psychology*, **22**(1): 40.

Rilling, J.K., Glenn, A.L., Jairam, M.R., Pagnoni, G., Goldsmith, D.R., Elfenbein, H.A. & Lilienfeld, S.O. (2007) Neural correlates of social cooperation and non-cooperation as a function of psychopathy. *Biological Psychiatry*, **61**(11): 1260–1271.

Rind, B., Tromovitch, P. & Bauserman, R. (1998) A meta-analytic examination of assumed properties of child sexual abuse using college samples. *Psychological Bulletin*, **124**(1), July: 22–53.

Rix, K. (2001) 'Battered woman syndrome' and the defence of provocation: two women with something more in common. *Journal of Forensic Psychiatry*, **12**(1): 131–149.

Roberts, K.A. & Herrington, V. (2011) 18 Police interviews with suspects. In J. Kitaeff (ed.), *Handbook of Police Psychology*. Hove, UK: Routledge, pp. 383–400.

Robertson, N., Davies, G. & Nettleingham, A. (2009) Vicarious traumatisation as a consequence of jury service. *The Howard Journal of Criminal Justice*, **48**(1): 1–12.

Roche, M., Shoss, N., Pincus, A. & Ménard, K. (2011) Psychopathy moderates the relationship between time in treatment and levels of empathy in incarcerated male sexual offenders. *Sex Abuse*, **23**(2), June: 171–192.

Rogers, T., Blackwood, N., Farnham, F., Pickup, G. & Watts, M. (2008) Fitness to plead and competence to stand trial: a systematic review of the constructs and their application. *Journal of Forensic Psychiatry & Psychology*, **19**(4), December:

Rose, V.G. & Ogloff, J.R. (2001) Evaluating the comprehensibility of jury instructions: a method and an example. *Law and Human Behavior*, **25**(4): 409–431.

Rothman, E., Decker, M., Reed, E., Raj, A., Silverman, J. & Miller, E. (2008) 'Running a train': adolescent boys' accounts of sexual intercourse involving multiple males and one female. *Journal of Adolescent Research*, **23**(1), January: 97–113.

Rountree, M. (2012) 'I'll make them shoot me': accounts of death row prisoners advocating for execution. *Law & Society Review*, **46**(3): 589–622.

Rule, A. (2009) *The Stranger Beside Me*. New York: Pocket.

Ruva, C. & LeVasseura, M. (2012) Behind closed doors: the effect of pretrial publicity on jury deliberations. *Psychology, Crime and Law*, **18**(5): 431–452.

Ruva, C., Mayes, C., Dickman, M. & McEvoy, C. (2012) Timing and type of pretrial publicity affect mock-jurors' decisions and predecisional distortion. *International Journal of Psychology and Behavioral Sciences*, **2**(4): 108–119.

Sackett, P.R., & Harris, M.M. (1984) Honesty testing for personnel selection: a review and critique. *Personnel Psychology*, **37**(2): 221–245.

Saladin, M., Saper, Z. & Breen, L. (1988) Perceived attractiveness and attributions of criminality: what is beautiful is not criminal. *Canadian Journal of Criminology*, **30**(3): 251–259.

Salfati, C.G. (2003) Offender interaction with victims in homicide: a multidimensional analysis of frequencies in crime scene behaviors. *Journal of Interpersonal Violence*, **18**(5): 490–512.

Salfati, C., James, A. & Ferguson, L. (2008) Prostitute homicides: a descriptive study. *Journal of Interpersonal Violence*, **23**(4): 505–543.

Salib, E. (2003) Suicide terrorism. *British Journal of Psychiatry*, **182**: 475–476.

Sanghara, K. & Wilson, C. (2006) Stereotypes and attitudes about child sexual abusers: a comparison of experienced and inexperienced professionals in sex offender treatment. *Legal and Criminological Psychology*, **11**: 229–244.

Santtila, P., Junkkila, J. & Sandnabba, N. (2005) Behavioural linking of stranger rapes. *Journal of Investigative Psychology and Offender Profiling*, **2**(2): 87–103.

Sarason, I.G. & Sarason, B.R. (1981) Teaching cognitive and social skills to high school students. *Journal of Consulting & Clinical Psychology*, **49**(6): 908–918.

Sarchiapone, M., Carli, V., Di Giannantonio, M. & Roy, A. (2009) Risk factors for attempting suicide in prisoners. *Suicide and Life-Threatening Behavior*, **39**(3): 343–350.

Savage, S. & Milne, R. (2007) Miscarriages of justice – the role of the investigative process. In T. Newburn, T. Williamson & A. Wright (eds), *Handbook of Criminal Investigation*. Cullompton, UK: Willan.

Savin-Williams, R. & Diamond, L. (2004) Sex. In R. Lerner & L. Steinberg (eds), *Handbook of Adolescent Psychology*. New York: Wiley, pp. 189–231.

Schank, R.C. & Abelson, R.P. (1977) *Scripts, Plans, Goals and Understanding: An Inquiry into Human Knowledge Structures*. Hillsdale, NJ: Lawrence Erlbaum Associates.

Schechter, H. (1994) *Depraved: The Shocking True Story of America's First Serial Killer*. New York: Simon & Schuster.

Schenk, A.M. & Fremouw, W.J. (2012) Individual characteristics related to prison violence: a critical review of the literature. *Aggression and Violent Behavior*, **17**(5): 430–442.

Schildkraut, J. (2012) An inmate's right to die: legal and ethical considerations in death row volunteering. *Criminal Justice Studies*, **26**(1): 1–12.

Schiltz, K., Witzel, J., Northoff, G., Zierhut, K., Gubka, U., Fellmann, H., Kaufmann, J., Tempelmann, C., Wiebking, C. & Bogerts, B. (2007) Brain pathology in pedophilic offenders evidence of volume reduction in the right amygdala and related diencephalic structures. *Archives of General Psychiatry*, **64**(6): 737–746.

Schlueter, G.R., O'Neal, F.C., Hickey, J. & Seiler, G.L. (1989) Rational vs. nonrational shoplifting types: the implications for loss prevention strategies. *International Journal of Offender Therapy and Comparative Criminology*, **33**(3): 227–239.

Schmall, L. (2012) Tribute article women on Death Row: a tribute to Dean Victor Streib. *Ohio Northern University Law Review*, **38**: 441–821.

Schröder, J., de la Chapelle, A., Hakola, P. & Virkkunen, M. (1981) The frequency of XYY and XXY men among criminal offenders. *Acta Psychiatrica Scandinavica*, **63**(3), March: 272–276.

Schwartz, J., Steffensmeier, D. & Feldmeyer, B. (2009) Assessing trends in women's violence via data triangulation: arrests, convictions, incarcerations, and victim reports. *Social Problems*, **56**(3): 494–525.

Schwartz, R., Fremouw, W., Schenk, A. & Ragatz, L. (2009) Psychological profiles of male and female animal abusers. *Journal of Interpersonal Violence*, **27**(5): 846–861.

Schwartzman, P., Stambaugh, H. & Kimball, J. (1994) *Arson and Juveniles: Responding to the violence. A review of teen firesetting and interventions*. Federal Emergency Management Agency–United States Fire Administration. Emmitsburg, MD: United States Fire Administration.

Schwarz, T. (2001) *The Hillside Strangler*. New York: Vivisphere Publishing.

Schweitzer, N. & Saks, M.J. (2007) The CSI effect: popular fiction about forensic science affects public expectations about real forensic science. *Jurimetrics*, **47**: 357–364.

Schweitzer, Y. (2003) *Female Suicide Bombers for God*. Tel Aviv: The Jaffee Center for Strategic Studies.

Scott-Moncrieff, L. & Vassall-Adams, G. (2006) Capacity and fitness to plead: the yawning gap. *Counsel*, October: 1–3.

Scully, D. (1990) *Understanding Sexual Violence: A Study of Convicted Rapists*. Boston, MA: Unwin Hyman.

Secret, M. (2012) Incarcerated fathers: exploring the dimensions and prevalence of parenting capacity of non-violent offenders. *Fathering: A Journal of Theory, Research, and Practice about Men as Fathers*, **10**(2): 159–177.

Segovia, D.A. & Crossman, A.M. (2012) Cognition and the child witness: understanding the impact of cognitive development in forensic contexts. *Current Topics in Children's Learning and Cognition*. InTech. Doi 10.5772153938.

Sellbom, M., Ben-Porath, Y. & Stafford, K. (2007) A comparison of MMPI-2 measures of psychopathic deviance in a forensic setting. *Psychological Assessment*, **19**(4), December: 430–436.

Serin, R.C. & Kuriychuk, M. (1994) Social and cognitive processing deficits in violent offenders: implications for treatment. *International Journal of Law and Psychiatry*, **17**(4): 431–441.

Serious Organised Crime Agency (2013) Organised acquisitive crime. http://www.soca.gov.uk/threats/organised–acquisitive–crime (retrieved 1.3.13).

Sharpe, J. (1996) Crime in England: long-term trends and the problem of modernization. In E. Johnson & E. Monkkonen (eds), *The Civilisation of Crime Violence in Town and Country since the Middle Ages*. Champaign, IL: University of Illinois Press, pp. 17–34.

Shaw, C.R. & McKay, H.D. (1969) *Juvenile Delinquency and Urban Areas*. Chicago, IL: University of Chicago Press.

Shneidman, E.S. (1981) The psychological autopsy. *Suicide & Life Threatening Behaviour*, **11**: 325–340.

Shoemaker, D.J. (1996) *Theories of Delinquency: An Examination of Explanations of Delinquent Behavior*. New York: Oxford University Press.

Siegel, L.J., Welsh, B.C. and Senna, J.J. (2006) *Juvenile Delinquency: Theory, Practice and Law*. Belmont, CA: Thomson/Wadsworth.

Sigusch, V. (2001) Lean sexuality: on cultural transformations of sexuality and gender in recent decades. *Sexuality and Culture*, **5**(2): 23–56.

Silovsky, J. (2002) Characteristics of young children with sexual behavior problems: a pilot study. *Child Maltreatment*, **7**(3), August: 187–197.

Silver, E. & Teasdale, B. (2005) Mental disorder and violence: an examination of stressful life events and impaired social support. *Social Problems*, **52**: 62–78.

Skeem, J. & Cooke, D. (2010) Is criminal behavior a central component of psychopathy? Conceptual directions for resolving the debate. *Psychological Assessment*, **22**(2): 433–445.

Skeem, J.L., Manchak, S. & Peterson, J.K. (2011) Correctional policy for offenders with mental illness. *Law and Human Behavior*, **35**(2): 110–126.

Skrapec, C. (1996) Sexual component of serial murder. In T. O'Reilly-Fleming (ed.), *Serial and Mass Murder: Theory, Research and Policy*. Toronto: Canadian Scholars' Press, pp. 155–179.

Slotboom, A.M., Hendriks, J. & Verbruggen, J. (2011) Contrasting adolescent female and male sexual aggression: a self-report study on prevalence and predictors of sexual aggression. *Journal of Sexual Aggression*, **17**(1): 15–33.

Smarty, S. (2009) Battered Child Syndrome. In A. Jamieson & A. Moenssens (eds), *Wiley Encyclopedia of Forensic Science*. London: John Wiley.

Smith, J. (2003) *The Nature of Personal Robbery.* London: Home Office.

Smith, P. (2008) Solitary confinement: an introduction to the Istanbul Statement on the use and effects of solitary confinement. *Torture*, **18**(1): 56–62.

Smith, S.F. & Lilienfeld, S.O. (2012) Psychopathy in the workplace: the knowns and unknowns. *Aggression and Violent Behavior*, **18**(2): 204–218.

Snell, T. (2011) *Capital Punishment, Statisical Tables*. Washington, DC: US Bureau of Justice.

Snook, B., Cullen, R., Bennell, C., Taylor, P. & Gendreau, P. (2008) The criminal profiling illusion: what's behind the smoke and mirrors? *Criminal Justice and Behavior*, **35**(October): 1257–1276.

Snook, B., Eastwood, J., Gendreau, P., Goggin, C. & Cullen, R. (2007) Taking stock of criminal profiling: a narrative review and meta-analysis. *Criminal Justice and Behavior*, **34**(April): 437–453.

Snook, B., Gendreau, P., Bennell, C. & Taylor, P. (2008) Criminal profiling Granfalloons and Gobbledygook. *Skeptic*, **14**(22): 36–41.

Snook, B., House, J.C., MacDonald, S. & Eastwood, J. (2012) Police Witness Interview Training, Supervision, and Feedback: A Survey of Canadian Police Officers 1. *Canadian Journal of Criminology and Criminal Justice/La Revue canadienne de criminologie et de justice pénale*, **54**(3): 363–372.

Snow, L. (2002) Prisoners' motives for self-injury and attempted suicide. *British Journal of Forensic Practice*, **4**(4):18–29.

Sobel, R. (1968) *The Great Bull Market: Wall Street in the 1920s*. New York: W.W. Norton.

Social Exclusion Unit (2002) *Reducing Re-offending by Ex-prisoners*. London: Social Exclusion Unit, 9.

Social Exclusion Unit (2004) *Mental Health and Social Exclusion.* London: Social Exclusion Unit.

Soothill, K., Ackerley, E. & Francis, B. (2004) The criminal careers of arsonists. *Medicine Science and the Law*, **44**: 27–40.

Spaans, M., Barendregt, M., Muller, E., de Beurs, E., Nijman, H. & Rinne, T. (2009) MMPI profiles of males accused of severe crimes: a cluster analysis. *Psychology, Crime and Law*, **15**(5): 441–450.

Spence, S.A. (2008) Playing Devil's advocate: the case against fMRI lie detection. *Legal and Criminological Psychology*, **13**(1): 11–25.

Spielvogel, J. (2007) *Western Civilization*. Vol. II: *Since 1500* (6th edn). University Park, PA: Pennsylvania State University Press.

Spouse, E. & Gedroyc, W.M. (2000) MRI of the claustrophobic patient: interventionally configured magnets. *British Journal of Radiology*, **73**(866): 146–151.

Steblay, N., Dysart, J., Fulero, S. & Lindsay, R.C.L. (2003) Eyewitness accuracy rates in police showup and lineup presentations: a meta-analytic comparison. *Law and Human Behavior*, **27**(5): 523.

Steblay, N., Hosch, H.M., Culhane, S.E., & McWethy, A. (2006) The impact on juror verdicts of judicial instruction to disregard inadmissible evidence: a meta-analysis. *Law and Human Behavior*, **30**(4): 469–492.

Stern, S. (2013) Actually, the Vicky Pryce jury did its duty admirably. http://www.guardian.co.uk/commentisfree/2013/feb/20/vicky–pryce–jury–did–its–duty (retrieved 21.2.13).

Stevens, J.A. (1997) *Standard Investigatory Tools and Offender Profiling. Offender Profiling: Theory, research and practice.* Chichester: Wiley.

Stevens, M. (2011) *Broadmoor Revealed: Victorian Crime and the Lunatic Asylum.* Reading: Berkshire Record Office.

Stewart, J. (2011) *Tangled Webs.* New York: Penguin Press.

Stotland, E. (1977) White-collar criminal. *Journal of Social Issues*, **33**: 179–196.

Strauss, A.L. & Corbin, J. (1990) *Basics of Qualitative Research.* Newbury Park, CA: Sage.

Streib, V. (2010) *Death Penalty for Female Offenders, January 1, 1973, through October 31.* Ada, OH: Ohio Northern University Press.

Sung, M.J., & Kim, J.H. (2011) A psychiatric review on kleptomania. *Journal of Korean Neuropsychiatric Association*, 50(3): 193–204.

Sutherland, E.H. (1939) *Principles of Criminology* (3rd edition). Chicago: JB Lippincott Co.

Swanson, J.W., Borum, R., Swartz, M.S. & Monahan, J. (1996) Psychotic symptoms and disorders and the risk of violent behaviour in the community. *Criminal Behaviour and Mental Health,* **6**(4): 309–329.

Swift, B. (2006) The timing of death. In G. Rutty (ed.), *Essentials of Autopsy Practice.* London: Springer, pp. 189–214.

Takahashi, A., Quadros, I., Almeida, R. & Miczek, K. (2011) Brain serotonin receptors and transporters: initiation vs. termination of escalated aggression *Psychopharmacology*, **213**(2–3): 183–212.

Tang-Martinez, Z. & Mechanic, M. (2001) Review of the book *A Natural History of Rape. American Anthropologist*, **103**: 1222–1223.

Tangney, J.P., Stuewig, J. & Hafez, L. (2011) Shame, guilt, and remorse: implications for offender populations. *Journal of Forensic Psychiatry & Psychology*, **22**(5): 706–723.

Tanzi, E. (1909) A *Text-book of Mental Diseases.* Authorized translation by W. Ford Robertson, MD, & T.C. Mackenzie, MD (Illustrated). London: Rebman Limited.

Tatar, M. (1998) *Sex and Violence: The Hard Core of Fairy Tales.* New York: W.W. Norton.

Taylor, E.R., Kelly, J., Valescu, S., Reynolds, G.S., Sherman, J. & German, V. (2001) Is stealing a gateway crime? *Community Mental Health Journal*, **37**(4): 347–358.

Taylor, J.L., Thorne, I. & Slavkin, M.L. (2004) Treatment of fire-setting behaviour. *Offenders with Developmental Disabilities*, **3**: 221.

Taylor, V.E. (1997) The psychiatric defense in military law. In R.G. Lande & D.T. Armitage (eds), *Principles and Practice of Military Forensic Psychiatry.* Springfield, IL: Charles C. Thomas, pp. 103–107.

Terry, M. (1987) *The Ultimate Evil: An Investigation into America's Most Dangerous Satanic Cult.* Garden City, NY: Doubleday.

Thomas, C.W. & Petersen, D.M. (1977) *Prison Organization and Inmate Subcultures.* Indianapolis, IN: Bobbs–Merrill.

Thomas, D. (2006) *Villains' Paradise: A History of Britain's Underworld.* New York: Pegasus Books.

Thompson, C. & Loper, A. (2005) Adjustment patterns in incarcerated women: an analysis of differences based on sentence length. *Criminal Justice and Behavior*, **32**: 714–732.

Thornhill, R. & Palmer, C. (2000) *A Natural History of Rape: Biological Bases of Sexual Coercion.* Cambridge, MA: MIT Press.

Thornton, D. (2002) Constructing and testing a framework for dynamic risk assessment. *Sexual Abuse: A Journal of Research and Treatment*, **14**(2): 139–153.

Thornton, D., Mann, R., Webster, S., Blud, L., Travers, R., Friendship, C. & Erikson, M. (2003) Distinguishing and combining risks for sexual and violent recidivism. *Annals of the New York Academy of Sciences*, **989**(1): 225–235.

Tibbetts, S.G. & Herz, D.C. (1996) Gender differences in factors of social control and rational choice. *Deviant Behavior*, **17**(2): 183–208.

Times (2010) Stephen Griffiths declares: I am the Crossbow Cannibal. *The Times*, 29 May, www.timesonline. co.uk (retrieved 30.5.10).

Tithecott, R. (1997) *Of Men and Monsters: Jeffrey Dahmer and the Construction of the Serial Killer* Madison, WI: University of Wisconson Press.

Tonglet, M. (2002) Consumer misbehaviour: an exploratory study of shoplifting. *Journal of Consumer Behaviour*, **1**(4): 336–354.

Tonkin, M., Santtila, P. & Bull, R. (2012) The linking of burglary crimes using offender behaviour: testing research cross-nationally and exploring methodology. *Legal and Criminological Psychology*, **17**: 276–293.

Torniero, C., Bernardina, B.D., Fontana, E., Darra, F., Danesino, C. & Elia, M. (2010) Electroclinical findings in four patients with karyotype 47:XYY. *Brain and Development*, **33**(5): 384–389.

Torry, Z. & Billick, S. (2010) Overlapping universe: understanding legal insanity and psychosis. *Psychiatric Quarterly*, **81**(3): 253–262.

Townshend, C. (2002) *Terrorism: A Very Short Introduction*. Oxford: Oxford University Press.

Treanor, J. (2012) Barclays sacked five staff over Libor manipulation scandal. *The Guardian*, 28 November, www.guardian.co.uk/business (retrieved 29.11.12).

Trojan, C. & Salfati, C. (2011) Linking criminal history to crime scene behaviour in single victim and serial homicide: implications for offender profiling research. *Homicide Studies*, **15**(1): 3–31.

Tromans, N. (2011) *Richard Dadd: The Artist and the Asylum*. London: The Tate Gallery.

Turvey, B. (2008) *Criminal Profiling: An Introduction to Behavioural Evidence Analysis*. London: Academic Press.

Tyler, N. & Gannon, T.A. (2012) Explanations of firesetting in mentally disordered offenders: a review of the literature. *Psychiatry: Interpersonal and Biological Processes*, **75**(2): 150–166.

Ullman, S. (2007) Comparing gang and individual rapes in a community sample of urban women. *Violence and Victims*, **22**(1): 43–51.

United Nations (1948) *Convention on the Prevention and Punishment of the Crime of Genocide, Resolution 260 (III) A of the United Nations General Assembly*, 9 December 1948, Paris. http://untreaty.un.org/cod/ avl/ha/cppcg/cppcg.html (retrieved 29.12.10).

United Nations (2003) *World Youth Report*. New York: United Nations.

US Bureau of Justice Statistics (2009) *Prisoners in 2008* (NCJ 228417). December 2009 report from the US Bureau of Justice by William J. Sabol, PhD, & Heather C. West, PhD (BJS statisticians).

US Department of Defense (2004) *Safeguarding Privacy in the Fight against Terrorism*. Report of the Technology and Privacy Advisory Committee, March. Washington, DC: US Department of Defense.

US Department of Justice (2009) *United States v. Bernard L. Madoff Case 1:09-cr-00213*. Department of Justice, http://www.justice.gov/usao/nys/madoff.html (retrieved 1.2.13).

US Supreme Court Center (1983) *Jones v. United States, 463 US 354*, Department of Justice, http://supreme. justia.com/us/463/354/ (retrieved 1.3.09).

van Lier, P.A.C., Vitaro, F., Barker, E., Koot, H.M. & Tremblay, R.E. (2009) Developmental links between trajectories of physical violence, vandalism, theft, and alcohol–drug use from childhood to adolescence. *Journal of Abnormal Child Psychology*, **37**(4): 481–492.

Van Lier, P., Vitaro, F., Barker, E., Koot, H., Hackett, S., Phillips, J. & Balfe, M. (2013) Developmental markers of risk or vulnerability? Young females who sexually abuse – characteristics, backgrounds, behaviours and outcomes. *Journal of Abnormal Child Psychology*, **37**: 481–492.

Van Ness, D.W. & Strong, K.H. (2010) *The Hillside Strangler*. New York: Vivisphere Publishing.

Van Tongeren, D. & Klebe, K. (2009) Reconceptualizing prison adjustment: a multidimensional approach exploring female offenders' adjustment to prison life. *The Prison Journal*, **90**(1): 48–68.

Van Wormer, K. & Odiah, C. (1999) The psychology of suicide–murder and the death penalty. *Journal of Criminal Justice*, **27**(4): 361–370.

Vandello, J.A., Ransom, S., Hettinger, V.E. & Askew, K. (2009) Men's misperceptions about the acceptability and attractiveness of aggression. *Journal of Experimental Social Psychology*, **45**(6): 1209–1219.

Vanderhallen, M., Vervaeke, G. & Holmberg, U. (2011) Witness and suspect perceptions of working alliance and interviewing style. *Journal of Investigative Psychology and Offender Profiling*, **8**(2): 110–130.

Vaughn, M.G., Fu, Q., DeLisi, M., Wright, J.P., Beaver, K.M., Perron, B.E. & Howard, M.O. (2010) Prevalence and correlates of fire-setting in the United States: results from the National Epidemiological Survey on alcohol and related conditions. *Comprehensive Psychiatry*, **51**: 217–223.

Verkampt, F. & Ginet, M. (2010) Variations of the cognitive interview: Which one is the most effective in enhancing children's testimonies? *Applied Cognitive Psychology*, **24**(9): 1279–1296.

Victoroff, J. (2005) The mind of the terrorist: a review and critique of psychological approaches. *Journal of Conflict Resolution*, **49**(3): 3–42.

Vidmar, N. & Diamond, S. (2001) Juries and expert evidence. *Brooklyn Law Review*, **66**: 1121–1180.

Vizard, E., Hickey, N. & McCrory, E. (2007) Developmental trajectories associated with juvenile sexually abusive behaviour and emerging severe personality disorder in childhood: three-year study. *British Journal of Psychiatry*, **190**(49): s27–s32.

Wagner, G.C., Beuving, L.J. & Hutchinson, R.R. (1980) The effects of hormone manipulations on aggressive target-biting in mice. *Aggressive Behavior*, **6**(1): 1–7.

Wakefield, H. & Underwager, R. (1991) Female child sexual abusers: a critical review of the literature. *American Journal of Forensic Psychology*, **9**(4): 43–69

Walker, L.E. (1990) Feminist scholarship and the training of psychoanalytic psychologists: a feminist psychotherapist's perspective. In M. Meisels & E. Shapiro (eds), *Tradition and Innovation in Psychoanalytic Education*. Hillsdale, NJ: Lawrence Erlbaum, pp. 233–243.

Walker, N. (1991) *Why Punish?* Oxford and New York: Oxford University Press.

Walker, T. (2009) *Eligible for Execution: The Story of the Daryl Atkins Case*. Washington, DC: Congressional Quarterly Inc (Sage).

Walklate, S. (2003a) Can there be a feminist victimology? In P. Davies, P. Francis & V. Jupp (eds), *Victimization: Theory, Research and Policy*. Basingstoke: Palgrave Macmillan, pp. 28–45.

Walklate, S. (2003b) *Understanding Criminology: Current Theoretical Debates* (2nd edn). Maidenhead: Open University Press.

Wallang, P. & Taylor, R. (2012) Psychiatric and psychological aspects of fraud offending. *Advances in Psychiatric Treatment*, **18**(May): 183–192.

Waller, J. (2007) *Becoming Evil: How Ordinary People Commit Genocide and Mass Killing* (2nd edn). Oxford: Oxford University Press.

Walmsley, R. (2010) *World Prison Population List* (8th edn). London: King's College.

Walsh, A. (2005) African Americans and serial killing in the media: the myth and the reality. *Homicide Studies*, **9**(4), November: 271–291.

Walsh, D. & Bull, R. (2010) Interviewing suspects of fraud: an in-depth analysis of interview skills. *Journal of Psychiatry & Law*, **38**: 99–135.

Walsh, D. & Bull, R. (2012a) Examining rapport in investigative interviews with suspects: does its building and maintenance work? *Journal of Police and Criminal Psychology*, **27**(1): 73–84.

Walsh, D. & Bull, R. (2012b) How do interviewers attempt to overcome suspects' denials? *Psychiatry, Psychology and Law*, **19**(2): 151–168.

Webster, S.D. & Beech, A.R. (2000) The nature of sexual offenders' affective empathy: a grounded theory analysis. *Sexual Abuse: A Journal of Research and Treatment*, **12**(4): 249–261.

Wecht, C.H. (2005) The history of legal medicine. *Journal American Academy of Psychiatry and the Law*, **33**(2): 245–251.

Weinstein, L. & Geiger, J. (2003) Insanity and its various interpretations. *Psychology and Education*, **40**(3–4): 19–24.

Wells, G.L. & Hasel, L.E. (2007) Facial composite production by eyewitnesses. *Current Directions in Psychological Science*, **16**(1): 6–10.

Welsh, B.C. & Farrington, D.P. (eds) (2006) *Preventing Crime: What Works for Children, Offenders, Victims and Places*. Netherlands: Springer.

Wessel, E.M., Bollingmo, G.C., Sønsteby, C., Nielsen, L.M., Eliersten, D.E., & Magnussen, S. (2012) The emotional witness effect: story content, emotional valence and credibility of a male suspect. *Psychology, Crime & Law*, **18**(5), 417–430.

West, S.G. & Feldsher, M. (2010) Parricide: characteristics of sons and daughters who kill their parents. *Current Psychiatry*, **9**(11): 20–38.

Wheatcroft, J. & Ellison, L. (2012) Evidence in court: witness preparation and cross-examination style effects on adult witness accuracy. *Behavioral Sciences and the Law*, **30**(6): 821–840.

White, J., Lester, D., Gentile, M. & Rosenbleeth, J. (2011) The utilization of forensic science and criminal profiling for capturing serial killers. *Forensic Science International*, **209**(1): 160–165.

Whitney, G. (1990) On possible genetic bases on race differences in criminality. In L. Ellis & H. Hoffman (eds), *Crime in Biological, Social and Moral Contexts*. Westport, CT: Praeger.

Widiger, T. & Trull, T. (2007) Plate tectonics in the classification of personality disorder: shifting to a dimensional model. *American Psychologist*, **62**(2), February–March: 71–83.

Williams, D. (1969) Neural factors related to habitual aggression. *Brain*, **92**: 503.

Williams, D. (2007) Effective CCTV and the challenge of constructing legitimate suspicion using visual images. *Journal of Investigative Psychology and Offender Profiling*, **4**: 97–107.

Williams, H., Cordan, G., Mewse, A., Tonks, J. & Burgess, C. (2010) Self-reported traumatic brain injury in male young offenders: a risk factor for re-offending, poor mental health and violence? *Neuropsychological Rehabilitation*, **20**(6): 801–812.

Williams, K., Poyser, J. & Hopkins, K. (2012) *Accommodation, Homelessness and Reoffending of Prisoners: Results from the Surveying Prisoner Crime Reduction (SPCR) Survey*. Ministry of Justice Report 3/12. London: Ministry of Justice.

Willig, C. (2001) *Qualitative Research in Psychology: A Practical Guide to Research Method*. Buckingham: Open University Press.

Winton, M. & Unlue, A. (2007) Micro-macro dimensions of the Bosnian genocides: the circumplex model and violentization theory. *Aggression and Violent Behavior*, **13**(1), January–February: 45–59.

Woldemicael, G. (2007) *Women's Status and Reproductive Preferences in Eritrea* (No. WP–2007–023). Rostock, Germany: Max Planck Institute for Demographic Research.

Wolfe, D. & Hermanson, D. (2004) *The Fraud Diamond: Considering the Four Elements of Fraud*. Atlanta, GA: DigitalCommons@ Kennesaw State University.

Wolff, S. & McCall Smith, R. (2000) Child homicide and the law: implications of the judgment of the European Court of Human Rights in the case of the children who killed James Bulger. Points of Law. *Child Psychology and Psychiatry Review*, **5**: 3.

Woodworth, M. & Porter, S. (2001) Historical foundations and current applications of criminal profiling in violent crime investigations. *Expert Evidence*, **7**: 241–261.

World Health Organisation (2011) *Health Topics*. Geneva: WHO.

World Health Organization (2013) *Adolescent Development*. http://www.who.int/maternal_child_adolescent/topics/adolescence/dev/en/ (retrieved 1.3.13).

Wrangham, R. (2009) *Catching Fire: How Cooking Made Us Human*. New York: Basic Books.

Wright, J. & Hensley, C. (2003) From animal cruelty to serial murder: applying the graduation hypothesis. *Inernational Journal of Offender Therapy and Comparative Criminology*, **47**(1): 71–88.

Wright, K. (1991) A study of individual, environmental, and interactive effects in explaining adjustment to prison. *Justice Quarterly*, **8**(2): 217–242.

Yang, M. & Coid, J. (2007) Gender differences in psychiatric morbidity and violent behaviour among a household population in Great Britain. *Social Psychiatry and Psychiatric Epidemiology*, **42**(8): 599–605.

Yanofski, J. (2011) Setting up a death row psychiatry program. *Innovative Clinical Neuroscience*, **8**(2), February: 19–22.

Yarber, A. & Sharp, P. (2010) *Focus on Single-Parent Families: Past, Present, and Future*. Westport, CT: Praeger.

Yokota, K. & Canter, D. (2004) Burglars' specialisation: development of a thematic approach in investigative psychology. *Behaviormetrika*, **31**(2): 153–167.

Yousafzai, A. & Siddiqui, M. (2007) Psychological perspective of suicide bombing. *Journal of the Pakistan Psychiatric Society Short Communication*, **4**(2): 121.

Zajac, R. & Cannan, P. (2009) Cross-examination of sexual assault complainants: a developmental comparison. *Psychiatry, Psychology and Law*, **16**: S36–S54.

Zajac, R., O'Neill, S. & Hayne, H. (2012) Disorder in the courtroom? Child witnesses under cross-examination. *Developmental Review*, **32**(3), September: 181–204.

Zamble, E. (1992) Behavior and adaptation in long-term prison inmates' descriptive longitudinal results. *Criminal Justice and Behavior*, **19**(4): 409–425.

Zapf, P., Zottoli, T. & Pirelli, G. (2009) Insanity in the courtroom: issues of criminal responsibility and competency to stand trial. In D. Krauss & J. Lieberman (eds), *Psychological Expertise in Court: Psychology in the Courtroom* (Vol. 2). Aldershot: Ashgate.

Zara, G. & Farrington, D. (2009) Childhood and adolescent predictors of late onset criminal careers. *Journal of Youth and Adolescence*, **38**(3): 287–300.

Zimbardo, P. (1971) *Stanford Prison Experiment*. Stanford, CA: Stanford University Archives.

Zimbardo, P.G. (2011) Lucifer Effect. In D. Christie (ed.), *The Encyclopedia of Peace Psychology*. Oxford: Wiley, pp. 603–607.

Zoroya, G. (2003) Her decision to be a suicide bomber. *USA Today*, **22**: 1.

Zuckoff, M. (2005) *Ponzi's Scheme: The True Story of a Financial Legend*. New York: Random House.

Index